Hoffa in Tennessee

MAURY NICELY

HOFFA
IN TENNESSEE

The Chattanooga Trial That Brought Down an Icon

The University of Tennessee Press / *Knoxville*

LIBRARY OF CONGRESS CATALOGING-IN-PUBLICATION DATA

Names: Nicely, Maury, author.
Title: Hoffa in Tennessee: the Chattanooga trial that brought down an icon / Maury Nicely.
Description: First edition. | Knoxville: The University of Tennessee Press, [2019] |
Includes bibliographical references and index.
Identifiers: LCCN 2018040735 (print) | LCCN 2018047398 (ebook) |
ISBN 9781621904762 (Kindle) | ISBN 9781621904779 (pdf) | ISBN 9781621904755 (hardcover)
Subjects: LCSH: Hoffa, James R. (James Riddle), 1913—Trials, litigation, etc. |
Trials (Bribery)—Tennessee—Chattanooga—History—20th century. |
International Brotherhood of Teamsters, Chauffeurs, Warehousemen,
and Helpers of America—History—20th century. | Kennedy, Robert F., 1925–1968.
Classification: LCC KF224.H6 (ebook) | LCC KF224.H6 N53 2019 (print) | DDC 345.73/0234—dc23
LC record available at https://lccn.loc.gov/2018040735

To my parents,
Steve and Karen Nicely

CONTENTS

ILLUSTRATIONS

following page 165

ACKNOWLEDGMENTS

My long fascination with the 1964 trial of Jimmy Hoffa began with a telephone call from US bankruptcy judge Shelley Rucker, who asked if I would be interested in working with a committee of the Federal Bar Association to produce a documentary on the trial for an upcoming Sixth Circuit Judicial Conference in Chattanooga. The resulting film, *Balancing the Scales: The Chattanooga Trial of* U.S. v. James R. Hoffa, was the acorn from which this book grew. Thanks to the members of the documentary committee, including Barry Cammon, Tonya Kennedy Cammon, Cameron Hill, Rita LaLumia, and John Medearis, for their hard work in unearthing long-hidden articles, images, and interviews to shed more light on the trial.

Thanks to US District Court Judges Curtis Collier and Sandy Mattice, whose interest and encouragement compelled forward the documentary project throughout 2007 and 2008. Thanks also to US Magistrate Judge Chris Steger, who recommended that the documentary would make a good book and gently nudged me to pursue the idea.

Several trial participants and their relatives proved willing to share their recollections and were patient in fielding a myriad of questions about minor details from a half century ago. Thanks to Marvin Berke, Judge William Brown, Jim Cole, Tommy Eason, Charlie Gearhiser, Pat Haverty, Harry Mansfield, Hayden Mauk, Jim Neal, Keith Partin, Betty Paschal, Cecil Pearce, John Sertel, Joanne M. Shobe, John Seigenthaler, Etta Williams, Tom Williams, Helen Wilson, and Randy Wilson for their time and knowledge. Thanks also to Mike Pare and Jerry Summers for their willingness to share their recollections of several of the attorneys, jurors, and witnesses from the trial.

As always, I relied heavily on any number of archivists, librarians, and experts to help to locate arcane pieces of information, tiny details, and images. Thanks to Kris Bronstad, modern political archivist, and the staff of the Baker Center at the University of Tennessee Libraries, Knoxville; Lynda Minks Hood at the Chattanooga Bar Association; Mary Helms, April Mitchell, and the staff of the Chattanooga Public Library; the staff of the Library of

Congress, Prints and Photographs Division; the staffs of the Michigan and Tennessee Bar Associations; Megan Adovasio-Jones and the staff of the Nashville Public Library; the staff of the *Nashville Tennessean;* Shane Bell at the National Archives in Morrow, Georgia; Lynda Edwards and the staff of the *Chattanooga Times-Free Press;* Thomas Wells, Elizabeth Crowder, Jon Boggs, and the staff of the University of Tennessee Press; and Rey Regenstreif-Harms, project archivist for the University of Tennessee at Chattanooga Library.

Thanks to the individuals who were willing to take the time to review all or parts of this manuscript in its various stages and also to offer their thoughts as to how to improve it. This book is better for their kind and thoughtful comments and suggestions. Also, thanks to all of my family, friends, and co-workers who shared encouragement and enthusiasm during what proved to be an extended period of time working on this project. I apologize to anyone I have inadvertently omitted.

Finally, and as ever, thanks to my wife, Jenny, and my sons, Charles and William, for their patient support throughout this project.

PROLOGUE

As US attorney general in the early 1960s, Robert F. Kennedy considered the president of the Teamsters Union, Jimmy Hoffa, a corrupt force who, in light of the organization's influence over the national economy, posed a threat to America. Convinced that Hoffa needed to be removed from power, therefore, he established a "Get Hoffa Squad" for the purpose of convicting the Teamster boss of wrongdoing. In so doing, Kennedy did not follow the general practice of identifying a crime and trying to determine who committed the act; instead, he began with *Hoffa* and then set out to determine whether he had engaged in some—any—criminal enterprise.

A unique defendant, Hoffa had the money and power to counter the efforts of the federal government, and several attempts to gain a conviction resulted in acquittal and disappointment. Undeterred, the Get Hoffa Squad persisted, year after year, to unearth some criminal act with which to nab the notorious Teamster leader. Over time, Hoffa and his lawyers became convinced that these efforts by Kennedy and his cronies had morphed into "persecution, not prosecution." Hoffa railed that government spies and informants had been used to report on his activities, witnesses had been threatened in order to sway their testimony, and wiretaps and recording devices had been used to listen in on confidential discussions within the Hoffa team.

To counter these aggressive tactics, Hoffa employed any number of courtroom strategies of his own. Celebrities appeared to shake hands with him in front of the jury. The testimony of government witnesses was blunted by accusations of racist behavior. Government agents were accused of surveilling and wiretapping Hoffa and his associates. As the government ramped up its efforts to "get Hoffa," the maneuvers the union boss was willing to employ in his effort to evade guilt likewise evolved. The result was a brutal, bare-knuckle brawl in which both sides appeared willing to dispense with not only the rules of civility, but also notions of right and wrong.

This struggle between Hoffa and Kennedy culminated in a six-week trial in a small federal courthouse in Chattanooga, Tennessee, in 1964. Wedged

1

between the two bitter factions was relatively new federal judge Frank Wilson, whose job it was to ensure a fair trial for Hoffa and his codefendants. The trial would prove to be a slugfest. Enraged by a belief that government agents and a turncoat Teamster had spied on Hoffa and his attorneys, and fearful that the trial was taking a negative turn, the defense team made a fateful decision. They would direct their rising ire toward the court itself in the hopes that the young judge would misstep, lose his temper, and cause a mistrial. The result was a bitter struggle, one that severely tested the court on a daily basis.

The story of the Chattanooga trial of Jimmy Hoffa is that of a lone, embattled judge struggling mightily to control a legal proceeding that teetered on the edge of bedlam, threatening to spin out of control. It also represents the first blow to Hoffa, a judicial setback that would tarnish his image and set in motion his downfall and disappearance a decade later. The following pages examine how—and whether—justice can prevail in the midst of an overwhelming assault on the judicial system itself.

ONE

Now some folks say he'll go to jail,
But others say, "We'll pay his bail"—
Now, we don't know who's right or wrong,
But a million drivers will sing his song.

Well, they're trying to get to Jimmy,
Trying to get to Jimmy,
Jimmy, they're coming after you;
Trying to get to Jimmy,
Trying to get to Jimmy –
Every politician and his brother, too.

—"The Ballad of Jimmy Hoffa," Smokey Stover (1960)[1]

AS THE SMALL aircraft taxied down the concrete runway toward the hanger, the crowd of blue-collar workers began to shout, clap, and wave homemade signs.[2]

"Welcome to Chattanooga!"

Built in 1930, the Lovell Field Airport consisted of a single hangar, an administration building, and a Standard Oil filling station. By the 1960s, the

3

antiquated airfield was in need of updating, and the landing strip had become a construction site. Touted as "one of America's most modern municipal airports" and the "Aerial Gateway of [the] Future," the contemporary airport was designed to "swallow up" the old structures, incorporating them into a sprawling building. The new terminal had only recently been completed, and the old lobby was being converted into a storage area for air freight.[3] At the ground breaking, local businessman T. A. Lupton Jr. characterized the airport as a "great step forward in increasing the strengths and advantages of Chattanooga." Floyd Delaney, president of the Chamber of Commerce, bragged, "Business leaders visiting us will get the impression they should get of Chattanooga."[4] With the arrival of a small aircraft on January 19, 1964, the city would be thrust firmly into the national spotlight, something that might have pleased those boosters.

Spotlights from the control tower flooded the runway. The door to the aircraft opened, and the crowd erupted. Jimmy Hoffa, president of the International Brotherhood of Teamsters (IBT), stepped down to the tarmac.

"We'll Always Be for Jo and Jimmy Hoffa"

Greeting supporters, Hoffa apologized for the late arrival; it had been a rough flight. Accompanying him were several members of his legal team and staff, as well as his wife, Josephine, his daughter, Barbara Crancer, and his son, James P. Hoffa. Asked about the others' presence, Hoffa replied, "We are a closely knitted family," adding that his wife and children were there "to give me encouragement." With his arm around his wife's shoulder, Hoffa smiled, waved to the crowd, and walked to a waiting Cadillac.[5]

"Thank You Jimmy for the Contract"

Only three days earlier Hoffa had enjoyed his finest hour. Less than one hour before a deadline set for six nationwide trucking companies to go on strike—a costly and destructive tactic from which Hoffa had not been willing to back down—the businesses had agreed to a National Master Freight Agreement, the first nationwide collective bargaining agreement in what had once been a completely decentralized industry. The contract created a common floor beneath which the wages of Teamsters members could not be reduced. It also established a common deadline for the expiration of bargaining contracts, maximizing Teamster leverage at the bargaining table. Hoffa, who calculated that the agreement would result in a forty-five-cent-per-hour pay increase for workers, pronounced it "a great contract." The *New York Times* assessed it as "a personal triumph for the union's president."[6]

"He Brings the Bacon Home—Our Wages Prove It"

It was not Hoffa's first visit to Chattanooga; he had swept through town only two days earlier. After answering "a barrage of questions from newsmen," he had been escorted downtown for a series of brief meetings before heading home to spend the weekend with his family. To his delight, Hoffa had been showered with support and thanks by crowds of union supporters. Now, on his return trip, he was scheduled to remain in Chattanooga not for hours but for weeks, a period of time that would prove to be one of the most pivotal of his public life.[7]

Leading the delegation of well-wishers on January 19 was George E. Hicks, the president of Teamsters Local 515 in Chattanooga. Beaming, Hicks greeted Hoffa enthusiastically, directing him to the car that would take him into town. A police motorcade escorted Hoffa and his entourage downtown to the Hotel Patten, where he greeted union members and their wives at a reception in his honor.[8] Jimmy Hoffa had arrived in triumph in the heart of the South. The following day, however, he would appear in federal court to answer charges that would threaten his freedom, his livelihood, and—most importantly—his grip on the Teamsters Union.

TWO

"You Have a Blessed Opportunity to Free
More Slaves Than Lincoln Did."

—Letter received by US senator John McClellan
during investigation of Teamsters Union[1]

ON THE MORNING of Tuesday, August 20, 1957, Jimmy Hoffa strode up the steps to the entrance of the old Senate Office Building in Washington, DC. With him was George Fitzgerald, who had been his legal representative for years. Inside, the two men proceeded up the curving marble staircase from the rotunda to the third-floor Caucus Room. Designed as an "audience hall," the Caucus Room featured Corinthian columns, glittering chandeliers, and a gilded ceiling. It had been adapted to host public hearings, including those examining the sinking of the *Titanic* (1912), the Teapot Dome Scandal

(1923), and the Army-McCarthy hearings (1954). In August 1957, the Caucus Room housed the McClellan Committee hearings, a public investigation into organized labor. The proceedings would create a national sensation, largely because they were broadcast to a wide audience through the new, modern medium of television.[2]

Hoffa and his attorney seated themselves at a table near the front of the room facing the committee members. The space was filled to capacity. Poster boards bearing titles such as "Teamster 'Paper' Locals, New York" surrounded Hoffa and Fitzgerald, as did microphones, television cameras, and a dozen reporters scribbling notes on pads of paper. One photographer crouched at the foot of the table to capture closeup images of the cantankerous Teamster. Hoffa pulled his chair close, resting his elbows on the table to size up the committee members as they made last-minute notes and whispered to one another. At precisely 10:30 a.m., Sen. John McClellan brought the Caucus Room to order.[3]

———

Congress did not begin its investigation of organized crime with an intention to examine the Teamsters. As the 1950s progressed, however, an investigation of the IBT became inevitable. Beginning in 1950, the criminal underworld was exposed to the glare of publicity when black-and-white television sets transmitted into American homes blurry images of hearings chaired by charismatic senator Estes Kefauver, a Tennessee Democrat who wore a coonskin cap on the campaign trail and served as Adlai Stevenson's running mate in the 1956 presidential race. Although eventually eclipsed by Joseph McCarthy's communist investigation, the work of the Kefauver Committee cracked open the door to public awareness of the connection between the Teamsters and organized crime.

It was revealed during the Kefauver hearings that Teamsters Local 985 in Detroit had been used as a front for the extortion of funds from jukebox distributors. In 1953, therefore, the newly elected Republican Congress pushed for further inquiry into Teamster locals in Detroit—Hoffa's home turf. Assigned to the task was the Hoffman Committee, named for its chairman, outspoken anti-labor Republican congressman Clare Hoffman. The central target of the inquiry was William Bufalino, a Pennsylvania-born lawyer who had reportedly married into the mob, relocated to Detroit, and acquired interests in the jukebox business. Companies that refused to pay initiation fees and dues to become "honorary" members of the union were picketed and, in some cases, firebombed. It was also alleged that the judge presiding over an extortion case against Bufalino had received a campaign donation of $6,200 shortly before acquitting the accused lawyer.[4]

In examining the Teamsters, the Hoffman Committee reportedly found a "gigantic, wicked conspiracy to, through the use of force, threats of force and economic pressure, extort and collect millions of dollars" from employers. Hoffa was swept into the investigation when it was learned that he had ordered the financial records of Local 985 to be destroyed, although he claimed that the disposal of the documents was a routine process "to save storage space."[5]

It seemed that Congress had the IBT on the ropes. However, internal conflict eventually crippled the Hoffman Committee. After the chairman was unceremoniously voted out, he was replaced by Wint Smith, a Republican from Kansas who shifted the committee's focus to a series of questionable investments Hoffa made with Teamster pension funds. It was during those hearings that Hoffa was first questioned about the Test Fleet Corporation, a financial interest that would plague him for much of the rest of his public life.

Hoffa and his close friend and business partner Owen Bert Brennan, a former truck driver from Chicago, had established Test Fleet in 1949. To distract attention from Hoffa, the ownership of the company was quietly placed in the maiden names of their wives. Test Fleet had allegedly been established with the help of another company, Commercial Carriers, in exchange for Hoffa's assistance in settling a potentially damaging Teamsters strike on beneficial terms for Commercial Carriers. It was also claimed that Commercial Carriers had lent $50,000 to Test Fleet for the purpose of purchasing equipment, and that the bookkeeper for Commercial Carriers had kept the books for Test Fleet for four years at no charge. The relationship between the two companies financially benefited Hoffa and Brennan, who realized a profit of $125,000 on their $4,000 investment over the first seven years of the company's existence. The problem? The ownership of a trucking company by a Teamsters official created a significant potential conflict of interest and violated the federal Taft-Hartley Act.[6]

Just when it seemed that Congress had latched onto tangible evidence of Hoffa's impropriety, the Smith Committee was abruptly disbanded on the basis that it lacked the jurisdiction to continue its investigation. Stepping away to answer a long-distance telephone call, Smith returned to the Caucus Room to announce that the hearings had been canceled. "The pressure comes from a way up there," the exasperated congressman told stunned reporters, "and I just can't talk about it any more specifically than that."[7]

In 1954, only months after the unexpected dismantling of the Smith Committee, a new set of hearings convened under the direction of Ohio Republican congressman George H. Bender. Critics referred to Bender, a candidate for the US Senate at the time, as "the Clown Prince" due to his silly antics such as conducting singing groups and rattling cowbells at public events. Once again, the hearings were quickly snuffed—or, as was said at the time, they were "recessed at the call of the chairman." This last claim raised eyebrows when the Ohio Conference of Teamsters, which had been supporting Bender's political opponent, hastily altered its position to support Bender in his Senate race.[8]

The Teamsters had slipped the noose.

———

Two months after his initial appearance before the McClellan Committee, on October 4, 1957, forty-four-year-old Jimmy Hoffa would be elected general president of the International Brotherhood of Teamsters in a landslide victory, receiving 72 percent of votes cast. In his acceptance speech, he stated, "[I promise] to do all in my power to lead you and this organization to a position of respect and honor in the eyes of the rank and file of labor, in the eyes of the nation, in the eyes of the world." Hoffa also took the opportunity to address critics of the IBT. "The 1,500,000 working American men and women who make up this International Brotherhood of Teamsters are your next-door neighbors," he assured his audience. "They aren't gangsters. They aren't hoodlums. . . . These people are Americans. I am proud to be one of these people." The rank-and-file membership adored their new, charismatic leader, who would be reelected for a second term in 1961. He was tailor-made for the job. Discussing his role as president of the union, Hoffa once remarked, "I like this job. Every hour I work [at it] is an hour of pleasure."[9]

In strictly numerical terms, Hoffa's presidency bore substantial fruit. The Teamsters added 132,000 new members (for a total of 1.567 million) in 1958–59, during a period of declining union membership in the United States. These increases translated into financial gains, and the Teamsters treasury contained $40 million by 1959. This was a high-water mark in terms of the union's finances. Given these developments, it was widely affirmed that Hoffa was "not just the most powerful man in labor, [but] the most powerful man in the country, next to the President."[10]

Hoffa would use this power to strengthen his ties to a dangerous partner—the mob. As early as 1941, faced with a need for "reinforcement manpower," i.e., muscle, to counter the violent tactics used by management to break strikes, Hoffa had devised a ready solution: affiliation with the criminal underworld. His relationship with organized crime had only expanded since that time. Publicly, Hoffa downplayed his ties to criminal figures, explaining, "You develop a relationship with 'em to where you don't interfere with their business and they don't interfere with your business." He naively believed that he could use organized crime to his advantage without the risk that it would actually worm itself deeply within the union.[11]

Hoffa considered organized crime a secure business partner, a safe bet for financial investments. Challenged on the basis that he had authorized loans to criminals out of the union's pension fund, he retorted, "I'll tell you one thing for damned sure. We had damned few defaults." In his mind, Hoffa was able to justify his questionable affiliations because business arrangements with the mob were profitable.[12]

Others, however, were not so comfortable with the ties developing between the Teamsters and suspected racketeers. Early on, Hoffa's underworld connections had led to two public trials. The first took place in 1941, when Hoffa pled no contest to allegations that he had assisted in forcing non-union wastepaper businesses out of operation. The following year, he was accused of extorting thousands of dollars from a mom-and-pop grocery store association that was using non-union labor to deliver its goods. Hoffa pled guilty after the charges were reduced to a misdemeanor, and he was required only to pay a fine. Neither trial resulted in jail time or negatively impacted Hoffa's status within the union. Nevertheless, he was coming to be recognized as a man willing to operate close to the line, if not over it.[13] As labor reformers began to examine the ties between organized labor and mob activities in the 1950s, it came as no surprise that Hoffa would be on their radar screen, particularly as he tiptoed closer and closer to the presidency of the Teamsters.

———

Although Congress's initial efforts to confront the Teamsters faltered—in part as a result of the political influence the union wielded—in time the federal government would identify a man undeterred in his relentless quest to implicate Hoffa in wrongdoing.

His name was Robert Francis Kennedy.

In January 1955, Democrats regained control of the US Senate. As a result, Sen. John L. McClellan (D-AK), now a member of the majority, was appointed to chair the Senate Permanent Subcommittee on Investigations.

A stern, ascetic man who had become a lawyer after serving in World War I, McClellan had sat in the US House of Representatives in the 1930s before his election to the Senate. During the infamous investigation of communistic infiltration into US affairs, McClellan had led a walkout of Democratic committee members to protest Joseph McCarthy's conduct. In McClellan, the subcommittee had found a firm, experienced chairman whose focus would not be easily diverted.[14]

Initially, the Teamsters were not the focus of the committee, which intended to scrutinize governmental operations. However, as investigators looked into the purchasing practices of the US armed forces, they stumbled upon information indicating that the criminal underworld was involved in the shipment of uniforms. It stood to reason, therefore, that attention would soon focus on the labor union dominating the trucking industry that shipped those items.[15]

As McClellan's committee was beginning to develop its evidence, public interest was aroused against the Teamsters in May 1956. Victor Riesel, an investigative journalist for the *New York Journal American*, had openly criticized the union on his daily radio show. He was subsequently blinded by a cup of acid thrown in his face on a New York sidewalk. Television viewers were taken aback when Riesel appeared on *Meet the Press* wearing dark sunglasses and thick bandages to cover the wounds on his face and hands.[16]

Journalist Clark R. Mollenhoff then exposed a scheme engineered by Hoffa and New York mobster "Johnny Dio" Dioguardi (who would also be implicated in Riesel's blinding). Hoffa and Dioguardi had planned to create a number of "paper locals"—local unions that existed nowhere but on paper—for the fraudulent purpose of boosting Hoffa's Teamster delegate totals and, therefore, his power within the union. Just as McClellan began to look into this irregularity, he received complaints that the committee was exceeding its authority. Critics claimed jurisdiction over labor racketeering issues properly lay with the Committee on Labor and Public Welfare. The idea of shifting the investigation to the labor committee was not favored, however, as it was suspected that labor committee chair John F. Kennedy (D-MA) would be soft on the union.[17]

To resolve these concerns, on January 30, 1957, the US Senate Select Committee on Improper Activities in the Labor Management Field, known informally as the McClellan Committee, was created. In light of the political problems previously experienced with the investigation of the Teamsters, half of the group's members were drawn from the Committee on Government Operations, and the other half from the Committee on Labor and

Public Welfare. The new committee would be bipartisan—four Democrats (McClellan, Kennedy, Sam Ervin [NC], and Pat McNamara [MI]) and four Republicans (Irving Ives [NY], Joseph McCarthy [WI], Karl E. Mundt [SD], and Barry Goldwater [AZ]).[18] The purpose of the McClellan Committee was twofold (and limited):

> To determine whether existing law is being properly administered, or if our present statutes are so defective and deficient as to permit improper practices and activities in the labor-management field; and

> To develop the facts and fortify the Congress with pertinent information necessary to enable it to enact remedial and strengthening legislation in those areas where present law does not prohibit or is inadequate to prevent actions that it deems to be improper or inimicable to the best interest of labor, management, or the public interest.[19]

Young lawyer Robert F. Kennedy, only four years out of the University of Virginia Law School and the brother of one of the committee members, filled the position of chief legal counsel. He established his headquarters in Room 101 of the Senate Office Building, which, cluttered with legal treatises and stacks of documents, resembled a "secondhand bookshop."[20] As might have been expected given the prior aborted attempts to corral the Teamsters, onlookers doubted whether the McClellan Committee would achieve anything consequential. With that in mind, Carmine Bellino, the "doggedly determined" chief accountant whose research would prove invaluable in tracking the documentary trail left by Teamsters leadership (and whom Kennedy referred to as "the best investigator in the country"), questioned the chief counsel.

"Unless you are prepared to go all the way," he cautioned, "don't start it."

"We're going all the way," Kennedy replied tersely.[21]

From the beginning, the McClellan Committee differed from its predecessors in tone and determination. Kennedy and his investigators "have the moral certitude, the fervor and lust for a better world that goes with youth," the *Saturday Evening Post* deadpanned. "These men condemn wrongdoing unequivocally. . . . There is something a little chilling about their moral certitude and zeal."[22] The committee established offices in eight cities, from which investigators pursued fifteen major inquiries at a time. They soon began uncovering real evidence as a result. Nevertheless, it would remain to be seen whether the results would be any different from those of the prior congressional committees that had confronted the Teamsters behemoth.[23]

In his 1975 autobiography, Hoffa attributed his legal problems to the efforts of a single man. His key mistake, Hoffa opined, was "coming to grips with Robert F. Kennedy to the point where [they] became involved in what can only be called a blood feud."[24]

The two men first met in the summer of 1956, when Kennedy and two of his aides appeared at the offices of Teamsters Local 299 in Detroit with a subpoena for the branch's records. According to Hoffa's version of the incident, when he informed the visitors that he was in a meeting, Kennedy, "a fellow with a big mop of brown hair," tried to push his way into the room.

Shoved back into the hallway, a flustered Kennedy stammered, "Do you know who I am? I'm Robert Kennedy."

Hoffa responded tersely, "I don't give a good goddamn who you are. If you want to see me you wait right out there in the hallway until we're through with our meeting."

In Hoffa's account, Kennedy "acted like a spoiled brat" after having been instructed to leave the office. And although he crowed when a local judge ultimately quashed the subpoena, Hoffa did recognize the significance of this initial contact, remarking, "[The] incident turned out to be the start of what was to become a blood feud. . . . I had stepped on a poison snake."[25]

Their next meeting occurred on February 19, 1957, at a dinner brokered by Eddie Cheyfitz, a Washington public relations staffer for Hoffa. Almost immediately upon arriving at Cheyfitz's home in Chevy Chase, Maryland, Kennedy and Hoffa reaffirmed their negative opinions of one another. Kennedy later wrote, "It seemed to me that he wanted to impress upon me that Jimmy Hoffa is a tough, rugged man." When the union boss informed him, "I do to others what they do to me, only worse," Kennedy felt that Hoffa was a "bully hiding behind a façade," a man whose lack of self-confidence compelled him to brag about his strength and vigor. For his part, Hoffa described Kennedy as "condescending" and "a damn spoiled jerk." Peppered with questions about how much money he earned and why he had not gone to college, Hoffa concluded that Kennedy was a pompous snob. "Here's a fella thinks he's doing me a favor by talking to me," he said.[26]

According to Hoffa, the evening reached its crescendo when Kennedy turned to the topic of physical prowess:

> I understand that you are supposed to be a very tough fellow . . .
> Hoffa, I'll just bet that I can beat you at Indian hand wrestling."

I hadn't heard anything so stupid since I was a kid. . . .
"Come on, come on," he said. "You're not afraid, are you?"
I let him strain for a couple of seconds. Then, like taking candy
from a baby, I flipped his arm over and cracked his knuckles on to
the top of the table. It was strictly no contest and he knew it. But
he had to try again. Same results. He didn't say a word. He just got
up, his face red as fire, rolled down his sleeve, put on his jacket,
and walked out of the room. He didn't even stay for dinner.[27]

In Kennedy's account, the dinner party came to a merciful close at 9:30 p.m. when his wife telephoned to report that a driver had hit a tree on their property and was sitting in their living room, hysterical. Kennedy said a quick good-bye and returned to Virginia. "Tell your wife I'm not as bad as everyone thinks," Hoffa remarked. Though smiling as he slid into his car for the drive home, Kennedy felt that Hoffa "was worse than anybody said he was." In the end, the February 1957 dinner, intended to allow Hoffa and Kennedy to clear the air, served only to pour fuel on the coals smoldering between them.[28]

"I'm damned certain in my heart," Hoffa concluded, "that Robert F. Kennedy became my mortal enemy that night."[29]

————

On a sidewalk outside of the Dupont Plaza Hotel in Washington on March 12, 1957, Hoffa approached a man wearing an overcoat and hat who handed him a large envelope. Hoffa gave the man $2,000 in cash, part of a sum promised in exchange for inside information about the affairs of the McClellan Committee. The following evening, the two men met again outside of the hotel, and Hoffa was handed another envelope stuffed with documents.

What Hoffa did not know was that FBI investigators stationed across the street from the hotel were photographing him. He was also unaware that his contact, forty-nine-year-old New York attorney John Cye Cheasty, had reported the bribery scheme to the federal government. A former IRS accountant, Secret Service agent, and disabled veteran, Cheasty had agreed to act as an informant. Hoffa was arrested on the spot.[30]

Later that night, sitting in a courthouse, Hoffa came face-to-face with Kennedy. In a bizarre, testosterone-soaked conversation, the two debated who could do more push-ups. Hoffa claimed that he could do thirty, while the younger, thinner Kennedy claimed fifty. Conceding the point, Hoffa snapped, "What the hell weight does it take to lift a feather?"[31]

Freed on bail of $25,000, Hoffa faced up to thirteen years in jail and a fine of $21,000 for attempted bribery and conspiring to influence and obstruct a federal investigation. In light of the FBI surveillance and the firsthand testimony of Cheasty, it seemed likely that Hoffa would be found guilty. "Anyone could try this case," prosecutor Edward Troxell boasted. Recognizing the corner into which Hoffa had been painted, a confident Kennedy quipped, "If Hoffa isn't convicted, I'll jump off the Capitol dome."[32]

Hoffa, however, was not prepared to concede. On Cheyfitz's recommendation, he secured the services of Washington attorney Edward Bennett Williams, who, despite being only thirty-six years of age, had become a well-respected trial litigator. His famous (and infamous) clients included Joseph McCarthy and criminal boss Frank Costello. Williams, nicknamed the "Magic Mouthpiece," would later go on to represent other newsworthy figures such as Hugh Hefner, Frank Sinatra, and John Hinckley Jr. Hoffa's decision to hire the charismatic Williams was arguably the brightest move made in the case.[33]

Hoffa admitted to hiring Cheasty but said he had done so in good faith, engaging him as a legal advisor due to his experience in handling Senate investigations. Hoffa said he had no intention to purchase inside information, and he claimed that he had not known that Cheasty was "a goddamn spy" who had obtained a job with the McClellan Committee. In light of the evidence amassed against him, this explanation might be difficult to buy. It pitted Hoffa's credibility against that of the patriotic, squeaky-clean Cheasty.[34]

Faced with sizably unfavorable facts, Williams chose to downplay the evidence and instead manipulate the jury's impressions of Hoffa and Cheasty. The fact that the jury hearing the charges included eight black members—largely because Williams had focused his jury challenges to exclude white panelists—assisted the defense. Examining the government's chief witness, Williams insinuated that Cheasty was a racist, asking whether he had used a fictitious name while employed in Tallahassee, Florida, to "break the bus boycott" and investigate the NAACP. Although the judge sustained objections to the questions, the mere accusation likely compromised the jury's opinion.

The judge learned that jurors had been given copies of the Washington *Afro-American* newspaper containing an article entitled "The Facts Behind the Hoffa Trial." The article referred to Hoffa as the "hardest-hitting champion" of the Teamsters Union, including its "167,000 colored truck drivers." It also deemed Williams the "White Knight" and the "Sir Galahad" of the civil rights movement and warned that Hoffa had been framed. In addition, the article labeled the judge (who was originally from Mississippi) and Senator McClellan (from Arkansas) puppets of Old South business interests. A photograph accompanying the piece showed Hoffa with Martha Jefferson, a black attorney from Los Angeles who had suddenly joined the defense team. Alarmed by the inflammatory content of the article, the judge ordered the jury to be sequestered for the remainder of the trial.[35]

The most notable episode, however, took place when former heavyweight boxing champion Joe Louis showed up in the courtroom. Embracing Hoffa, whom he called "my good friend," Louis declared that he had come from Detroit to see how things were going. When accused of trying to influence the star-struck jury with celebrity appearances, the defense pointed out that the boxer had simply come to visit Martha Jefferson (who did become his wife in 1959). Nevertheless, it was later revealed that the Teamsters had paid Louis's travel expenses. The episode was significant enough to lead McClellan Committee member Barry Goldwater to sarcastically remark, "Joe Louis makes a pretty good defense attorney."

In retrospect, the tactics of the defense team seem transparent. Nevertheless, even before closing arguments, the conclusion seemed foregone, and the jury deliberated for only four hours before acquitting Hoffa.

"Jimmy," remarked reporter Clark Mollenhoff outside the courthouse, "you are a lucky bastard."

"I just live right," Hoffa smirked.

Unable to restrain himself, a gloating Williams sent Kennedy a present wrapped up with a ribbon. When the chief counsel opened the package, he found a toy parachute intended to assist in his promised leap from the Capitol dome.[36]

The unorthodox tactics Hoffa employed in the 1957 trial foreshadowed the no-holds-barred approach that he and his lawyers would bring to the various legal attempts to bring him to justice in the 1950s and 1960s. Over time, the lawfulness of some of those bruising maneuvers themselves would be called into question.

———

Hoffa's surprising acquittal would not resolve all of his legal entanglements. In fact, he was soon spending so much of his time fending off legal threats that he commented sardonically, "I'm going to be able to hang out a shingle as a lawyer myself before long."[37] In late 1957, Hoffa was tried in New York City on allegations that he and his business partner, Owen Bert Brennan, had hired a wiretap specialist, Bernard Spindel, to install listening devices to illegally monitor IBT employees in Detroit. Spindel also informed a New

Jersey legislative committee that he had been paid to strap minirecorders to union officials so that Hoffa could review their grand jury testimony. Edward Bennett Williams would not repeat his performance on behalf of Hoffa. "I've about had it," he confided to Mollenhoff. "I didn't know what I was getting into with Hoffa and his friends." Nevertheless, after thirty hours of deliberations the jury reported that it was "hopelessly deadlocked," causing the judge to declare a mistrial. It was later revealed that eleven members of the jury had favored conviction, with only a single holdout. Once again, Hoffa had narrowly dodged a guilty verdict.[38]

The case was retried in the spring of 1958, but it was diluted by a ruling of the US Supreme Court in *Benanti v. United States* that evidence obtained by wiretapping was inadmissible in federal trials. Because most of the supporting evidence had been obtained by wiretaps, it was a much weaker case the second time around. During the retrial, moreover, the defense presented twenty-seven new witnesses who testified that on the day in question Hoffa had been in Seattle, and not Detroit. After the verdict, a note bearing the words "Hoffa was acquitted" was passed to Kennedy. Reporters noted that his face went sallow at the unhappy, but by now familiar, news.[39]

These successes did not come without a cost. As federal investigators' efforts to snare Hoffa intensified, his efforts to elude conviction escalated. Hoffa was compelled to retain as many as 150 lawyers experienced in labor, transportation, and (increasingly) criminal law, leading him to comment that he had "single-handedly doubled the average standard of living for all lawyers in the country." The ever-inflating Hoffa legal team came to refer to itself as the "Teamsters' Bar Association." In a wry nod to his ongoing legal battles, moreover, Hoffa kept a plaque on his desk featuring the Latin phrase *Illegitimi non carborundum*—"Don't let the bastards wear you down."

Since the McClellan Committee had begun its investigation, Hoffa had faced three criminal trials and one additional indictment. All had ended ingloriously for Kennedy and his federal investigators. Hoffa appeared unbeatable.[40] The chief counsel bumped into the union boss in a courthouse elevator during his New York wiretapping trial. Kennedy asked Hoffa how the case was going. "You never can tell with a jury," Hoffa responded slyly. "Like shooting fish in a barrel."[41]

———

Despite his legal disappointments, Kennedy could take solace in the fact that he would have his own opportunity to question Hoffa before a national audience. The televised McClellan Committee hearings had captured the attention of the nation, so much so that the committee, initially authorized for one year, secured renewal for two additional years, through March 1960. The McClellan hearings would pit Hoffa and Kennedy against one another, increasing their mutual animosity. Over time, the two slowly became obsessed with one another, each trying doggedly to get the best of the other at every turn. "My first love is Jimmy Hoffa," Kennedy remarked at one time, conceding his fixation with "getting" the Teamster leader.

It was a family obsession. Ethel Kennedy was reported by the gossip column of the *Washington Post* to have engaged in a lighthearted call-and-response with her children while driving past Teamsters headquarters:

> "What's up there?" she asked.
> "The Teamsters Union!"
> "And what do they do?"
> "Work overtime to keep Jimmy Hoffa out of jail!"
> "And?"
> "Which is where he belongs!"[42]

The jokes were not all at Hoffa's expense. While driving home following his normal eighteen-hour workday, Kennedy spied a light on in Hoffa's office. Unable to allow his rival to outwork him, Kennedy returned to his own office to try even harder to unearth some piece of incriminating evidence. After that episode, it was said, Hoffa sometimes left his office lights on at night to trick Kennedy into thinking he was up there working, even if he was long gone.[43]

Over time, the rhetoric Hoffa and Kennedy employed deteriorated into a morass of nasty condemnations. Kennedy famously labeled the Teamsters a "conspiracy of evil" and its leader "a dangerous influence in the American labor movement." He catalogued the dangerous power possessed by the union with respect to the US economy: "Between birth and burial, the Teamsters drive the trucks that clothe and feed us and provide the vital necessities of life. They control the pickup and deliveries of milk, frozen meat, fresh fruit, department store merchandise, newspapers, railroad express, air freight, and of cargo to and from the sea docks. Quite literally, your life—the life of every person in the United States—is in the hands of Hoffa and his Teamsters. The fact that this power is now lodged in the hands of a man such as Hoffa," Kennedy prophesied grimly, "[is] tragic for the Teamsters union and dangerous for the country at large."[44]

For his part, Hoffa publicly professed contentment: "[I'm] happy with the free advertising that Bobby Kennedy is giving me. I couldn't buy that kind of publicity for a million dollars." He could not disguise, however, his contempt for the chief counsel, whom he described as "a vicious bastard" and "a spoiled brat who never had to work for a living and who never tried a case in court." Hoffa felt that Kennedy had developed a psychotic fixation on him, seeking to charge him with some crime—any crime—at any cost. That attitude did not soften with time. "Hell, I hated the bastard," Hoffa wrote bitterly years later, long after Kennedy had died and Hoffa had relinquished the reins of the Teamsters Union.[45]

Hoffa appeared before the McClellan Committee on four separate occasions, enduring thirteen days of questioning. Although the topics broadened over time, the initial focus in August 1957 was "his [Hoffa's] and his wife's investments in a variety of enterprises ranging from trucking to partnership in a girls' camp and a heavyweight boxer"—and including the Test Fleet Corporation. When the committee challenged his motivation for stepping into the Commercial Carriers strike, Hoffa insisted that "the strike was illegal, and he had gone into the situation only for that reason," and not as a quid pro quo for financial support for his own corporation. Asserting that he saw nothing wrong with maintaining business interests in an industry (trucking) in which his own union operated, Hoffa nevertheless offered to "rid himself of any family investments in the trucking business."[46]

That concession notwithstanding, Hoffa employed any number of evasive tactics to stymie the committee's investigation. The questioning devolved into a frustrating attempt to extract information from an obstinate witness who professed to remember very little about the subject of the inquiry. Numerous other witnesses at the hearings employed obstacles to hinder the work of the committee. Of the 1,526 individuals who offered their testimony in the Caucus Room of the old Senate Office Building, an astonishing 343 took refuge behind the Fifth Amendment, which provides that "No person . . . shall be compelled in any Criminal case to be a witness against himself."[47]

One noteworthy exception, interestingly enough, was Hoffa. As the rising president of the Teamsters Union, Hoffa had political reasons for avoiding misuse of the Fifth Amendment, which could jeopardize the standing of the union in the eyes of the AFL-CIO, as well as his own ability to remain in office. Hoffa did not "take the Fifth" a single time during his testimony. Instead, he simply professed a lack of memory in response to the questions hurled at him. To that end, during his testimony in August 1957 it was said that Hoffa "either avoided or equivocated" when responding to 111 questions.[48] This shrewd (but somewhat transparent) strategy eventually led the vice-chairman of the committee, Irving Ives, to remark upon the witness's "forgettery." For his part, McClellan lamented that Hoffa "was a direct man everywhere but in the witness chair." The senator eventually grew so infuriated with Hoffa's evasiveness that he considered bringing perjury charges against the IBT president.[49]

After Hoffa's appearance in August 1957, McClellan read out a forty-eight-count indictment against the witness. In addition to detailing conflicts of interest, questionable associations, paper locals, dubious expenses, and evasive responses to the committee's questions, the indictment devoted five paragraphs to the Test Fleet Corporation. Thirty-four additional counts supplemented the indictment in September 1957. At the conclusion of the 1957 hearings, the committee issued an interim report concluding that "President [Dave] Beck and Vice-President Hoffa used their official union position for personal profit and advantage, frequently to the direct detriment of the Teamster Union membership."[50]

If one objective of those chastisements was to encourage the recalcitrant witness to be more forthcoming, the committee was to be sorely disappointed. To the contrary, as time progressed, Hoffa added additional dilatory techniques to his arsenal:

> "Proxy pleading" of the Fifth Amendment, by which Hoffa would profess to have no recollection of a topic and refer the committee to another witness who would take the Fifth Amendment himself;

> The "stout denial." "That isn't in the record," Hoffa would remark after listening to a summary of a prior witness's testimony. "I have read the record and nothing like that is in there." This would force the committee to either take the time to pause the proceedings and search for the testimony or abandon the question; and

> The "long tangent," going off on a long, vague, and ultimately unresponsive digression.[51]

These various strategies led a frustrated Ives to remark, "You haven't taken the Fifth, but you're doing a marvelous job of crawling around it."[52]

Over the course of the hearings, the animosity between Kennedy and Hoffa continued to escalate, at times boiling over publicly. By the occasion of his final appearance before the committee on July 14, 1959, Hoffa had perfected one additional strategy—a disconcerting, inexhaustible stare directed toward the chief counsel. As Kennedy recalled in his 1960 book *The Enemy Within*:

I called it "the look." . . . During the afternoon I noticed he was
glaring at me across the counsel table with a deep, strange, pen-
etrating expression of intense hatred. I suppose it must have
dawned on him about that time that he was going to be the subject
of a continuing probe—that we were not playing games. It was
the look of a man obsessed by his enmity, and it came particularly
from his eyes. There were times when his face seemed completely
transfixed with this stare of absolute evilness. It might last for five
minutes—as though he thought that by staring long enough and
hard enough he could destroy me. Sometimes he seemed to be
concentrating so hard that I had to smile, and occasionally I would
speak of it to an assistant counsel sitting behind me. It must have
been obvious to him that we were discussing it, but his expression would not change by a flicker. . . . And now and then, after a
protracted, particularly evil glower, he did a most peculiar thing:
he would wink at me. I can't explain it. Maybe a psychiatrist would
recognize the symptoms.[53]

Hoffa claimed to have used the last tactic to aggravate the chief counsel.
"I used to love to bug the little bastard," he explained. "Whenever Bobby
would get tangled up in one of his involved questions, I would wink at him.
That invariably got him."[54]

By the conclusion of the McClellan Committee hearings, what had begun as an apprehensive relationship between two polarized and extremely
competitive personalities had devolved into carping, public disparagement,
and mutual loathing.

———

Years later, Hoffa complained that the methods of the McClellan Committee
and its offspring constituted "persecution[,] not prosecution." He was not
the only critic, as a number of other observers questioned the group's tactics in its vigorous pursuit of the Teamsters.[55] The most significant censure
involved the manner in which the McClellan Committee selected topics to
investigate. It is generally expected that an investigation should begin with
a crime; the purpose of the investigation, then, is to determine who committed that crime. Kennedy, critics charged, had "placed the mule in front
of the cart" by latching on to an individual he wanted to prosecute—such as
Hoffa—and then searching for *any* evidence to convict him of a crime. Noting that a savvy investigator could probably dig up enough dirt on anyone by

looking hard enough, critics lamented that this process of "selective justice" risked upsetting the foundations of the US justice system.[56]

Supporters rose to Kennedy's defense, characterizing the labor racketeering investigations as unique, involving "known criminals but unknown crimes." Investigator Walter Sheridan explained the situation as follows: "It was not a vendetta. It was, rather, a determined and dedicated effort by Bob Kennedy, as chief counsel of the Committee and later as Attorney General of the United States, to cope with a uniquely talented man who used his almost limitless power and resources to perpetuate a racket-infested nationwide empire; to corrupt public officials and private citizens; and to arrogantly violate his own fiduciary trust and the laws of the land for the benefit of himself and his associates and to the detriment of his union members and the public good. For Kennedy to have done less than he did would have been a violation of his own public trust and a dereliction of duty." From a goal-focused point of view, one commentator opined, Kennedy's methods accomplished "useful social results that might not have been achieved otherwise." Thus, the end result—convicting Hoffa—would justify any overreaching or aggressive tactics.[57]

Of course, Hoffa did not accept that self-serving explanation for what he considered government oppression. In his mind, Kennedy had made him the target of one of the largest-ever federal investigations solely because of a personal vendetta and a political desire to punish the Teamsters for supporting Republican candidates. As Hoffa stated in 1959, "Something is wrong when a man may be judged guilty in a court of public opinion because some enemy or some ambitious person accuses him of wrongdoing by hearsay or inference."[58]

Or, as he put it in his autobiography, "It was a witch hunt, pure and simple."[59]

———

One result of the McClellan hearings was the public conclusion that Hoffa was a dangerous influence on the US labor movement. In its second interim report (1959), the committee noted, "If Hoffa remains unchecked he will successfully destroy the decent labor movement in the United States." As the hearings quietly wound down in early 1960, the committee reiterated this opinion: "The testimony is crystal clear that in his unrelenting drive for power Mr. Hoffa had repeatedly shunted aside the interest and welfare of rank-and-file union members while making deals with major employers and the trucking industry. . . . He and his racketeer—and in some instances gangster—associates continue to do business at the same old stand, in the same arrogant and defiant way, despite the overwhelming demands of the citizens of this country for a cleanup, and the elimination of corruption and disreputable practices for this, the Nation's most powerful union."[60]

The work of the McClellan Committee resulted in numerous criminal convictions. All told, 201 Teamster officials and conspirators were indicted as a result of the hearings, and by 1964 more than 125 of those individuals had been convicted. Even so, one key objective of the committee had gone unfulfilled: Hoffa remained a free man, and he was still the president of the Teamsters Union.[61]

Upon the close of the hearings, Kennedy resigned as chief counsel in order to assist with his brother's race for the presidency and to write a book about his experiences, published in 1960 as *The Enemy Within*. However, he could not forget about Hoffa. "We have fought the evil that Hoffa represents for two and a half years," he told his supporters. "It's been a hard grind all along—for the people who work on our committee and for myself. I am not going to lie down and see all that work go to waste." It was not an idle threat. Kennedy simply could not let Hoffa go.[62]

———

Kennedy would not have to wait long for his next shot. On December 16, 1960, President-Elect John F. Kennedy appointed his brother attorney general. As might have been anticipated, criticism of the thirty-five-year-old focused on his lack of legal experience. "If Robert Kennedy was one of the outstanding lawyers of the country, a preeminent legal philosopher, a noted prosecutor or legal officer at Federal or State level, the situation would have been different," one critic noted. "But his experience . . . is surely insufficient to warrant his present appointment." While some detractors may have questioned Kennedy's experience and qualifications, the news of the his appointment must surely have concerned Hoffa, who had personally experienced his tenacity and determination. Even as he insisted that the "attorney general's job [would] not be another subcommittee for the Senate," Hoffa must have recognized that it would now be the executive branch of the US government, and not simply a legislative committee, placing him in its cross hairs.[63]

It came as no surprise, then, when the newly appointed attorney general assembled an interagency team of attorneys and investigators for the single-minded purpose of continuing the pursuit of the Teamsters president. The

members of this group, which came to include sixteen attorneys and approximately thirty investigators, jokingly referred to themselves as the "Terrible Twenty." To others, however, they were known simply as the "Get Hoffa
Squad."[64]

Outraged, Hoffa complained that Kennedy had "assigned an elite squad
of 23 deputy attorneys generals" to get him. For the first time, Hoffa began
to sound paranoid, complaining that "FBI agents followed him wherever he
went, tapped his phone, opened his mail, and beamed electronic listening
devices on him from half a mile away, aided by invisible powder they had
rubbed into his clothes." "You are walking on a picket line," he explained to
curious reporters, "and an FBI agent comes up and rubs this white chemical
on you and you're wired from then on. They can pick up everything you say
until you have the suit cleaned." "FBI agents say they are mightily intrigued
by such a chemical," a news account reported, "but equally unaware of its
existence. If Hoffa has the formula, they wish he'd share it."

In reality, the efforts of the Get Hoffa Squad were not quite so scintillating. For the most part, investigators spent their time painstakingly reviewing
piles of documents—ledgers, receipts, and canceled checks documenting
Teamster activities—searching for evidence of inappropriate conduct. It was
a meticulous, boring process with little resemblance to the cloak-and-dagger
exploits of secret agents the public imagined.[65]

Even if Hoffa was exhibiting signs of paranoia, though, his feelings of
persecution were to some degree grounded in fact. He correctly believed
that the new administration had placed him squarely in its sights. Despite
the dissolution of the McClellan Committee, Kennedy was still working to
get Hoffa. The question that hung in the air was from which quarter the next
indictment would come, and when.

It would not take long for that question to be answered.

THREE

"They're fixing to get at the jury."

—Edward Grady Partin[1]

FOLLOWING THE QUIET dissolution of the McClellan Committee, Hoffa was free to focus on union affairs for the first time since assuming the Teamsters presidency. Reelected in 1961, he pushed through a series of revisions to the IBT constitution that served to solidify his power and influence. He also continued to work toward his ultimate goal—a single nationwide trucking contract for all IBT locals. Confident that he had sidestepped the various traps the federal government had laid for him, Hoffa proclaimed,

"[Kennedy] ought to recognize now that the time and effort they've put in trying to destroy the Teamsters have completely failed. It was a waste of time."[2]

Within the Department of Justice, however, a team of attorneys and investigators was laboring day and night, reviewing the voluminous transcripts of the McClellan hearings to determine how to best exploit Hoffa's testimony to bring new charges against him. Eventually, a scheme involving Sun Valley, the "Teamsters model city of tomorrow," offered the best opportunity for successful prosecution.[3] The Sun Valley project consisted of a strip of undeveloped land located in Titusville, Florida, a few miles south of Cape Canaveral, that had been purchased for $150,000 ($18.75 per lot) by Henry Lower, an "escaped convict and narcotics dealer" from Detroit. Lower offered the property as a retirement paradise for rank-and-file Teamsters. Two thousand union members purchased lots for $150 each, and the remaining 75 percent of the lots were placed on the public market for $550 each. Unbeknownst to rank-and-file investors, however, Hoffa and his business partner, Owen Bert Brennan, had privately arranged to purchase up to 45 percent of the property at the deflated price that Lower had originally paid, thus allowing them to make a considerable profit.[4]

To fund the project, Lower needed a bank loan. Hoffa withdrew $500,000 from the bank accounts of Teamsters Local 299, which was deposited into the Florida National Bank of Orlando, supposedly to stand as collateral for the loan. Of course, the diversion of union funds for that purpose was illegal. Complicating matters, after claiming $90,000 for his own services, Lower redirected $250,000 to other business enterprises, allegedly with Hoffa's approval. At the end of the day, Sun Valley never benefited from the promised improvements. The project deteriorated into a Sunbelt ghost town, with only six homes ever built. After Sun Valley filed for bankruptcy and defaulted on the remaining balance, the bank understandably refused to allow Hoffa to withdraw the union funds that had been deposited as part of the scheme.[5]

The Sun Valley fiasco came to the attention of investigators in September 1957. An investor identified only as "Oscar" contacted the government to report that he had visited the property and found no improvements. Moreover, while developers had advertised the area as "all on high, dry and rolling land," many of the lots were "so low and permeated with water as to make them unsuitable for construction of homes."[6]

Initially, Hoffa held investigators at bay by offering his political support to presidential candidate Richard M. Nixon, who stifled any real inquiry into the Sun Valley sham. After Kennedy defeated Nixon in the 1960 election, however, the protection the Republican candidate offered evaporated. On

December 7, 1960, Hoffa, Lower, and Detroit banker Robert E. McCarthy Jr. were indicted on twelve counts of mail fraud. On December 16, Hoffa appeared in a federal court in Orlando and pled not guilty to the charges, which carried a potential penalty of sixty years in jail and a fine of up to $12,000.[7]

The Sun Valley scheme was a public relations nightmare. In an article entitled "Hoffa's Hornswaggle," *Time* magazine pinpointed the problems the development plan created: "In all his brushes with courts, congressional committees, ethical practices committees and assorted reformers, Teamster Boss James Riddle Hoffa has earned a reputation as a thoroughly bad egg. But, curiously, even some of his critics pay him at least one grudging compliment: despite his many faults, they say, Jimmy Hoffa always takes good care of his Teamsters. Last week a federal grand jury in Florida leveled charges against Hoffa that, if proved, should smash forever the notion that he cares a hoot about the welfare of his union's members." Hoffa must have cringed when he pictured rank-and-file Teamsters reading articles discussing his self-serving manipulation of the Sun Valley project. Nevertheless, he addressed the charges with accustomed aplomb. "Nobody got defrauded out of a quarter," he insisted. "So where's the problem?" To reporters he explained, "Stories about the Orlando case make it look like Hoffa put $500,000 in his kick. Which ain't bad if you can do it, but I didn't." What was wrong with using union funds to invest in potentially lucrative Florida property?[8]

A second legal issue arose on May 17, 1962, when Hoffa was arrested for assaulting a subordinate, Samuel Baron, the field director of the IBT warehouse division. Accurately suspecting Baron of leaking information to the Get Hoffa Squad, Hoffa had cursed and shoved him, blackened his eye, and given him a bad cut under his right eyebrow. Hoffa was released on $500 bail. If found guilty, he would be subject to up to a year in jail and a $500 fine; even more significantly, under the IBT constitution the striking of a fellow union member was grounds for expulsion from office.[9]

Only two days later, a Nashville grand jury indicted Hoffa yet again, this time for labor extortion stemming from the Test Fleet situation. Misdemeanors, the two counts of the indictment carried potential penalties of up to a year in jail and a fine of $10,000. The government made a shrewd decision in selecting Nashville as the site for the trial. Either Nashville or Detroit would have been a suitable location; Test Fleet was chartered in Tennessee, while Commercial Carriers was based in Michigan. It was clear, however, that the prosecution would prefer to conduct the trial far from Hoffa's home turf. In addition, Kennedy's former administrative assistant John Seigenthaler edited the *Nashville Tennessean*, which would cover the trial.

On July 19, 1962, a federal court in Washington held that union funds could not be used to pay a union official's legal bills. Hoffa's continuing legal battles would force him to dip into his personal savings.[10] One piece of good news did arrive in mid-1962. The government elected not to move forward with the Sam Baron assault case, largely because all six witnesses to the incident either refused to testify or claimed that Baron, and not Hoffa, had been the aggressor. In the wake of this stunning reversal, one Teamster attorney labeled such Hoffa devotees, who were apparently willing to perjure themselves to support the IBT president, as the Teamster boss's "improvers." These individuals had "a facility for improving misdemeanors into felonies"—while assault was a misdemeanor, obstruction of justice and perjury were felonies. This notion would prove to have an eerie resonance in subsequent years.[11]

Even after the failure of the Baron case, a delicate question remained as to how two trials (in Orlando and Nashville) could be scheduled for prosecution in the same time frame. Soon, that issue would resolve itself in Hoffa's favor. When the US Congress passed a bill creating a new Middle Judicial District in the State of Florida, all cases scheduled for trial prior to October 29, 1962, were delayed until a conference could be held to consider the effects of the change. The Sun Valley case, set to begin on October 15, was removed from the trial calendar.[12] In this manner the way was cleared for the government to proceed with the Test Fleet case. Given the gravamen of the charges (mere misdemeanors), it appeared that circumstances had unexpectedly benefited Hoffa once again.

———

On October 21, 1962, the day before the Test Fleet trial was set to begin, Hoffa arrived at the Nashville airport, where Ewing King greeted him. Hoffa had helped King secure the presidency of Teamsters Local 327 in Nashville. Climbing into King's red Thunderbird, Hoffa was escorted to the Andrew Jackson Hotel, where a block of rooms on the seventh floor would serve as the IBT's de facto headquarters throughout the trial.[13]

"The people of Nashville just were not that interested [in the Test Fleet trial]," Get Hoffa Squad member Walter Sheridan reflected. Perhaps one reason was the competing national news during the same time frame. On October 22, the first day of the trial, President Kennedy announced the discovery of missile installations in Cuba, ninety miles off the coast of Florida. According to the President, the United States intended not only to quarantine Cuba but also to retaliate with force against any aggressive action by the Soviet-backed island nation. For the next week, the country was riveted to the crisis, which would become the apex of the Cold War—quite possibly the closest that the United States and the Soviet Union came to nuclear war. The crisis was not resolved until October 28, one full week into Test Fleet proceedings. From a public relations perspective, the affair blessed Hoffa's team by diverting Americans' attention from the trial in Tennessee. Yet again, it seemed that luck clung to Hoffa's coattails when it came to legal matters.[14]

The chief attorney for the prosecution was Jim Neal, a "stocky, cigar-chomping ex-Marine with a Tennessee drawl" who had graduated first in his class from Vanderbilt University Law School in 1957. Neal's "native intelligence and aptitude for painstaking research" made him the first man recruited to the Get Hoffa Squad. When Kennedy approached him about the possibility of trying organized crime cases, Neal protested, pointing out that he had no experience with such matters. "That's all right," Kennedy replied, "I don't have any experience being attorney general." Neal acquiesced and agreed to join the team. Prior to Test Fleet, he had won a bankruptcy fraud case against Hoffa associate Benjamin Dranow in Minneapolis. Also, Neal had initially recommended that an indictment be pursued in the Test Fleet case. In time, Hoffa would refer to Neal as "one of the most vicious prosecutors who ever handled a criminal case for the Justice Department."[15]

Assisting with the prosecution was the youthful Charlie Shaffer, a twenty-six-year-old assistant US attorney who had recently graduated at the top of his class from Fordham Law School. US attorney Kenneth Harwell rounded out the government team. The Test Fleet trial would be the largest and highest-profile legal matter in which they had been involved. They would hole up at the Noel Hotel, only a few blocks from the courthouse.[16]

Across the aisle, forty-four-year-old William Bufalino, the "fiery and headstrong" counsel who had represented the IBT in a number of previous legal matters, represented Hoffa. The son of a Pennsylvania coal miner (and the cousin of crime boss Russell Bufalino), William Bufalino had studied for the priesthood before opting for a legal career. After serving in the army's Judge Advocate General (JAG) Corps during World War II, he had moved to Detroit, married into the Angelo Meli mob family, and opened his law office. In addition, Bufalino been a principal target of the "jukebox locals" investigation into criminal extortion in 1953. A veteran of Hoffa's prior trials, he would bring a brash, aggressive style to the defense.[17]

The defense also included sixty-five-year-old James E. Haggerty, a well-respected veteran attorney from Detroit who had once been president of the Michigan Bar Association. Meticulous and white-haired, Haggerty was rarely seen outside the courthouse without a hat and cigarette. Some Hoffa associates referred to him as "the Bishop." Primarily an antitrust lawyer, Haggerty had joined the defense team following the Sun Valley indictment.[18]

Z. T. "Tommy" Osborn, a Nashville lawyer familiar with local customs as to courtroom procedures, served as local counsel for the defense. A "highly regarded Nashville native," Osborn had recently won the landmark *Baker v. Carr* case (1962), a divisive, politically charged decision in which the Supreme Court established the "one person, one vote" standard for legislative redistricting, increasing the political power of urban areas (and black voters) vis-à-vis rural districts. "At forty-two," therefore, Osborn "became the new darling of local politics, one of the few people in [Nashville] welcome at both newspapers and in both political factions." Osborn had received his law degree from the YMCA Night Law School. A former city attorney who had defended Nashville Teamsters from time to time, he was known to have an affinity for underdogs—he was willing to take cases for little pay if he felt that a litigant needed his help. Well-liked throughout Nashville, even by those who opposed him in court, Osborn was a rising star in the legal community.[19]

Federal district court judge William E. Miller, a native Tennessean whom Eisenhower had nominated in 1955, presided over the trial. Miller was known for his "uncompromising integrity," so much so that a purported Chicago-based plot to bribe him was said to have failed because no one had the courage to approach him.[20] Due to a preexisting heart condition, Judge Miller announced that court would be held for only four hours each morning. While this decision afforded the attorneys a great deal of time to prepare for each day's proceedings, it also caused the trial to draw out for an excruciating nine weeks.[21]

———

On October 26, opening statements began in the Test Fleet trial. Speaking on behalf of the prosecution, Charlie Shaffer summed up the government's position: "The proof in this case will show that beginning in 1947 and up until 1958 Hoffa, his union associate and business partner, Bert Brennan, and several people connected with a company who employed Teamsters Union members represented by Hoffa all participated in a long-range plan, whereby Hoffa would be continuously paid off by the employer."[22] The United States would offer several witnesses to testify as to the organization of the Test Fleet Corporation. Their testimony would challenge the notion that the wives of Hoffa and Brennan were the real owners of (or in any way involved in) the company.

The defense offered several answers to the charges. Hoffa and Brennan had received legal advice indicating that there was nothing wrong with their wives' owning a trucking company. Once the arrangement had been challenged during the McClellan Committee hearings, the women had withdrawn from the company. Hoffa's lawyers—including Jacques Schiffer, who would later play a prominent role in the union boss's Chattanooga trial—confirmed that they had deemed the arrangement lawful. Brennan's widow[23] testified that she and Jo Hoffa had owned the Test Fleet Corporation, although on cross-examination she admitted that she knew little about the company or its business practices. The defense argued that the strike against Commercial Carriers had been settled because it was an illegal strike, and not because of any business arrangement with Hoffa. Finally, the defense claimed that the attacks on Test Fleet were motivated by the attorney general's all-consuming desire to get Hoffa at any cost, and not by any legal shenanigans by Hoffa or his partners.[24]

Despite the prominence of the litigants and the fiery accusations leveled back and forth, outside observers considered the Test Fleet case no more than a dry, tedious piece of litigation involving a litany of details concerning the ownership and control of a business entity. Perhaps it was for that reason that Nashvillians seemed uninterested. As the trial progressed, however, it was clear that the Test Fleet hearings would be anything but dull. The first sign that the trial would be unorthodox was immediately apparent. On the evening of the proceedings' first day, US attorney Ken Harwell received a phone call from a prospective juror who had been contacted by a "Mr. Allen" from the local *Nashville Banner* newspaper. Allen asked him several questions about the trial, some of them concerning her feelings about Hoffa and the Teamsters. Of course, such a contact with potential jurors was highly improper. The curious thing about the call? There was no reporter at the *Nashville Banner* with the surname of Allen.[25]

Informed of the situation, Judge Miller dismissed the juror who had reported the improper contact. When he asked others whether they had received similar calls, several raised their hands and were likewise excused. Miller instructed the remaining jurors not to talk with anyone, watch the television news, or read newspaper articles about the trial. Fearing damage to the *Banner*'s reputation, the newspaper's editor printed a front-page editorial denying involvement and offering a $5,000 reward for information leading to the arrest of the perpetrator(s).[26]

"I swear to God that neither I nor any of my lawyers knew anything at all about these attempts," Hoffa insisted in his autobiography. The "Allen from the *Banner*" calls, though, signaled the opening salvo in what would become a serious, ongoing attempt to influence the Test Fleet jury. Significantly, the incident also represented the first time that one of the members of Hoffa's camp quietly fed information to the government about the very same attempt.[27] That man was Edward Grady Partin.

———

The Get Hoffa Squad first became aware of Partin, the head of Teamsters Local 5 in Baton Rouge, Louisiana, on January 1, 1962, when he called a dissident former Teamster to report threats of violence by Hoffa, as well as bribes being paid to fix NLRB elections. Ironically, the FBI was already investigating Partin on unrelated issues. Because he was a close associate of Hoffa who had refused to cooperate with prior investigations, his claims were ignored. The call was completely forgotten when a grand jury indicted Partin for forging the name of a Local 5 member on a union withdrawal card.[28]

The indictment was not Partin's first brush with the law. He had acquired a lengthy rap sheet dating back to his discharge from the Marine Corps at age seventeen after stealing a watch. When Partin was charged with auto theft in Oregon one month later, the case was dismissed with the stipulation that he leave the Pacific Northwest and return home to Natchez, Mississippi. Just two years later, however, Partin was back, pleading guilty to second-degree burglary. He served three years in the Washington State Reformatory, and one year after his release, he served an additional ninety days on a plea for petit larceny.

It was at that point that Partin's life was said to have turned around. He married his wife, Norma Jean, in Baton Rouge and joined the Teamsters Union, rising to the presidency of Local 5 by 1952. He also became an avid Hoffa supporter.[29] Partin's legal entanglements, however, had not ceased. On June 22, 1962, a federal grand jury in New Orleans indicted him for embezzling $1,659 in union funds. On September 26, he was charged with vehicular manslaughter and leaving the scene of an accident in Alabama. The following day, Partin was arrested on a charge of kidnapping and held without bail. Although the matter concerned a family quarrel involving a Teamster member (and not a true kidnapping), the allegation was a serious one, particularly for a man with a lengthy rap sheet.[30]

Three days after Partin was jailed on the kidnapping charge, Walter Sheridan received a call from Department of Justice attorney Frank Grimsley, who reported that Partin wanted to talk to a department official about a national security issue. Grimsley agreed to a meeting in the middle of the night on October 1. Partin recounted a disturbing encounter between himself and Hoffa. "I've got to do something about that son of a bitch Bobby Kennedy," Hoffa had grumbled. "He's got to go." During the same meeting, Partin claimed, Hoffa had asked him what he knew about plastic bombs and had commented that he knew where to get a silencer for a gun. For whatever reason, either patriotism or self-preservation, one of Hoffa's associates was suddenly willing to turn on the IBT president.

Still somewhat suspicious, the FBI administered a lie detector test. Partin passed.[31] After using his influence to see that the "kidnapped" children were returned to their mother, Partin was released on bond. He called Hoffa on October 8 to report his release from jail, then again on October 18, as the Test Fleet trial loomed on the horizon. Unbeknownst to Hoffa, the calls were tape recorded. As Hoffa later related, Partin said that "he was being hounded by federal investigators 'because [he was] a loyal Hoffa man.'" He also requested a meeting, to which Hoffa assented passively. Partin was told to come to the Andrew Jackson Hotel, where the defense team was setting up camp. The question as to who had invited Partin to Nashville would become a critical issue in examining the events of the Test Fleet trial.[32]

Almost unwittingly, the government had stumbled on the key to getting Hoffa. Partin would go to Nashville and keep an eye open for jury tampering or other illegal activities. If he saw anything inappropriate, he was to call the federal office in Nashville and use the code name "Andy Anderson," which investigators would recognize.[33] Surprisingly, and despite the various charges hanging over his head, Partin did not make any demands in exchange for his cooperation. "Most of the sources I had dealt with in the past had asked for anonymity and for promises that they'd never be called to testify," Sheridan later recalled. "Partin made no such request."[34]

It would not take long for Partin to call the FBI. On the evening of October 22—the first day of the trial—Sheridan spoke with him. "They're fixing to get at the jury," Partin said, explaining that two ostensible Hoffa associates,

Allen Dorfman and Nicholas Tweel, were in Nashville conspiring to influence members of the jury. When they conferred later that evening, Sheridan learned that Partin had met with Hoffa during the day. When asked about Tweel, Hoffa had said, "[He's] up here to help me." Hoffa also remarked tellingly, "We're going to try to get a juror—or a few scattered jurors—and take our chances." He added that Nashville Teamster leader Ewing King was holding a meeting that very evening to discuss the jury.[35]

The next day, Partin informed Hoffa that he needed to return to Baton Rouge for a few days to handle some union business. According to Partin, Hoffa responded that he might want him to "pass something" when he returned to Nashville. As he spoke, the Teamster boss patted his hip pocket to insinuate that Partin might be asked to deliver money to someone. From the very beginning, Partin said, Hoffa was drawing him into an intricate web of malfeasance.[36] As Hoffa saw it, though, Partin was a nonentity, a mere hanger-on who played an insignificant role during the trial: "Partin arrived in Nashville on October 22, the day before the trial started, and hung around like a leech the whole time. He was in court every day and came up into my suite every night while I was conferring with my lawyers. Partin was kind of like the furniture. He was around but you hardly knew it."[37]

Whatever role Partin played, events soon appeared to confirm his claim that the defense was planning to taint jurors. The first direct attempt to influence a juror occurred on the morning of the third day of trial (October 24). Prospective jury panel member James Tippens informed Judge Miller that he had been approached by a neighbor, Lawrence "Red" Medlin, who had offered him $10,000 to vote for acquittal. Tippens was immediately excused from jury service, and Miller asked the FBI to locate and interview Medlin.

Judge Miller held a meeting with the parties and their attorneys in chambers that morning. Carefully noting that he was not accusing anyone of misconduct, he expressed concern about the reported approach to Tippens. When prosecutor Jim Neal asked that the jury be sequestered to avoid similar future incidents, Tommy Osborn objected, speculating that independent "do-gooders" trying to help Hoffa were behind any misguided attempt to contact the jury. Miller ruled that the jury would not be locked up, although he expressed his hope that no further incidents would occur during the trial.

In that, the judge was to be sorely disappointed.[38] After the proceedings had concluded on October 24, Partin reported to Sheridan, Hoffa had been extremely upset that Tippens could not be bought.[39]

———

After the abortive Tippens incident, things were quiet for almost a month. Then, on November 17, FBI agents tracked Ewing King—code-named "Top-cat"—as he set out to meet with a Tennessee state highway patrolman on a deserted road late at night. Unaware that he was being followed, King swapped his Thunderbird for the drab sedan of another local Teamster official. He then drove to the home of the patrolman, James Paschal, whose wife, Betty, just happened to be one of the jurors in the Test Fleet trial. Although there was no evidence that money had changed hands, the mere fact that contact had occurred between a Teamster official and the husband of a juror was enough to raise eyebrows.

Partin tipped off the government about the clandestine meeting, reporting that King had been "talking about approaching a female juror whose husband was a highway patrolman." This tip helped Sheridan identify Betty Paschal, juror number ten, who had noted on her jury questionnaire that her husband was a "State Highway Patrolman." The government had tailed King's Thunderbird as a result.

Neal requested Paschal's removal from the jury on the grounds of "compelling, suspicious circumstances indicating an improper approach." During a four-hour hearing, the windows in the courtroom doors were taped over with newspapers to thwart curious reporters. Ultimately, Judge Miller agreed to remove Betty Paschal from the jury. Taken into custody, King took the Fifth Amendment when asked about his contacts with the patrolman—allegedly after receiving a suggestive five-fingered gesture from Hoffa. Initially denying that he had spoken to King, James Paschal later changed his tune and admitted that King had offered to help him obtain a promotion—but insisted that the Hoffa trial had not been mentioned. When asked whether he had found it strange that a complete stranger had offered to do such a good deed for him out of the blue, King mumbled, "I don't know."

Understandably upset, Betty Paschal expressed surprise at her dismissal from the jury and insisted that she knew nothing about the allegations.[40] It was less than a month into the trial, and two jurors had already been dismissed.

———

If the Test Fleet trial had already been quite unusual (at least behind the scenes), on December 5 the case would take an even stranger turn—this time in public. That morning, twenty-eight-year-old Warren Swanson, an itinerant restaurant worker and former mental patient, entered the Nashville courthouse and took the elevator to the top floor. In doing so, he was just like any other spectator wishing to get a glimpse of the Hoffa trial. Swanson, though, was no ordinary spectator. Six months earlier, while he was wasting away in a Cincinnati hotel room and staring at a sign advertising a local Teamsters convention, a voice had popped into his head and told him to kill Jimmy Hoffa. A *Sports Illustrated* ad for a high-powered gas pellet gun buoyed Swanson with its promise that the weapon would "drive[ ] pellets through four-inch blocks of wood." He sent off for the pistol and waited.

When Swanson entered the Nashville courtroom on December 5, a hearing was in progress, and the jury was not present. No one tried to stop him as he strode up to the defense table. Without a word, he pulled the gun out from under his raincoat. Stunned, no one moved. Swanson leveled the gun at Hoffa and pulled the trigger three times from point-blank range. Yet Swanson had made a critical mistake. Although he had pumped up the air gun as instructed, he had left it to sit overnight, allowing the gas pressure to dissipate. The pellets simply bounced off of Hoffa's face and arms. The Teamster jumped up and began swinging. "You always run away from a man with a knife," he said when recounting the situation, "and toward a man with a gun."

A courtroom marshal subdued Swanson with the butt of his own revolver, while Hoffa's assistant, Chuckie O'Brien, leapt over a table and began pounding and kicking Swanson until Hoffa himself yelled for O'Brien to stop. The courtroom paused in stunned silence. After a few tense moments, the court reporter, dutifully taking down everything that was said, recorded the words of Judge Miller: "Will somebody clean up all that blood?" The failed assassin was handcuffed and taken to a federal medical center in Missouri. He would require fourteen stitches in his scalp.

Hoffa curtly summarized the incident: "Some goddamned kook came right into the courtroom and tried to kill me." Two days later, however, the defense filed a motion for a mistrial. Accompanying the motion was an affidavit signed by Hoffa, in which he contended that he had suffered "such shock, stress, and strain" that he would be unable to communicate fully with his lawyers during the remainder of the trial. Judge Miller denied the motion, finding it "utterly groundless if not fantastic." He also recalled that Hoffa had acted "with unusual composure considering the circumstances." It was simply unbelievable that, after pummeling Swanson and coolly advising his attorneys how to handle the situation, the union boss had subsequently developed an incapacitating emotional distress due to the incident. Despite the escalating flurry of bizarre events associated with the case, it would press on. Judge Miller did, however, order the jury to be sequestered for the remainder of the trial.[41]

———

The third strike occurred on November 21. Once again, a juror was dismissed based on information Partin relayed—Hoffa had remarked that he had "the colored male juror in [his] hip pocket." As Partin reported, a black business agent from Local 299, Larry Campbell, had traveled to Nashville, where his uncle Thomas Ewing Parks lived. Apparently, Parks knew the only black male juror on the panel, retired railroad worker Gratin Fields. In attempting to corrupt Fields, however, Campbell had made a critical mistake: he did not follow instructions to only use untraceable pay telephones. The FBI tracked a record of his credit-card calls and found that Carl Fields, Gratin Fields's son, had been offered $5,000, and another $5,000 for his father, if Gratin Fields voted in favor of acquittal. To confirm the sincerity of the offer, one hundred dollars had already been passed to the son.[42]

Sheridan and his team hastily assembled a timeline of calls between Brown's Tourist Home in Louisville, where Larry Campbell was staying, and Parks's residence. Importantly, the investigators also discovered a number of calls from Brown's Tourist Home to Hoffa's unlisted telephone number in Detroit. Campbell's negligence had created a vital (and until that point nonexistent) link between Hoffa and the attempts to contact jurors in the Test Fleet case.

Once again, Neal acted to remove a juror from the panel. This time, though, he produced a sealed affidavit signed by the government's secret informant (Partin) clarifying that Hoffa had made comments about Gratin Fields. Hoffa's attorneys objected, believing that the document would confirm illegal government monitoring of their conversations with their client. Of course, the lawyers' suspicions were not paranoid; each time an effort to manipulate the jury had been initiated, the government seemed to know about it almost instantaneously. Little did the Hoffa team know that the supposed wiretaps did not exist; the information was coming from *inside* the Hoffa camp.

Gratin Fields was immediately sent home. Like Betty Paschal, he told reporters that he did not know why he had been dismissed, and he insisted that no one had ever contacted him about the trial. Judge Miller commented, "This is the most astounding, most amazing set of circumstances that I have ever seen."[43] Concerned about security in the wake of this third dismissal, Hoffa placed a guard at the door to his hotel suite.

The man he chose for the job was Edward Grady Partin.[44]

————

On December 21, after forty-two days of testimony and argument, the Test Fleet case was handed to the jury. The seventeen-hour deliberations would drag on into the weekend. While seven jurors reportedly favored acquittal, they could not convince the remaining members of the panel to agree. On three separate occasions, the jury reported that it was unable to reach a verdict, and each time the frustrated jurors were sent back to consider the case further.

Finally, on Sunday morning, December 23, the jury sent a note to the judge reporting that it was "hopelessly deadlocked." By that time, the court was facing considerable pressure to wrap things up. The case had been dragging on since October; it was now almost Christmas. In addition, an unusual winter storm had thrown Nashville into disarray, unloading five inches of snow, ripping down power lines, and starting fires throughout the city. Left with no other reasonable choice, Judge Miller declared a mistrial. "There comes a time when if the members of the jury cannot agree, they cannot agree," he said, "and that is it."[45]

Hoffa had won again. On four separate occasions, the federal government had brought criminal charges against the Teamster leader, and on four occasions he had escaped conviction. The prosecution team left Nashville empty-handed as their victorious prize returned to Detroit. Hoffa wished "everybody connected with the trial a Merry Christmas" and left Nashville as a free man. "Santa Claus has simply refused to put Jimmy Hoffa in Bobby Kennedy's stocking," Bufalino crowed to reporters.[46]

Judge Miller, however, tempered the exuberance of the defense by reading a lengthy statement at the close of the trial:

> I feel that it is my duty to make a statement as to some of the unfortunate events which have marked the trial from its inception. . . . From the very outset, while the jury was being selected from a list of those summoned for jury service, there were indications that improper contacts have been made and were being made with prospective members of the jury. In one instance the Court was required to excuse a prospective juror who had been examined on

voir dire after he very commendably disclosed to the Court that he
had been improperly approached.

After the jury was finally empaneled and while the trial was un-
derway, two sessions of the Court were held when all persons were
removed from the courtroom except the defendant, the attorneys
for both parties, the official court reporter, the courtroom clerk
and any witnesses called to testify. At these sessions evidence was
presented to the court indicating that illegal and improper attempts
were made by close labor associates of the defendant to contact and
influence certain members of the jury. . . . I have signed orders to
convene another grand jury soon after the first of the year to investigate fully and completely all of the incidents connected with this
trial indicating illegal attempts to influence jurors and prospective
jurors by any person or persons whomsoever and to return indictments where probable cause therefore exists. . . . The right of a
defendant in a criminal case to be tried by a jury of his peers is one
of the most sacred of our Constitutional guarantees. The system
of trial by jury, however, becomes nothing more than a mockery
if unscrupulous persons are allowed to subvert it by improper and
unlawful means. I do not intend that such shameful acts to corrupt
our jury system shall go unnoticed by this Court.[47]

Although Hoffa could revel in yet another failed effort at prosecution, it
appeared that the steps taken to secure that victory might have serious repercussions. On Christmas Eve, Hoffa taped an interview with Detroit station
WWJ-TV, railing that Judge Miller was prejudiced against him, condemning
the allegation that he had done anything to tamper with the Test Fleet jury
and labeling it a "disgrace . . . for anyone to make a statement that this jury
was tampered with."[48]

While 1962 was ending on a positive note, 1963 would begin with yet another grand jury—and this time, it would be investigating the possibility of
felony charges against the Teamster president.

FOUR

"If he wants that deal, he's got it."
—Z. T. "Tommy" Osborn[1]

ON NOVEMBER 8, 1963, FBI agents watched as Nashville police officer Robert Vick walked into the law office of Tommy Osborn, Hoffa's local counsel during the Test Fleet trial. An hour later, Vick emerged from the building. FBI agents followed him to a waiting car that sped to a federal government office. There, Walter Sheridan and a handful of members of the Get Hoffa Squad watched as agent Bill Sheets carefully removed the listening device that had been taped to the small of Vick's back. The frustrated agents sank back into their chairs; the ribbon within the recorder had unraveled.

They tried to listen to the tape, but while they could hear the receptionist greet Vick as he entered the office, the recording went dead at that point.

The initial attempt to obtain Osborn's admission of jury tampering had failed.[2]

———

Following the disappointing conclusion to the Test Fleet trial, members of the Get Hoffa Squad reconvened in Nashville to study the evidence of jury tampering. The details were rough, leaving unanswered questions and holes in the proof that needed to be resolved to obtain an indictment. While confident that they had unearthed strong evidence of a series of attempts to contact jurors, federal agents still needed to prove that Hoffa had been in on the plot. The government did have one valuable asset—Edward Grady Partin had continued to work with the Get Hoffa Squad in the aftermath of the trial. Hoffa still had no idea that Partin had become a government informant. It was critical to the government, and certainly to Partin, that his identity remain secret as long as possible.

On January 17, 1963, a special grand jury was convened to examine the allegations of jury tampering. Through a parade of witnesses, including police officers, bar owners, and hotel workers, the government began to piece together many of the questionable contacts that had been made with jurors during the Test Fleet trial. Voluminous telephone records from pay phones and tourist courts were linked to callers; even more importantly, government attorneys were starting to link those callers to members of the Hoffa camp. "It was a slow, day-by-day, piece-by-piece process," Sheridan reflected, but the evidence was slowly starting to come together.[3]

One touchy question was what to do with Partin during the grand jury proceedings. Other members of the Hoffa team were receiving subpoenas, and Partin's omission might inadvertently reveal his identity as the government's secret witness. Therefore, he was ordered to appear before the grand jury, just like any other witness. When he received his summons, Partin asked Hoffa what he should do. When Hoffa wanted to see him in Washington the following day, everyone became worried—doubtless including Partin himself. What did Hoffa know? What might happen?

Sheridan greeted an anxious Partin at Washington National Airport, then drove him to the Justice Department. An attempt to fit Partin with a tiny recording device failed—it created a noticeable lump under his clothing. The effort to record the meeting with Hoffa was abandoned. Undaunted,

Sheridan drove his informant to Union Station, only a few blocks from Teamsters headquarters.

"Call me as soon as you get out," Sheridan instructed.

"You mean, *if* I get out," Partin countered grimly.

By the time a worried Sheridan received the promised telephone call, it was midafternoon. However, there was nothing to fear; no one within the Teamsters' leadership seemed to suspect that Partin had turned on Hoffa.[4] According to Partin, the union boss was preoccupied with other business and only met with him for a few minutes, cautioning him to be careful to whom he talked to, as he suspected that information was somehow being leaked to the government. Hoffa also told Partin to meet with William Bufalino about the grand jury hearing. Bufalino instructed Partin to take the Fifth Amendment when questioned, gave him a card detailing the language to use when taking the Fifth, and told him to contact Tommy Osborn in Nashville prior to the hearing.

A week later, on February 14—Hoffa's fiftieth birthday—Partin appeared before the Nashville grand jury and took the Fifth. He had toed the Teamsters line, as instructed. Everything was going as planned.[5]

———

On March 5, 1963, Walter Sheridan appeared before the twenty-one-member grand jury to present his own testimony. As the principal link between Partin and the prosecution during the Test Fleet trial, Sheridan was a crucial witness. He was one of the few able to explain how all of the pieces of evidence fit together, and how they ultimately pointed to a master plot to compromise the jury and secure an acquittal for Hoffa. Sheridan was a dogged fact finder whom Hoffa labeled a "slimy, sleazy rat." Kennedy, on the other hand, had referred to Sheridan as "one of our best and most relentless investigators," asserting, "In any kind of fight I would always want him on my side." [6]

Marked as secret and barred from disclosure for more than forty years, Sheridan's grand jury testimony was made available by court order in 2009. The twenty-six-page transcript, enigmatically titled "In the Matter of: John Doe," contains 138 redactions, mainly the names of witnesses. Nevertheless, the document reveals that the government was slowly beginning to piece together the Test Fleet puzzle.

Questioned by Jim Neal, Sheridan immediately drew a bead on Hoffa. "Starting on the first day of the trial, October 22," he recounted, "James R. Hoffa made the statement that 'We will have to get to one of the jurors, or we will get to a scattered few and take our chances.'" Careful to avoid exposing Partin, who was referenced throughout the transcript as the government's "source of information," Sheridan provided details that he said could only have come from within the Hoffa camp. By way of example, he said, "On October 29 Mr. Hoffa made the statement that he would be willing to pay $15,000–$20,000, whatever it took [to secure the cooperation of a juror]."[7] From the get-go, there would be no confusion as to Hoffa's involvement in the efforts to taint the Test Fleet jury.

Sheridan described four separate efforts to influence the jury. In so doing, he implicated a number of Hoffa associates, including Local 327 president Ewing King and Local 299 member Larry Campbell. In each case the evidence identified Hoffa as the man holding the puppet strings. Sheridan also made the wise decision to reference Partin's presence during the trial. Ignoring the man who had guarded the door to Hoffa's suite during the proceedings might have raised suspicions about the government's shadowy "source of information."

Asked whether his anonymous source would be willing to testify at a possible future trial, Sheridan responded affirmatively. He also vouched for the informant's credibility. "The voluminous information he furnished, that which was subject to corroboration, was corroborated one hundred per cent," he pointed out. "We have never found him to be wrong in any instance." It was becoming clear that this anonymous individual held the key to Hoffa's prosecution. The majority of the information concerning efforts to sway the Test Fleet jury came from the government's source, a man who had yet to be revealed to anyone outside the Get Hoffa Squad.[8]

By the time Sheridan finished testifying, he had sewn together an intricate patchwork of details relating to the efforts to influence Test Fleet jurors. Travel receipts, witness testimony, call records from coin-operated telephone booths, evidence from government surveillance, and, above all, information received from shadowy informants were for the first time woven together into a seamless narrative. And at each step Sheridan punctuated the story with references to the man behind the effort. In the twenty-six pages of his testimony, Sheridan made at least sixteen references to Hoffa's comments and reactions during the trial. As Sheridan made very clear, Hoffa—and Hoffa alone—was at the center of the plan to shipwreck the Test Fleet jury.

This time, the government would take no chances that Hoffa would slip through its fingers.

———

Hoffa was neither cowed nor intimidated by federal efforts to ensnare him. In speeches given in early 1963, he only intensified his vitriol toward the government and his chief antagonist. "Something is happening in this country by the name of Bobby Kennedy," Hoffa remarked at an appearance before 1,800 Teamsters in Pittsburgh on February 28. "One man has assigned an elite squad of 23 deputy attorneys general to work his dictates on me." In Wilmington, Delaware, Hoffa boasted that he had held off the federal government's $50 million effort to bulldoze him, while spending only $170,000 of his own money in legal costs. "Do you think if Hoffa really did all those things," he asked the audience, "that he'd be standing here today?" The crowd roared its approval. "Instead," he shouted over the enthusiastic throng, "Bobby Kennedy is going crazy because he doesn't know how to put Hoffa away."[9]

On April 1, Hoffa appeared on the nationally televised *David Brinkley Journal* and once again took the offensive. After leveling the by-now-familiar refrain that Kennedy was "a spoiled young millionaire that never had to go out and find a way to live by his own efforts," he offered a rare compliment to the attorney general. "There's only one thing I like about Bobby Kennedy," he allowed, "his willingness to work and to fight to win." "Outside of that," Hoffa quickly added, lest he seem too conciliatory, "I don't have any use for him."[10]

———

While Hoffa publicly decried their efforts to ambush him, government attorneys were trying to determine whether they had him cornered. In April 1963, Jim Neal began to prepare a prosecutorial memorandum detailing the assembled evidence. On April 10, Sheridan, Neal, and attorneys Charlie Shaffer and Nat Lewin traveled to Washington to meet with Kennedy and Jack Miller, the chief of the Justice Department criminal division, to discuss pursuing an indictment. No final decision was reached at that time.[11]

Believing that an experienced Tennessee trial attorney should be involved in the case, Kennedy was considering prominent Nashvillians John J. Hooker Sr. and Jack Norman. He called Hooker, whom he knew personally, and invited him to Washington to discuss the evidence. Along with Norman, the sixty-three-year-old Hooker was considered "one of the two giants of the criminal bar" in Nashville. He had obtained his bachelor's and law degrees from Cumberland University in Lebanon, Tennessee, taught law at his alma mater, and served a single term in the Tennessee legislature before opening a law office in Nashville in 1930. Hooker was twice elected president of the Tennessee Bar Association.[12]

Hooker was also a natural raconteur. One admiring journalist recalled his "intelligence and supreme confidence . . . actor's animation, and . . . distinctive voice that could boom, screech, or flow like warm honey depending on the desired effect." He was an immaculate dresser, wearing expensive three-piece suits with a gold watch chain and fob; in the summer, he substituted a seersucker suit and straw boater. With his thinning hair, ruddy face, and bulbous nose, he was a familiar character in Nashville courtrooms. *Nashville Tennesseean* editor John Seigenthaler described him as a "hulking man, barrel-chested, with a barrel belly right underneath it." While sharing an anecdote, he had a habit of hooking his thumbs in the breast pockets of his suit coat, rocking back and forth on his heels, holding the audiences at rapt attention as his voice rose and fell with the rhythms of a story. The powerful orator and advocate for his clients was admired for the courtesy and down-home style he brought to the adversarial practice of law.

One of Hooker's most fascinating cases involved defending Jack Daniel's whiskey proprietor Lem Motlow in 1924 on charges that he had murdered a Louisville and Nashville Railroad conductor. Motlow contended that his pistol had discharged accidentally when he was jostled. However, he admitted that he had been drinking and had drawn his pistol after a black porter had demanded to see his ticket (which he could not find). Convincing the jury that the key eyewitness, a circuit-riding preacher, was biased because the railroad had allowed him to ride for free, Hooker helped secure Motlow's acquittal. In return for his services, Hooker received shares in the distillery.[13]

Listening to Kennedy's pitch, Hooker indicated that he would need to meet Partin in person. The next week, Hooker flew to Atlanta, where he spent two hours talking with the informant on a bench in the airport lobby. Hooker reported that he "thought that the evidence was strong and that Partin would make an excellent witness," but he still wanted more time to think it over.[14] On April 19, a group of Kennedy's top legal advisors joined the lawyers in Washington; it had become a common practice for this group to gather informally to discuss the merits of various legal strategies. "We'd kick it around," Sheridan explained, "and then [Kennedy would] ask these people for their opinion."[15]

With respect to the jury tampering indictment, the group was unable to arrive at a unanimous recommendation. As Sheridan recalled:

> Ramsey Clark, I think, [opposed indictment] on the Sixth Amendment ground. And Bill Hundley, I think, he just didn't think we could win it. But Archibald Cox, who was the solicitor general,

voted for it and said he'd be happy to argue it before the Supreme
Court. . . . I think there were only two, maybe three, dissent-
ers, because [Hoffa] had already been tried three times in federal
court—four times—three under Eisenhower and one under us. I
think there was a pretty strong feeling that if you went again, it had
to be something strong and heinous, and this was both. But there
were problems with it. One witness against Hoffa, Ed Partin, was,
you know, the only one who could really tie him into it. And there
were problems of Sixth Amendment nature, whether he'd been
planted in the Hoffa camp.[16]

The most serious hurdle was the fact that the case would hinge on the
testimony of a witness (Partin) who had potentially been present during
confidential discussions between Hoffa and his attorneys. Among other
things, the Sixth Amendment to the US Constitution provides the accused
with the right to legal counsel, a right that has been interpreted to protect
the confidentiality of attorney-client communications. If the government
had *planted* Partin in the Hoffa camp, a court might invalidate any evidence
derived from his presence. Thus any effort to convict the union boss would
be all but doomed. Even absent an intentional effort to establish him in
Hoffa's inner circle, if Partin had passed on any information relating to trial
strategy or attorney-client conversations, then any verdict obtained against
Hoffa would be tainted and overturned. Before seeking an indictment, the
Get Hoffa Squad would have to ensure that Partin's information was beyond
challenge—and admissible at trial.

At Kennedy's request, Sheridan examined his notes from the Test Fleet
trial with Asst. Atty. Gen. John Douglas. After reviewing material scrawled
on notepads, envelopes, and napkins, the two concluded that 85 percent of
Partin's information related directly to efforts to tamper with the Test Fleet
jury. The remaining 15 percent consisted of mundane remarks concerning
various people's comings and goings. Confident that the government did
not possess privileged information, Kennedy's advisors voted on whether
to proceed. The majority voted to indict; Kennedy concurred, announcing
that he would recommend indictment to the grand jury.[17]

Kennedy telephoned Hooker, who had remained undecided about taking the case, and invited him to return to Washington. On April 22, after
lengthy discussion, Hooker joined the prosecution. He would be joined as
lead counsel by Jim Neal. "We divided it up pretty equally," Neal recalled.
"I would suppose if you look at the grunt work, I did most of that, but he

[Hooker] was invaluable." The following day, the prosecution gathered in Nashville to prepare the case against Hoffa and his colleagues.[18]

On May 9, the grand jury delivered a five-count indictment against Hoffa and five coconspirators for attempted jury tampering during the Test Fleet trial:

> The first count accused Hoffa of conspiring to tamper with the Test Fleet jury.
>
> A second count charged Hoffa and Nashville sandwich shop owner Lawrence "Red" Medlin with attempting to bribe James Tippens in exchange for an acquittal.
>
> In the third count, Hoffa, Larry Campbell, and Thomas Ewing Parks were charged with attempting to influence juror Gratin Fields through his son, Carl Fields.
>
> The fourth count alleged that Hoffa and two associates, Allen Dorfman and Nicholas Tweel, had offered a bribe to Nashville tavern owner Dallas Hall in order to influence the jury.
>
> The final count accused Hoffa and Ewing King of attempting to bribe patrolman James Paschal to urge his wife, Betty Paschal, to vote for acquittal.

Notably, while the indictment charged Hoffa with "aiding, abetting, counseling, commanding, [and] inducing" the attempts to manipulate the jury, none of the counts claimed that he had made an illicit contact himself.

Four days later, Hoffa appeared in a Philadelphia federal court to plead not guilty. He was released on $10,000 bond, and while talking with reporters, he renewed his claim that he was being persecuted. "Of course I'm not guilty," he pronounced. "This indictment talks about ten people and I know only three of them. Two of them worked for me as Teamster officials and the other is an insurance agent who represents our central Teamsters conference. Outside of that I wouldn't know the other seven persons if they walked down the corridor of the courtroom."[19]

Undaunted by Hoffa's protestations, the prosecutors handed down three additional indictments on May 19.

> A trio of men from West Virginia—Herman Frazier, Nelson Paden, and Albert Cole—were charged with posing as reporters for the *Nashville Banner* and making calls to prospective jurors.
>
> Cole was also charged with perjury for lying to the grand jury, testifying that he had not told FBI agents that he had traveled to Nashville to contact and influence prospective jurors

Two additional men, Henry "Buster" Bell and William T. Morgan, were charged with conspiring to bribe prospective juror William B. Morgan to influence jurors Gratin Fields and Mrs. Matthew Walker.[20]

On June 10, Hoffa and his alleged coconspirators were arraigned in Nashville. As he had done any number of times, Hoffa pled not guilty. He also spoke to reporters of his frustration. "I think it would be difficult to get a fair trial anywhere because of the constant harassment of the Justice Department," he said. "It's just another one of Bobby Kennedy's shenanigans."[21] Kennedy's plans, however, were just starting to percolate. On June 25, Hoffa was arraigned in a separate case in Chicago, where he and several coconspirators allegedly defrauded the Teamsters pension fund by diverting monies for personal use. Asked which case they intended to prosecute first, federal attorneys responded that they planned to prioritize the jury tampering case in Nashville. The government was lining up a series of cases against Hoffa; if it could not get him in one, it would have another charge waiting in the wings.[22]

Yet the public did not unanimously condemn the Teamsters president. On the day Hoffa was indicted in the jury tampering case, columnist William Loeb published a front-page editorial in his *Manchester Union Leader* entitled "Moving Toward Dictatorship." Loeb viscerally criticized the newest attempt to ensnare the nation's central labor figure:

> The latest attack by Attorney General Robert Kennedy on James Riddle Hoffa, the head of the Teamsters Union, makes you think of the kids who lost the ball game and then accused the other side of cheating. Last December, in Nashville, Tenn., almost on Christmas Eve, Bobby Kennedy lost another of his many attempts to "hang" something on Hoffa. The jury couldn't agree. Now the government has just indicted Hoffa on the grounds that he and some of his associates conspired to fix the jury . . .
>
> The government has now indicted Hoffa numerous times. Each time Hoffa has either been acquitted or, as in the last case, the jury was divided and a mistrial declared. Under any just and fair system of government it would seem that his persecution of Hoffa should cease, since the only "crime" that Hoffa seems to be guilty of is that he will not knuckle under to the Kennedys and give them slavish obedience, that other labor unions in the United States do. The Teamsters and the head of the Teamsters, James Riddle Hoffa, are as independent and proud as the Kennedys, but since when has that been a crime in this country?

The fight of James Hoffa against the Kennedys is becoming the
fight of all Americans who want to stay free men and women.

It was soon revealed that the *Manchester Union Leader* had, five weeks earlier,
received a $500,000 loan from the Teamsters pension fund.[23]

––––––

As summer crept along, Hoffa decided to go on the offensive, firing off a series of motions. At a July 22 hearing, the defense asked that the indictment
be dismissed, arguing that pretrial publicity had made it impossible for the
defendants to receive a fair trial; that unlawful wiretaps had been used to
develop evidence in the case; that the prosecution had threatened witnesses;
and that Sheridan (who was not an attorney and therefore should not have
been present) had improperly attended the grand jury proceedings.

During the course of a three-day inquiry, the defense requested the right
to review the mysterious contents of the sealed envelope Judge Miller had
received during the Test Fleet trial. Hoffa's lawyers believed those materials
would confirm the FBI's use of wiretaps. Although the defendants' suspicions
were understandable given the information the government seemed to have
about the various approaches to the jury, the envelope contained only Partin's
secret affidavit. Judge Frank Gray, who had stepped in after Judge Miller had
recused himself, reviewed the envelope's contents and denied the defendants'
request and the various motions to dismiss. He also set the jury tampering
trial for October 14, 1963. Of course, the defense found this mysterious handling of the sealed evidence fishy and underhanded.[24]

––––––

The government's top-secret witness was not present at the hearing in Nashville. On July 2, Partin met with Sheridan in Atlanta to discuss the trial.
Although Hoffa did not seem to suspect him of any betrayal, Partin said he
would feel more comfortable if he were hidden away prior to the proceedings.
He also reported that he could not make required monthly payments to his
estranged wife while hiding out. "Inasmuch as Partin was entitled to reimbursement from the government for all the expenses he had borne during the
Nashville trial and would continue to bear," Sheridan explained, "I decided
that we would offset these expenses by making the monthly payments to
his wife when he was unavailable." Withdrawn from a confidential fund, the

monies were funneled to Partin's unsuspecting spouse. It would certainly have
been inappropriate for the government to pay Partin for his testimony. Yet
by labeling the payments as reimbursement for expenses, Sheridan believed
he had sidestepped any questions as to improper influence of the witness.
Even so, questions concerning the payments would flare up as the case proceeded to trial. Having confirmed Partin's continuing cooperation, Sheridan
returned to Washington and notified Kennedy that the case was on track.[25]

As the case lurched toward trial, Sheridan learned of what would become
the most astonishing scandal of the Test Fleet case. The first hint came on
August 23, when he received a telephone call from Nashville police officer
Robert Vick. Vick and others had conducted background investigations of
potential jurors during the Test Fleet case, a relatively common (and legitimate) practice aimed at discovering whether individuals held a belief or
prejudice that would create bias. Cautious but curious, Sheridan spoke with
Vick. Without providing specific details, the officer implied that the Test Fleet
trial might have involved even more jury tampering than the government
thought. After the meeting, Sheridan departed for Washington, armed with
this nebulous information and Vick's promise to be in touch.[26]

Vick resurfaced on November 7, informing Sheridan that Nashville counsel Tommy Osborn had instructed him to offer a prospective juror in the
looming jury tampering trial $10,000—$5,000 up front and $5,000 after the
verdict—to vote for acquittal. The following morning, Vick sat down with
Sheridan, Neal, Hooker, and FBI agents Ed Steele, Bill Sheets, and Al McGrath
in Nashville. The policeman recounted that he had visited Osborn's law office
the day before to review the panel of prospective jurors for the upcoming
trial. When Vick had told Osborn that he knew one of the names on the list,
Ralph Elliot from Springfield, Tennessee, Osborn had asked Vick to offer
Elliot money to vote for acquittal. The idea that a respected attorney like
Osborn would blatantly attempt to tamper with a jury—in a jury tampering
trial, no less—stunned the men in the room. "Walter[,] that's just a lie," Neal
said. "Tommy wouldn't do something like that." Sheridan quietly nodded;
he did not want to believe that Osborn had done any such thing.[27]

If government prosecutors found Vick's story hard to swallow, so would
a judge or jury. The case would likely boil down to Osborn's word against
Vick's, a dispute in which the well-regarded lawyer would certainly hold a
distinct advantage. One way to remedy that problem, the prosecutors decided,

was to get Osborn to repeat his clandestine offer. Steele presented a stunned Judge Miller with a sworn affidavit signed by Vick. Miller then authorized the FBI to place a recording device on Vick, and investigators made their first attempt to tape-record Osborn that same day (November 8). It was on that occasion that the tape recorder malfunctioned, causing the tape to spill out of the device. However, Vick did report that Osborn had repeated his illicit instructions.[28]

Undeterred, Vick and federal agents tried again the following morning. Special Agent Bruce Fischer arrived from Washington with a new recording device, which was taped to Vick's back. As it was a Saturday, however, Osborn was not in his office. On Monday morning, November 10, Vick and the FBI made a third attempt to catch the lawyer. The policeman ventured to Osborn's office at 9:30 a.m. and emerged a half hour later. Back at the government office, agents crowded around the recorder Vick had worn and held their breath while they waited for the tape to play. Amid the sound of rustling clothes, wide-eyed investigators heard the beginnings of a conversation between Vick and Osborn:

Osborn:	Did you talk to him?
Vick:	Yeah. I went down to Springfield Saturday morning and talked to him.
Osborn:	Elliot?
Vick:	Elliot . . .
Osborn:	Is there any chance in the world that he would report you?
Vick:	That he will report me to the FBI? Why of course, there's always a chance, but I wouldn't got into it if I thought it was very, very great.
Osborn:	(Laughed.)
Vick:	You understand that.
Osborn:	(Laughing.) Yeah, I do know. Old Bob first.
Vick:	That's right. Don't worry. I'm gonna take care of old Bob and I know, and of course I'm depending on you to take care of old Bob if anything, if anything goes wrong.
Osborn:	I am. I am. Why certainly . . .
Vick:	Well, I'm gonna play it slow and easy myself and er, anyway, we talked about er, something about five thousand now and five thousand later, see, so he did, he brought up five thousand see, and talking about about [sic] how they pay it off you know and things like that. I don't know whether he suspected why I was there or not cause I don't just drop out of the blue to visit him socially, you know. We're friends, close kin,

cousins, but I don't ordinarily just, we don't fraternize, you know, and er, so he seemed very receptive for er, to hang the thing for five now and five later. Now, er, I thought I would report back to you and see what you say . . .

Osborn: Then tell him it's a deal.

Vick: It's what?

Osborn: That it's a deal. What we'll have to do—when it gets down to the trial date, when we know the date, tomorrow for example if the Supreme Court rules against us, well within a week we'll know when the trial comes. Then he has to be certain that when he gets on, he's got to know that he'll just be talking to you and nobody else . . .

Vick: All right. You want to know it when he's ready, when I think he's ready for the five thousand. Is that right?

Osborn: Well no, when he gets on the panel, once he gets on the jury. Provided he gets on the panel.

Vick: Yeah. Oh yeah. That's right. That's right. Well now, he's on the number one [on the jury panel] . . .

Osborn: All right, so we'll leave it to you. The only thing to do would be to tell him, in other words your next contact with him would be to tell him if he wants that deal, he's got it.

Vick: O.K.

Osborn: The only thing it depends upon is him being accepted on the jury. If the government challenges him there will be no deal.

Vick: All right. If he is seated.

Osborn: If he's seated.

Vick: He can expect five thousand then and—

Osborn: Immediately.

Vick: Immediately and then five thousand when it's hung. Is that right?

Osborn: All the way, now!

Vick: Oh, he's got to stay all the way?

Osborn: All the way . . .

Vick: Now, I'm going to play it just like you told me previously, to reassure him and keep him from getting panicky, you know. I have reason to believe that he won't be alone, you know.

Osborne: You assure him of that. One hundred percent.

Vick: And to keep any fears down that he might have, see?

Osborn: Tell him there will be at least two others with him. . . . We'll keep it secret. The way we keep it safe is that nobody knows about it but you and me—where could they ever go?[29]

Back in Washington, the Get Hoffa Squad reviewed the tape. Neal tele-phoned Judge Miller, who was at a judicial conference in New York, to re-port the situation. The judge returned to Nashville the following morning, reviewed the transcript and recording of the conversation, and indicated that it was necessary to inform Judge Gray of the situation.[30]

It would not take long for the matter to come to a head. The following morning, Osborn was summoned to Judge Miller's chambers, where two judges awaited him. They informed the surprised lawyer that they had re-ceived information "of a substantial nature"—someone had tried to tamper with the jury in the upcoming trial, and he had been implicated. Was he aware of any such attempts? Osborn responded in the negative. The judges questioned him more directly: Had he engaged in any effort to tamper with the jury? Again, Osborn denied any knowledge of the situation. Honing in even further, the judges asked whether he had discussed influencing a juror named Elliot. Once again, Osborn denied all knowledge. The judges served him with a show cause order to demonstrate why he should not be disbarred from practicing law. Given the choice of an open hearing or a private one in the judge's chambers, he chose the latter (and confidential) option.[31]

Although he had managed to maintain his composure during the meeting, after leaving the courthouse Osborn fell apart. Repeatedly, he tried and failed to telephone Vick, who had been spirited away to a Nashville hotel. When retired Treasury agent John Polk ventured to Vick's house the next morn-ing, he was met at the door by stony-faced, cigar-chomping FBI agent Elmer Disspayne, who informed him that Vick was not there and could not be con-tacted. Starting to put the pieces together, Osborn asked to meet Judge Gray in his chambers. Flanked by his law partner Raymond Denny and attorney Jack Norman, Osborn requested the information forming the basis for the show cause order. Judge Gray provided the details, including the affidavit signed by Vick, the FBI investigation, and the tape recording obtained at Osborn's office.

Osborn was floored. Over the weekend, he and his attorneys worked fran-tically to mend the situation. However, it appeared to be all but a foregone conclusion that his career was in jeopardy. When Osborn met with Hooker to brainstorm his options, he learned that the government would not prosecute him if he confessed and testified against Hoffa. Osborn refused the offer.[32] On November 18, he contacted Judge Gray, indicating that he was prepared to make a statement in chambers. Standing before the judges, he admitted to conversations with Vick about influencing Ralph Elliot, and he confirmed that the voice on the recording was his own. While Osborn claimed that *Vick* had devised the idea to approach Elliot, the lawyer's defense was halfhearted. As Hoffa became more of a friend than a client, Osborn explained, he had unexpectedly realized that his client was being "abused" and "persecuted" by the government. He thus tried to protect his friend.

The following day, Judge Miller disbarred Osborn from further practice in federal court. Judge Gray issued a concurring opinion detailing the efforts to approach the prospective juror, as well as Osborn's false responses to the court's initial inquiries and failure to fully disclose information concerning the attempted jury tampering. "[That] the respondent," the memorandum concluded, "in the light of this immediate history [the indictment for jury tampering in the Test Fleet trial] and in this context and atmosphere did himself engage in a brazen attempt to bribe and improperly influence a prospective juror is an indication of such a callous and shameful disregard of duty, such a lack of moral fitness and sense of professional ethics as to warrant no lesser punishment than the removal of his name from the roll of attorneys permitted to practice law in this court."[33]

Nashville Tennessean editor John Seigenthaler said of Osborn, "[He was] one of the brightest, most intelligent, decentest men I've ever known." As such, he sadly recalled, "when I read the transcript [of the conversation between Osborn and Vick] . . . I just felt a tightening of the chest." "This is devastating," Neal lamented, "just unbelievable to me."[34] Nashville lawyers also reacted with stunned disbelief. Only months earlier, Osborn had been elected to the American College of Trial Lawyers, an honor reserved for 1 percent of the attorneys in the state. Moreover, he was expected to become the next president of the Nashville Bar Association. "Tommy would have been elected," one organization representative told the *Tennessean*. Now, in a matter of only a few short days, he had found himself disbarred and disgraced. As a result, the newspaper noted, the local legal community was in "a profound state of shock."[35]

Less than a week later, their attention—and that of the entire nation—would be abruptly diverted to a completely different tragedy.

———

November 22, 1963. Hoffa was in Miami Beach discussing the terms of the national trucking agreement he had worked on for a decade when he learned that President Kennedy had been shot in Dallas. For Hoffa, who felt that the Kennedy brothers had unfairly singled out and persecuted him for years, the news was not unwelcome. "Hoffa was in Miami in some restaurant when the word came of the assassination," Sheridan explained, "and he got up on a table and cheered."[36]

As the nation collapsed into mourning for the slain President, Hoffa insisted that it would be business as usual for the Teamsters Union. At IBT headquarters, a weeping Larry Steinberg ordered the American flag lowered to half-mast and sent employees home for the day. When Harold Gibbons read him a draft statement of condolence on behalf of the union, Hoffa was enraged, believing that any such announcement would be hypocritical; the Teamsters boss forbade them to comment and berated his personal secretary for crying. The day of the funeral was a national day of mourning. As with other businesses and public institutions, Teamsters locals throughout the country were closed. In Detroit, however, Teamsters Local 299 remained conspicuously open all day long. In Nashville, only blocks from a memorial service to honor the late president, Hoffa attended a buoyant rally for local union leader (and codefendant) Ewing King.[37]

Denying descriptions of his gloating response to the assassination, in his 1975 autobiography Hoffa claimed, "I never felt any great animosity toward John Fitzgerald Kennedy. . . . So I felt bad along with the rest of the nation when JFK was assassinated in Dallas." Of course, this assertion stands in stark contrast to Hoffa's reaction when he heard the news of the president's death: "I hope the worms eat his eyes out."[38]

———

On December 2, as the nation climbed unsteadily to its feet, the grand jury convened in Nashville to consider the claims against Osborn. During the proceedings, yet another attorney was swept up into the accusations of jury tampering. Harry Beard Jr., a "mediocre country lawyer" from nearby Lebanon, Tennessee, admitted to meeting with Osborn during the Test Fleet trial. At that time, Osborn told Beard to offer $10,000 to the husband of a juror if his wife would vote for acquittal. Beard claimed he had been flattered that Osborn had contacted him, and he had agreed to use what influence he had to help out. Conveniently, Beard also maintained that he had never intended to do anything and had simply humored Osborn. He said that he had eventually told Osborn a false story, informing him that the husband had demanded $50,000. Beard figured that Osborn would reject the figure for being too expensive. Armed with this damning information, the court denied Osborn's petition for a rehearing.

On December 6, the grand jury indicted Osborn on three counts of jury tampering: (1) instructing Vick to offer $10,000 to prospective juror Ralph Elliot; (2) instructing Beard to offer $10,000 to D. M. Harrison for influencing his wife to support acquittal in the Test Fleet case; and (3) instructing investigator John Polk to set up a meeting with Virgil Rye, whose wife also served on the Test Fleet jury, to attempt to influence her vote.[39] On December 14, the Tennessee Bar Association instigated disbarment proceedings against Osborn. The Nashville Bar Association informed reporters that Osborn had agreed not to practice law in Tennessee state courts and to surrender his law license if his federal disbarment was upheld, as it would be.[40] On December 18, Judges Miller and Gray also disbarred Beard. "We are painfully conscious in this case, as in any case of a similar nature, of the deep tragedy involved to the attorney personally and to the members of his family," they wrote. "Yet if the courts are to survive as instruments for the administration of justice, the strictest disciplinary action in such cases is imperatively required and demanded."[41]

Speaking to a Nashville television reporter, Hoffa remarked with familiar outrage, "It's just a travesty of justice. That the government, the local officials, and the judges should have any part of trying to set up and entrap him [Osborn] and be able to take away from me a competent lawyer to represent me in my case." This brash finger-pointing seemed to ignore the very serious jeopardy Hoffa's lawyer faced.[42]

———

On December 11, Hoffa filed a motion for delay in the upcoming jury tampering case to allow himself time to replace Osborn. The motion also demanded that Judge Gray recuse himself, on the basis that he was biased and had already concluded jury tampering had occurred. Finally, the motion asked for a change of venue on the grounds that recent publicity would prevent Hoffa from receiving a fair trial in Nashville. Judge Gray denied that he was in any way biased; however, out of an abundance of caution, he voluntarily withdrew. As Judges Miller and Gray had recused themselves, it was necessary to bring in an outside jurist to preside over the trial. Frank Wilson, a US district judge in Chattanooga, 120 miles southeast of Nashville, was chosen for the job.

Born in Knoxville in 1917, Judge Wilson received his undergraduate and law degrees from the University of Tennessee. After serving in Italy as an air force staff sergeant during World War II, he had become "the first lawyer in Oak Ridge," the city established in 1942 as a top-secret research site for the atomic bomb. In 1950, Wilson had run for Congress as a Democrat, but Howard Baker narrowly defeated him.[43] Nominated by Kennedy, Wilson was confirmed on June 14, 1961, as US district judge for the Eastern District of Tennessee. Tall and soft-spoken, with a black shock of hair swept across his forehead, he immediately earned the respect of the local legal community with his calm demeanor, meticulous attention to detail, and unquestionable integrity. Wilson's rulings had only been reversed on two occasions. "He had a wonderful sense of humor, intellect, and respect for his fellow man," remembered law clerk Charlie Gearhiser. Tellingly on that point, convicts whom Wilson had sentenced to prison often visited him at the courthouse and discussed how he had helped them change their lives. Yet despite Wilson's quiet conduct, it was remarked, "There is steel underneath his mild and courteous manner."[44]

In addition to handling the seemingly endless parade of criminal cases that made up the bulk of the court's docket, Wilson had found himself mired in the tumultuous social issues of the civil rights era. *James Jonathan Mapp, et al. v. Board of Education of the City of Chattanooga* concerned black residents' 1960 suit to protest delays in school desegregation. As a new appointee, Wilson reviewed three integration plans and selected one that would accomplish full desegregation by 1969; following objections, he amended the date to 1966. Even so, the case would drag out for twenty-six years, becoming the longest one in the nation's history. During the tortuous, exceedingly stressful process, Wilson received numerous death threats. The lead plaintiff suffered not only threats but also the firebombing of his home. Wilson would later remark that the Mapp and Hoffa cases had taken ten years off of his life.[45]

Informed of his new and thankless assignment, Judge Wilson set a hearing on December 20 to address any pending motions. On Christmas Eve, he issued an order resetting the start of the jury tampering trial to January 20, 1964. The judge also granted a defense request for a change of venue, transferring the case to Chattanooga.[46]

———

For Tommy Osborn, the Test Fleet trial had initiated a series of events that continued to spiral out of control as the new year began. During the jury tampering trial, he would be present in Chattanooga—as an unpaid advisor. He would never act as an attorney again.[47] On May 25, 1964, Osborn's own trial would take place in Nashville. Jim Neal and a reluctant, saddened John J. Hooker prosecuted the case. Feeling responsible because he had introduced

Osborn to Hoffa, attorney Jack Norman agreed to defend the disgraced attorney. One last attempt was made to allow Osborn to dodge prosecution. Though he could plead guilty to one count of obstruction of justice to avoid prison time, he somewhat inexplicably refused the offer. Osborn blindly believed that he had been set up and would somehow be proven innocent. If he pled guilty, he insisted, he could not apply for the reinstatement of his legal license. Forsaking his status within the Nashville legal community was not an option.[48]

At trial, FBI agents summarized their investigation, and Vick testified as to his conversations with Osborn. The defense countered with some thirty witnesses who emphasized Osborn's good character. As expected, the defense also attacked Vick's credibility, claiming that Osborn had been entrapped. Norman's brutal, brilliant cross-examination eviscerated Vick's character, highlighting his shiftiness and opportunism. The closing arguments were masterful. "It has been said that in the Louvre of Paris," Norman rumbled, "there are twelve different pictures of Judas Iscariot . . . and there are no two of the twelve that look alike." He pointed his finger at the government's key witness. "But surely they must all look like Vick."

Rising, Hooker slowly surveyed the gathered crowd. "Jack Norman," he began, "you and I have been friends for many years. You are a great speaker. Your voice is like an affidavit." Yet Hooker declared Vick's questionable character irrelevant. "You don't catch anybody trying to fix a jury with an elder or a deacon of a church," he offered.[49] He cast his gaze on the jury box, leaving no question that the case had touched him personally. "This is a sad, dark day, but there was a sad, dark day before this—and that was the day that Tommy Osborn got mixed up with Hoffa." Hooker brought his hand down on the podium. "Ever since he came into the courts of Tennessee, there has been a trail of jury fixing across this state."[50]

Finally, Neal offered his own brief summation. Addressing the claim that Osborn had been entrapped, Neal retorted, "It is foolish to believe that a brilliant, well-educated lawyer who was a former prosecutor could be led by a man like Vick. It's like saying a jackass led a fox into a trap." Osborn, and Osborn alone, was responsible for the position in which he had found himself.[51]

Ultimately, Osborn was convicted by a simple and most damning piece of evidence—his own voice. After deliberating for two hours and fifty-two minutes, the jury found him guilty of jury tampering.[52] Osborn appealed the verdict, but the US Court of Appeals for the Sixth Circuit upheld it in 1965. "The transcript does not mirror the inducing of an unwilling party to commit a crime," the court concluded, rejecting the claims of entrapment, particularly given Osborn's intimation to Vick that "at least two others" would be contacted. While the court did find that Vick exhibited "moral flexibility," that was not enough to overcome Osborn's own words.

His appeals exhausted, Osborn was sentenced to three and one-half years in prison in Alabama. One poignant footnote occurred when John Jay Hooker Jr.—the son of Osborn's reluctant prosecutor—announced his candidacy for Tennessee governor in 1966. Writing from jail, Osborn wished Hooker luck and enclosed twenty-seven dollars he had earned working in the prison laundry.[53]

When Osborn was released from prison in 1969, he still hoped for a new trial and the chance to practice law again. The prior year, it was revealed that Vick had bragged about Sheridan promising him "thirty-five dollars a day during the trial, a job, money, and education for his children" in exchange for his testimony. It was true that Sheridan had given the friendless, destitute Vick $3,000 in cash. Later, Sheridan said, he had thought better of the decision and recovered the money. Yet the district court concluded (ironically), "Vick has apparently made wild and untrue statements when not under oath on a number of occasions," thus discounting his braggadocio about government payouts. His blatant moral failings were insufficient to overcome the hard evidence against Osborn.

In 1969, Osborn was expelled for life from the Tennessee bar. Any hopes for absolution were dashed in 1970, when the Supreme Court refused to hear his case.[54] On February 2, 1970, Osborn, a man who "could talk a vine out of climbing a wall," placed a police revolver under his chin and pulled the trigger. His wife found his body in their Nashville home.[55] Despite his efforts to salvage his life and his career, Osborn was ultimately unable to escape the shadow cast by his fateful involvement with Hoffa.

FIVE

"We were all going to be dancing the 'Chattanooga
Choo Choo' for the new year."

—Frank "The Irishman" Sheeran, Hoffa associate and bodyguard[1]

AS 1963 CAME to an end, another Hoffa trial loomed on the horizon. Judge Wilson's first significant decision was to transfer the trial to Chattanooga. The move was necessary in light of the publicity the Test Fleet trial and the Osborn situation garnered. "Once the public read it [the transcript of the conversation between Osborn and Robert Vick], it was impossible to give Jimmy Hoffa a fair trial in Nashville," conceded *Nashville Tennessean* editor John Seigenthaler. "A change of venue was natural, and automatic, and necessary."[2]

By the 1880s, industrial growth had earned Chattanooga, situated in the southeastern corner of the state, the nickname "Dynamo of Dixie." The town Hoffa entered in January 1964 was a heavily unionized manufacturing center. In fact, Chattanooga was the tenth-largest manufacturing city in the nation, and the defense team was "more than pleased" with the change. Moving the trial away from Nashville would also insulate Hoffa and his codefendants from Kennedy cronies like Seigenthaler and his *Nashville Tennessean,* which had universally criticized Hoffa.[3] When asked for his reaction to the change of venue, lead Hoffa attorney James Haggerty smiled and responded, "I am pleased." Asked about his client's reaction, he replied, "I'd say he [Hoffa] was more pleased than he was when the case was set for trial in Nashville."[4]

Both sides could agree that they were satisfied with the appointment of Judge Wilson, "a tall, soft-spoken forty-seven-year old Tennessean with a reputation for painstaking research and judicial scholarship." "From the reputation which has preceded him," William Bufalino remarked effusively, and with no small bit of hyperbole, "I believe he is as just and fair a jurist as ever walked in shoe leather."[5] Even Hoffa was cautiously optimistic. "We knew that federal Judge Frank W. Wilson, in Chattanooga, had been appointed to his post by [John F.] Kennedy," he later explained, "but my attorneys thought this would cause him to lean over backward in being completely fair." On the other side of the fence, the prosecution may have had reason to be skeptical—prolabor senator Estes Kefauver had nominated Wilson. But the general reaction to his assignment was positive.[6]

———

On the eve of the new year, reporter Edward Woods of the *St. Louis Post Dispatch* reported that Hoffa had approached the government offering to resign as Teamsters president if the charges against him were dropped. However, federal officials had rejected the proposal. In an interview with station WWJ-TV in Detroit, Hoffa stridently denied the allegation. His camp had made no such approach; in fact, the reverse had been the case. "People representing the federal government approached our office, and me in particular, to make an arrangement whereby I would leave office, several aides would leave and they would drop the grand juries and pursuit of the Teamsters Union," he countered. "And we refused to do it." Asked whether he had any intention of stepping down, he replied, "[I will remain the Teamster president] as long as I have enough sense to understand the problems, I'm physically able and the members want me."[7]

On January 4, Judge Wilson issued his pretrial order. Two days earlier, he had issued a "sharp warning"—not unexpected given the nature of the case—for the attorneys to avoid communicating with prospective jurors. In addition, he announced that all oral arguments would be made in the order in which the defendants appeared in the indictment. This would give Hoffa's counsel the significant advantage of taking the first shot at any arguments made before the court. The new order directed defense attorneys to "consult among themselves to determine if they [could] agree upon designation of one counsel to act as spokesman for all defendants in making motions and objections that [would] pertain to all defendants." Nashville attorney Cecil Branstetter stated firmly that he would "object to another attorney speaking for his client." This remark signaled the opening note of the six defendants' growing disagreement on a variety of issues.[8]

As reflected in the pretrial order, Judge Wilson readily grasped the gravity of the situation. The Test Fleet case had taken nine long weeks. This one, with multiple defendants and a number of separate factual allegations, might take far longer. The media and the general public would scrutinize every ruling, every comment. Helen Wilson, the judge's wife, surely minimized the challenges of the case when she remarked years later, "He knew it was going to be a lot of work." To help with the additional caseload, Judge Wilson contacted the Department of Justice to ask for permission to hire an extra law clerk. He was granted this request and sought out his former assistant John Hennis for a temporary assignment. As his clerk at the time, Charlie Gearhiser, reminisced, "We had two law clerks during that trial—and we needed more than two, probably."[9]

Accompanied by Bufalino, who would oversee IBT operations from Chattanooga during the trial, Haggerty made his initial visit to the city on January 6 to identify local counsel to assist with the defense. Cornered by anxious reporters, Haggerty revealed that he had been given the names of a number of local attorneys. "I intend to take my time and select the man who, in my judgment, is the best lawyer," he explained. "I expect to spend two or three days here."[10] Haggerty added that he was "astounded at the number of good lawyers in a city the size of Chattanooga." He did note that Chicago probably had more good criminal lawyers than any other city, pausing before delivering his punch line: "They probably get more work." The sixty-five-year-old Haggerty acknowledged that the case would probably take several weeks. That prospect did not bother him, he quipped, as he typically lost fifteen to twenty pounds during the course of a trial.[11]

Turning to more serious matters, Haggerty indicated that his only disagreement thus far was the date set for the trial. "I would like a couple of months [to prepare]," he said. Asked whether he intended to file a motion for continuance, though, he responded that he had not yet decided. He "wanted to see whether 'the newspapers' [were] going to try the Teamsters Union President." When a reporter commented that local papers had been printing only basic factual information about the trial, Haggerty replied acerbically, "It will be the first time Hoffa was not tried by the newspapers if that happens as you say." To ensure that potential jurors were not prejudiced by publicity, he added, Philadelphia attorney Jacob Kossman had been hired to review all media accounts of the trial.[12] Finally, Haggerty agreed with the "very proper" order instructing the parties not to discuss the case with prospective jurors, a practice which he said "should exist without a court order." He also estimated that the defense "ought to be able to get . . . proof in a week's time" if the government did not unduly prolong the examination of the witnesses.[13]

While Haggerty was visiting with reporters and assessing his local counsel options, the prosecution team was meeting with Ed Partin in nearby Columbia, Tennessee. The defense still had no idea of the critical role Partin would come to play in the case.[14]

———

On January 7, the defense proposed a sixty-day "cooling-off period" to allow the publicity surrounding the trial to die down, and to provide additional time for defense lawyers to prepare. Interestingly, much of the day's local newspaper coverage related not to the jury tampering trial, but rather to the ascension of George Hicks to the presidency of Teamsters Local 515 in Chattanooga. Hicks was a close friend of defendant Ewing King and a devotee of Hoffa.[15]

The attorney general and the Get Hoffa Squad were well acquainted with Teamsters Local 515. In the 1950s and 1960s, the Teamsters Union was one of the most prominent labor organizations in the area. Local 515 members tended to support Hoffa, joining many IBT rank and file in saying, "We know he's not a saint, but look what he does for us." In the coming weeks, members would volunteer to do anything they could to help support Hoffa. Just how they might "help" presented an intriguing question, as Local 515 was well known for violence and criminal activity.[16]

During the McClellan Committee hearings, a number of Tennessee union members had testified about threats and violence at the hands of Teamster supporters. These revelations had first alerted John Seigenthaler to potential corruption within the union. Recognizing the personal risks they took by testifying, Kennedy held those Tennessee informants in high regard. "Tennessee people must be the most honest people in the world," he wrote in *The Enemy Within*. "I can't ever recall having as many people who sat down and just told the plain truth, regardless of whom it hurt—even their friends or themselves."[17]

The president of Local 515 during that period was Glenn W. Smith, whom Kennedy described as "an ex-convict who had twice served terms for burglary and robbery before joining the Teamsters union." Smith was not averse to using bricks, bats, and dynamite to keep his opponents in line. "The publicity that the Teamsters [Local 515] generated back then was not advantageous to either them or Mr. Hoffa," explained Gearhiser. "It was bad publicity. It was publicity incident to bombings and things like that."[18] Charged (along with twelve others) with conspiring to commit labor violence, Smith had admitted to using $20,000 in Teamster funds to bribe a Chattanooga criminal court judge to acquit him and his codefendants. The judge, Raulston J. Schoolfield, was a colorful character in his own right. "So adept as a lawyer that seemingly he could take either side of a lawsuit and win," Schoolfield had been elected as criminal court judge in 1948. Upset by the *Brown v. Board of Education* desegregation decision, he had run for Tennessee governor in 1954 on a segregationist platform. Despite that fact (and the frequent racial jokes permeating his chambers), he reportedly "took great pride in the fact that he [had] impaneled the first black juror to serve in Hamilton County since Reconstruction days."

Summoned to appear before the McClellan Committee, Schoofield declined the invitation. A year later (1958), special investigator Jack Norman charged him with "corrupt and injudicious conduct" stemming from the Glenn Smith matter. Claiming that the *Chattanooga Times* and *New York Times* had slandered him, and labeling himself the victim of political enemies and "invidious national forces," the fifty-two-year-old chose to defend himself. During the ensuing impeachment trial, even Kennedy said that he had been "impressed with the agility of his [Schoolfield's] mind and his shrewdness." While Schoolfield was acquitted, new charges were lodged against him. It was found that he had accepted a car from criminal defendants and had "forc[ed] gamblers and racketeers with charges pending against them to help in his election campaign" in order to avoid conviction. Ultimately, Schoolfield was found guilty of three counts of judicial misconduct (accepting the gift of a 1950 Pontiac automobile, engaging in partisan political activity, and using profane language) and was removed from office and disbarred.[19]

Unlike Schoolfield, Glenn Smith appeared before the McClellan Committee, although he consistently took refuge behind the Fifth Amendment. Later indicted for tax evasion, Smith was acquitted on the basis that the $20,000 bribe was not income, as he had either served as a "pass through" for the funds or embezzled them. Learning of this outcome, Hoffa was said to have shrugged, dismissing any concerns on the ground that Smith had been cleared of wrongdoing. In his summary of the McClellan Committee hearings, Senator McClellan referred to the Glenn Smith saga as "the prize situation of them all." When asked why he retained people like Smith in leadership positions, Hoffa reportedly remarked, "We need somebody down there to kick those hillbillies around."[20]

After Smith was finally removed from office in 1959, William A. Test replaced him. George Hicks, who had previously held a "minor appointive position" in the 1,700-member local, assumed the role of secretary-treasurer. Four years later, Hicks challenged Test for the position of president and won the job in a 688–406 vote. Following the election, Hicks publicly declared his allegiance to Hoffa.[21]

———

On January 9, it was announced that Hoffa's pet project, the national trucking agreement, had been defeated in a 584–185 vote. Hoffa angrily informed a group of six national trucking companies that he would call a work stoppage if the agreement was not approved, with the expectation that "the strike [would] spread to their operations throughout the country" and therefore impact the national economy.[22]

In addition, Hoffa was personally disappointed to learn that Bobby Kennedy intended to stay on as US attorney general until the presidential election later that year. Although Kennedy admitted that "he had no heart for his work for weeks after the assassination," an assistant explained, "He has made peace with his situation, and with himself." If Hoffa held out any hope that his days of fending off Kennedy and the Get Hoffa Squad were past him, this news must have deeply frustrated him.[23]

The defense received one piece of good news in early January. After screening a number of Chattanooga attorneys, Haggerty found the lawyer who would serve as local counsel during the trial. Fifty-two-year-old Harry Berke had been "on the winning side of some of the largest judgments in civil cases to be recovered in Hamilton County." A graduate of the University of Tennessee and the Chattanooga College of Law, he had opened his law office in 1934. Berke was recognized as one of the sharpest attorneys in the Chattanooga bar. "He'd take a case, he'd get fifty percent [of any damage award]," one local resident later said. "He was that good, but he'd never take a case except he could win it."

However, Berke's career had not lacked controversy. In the mid-1950s, he and his wife were cleared of fraud charges by a US tax court after paying $23,197 to rectify what Berke characterized as "technical adjustments based on net worth computation." In 1960 the Tennessee Bar Association had brought disbarment proceedings against him following what was considered a conspiracy to conceal and launder stolen monies. In this matter, the Tennessee Supreme Court had ruled in his favor.[24]

Berke immediately leapt into preparations for Hoffa's trial. "I have made a study of the case, but it has not been a detailed one," he informed the media. "I believe it would take a month to get the case properly prepared. But if we are forced to go to trial on January 20 we will give Mr. Hoffa the best possible defense we can." Haggerty reported that he was considering requesting a two-month delay to get Berke up to speed.[25] Meanwhile, FBI agents in Chattanooga were edgy and nervous. Sheridan later revealed a startling development that was withheld from the press at the time. On January 11, less than ten days before the start of the trial, a "prominent political individual" offered $5,000 to Judge Wilson's former law partner to influence a sixty-day delay in the trial. According to Sheridan, the offer was promptly rejected.[26]

Were Hoffa's "improvers" at it again?

———

January 10 saw the addition of two hundred names to the jury pool for the trial. As each name was drawn, only the first initial and last name were declared. "The address of the prospective juror was not announced, nor did the persons drawing the names announce whether the juror was a man or woman." After the session, the information was sealed and locked away.[27] "In view of the past history of trials in which Mr. Hoffa has been charged with crimes by the federal government," the *Nashville Tennessean* editorialized, "these steps offered by Judge Wilson are not surprising. Again, the federal courts in Tennessee—in Chattanooga as in Nashville—have moved with every effort to protect the rights of Mr. Hoffa, the rights of the public and the integrity of the court."[28] Yet the defense was not so pleased. Without any firm substantiation, Hoffa later charged that the government, unlike the defense, had received detailed information about the jurors. "The jury panel of 200 names had been sent to three Chattanooga industrialists for 'screening,'" he claimed. "The list was then turned over to the FBI to have each prospective juror checked out." The government denied the accusation.[29]

As anticipated, on January 13—one week before the start of the trial—Harry Berke filed a motion for continuance. He argued that the "running barrage and saturation of prejudicial publicity disseminated in the various news media consisting of magazines, newspapers, radio and television in the Chattanooga area" should be allowed to die down before the case was heard. In support of the motion, Berke referenced a December 30, 1963, *Nashville Tennessean* article that stated, "Newspapers, television and radios in Chattanooga have closely followed the account of Hoffa's US court proceedings here." Berke asserted that Hoffa could not obtain a fair trial due to "exposure to this widespread defamatory and inflammatory publicity." He added that "a great deal of the prejudicial publicity was engendered by public statements and acts of Department of Justice officials and others acting in concert with them." Furthermore, the two Chattanooga newspapers, which were largely responsible for creating the prejudicial environment, had a "wide circulation in the division" from which the jury pool would be drawn.

Finally, the motion alleged that Hoffa had been deprived of the assistance of his prior counsel (Osborn), who had been interviewing witnesses. As a result, Hoffa had found it necessary to secure alternate counsel (Berke), who would need more than twenty days to prepare the case. A thirty-one-page exhibit and two large scrapbooks filled with an eighteen-month survey of local newspaper clippings accompanied the defense's request.[30]

It was unlikely that the motion would be granted. Judge Wilson had already commented that he would look unfavorably on further delays. Neal hinted that the government would strenuously oppose any attempt at postponement, stating, "We think it has been delayed too long."[31] Nevertheless, the other defendants filed their own motions and added ballast to Berke's claims. On January 14, Cecil Branstetter requested a twenty-five-day delay because the full names and occupations of the members of the jury pool were unavailable for review. He moved for postponement "so he [could] determine whether due consideration was given to race, social and economic background and other factors in selecting the jury panel." Branstetter also stated that the court's procedure prevented the defense from evaluating the jury array to verify whether there had been a systematic exclusion of "any class" of people. Given the fact that his client (Larry Campbell) was black, the composition of the jury was of obvious importance to Branstetter.[32]

Objections to the jury notwithstanding, it came as no surprise when on January 16 the court denied the requests for continuance. Local reports about the trial, Judge Wilson explained, "rarely were given front-page treatment," and the coverage "related wholly to pretrial procedures and trial preparations, free of prejudicial content." Noting Hoffa's status as a nationally well-known figure, he added, "Publicity given a public figure upon matters unrelated to the issues upon which he stands for trial will not ordinarily form a basis for delay in the trial. Otherwise, no public figure could be tried until he ceased to be a public figure."[33]

As for the allegation that Hoffa had been denied counsel, the court responded that he had numerous attorneys, most of whom had long represented him. Moreover, an examination of the newspaper articles submitted by the defense revealed that "local counsel [Berke] had made extensive review of the case for some time prior to formally associating in the defense of the case." Finally, the court declared, "Much of the recent publicity cited by the defendant in his motion has consisted of statements made on behalf of the defendant by his own counsel. Those statements have been anything but prejudicial to the defendant." The motion was therefore denied. The trial would begin as scheduled on January 20—in four days.

Even that disappointing news could not dim Hoffa's enthusiasm when, less than one hour prior to the deadline set for his national trucking strike, the Master Freight Agreement that had been his goal for decades was approved. Referred to as "Hoffa's finest hour," this feat was immediately recognized as "history in the making for the labor movement." The agreement would cover four hundred thousand employees throughout the country. Hoffa estimated that it would cost $400 million to trucking companies, with a corresponding benefit to the Teamsters rank and file.[34]

Critics charged that the Master Freight Agreement would concentrate undue power in the hands of the Teamsters president. This, in turn, would create dangerous consolidation within the trucking industry, resulting in fewer, larger corporations; only massive conglomerates would be able to match the economic power of the union. As a result, the economy would face nationwide strikes, shutdowns, and "national emergencies." Dire predictions aside, Hoffa had indisputably seized his prize.[35]

Chattanooga buzzed with excitement on January 17 when Hoffa made his first appearance in the city. After posing for pictures amidst a cheering crowd that "resembled a labor rally more than preparation for a trial," he climbed into a waiting car. A motorcade led by Bookie Turner, the commissioner of fire and police, escorted the vehicle downtown.

Reporters elbowed into the mob surrounding Hoffa as he made his way to meet with his lawyers. As to whether he could get a fair trial in Chattanooga, Hoffa opined, "A man can get a fair trial any time twelve people sit down who are not saturated with false propaganda." Asked for his assessment of local news coverage, he spoke of the city's newspapers: "I must say they have been fair." Hoffa added that unfair publicity would occur only if there were "a saturation of unfair stories from other places"—such as the *Nashville Tennessean*. He reiterated the old charge that Kennedy was behind the claims against him, adding that the union had spent over $500,000 to counter the $5 million the government had devoted to railroading him. But he was not worried, asserting, "I'm not guilty."[36] Hoffa then pointed a finger at the reporters. "I want no favors," he insisted, "just a fair trial."[37]

That evening, surprised audiences in Chattanooga saw Jimmy Hoffa give a live half-hour interview in a local television studio. During this relatively unheard-of event, Hoffa discussed a variety of topics, including the National Freight Agreement, the looming trial, and, of course, his persecution at the hands of the attorney general. Parading a charismatic, engaging Hoffa in front of local viewers—including potential jurors—was a "big propaganda plus" for the defense team. By conducting the interview only three days before the start of the trial, Hoffa carried off a well-calculated publicity stunt, perhaps one of the finest strategic decisions leading up to the trial.[38]

––––––––

Anxious to avoid the mistakes that had plagued the Test Fleet case, the FBI summoned an additional thirty to forty special agents to Chattanooga. Though these operatives came from various districts throughout the eastern United States, most came from Hoffa's home base in Michigan. As one investigator recalled, "The agents and persons in the Detroit office were more familiar with Hoffa's activities than we were here."[39]

FBI agents surveilled persons deemed suspicious. Three such individuals were followed prior to the trial: George Hicks, the president of Teamsters Local 515; William Test, the former president of the local; and John

Cleveland, "a heavyset black Teamsters official from Washington, D.C., who had arrived in town the previous evening (January 19) and who did not seem to have any obvious reason for being there." This surveillance did not go unnoticed by the defense. "Some car's been following me wherever I go," Hicks muttered to a *Wall Street Journal* reporter. "Just goin' to the post office for some stamps," he shouted as the car rolled past. "You can wait for me."

The federal government denied accusations that it had monitored the defendants and their legal counsel. "The agents were specifically instructed not to surveil any defendant or attorney," Sheridan insisted. "We were specifically instructed not to surveil Hoffa or his attorneys," FBI special agent Jim Cole corroborated, adding, "they were not surveilled during the whole trial . . . because we were ordered not to do it."[40] Despite these protestations, the subject of government surveillance would become a festering topic of contention throughout the trial.

———

On January 18, a dozen attorneys converged on the Joel W. Solomon Federal Building in Chattanooga, coming face-to-face for the first time. Before passing into the building, they saw "the Great Seal of the United States, emblazoned above the doors," a stern reminder of the weight of justice.[41] The final pretrial conference is something akin to the weigh-in before a prizefight. The combatants face one another—at least the attorneys do (typically, the parties are not required to attend)—to address final pretrial matters, and the court establishes preliminary rules.[42] A day earlier, a Cincinnati federal appeals court had issued a pair of important rulings. First, the court upheld the denial of defense motions for delay, clearing the way for the trial to begin on January 20. In addition, and more significantly, the court severed the claims against Lawrence "Red" Medlin, the fifty-two-year-old sandwich shop owner accused of offering $10,000 to prospective Test Fleet juror James Tippens. Medlin's request to be tried separately in Nashville allowed him to step out from under the shadow cast by Hoffa.[43]

After dispensing with some minor introductory issues, Judge Wilson addressed the number of peremptory challenges—the automatic removal of prospective jurors without providing a basis for the challenge—each party would be allowed. Branstetter directed Wilson's attention to a case in which *unlimited* challenges were allowed because "there had been considerable amounts of publicity over just a two-day period preceding the trial." As Hoffa's very public case had been accompanied by an ongoing deluge of publicity,

Branstetter argued, a similar approach was warranted.[44] Berke concurred, referring the court to a case in which a *single* defendant had been given forty-two challenges. Here, he argued, where the case involved six defendants with distinct interests, even more latitude was justified. Neal adamantly disagreed with the concept of unlimited challenges, which would slow jury selection to a crawl. He asked that the defense be limited to a total of ten challenges.[45] Without issuing a final decision, Judge Wilson announced that he would not allow *unlimited* peremptory challenges. The defense was disappointed to have been denied what they viewed as a reasonable request under the circumstances.[46]

Neal then raised the subject of the self-serving publicity the defense had created in advance of the trial: "I would like to at this time to call the court's attention to an interview of one of the defendants last night on a local TV station that touches directly on this matter of publicity. Personally, I think that it was a highly improper thing to do. I think the defendant could have controlled it himself and in that regard, I would like to suggest to the Court for the Court's consideration that we obtain a copy of that tape of that interview and let it become a part of the record in this case."[47] Hoffa's codefendants used the moment to interject their own concerns about the unique nature of the very public trial. The conduct of one celebrity defendant, Chicago attorney Harvey Silets contended, should not be attributed to the other defendants, including his client Allen Dorfman. In fact, Silets said, his client had been improperly joined with Hoffa. It was unfair to lump them together, as Hoffa's television appearance only highlighted.

At the very least, New York attorney Jacques Schiffer chimed in, the additional publicity should merit additional peremptory challenges. "In the event the Court should in its discretion decide to listen to the tape [of the interview]," he warned, "I would then be forced to revise my estimate of fifty additional challenges to five hundred because there is no question in my mind, Your Honor, anyone in the general public who may have been asked to appear in this case as a prospective juror would have of necessity . . . carr[ied] that prejudice over against the Defendant Parks."[48] When Neal asserted that the "community of interest" among the defendants would make additional challenges unnecessary—all had allegedly engaged in jury tampering on Hoffa's behalf—Silets demurred. There was no community of interest, he insisted. The defendants were not all union men; some did not know Hoffa and were not affiliated with him. In fact, he pointed out, he had met some of the defendants for the first time that very morning.[49]

Silently, Judge Wilson listened. Without arriving at a final decision, he turned to the examination of potential jurors. "The Court intends to leave the voir dire[50] to counsel very largely," he explained. However, he reserved the right to take over the examination of jurors at any stage of the proceedings.[51]

Undaunted by the prior rejection of several similar requests, Schiffer asked the court to delay the case until January 22. When Wilson inquired as to the reason, Schiffer answered that he was required to be in Washington for another case, which would leave his client without assistance of counsel. "Why was this not raised at the hearing held on December 20?" the court asked.

Schiffer shrugged. "We thought we would settle [the other case]."

Neal opportunistically pointed out that the Chattanooga trial had been set *before* the other case, and that the conflict had not been previously mentioned.

"Now I should like Mr. Neal to state then for the record," an affronted Schiffer said, "does he want Mr. Parks to appear here on Monday without an attorney?"

"Well," Judge Wilson drawled, "the Court will expect this trial to begin on Monday at nine o'clock as scheduled"—Schiffer or not.[52]

After dispensing with the various pretrial motions, the parties stepped from the judge's chambers into the "ceremonial courtroom" to familiarize themselves with the space. The walls of the third-floor room feature the portraits of prior federal judges who presided over the court.[53] Behind the judge's bench is the New Deal–era *Allegory of Chattanooga*. The eighteen-by-five-foot mural illustrates the rich history of the area, featuring Cherokees, Confederate soldiers, frontiersmen, a locomotive, and a hydroelectric dam. One architectural historian notes that the mural's "conjunction of images representing hard work in the past and contemporary technology reinforces the optimistic New Deal message that a bountiful future was still attainable." Throughout the trial, day in and day out, this colorful image would loom above Judge Wilson.[54]

After some discussion as to the layout of the courtroom, the three-hour hearing concluded, and the lawyers departed to complete their final preparations.[55] Reporters engulfed Hoffa and his attorneys as they exited the building. Berke presented the grateful correspondents with a publicity bombshell, announcing that the defense intended to call, as worded by *Time* magazine, "a monumentally hostile witness for the defense—old Hoffa baiter Robert Kennedy." Reminded that the attorney general was at that time in Asia, Berke responded, "The Court will be asked to use whatever power it may have to compel his attendance." It appeared that the Hoffa trial would not disappoint journalists looking for good fodder for the mill.[56]

SIX

"The atmosphere in the courtroom was fully charged
from the first day of jury selection."

—Marvin Berke[1]

THE WOMAN STEPPED briskly to the front of the line that snaked along Georgia Avenue in front of the courthouse. She rose to her full height of nearly five feet and handed a card reading "No. 5" to the deputy marshal guarding the entrance. "Tennessee's most persistent, flamboyant, indefatigable reporter," Nellie Kenyon was the sole female journalist to cover the Hoffa trial.

"Miss Nellie" was known for her investigative tenacity. In the summer of 1925, the so-called girl reporter covered the Scopes Monkey Trial in nearby

Dayton, Tennessee, interviewing chief attorneys Clarence Darrow and William Jennings Bryan. She also hobnobbed with vituperative journalist H. L. Mencken, who scorned the southern backwardness of a "Holy Roller" meeting they attended but was impressed with Kenyon. "There's a girl in Chattanooga," he wrote, "who can dig up more news and write it better than any girl reporter I ever saw." In fact, Kenyon—not Mencken—was the first journalist to reveal that local businessmen had "cooked up" the trial as a publicity stunt.

In 1932, Kenyon interviewed crime boss Al Capone after his conviction for income tax evasion. When she asked him who would handle his business affairs, he cracked, "You are, cutie." In 1940, Kenyon left the *News* in Chattanooga for the *Nashville Tennessean,* where she would cover cases in local federal courts. A series of her articles uncovered a $1 million "baby selling racket" based in Shelby County (Memphis), Tennessee. "Baby thief" Georgia Tann persuaded and in a few cases forced mothers to surrender their children—often before the women had recovered from anesthesia. Hollywood movie stars purchased some of the infants. Kenyon's revelations led to national outrage, criminal charges, and the tightening of Tennessee's adoption laws.

By the time of the Hoffa trial, Kenyon was in the twilight of her noteworthy career. Each morning, she presented her credentials as the fifth reporter afforded a reserved seat. She occupied her customary front-row spot in the courtroom throughout the long trial, and she called in to the *Tennessean* every evening to report the day's events. Over time, Kenyon developed a collegial relationship with Hoffa, who labeled her "the most persistent woman [he'd] ever known." On one occasion, it was said that Hoffa encountered her in a hotel lobby and called over to her with a jocular "Nellie, dear." Miss Nellie vigorously denied referring to him as "Jimmy, dear."[2]

While reporters from far-flung cities flocked to Chattanooga in early 1964, members of the local press enthusiastically welcomed the trial to town. Among those poised to take advantage of the unique opportunity was Fred Hixson, the barrel-chested, guffawing political reporter for the *Times.* Notably, Hixson had developed a friendship with Franklin D. Roosevelt during his visits to Chattanooga. "The guy who was most thrilled about the transfer of this case to Chattanooga," Charlie Gearhiser laughingly recalled, "was . . . Fred Hixson, who had a law degree and was a legendary writer for the *Chattanooga Times*[,] and he actually was doing back flips about the case coming down here."[3] Staff members at the competing *News-Free Press,* including Julius Parker, were equally excited. The forty-nine-year-old Parker was a former professional wrestler, a World War II veteran, and a twenty-year newsroom veteran. His down-to-earth rapport with the common man helped him uncover information well below the surface of a story. Throughout the trial, local newspapers would carry daily bylines from Hixson and Parker.[4]

––––––

Monday morning, January 20, 1964. Fifty-eight days after the Kennedy assassination. By eight o'clock, when the doors to the courthouse officially opened, the line of hopeful onlookers stretched around the block. Most of them carried umbrellas, and some brought their lunches. Little else was allowed into the courthouse. "You could take your car keys," one spectator observed, "but nothing else."[5] Chattanoogans were inexhaustibly intrigued by the trial of Jimmy Hoffa; visitors lined up day after day to witness the proceedings. A deputy marshal later remarked, "I worked the Dr. Spock trial in Boston [alleging the encouragement of young men to evade the Vietnam draft], but it wasn't nothing compared to the Hoffa trial. The Hoffa trial was the biggest thing that ever happened in this area."[6]

The court maintained its customary "no standing" rule, which limited the courtroom's capacity to roughly one hundred spectators. Reserved seats for the press further limited available space. Yet a throng of spectators waited patiently in the hallways every day, in case someone left and opened up a seat. One deputy marshal recalled, "People started bringing their lunches in and wouldn't leave because they'd lose their seat. So, it was making such a mess we cut that out and made everybody leave."[7]

Harry Mansfield was the US marshal in charge of security. Endorsed by labor, the former Merchant Marine and World War II veteran had served two terms in the Tennessee legislature in the 1950s before President Kennedy had appointed him a US marshal in 1961. Mansfield was affable and gregarious; the son of one of his deputies recalled that he was "a lot of fun to be around . . . just joyful . . . A super nice guy."[8] In performing his responsibilities, though, Mansfield was firm and unflappable. He understood that his job was to ensure a fair trial for Hoffa and his codefendants with no slipups. The assassination attempt during the Test Fleet case was surely on his mind as he contemplated the upcoming case. As soon as Mansfield learned that the trial would be held in Chattanooga, he had gone directly to Judge Wilson: "I said, 'Judge, I understand we're going to have the Hoffa trial here. I know it's going to be a big trial, a long trial, probably a sequestered trial. What instructions do you have for me?' He was a very tall man. He stood up, and he said, 'Harry, don't let the marshal service cause a mistrial.' That was my instructions. That lived with me the whole time of that trial.[9]

The large crowds swarming around the courthouse led Mansfield to make an important early decision that led to repeated objections by the defense. Given the scale of, and general interest in, the Hoffa case, Mansfield believed the ten marshals the Eastern District of Tennessee usually employed would be insufficient. With that in mind, he telephoned the director of the Marshals Service in Washington to ask for additional officers. "I'll send you all the help you want," the director responded.[10] The result was an influx of deputies into Chattanooga. "We had around fifty . . . to come in every two weeks," deputy US marshal Granville Sertel recounted. "We changed every two weeks and some of them changed." Mansfield personally interviewed each one, outlining his expectations.[11]

On the morning of January 20, a dozen marshals were stationed at the courthouse doors to survey the swollen crowd. There were no metal detectors or X-ray machines to prevent dangerous items from entering the building, and no one was to be frisked or patted down. Instead, deputy marshals checked credentials, searched for contraband items, and eyeballed the crowd for suspect individuals. Still, Mansfield said, "no one could carry any kinds of handbags or anything into the courtroom, and then if we saw someone that looked suspicious or we thought they might be suspicious, I had a deputy go in and have a seat. And we made arrangements to have a deputy [sit beside that person in the courtroom]."[12]

———

As the clock ticked toward nine o'clock, a clamor arose along Georgia Avenue. Flanked by members of his family and his legal team, Hoffa was making his way to the courthouse. Photographers and reporters raced toward him as he crossed Tenth Street in front of the offices of the *Chattanooga Times*. Video photographer Cecil Pearce was among that crowd. "The media here was very hungry for good news stories," he recalled a half century later. "And you get a blockbuster like this, you play it as much as you want, as far as doing everything in the world to get it on TV and as much of it as you can. It was a circus out there on the street when he was walking back and forth. . . . We were burning film, just as fast as you could wind it up and shoot it."[13]

Hoffa swept into the courthouse and up to the third-floor courtroom, which, according to Mansfield, was "more than full." No room remained for members of the Hoffa family; they remained in the hallway.[14] As the bells of nearby St. Peter and Paul's Catholic Church struck nine o'clock, the onlookers stiffened in their seats, and a stillness fell over the room. "It was very quiet," remarked local schoolteacher Etta Williams, who had been lucky enough to secure a place for the first day of the trial. "You could hear a pin drop." Moments after the sound of the bells faded, a side door flew open. "All rise." The squeaking of long, wooden benches as the crowd stood. Black robe swirling behind him, Judge Wilson strode into the courtroom. Bailiff James Stookesbury began the proceedings by calling case number 11,989. As the expectant audience members settled back into their seats, the trial of James R. Hoffa began.[15]

The charges were read. Each involved Title 18 of the United States Code, Section 1503, which states, "Whoever corruptly endeavors to influence, intimidate, or impede any petit juror in the discharge of his duties or corruptly endeavors to influence, obstruct, or impede the administration of justice, shall be punished as provided by law." Count one of the indictment set forth the general charge of jury tampering. The details followed in the remaining charges. Count two charged Hoffa and Lawrence "Red" Medlin with offering prospective juror James Tippens $10,000 to vote for acquittal in the Test Fleet case. Of course, Medlin would not be present, as the charges against him had been split off and relocated to Nashville. Haggerty and Berke represented Hoffa at trial. Count three alleged that Hoffa, Larry Campbell, and Thomas Ewing Parks had offered Carl Fields $5,000 for himself and $5,000 for his father (Gratin Fields) if his father would vote to acquit Hoffa. Nashville attorney Cecil Branstetter represented Campbell, and Jacques Schiffer of New York appeared on behalf of Parks. The fourth count accused Hoffa, Nicholas Tweel, and Allen Dorfman of offering to pay nightclub owner Dallas Hall to influence the Test Fleet jury. At trial, Nashville lawyer Dave Alexander and Chattanooga attorney Henry Grady represented Tweel. Harvey Silets of Illinois served as Dorfman's counsel. Finally, count five charged Hoffa and Ewing King with offering patrolman James Paschal a promotion to influence his wife, Betty, to vote for acquittal. At trial, King was represented by Chattanooga lawyer Harold Brown, a last-minute substitution who promised the court that his late addition was not for purposes of delay.[16]

Government attorneys made their appearances across the aisle. These lawyers included Neal, Hooker, and Jack Reddy, the US attorney for the Eastern District of Tennessee into whose lap Hoffa's case had dropped. Behind the scenes, Jim Durkin and Nat Lewin assisted the prosecution attorneys.

Durkin's agreement to help out "for a few weeks" had evolved into a two-year involvement with the Get Hoffa Squad. Lewin's stunning ability to produce on-point legal citations at a moment's notice had earned him the nickname "Instant Law."[17]

In all, thirteen lawyers crowded the broad wooden tables where the parties sat. This figure did not count the scores of behind-the-scenes attorneys, researchers, and assistants clustered throughout the courtroom and back at the hotels. Those individuals monitored the proceedings in order to research legal questions, investigate issues as they arose, and provide timely written materials. As Marvin Berke, a young lawyer who assisted his father during the trial, reminisced, "[There were] lawyers all over the place."[18]

With so many lawyers in and out of the courtroom, the making of motions would soon become a familiar, repetitive background music to the trial. To that end, a chorus of voices met Judge Wilson's routine inquiry about pretrial motions. Silets stood first. The Chicago native had attended the University of Michigan Law School, served in the army, and joined the US Attorney's Office in Chicago, becoming chief of the tax division. In the early 1960s, he had entered private practice. Probably the most bookish of the defense attorneys, Silets was widely regarded as hardworking and detail oriented.[19]

Silets objected to the layout of the courtroom: he was seated too far from the jury, and the lectern obstructed his view of the witness stand. "It is an unusually poor arrangement," Haggerty agreed. Judge Wilson denied the motion—but he allowed the lawyers to move their chairs so as to better see.[20] Silets also protested the number of US marshals in the courtroom: "With the marshals standing by each door with folded arms I think the jurors . . . may infer some evil or intent or motive by the defendants." Neal retorted that the marshals were wearing ordinary street clothes and had no visible weapons. Objections to the marshals' presence and behavior would resurface periodically throughout the trial.[21]

Branstetter then repeated his objection to the jury array. "Prior to this morning at 8:10," he complained, "counsel for defendants did not have names of jurors." When questioned, he reluctantly admitted that he had not asked for such information, then turned his attention to the *composition* of the jury pool. Only four of the eighty jurors present were black, Branstetter said. While 18–20 percent of Hamilton County residents were black, less than 5 percent of the jury pool met that qualification. The fact that only one member of the panel was a carpenter (while 6 percent of local residents held that job), he added, constituted "systematic exclusion of the blue-collared worker."

"No defendant has a right that a particular jury box," Neal countered, "much less a particular panel, include a representation of every cohesive group in the community." While no group should be *excluded* from jury service, the process was not guaranteed to select a jury representative of the community in which the court was located. Without comment, Judge Wilson overruled the defense's motion, noting that no party had made any pretrial effort to ascertain facts about the process for selecting the jury panel. It was unreasonable to now challenge the jury array for unfairness.[22]

Haggerty then moved to sever count two. Because the principal defendant (Medlin) was not on trial in Chattanooga and could not be subpoenaed to testify, he argued, the accomplice (Hoffa) could not be found guilty. Neal responded that the aider and abettor could be tried separately, even before the principal's trial. Judge Wilson took the matter under advisement.[23] At that point, Silets made a seemingly offhand comment about the court's plan for keeping watch over the jury. "Well, gentlemen," Wilson drawled, "the court proposes in this case to sequester the jury throughout the proceedings." It was not a surprising decision, particularly for a jury tampering case. Still, the defense erupted.[24]

Attorney Jacques Schiffer, "a vociferous flame-thrower" educated at Columbia and New York Universities, was known for earsplitting courtroom outbursts and rambling rants. The choice of Schiffer to represent Parks, with whom he seemed to have little in common, seemed peculiar, and questions would be raised during the trial as to how Parks, a Tennessean with very limited funds, came to hire a high-priced New York attorney. Behind the scenes it was well understood that Hoffa had engaged the high-priced lawyer for the impecunious Parks. Schiffer had come to Hoffa's attention years earlier, when he had represented three Teamsters in a criminal trial and held daily press conferences attacking Kennedy. The presiding judge had threatened "severe disciplinary measures" for Schiffer's "vile soap box oratory." Schiffer had then represented the Teamsters president in several matters and served as one of the first witnesses at the Test Fleet trial, defending Hoffa's dealings with Commercial Carriers as a legal, "ordinary way" of doing business.[25]

Parks's counsel exploded at the decision to isolate the jurors: "A sequestration of the jury at this time in the present atmosphere . . . would hamper, if not seriously affect, my defendant and would surely lead to his conviction because this jury would . . . feel that they were being sequestered for reasons that may have arisen out of Nashville. They read the newspapers. This place has been saturated with the gravamen of the charge in this very case[,] and the fact that they would be sequestered . . . for possibly two months could do nothing else but prejudice this defendant Parks without any question in any reasonable person's mind." In other words, telling jurors they needed protection would make them suspicious of the defendants. While Schiffer referenced sequestration as "one of the most crucial effective weapons to be used by the government in this case," the judge was unpersuaded.[26]

———

Court clerk Robert Dale swore in the first panel of one hundred jurors. Nine of them offered reasons why they could not serve on the jury. One was immediately excused because he was a judge in nearby Meigs County. Four others were passed to the end of the jury list due to work obligations. On the other hand, one hearing-impaired juror was retained, as was another who indicated no one could run his barbershop in his absence. Two jurors who professed strong feelings about the case, including one who reported, "I have already formed an opinion and in my mind a very definite opinion," were likewise retained, at least for the moment.[27]

Judge Wilson announced that the government would be given four peremptory challenges, while each of the defendants would be given two—not the unlimited number they had hoped for.[28] One by one, the clerk pulled the names of twelve jurors. Mildred E. Opdyke, who had professed a very strong opinion about the case, was among them. Frank McDaniel Raulston was promptly dismissed for living outside the court's jurisdiction, and Schiffer protested the entire jury panel on the basis of this mistake.[29] The jurors were again asked whether they had "formed or expressed an opinion with respect to the guilt or innocence of any defendant." Opdyke reiterated her prejudice, and another individual revealed that he was a member in the International Brotherhood of Electrical Workers (IBEW) and therefore sympathetic to the cause of labor. Wilson quietly noted their comments.[30]

The court then called juror number 111, electrician George H. Baber Jr. The relatively expeditious jury selection process dragged on in the Hoffa case, in part because each defendant, as well as the government, could question each juror. Hooker began the examination, followed by Haggerty, who conducted an exhaustive two-hour inquiry. Baber revealed his past union membership. He also offered that he had once been accused of involuntary manslaughter but not convicted.[31] "Would the fact that the defendant Hoffa may have been or may not have been over-zealous in advancing the cause of labor prejudice you against him?" Haggerty asked.

"No," Baber responded curtly.[32]

Branstetter then asked, "Does the fact that my client is a union official or Negro affect your ability to be giving him a fair trial?"

"No," Baber said.[33]

Schiffer spoke next, offering an interesting hint of his behavior at trial. "Now, if you heard me say there was a flock of Washington lawyers coming in representing the government, who had deliberately come down here in this case to frame my client, Mr. Parks," he smirked, "would you feel that I shouldn't say something like that?"

"I thought you were free to speak your mind in here," Baber replied.

"Would you feel that it was my obligation to give my best?"

"Yes."

"And that wouldn't offend you?"

"No."[34]

There was not much left to explore about juror 111, but each defense attorney would try. Silets asked Baber, "Do you feel as you sit here now that unless you vote for conviction of Mr. Allen Dorfman that the Internal Revenue Service will show up at your door?" Shaking his head, Baber responded that the idea had never occurred to him.[35]

Chattanooga defense attorney Henry Grady replaced Silets at the podium. One of the more prominent criminal defense attorneys in Chattanooga, Grady was low-key and eccentric. He was notorious for his cheap attire; it was speculated that he owned a single suit, which he complemented with wash-and-wear rayon shirts and skinny ties. As an assistant district attorney, Grady had been one of "Morgan's Raiders," hunting bootleggers and gambling joints under district attorney Fletcher Morgan. On the weekends, he also raced stock cars, a hobby that did not sit well with Morgan, who scolded that it was improper for a legal officer to hobnob with known bootleggers. He was instructed not to race under his name. The following weekend, therefore, Grady raced under a nom de guerre: "Fletcher Morgan."

Addressing Baber, Grady immediately took a swipe at the Get Hoffa Squad. "Do you believe in the idea of law enforcement that to catch a crook you have to be a bigger crook?"

"No," Baber responded.

After a few follow-up questions, Grady took his seat.

After all of the attorneys had questioned Baber, the mind-numbing process began again with the next juror.[36] For the third time, Mildred Opdyke indicated her prejudice about the case, firmly stating, "I am an avid reader . . . you normally form certain opinions, very definite opinions." With that, Judge Wilson finally excused her from further service.[37] By late afternoon two more jurors were excused, one because he was a Seventh-Day Adventist and could not participate in the trial on Saturdays, and another because the jury's sequestration would leave his wife alone in a remote area. Another juror worried about leaving his wife to run his business, but he acknowledged that he *could* serve on the jury and was therefore retained.[38]

As the first day of trial drew to a close, Judge Wilson called forth the seventeen marshals who would oversee the jury. Drawn from districts as far-flung as Ohio, Indiana, Arkansas, and Florida, they introduced themselves to the eight individuals who would be in their care that night. "Now," Wilson said to the jurors, "you feel free to ask any reasonable request of these officers. They are here for your service and to wait upon you." At 4:52 p.m., court was adjourned.[39]

A flock of reporters clustered around the courthouse, waiting for the key players, especially Hoffa. The union boss reported that his wife had fainted at the hotel during the lunchtime break. "I told her the courtroom was no place for her and she should go right back home," he said. He explained that she was returning to Washington.

"If it's that hard on her," he asked the crowd, "what will it be for the jurors?"[40]

———

As reporters jostled in front of the courthouse, a line of jurors quietly crossed Georgia Avenue, moving west along Ninth Street. Marshals stopped traffic in the intersections and ran ahead to turn magazine racks and newspaper boxes to conceal headlines relating to the trial. Crossing Broad Street, the jurors entered the Read House hotel, where they would stay for the duration of the proceedings, repeating this two-block walk four times a day. "After they said, 'you are on the jury,'" one juror later remembered, "we didn't get to go home. They sent someone with us and had a bag packed and came back out of the house and went to the hotel and that's where we lived."[41]

Informed that Judge Wilson was contemplating sequestration, Mansfield had asked the hotel manager to reserve the top floor. The floor below was purposefully kept empty and occupied only by federal marshals. The jury's living quarters were restricted; visitors had to be accompanied by marshals to even take the elevator to that floor. As deputy marshal Granville Sertel recalled, "We had marshals in all exits, like the freight exit or the fire escape exit, and they stood in front of the elevator where the elevator operator knew not to let anybody off on the eighth floor unless they had credentials and they were marshals."[42] Indeed, the marshals were a constant, ubiquitous presence, even entering jurors' rooms while housekeepers made up the beds.

Prospective juror T.O. Gordon said that "it was more marshals sometimes than there was jurors."[43]

Jurors took all meals at the hotel, where the food was inspected before being served. Mealtime was a welcome, sociable respite for jury members; they would recall that "the eating table was the most relaxed place" they encountered during the trial. One of them commented that the food at the Read House was so good that he gained six pounds during the first weeks of the trial.[44]

Jurors' rooms contained no means of communication with the outside world. Marshals examined all reading materials and clipped out articles referencing the trial, Hoffa, or the Teamsters Union. Some jurors read the Bible—which presumably had not been censored. While marshals provided phonograph players and records, telephones and television sets were removed from the rooms. One juror described the situation as follows: "They had one television room, and it was pretty crowded usually in the evenings, but one of the federal marshals sat beside the set—and if a newscast came on at all, the television went off. We were not allowed to see anything that he was suspicious of, and they would cut it off in a flash."[45]

Cordoned off from the rest of the world, jurors had no sense of Walter Sheridan's behind-the-scenes jockeying. He hovered around the fringes, working out of a vacant office across the hall from the Marshals Service so that he could keep an eye on things for the attorney general. Sheridan's desire to maintain control over the trial led to an early clash with Mansfield regarding supervision of the jury:

> I discovered one day that the marshal from the Middle District of Tennessee, Elmer Disspayne, and practically his entire staff, was here in town. Well, my deal was that when anyone came in on special assignment here I met with them personally . . . and that surprised me. So next thing I know, Mr. Sheridan says that he wanted those marshals from Nashville to be in charge of the jurors' quarters.
>
> And I said right quick, "No, Mr. Sheridan, they're not going to be in charge of their quarters. I'm the marshal here, I've got my instructions from the judge, and I'm gonna say who's gonna be over there on that floor and who's gonna run that floor." Because I know from past experience that jurors can be swayed by the actions of those that look after them ... by word or deed, or not doing something . . . they were my people from my district in charge of that.
>
> He wasn't pleased with that, but he knew that I meant business.

Later, it was revealed that Judge Wilson had experienced similar pressure to assign Disspayne, a former football player for the University of Tennessee who had clashed with Hoffa during the Test Fleet trial, to oversee security in Chattanooga. Wilson, however, stood by Mansfield, and "he did not yield to that [pressure] at all." In time, as emotions ran higher and tempers began to flare, that decision would prove prescient.[46]

———

As the second day of the trial dawned, observers had already realized that it would be a long time before anything eventful might occur. Still, the courtroom was packed. Judge Wilson began the day by announcing that he would not strike the second count from the indictment. Hoffa would be tried as an accomplice, even if Medlin was not present to testify.[47] Then Branstetter once again addressed the composition of the jury. Having reviewed the panel in detail, he noted that, "of 200 names, there were seven merchants, five machine operators, [and] fourteen married females, none of whose husbands worked in the blue-collar class, all were either insurance men, bankers' wives or in the executive end of industry." He continued:

> There was one teacher, there were six clerks, there were nine farmers, fifteen retired persons, four electrical engineers, one sales consultant, seven TVA electricians, four maintenance engineers, six supervisors or foremen, one Bell Telephone Company employee, one restaurant employee, one cost accountant, fifteen salesmen, two barbers, two managers, two draftsmen, two listed simply as professionals, sixteen listed as executives, six listed as mechanics, one painter, two bankers, two government officials, one city employee, one employment officer, one stockman, two butchers, two bookkeepers, three employees general, two truck drivers, one inspector and one tree farmer.

This variety of individuals, he concluded, "does not even come close to representing a fair cross-section of employment categories in this community." Yet no guarantees were provided that a given jury would proportionally represent all occupations. Moreover, no *purposeful* exclusion of any category of persons had been proven. The court overruled the objection and called the next juror for questioning.[48]

Insurance company field manager Patrick J. Haverty, juror number 193, would later become the last-surviving jury member to have heard the case.[49]

He handled the defense attorneys' questioning well, responding simply and amiably to a barrage of inquiries about his background, family, and views of the government, Hoffa, and organized labor. For example, Berke inquired about the tactics of the attorney general's office: "Do you start with a premise that government agents can do no wrong?"

"No, sir."

"Do you recall reading a promise by Attorney General Robert Kennedy that he would have Mr. Hoffa in jail by 1964?"

"No."[50]

Taking over the questioning, Branstetter confirmed that Haverty would not be prejudiced by his client Larry Campbell's race, then asked, "Do you want to serve on this jury?"

In later years, Haverty would claim reluctance to be a juror in the trial. When asked in January 1864, however, the young man said he did want to join the jury, remarking, "Well, first of all, I think it would be a real interesting experience and I guess that's the basic reason."[51]

Obviously, prospective jurors' union membership was important to Hoffa, the president of the Teamsters Union. Haverty noted that he was not a union member but declared, "I certainly am not opposed to them because they fed me for most of my life"—his father was a unionized motion picture projectionist.[52] The process continued for hours, with Haverty fielding questions from Schiffer, Silets, Grady, and Brown. "Have you attached any particular significance to this trial because of the individuals involved?" Brown asked. Nodding to Hoffa, Haverty admitted that "he [Hoffa] has been in the news for years." That was simply not enough to remove him from the jury, and there were no objections to Haverty. A second member of the panel had been tentatively accepted.

There were still ten to go.[53]

During the second day ten jurors were examined, largely due to Judge Wilson's admonishing lawyers to quicken the pace of questioning or relinquish the task to him.[54] One juror was excused for health-related reasons, and four were dismissed for cause. A former IBEW member reported that he favored Hoffa, who he thought "did a good job on TV." Another juror stated that he held an opinion about the case and "would have to hear more than [he knew]" to be impartial, while dairy farmer John Wheeler revealed, "I think sometimes they [labor unions] go too far." The prejudice went both ways. Trust officer and former naval officer Alvin Richardson was excused after declaring, "I'm not an admirer of the Attorney General, sir."[55]

A somewhat heated exchange occurred during the examination of T. O. Gordon, the sixty-one-year-old owner of a local variety store. "Do you think it would be your patriotic duty [or] that you were being patriotic if you convicted any of the defendants in this case," Schiffer asked him, "because the government wanted you to do that?"

Gordon responded with a customary "No, sir."

Tired of suggestive questions about government motives, Neal stood and posited, "The government wants a fair trial."

"Well," retorted a trigger-ready Schiffer, "I seriously object to the fact that the government has stated they want a fair trial. I say they don't want a fair trial and—"

Judge Wilson asked him to take up a new topic.[56]

———

One juror who generated considerable discussion was Elizabeth Gilliland, the wife of the police beat reporter for the *Chattanooga News-Free Press*. Asked what she thought about the number of marshals in Chattanooga, she responded, "The problem lay in not enough security another time [the Test Fleet trial] and . . . in order to prevent the same thing recurring . . . they have made some guards here." When Berke asked whether she would attach any significance to a witness taking the Fifth Amendment, Gilliland responded that this would, in fact, alter her feelings about that person. "You can rest assured," Berke smiled confidently, "that my client will not take the Fifth Amendment." Later that afternoon, Silets challenged Gilliland for cause, citing her response concerning the Fifth Amendment and the fact that she had school-age children at home. The court denied the challenge.[57]

As the second day wound down, Judge Wilson met with the attorneys. "All right gentlemen," he said, "I think you have done some better today in sticking to the material issues." Instructing them to keep the questioning of jurors "down within reasonable limits," he adjourned the proceedings at 4:33 p.m.[58] Six jurors had been *tentatively* accepted: George Baber; Patrick Haverty; T. O. Gordon; Elizabeth Gilliland; disabled World War I veteran and retired union member Marvin H. Vick; and insurance salesman Grady Jones.

———

Throughout jury selection, Hoffa remained in the background, scribbling notes, whispering to Berke, and watching the proceedings intently.[59] After adjournment each day, Hoffa turned to IBT affairs at the Hotel Patten, but he also passed the time by exercising. The January 22 edition of the *Detroit News* featured a photograph captioned "Gymmy Hoffa" in which the Teamster wore a skintight T-shirt emblazoned with "Chattanooga Y.M.C.A." and lifted a heavy dumbbell over his head. As one newspaper explained, Hoffa wanted to work out because "attendance in courts and behind bargaining tables with truckline operators [had] kept him out of gymnasiums." His hometown newspaper explained that he exercised each day, and that he "lifts the dumbbells with ease." *Time* magazine, however, ribbed that "he started with relatively short, painless sessions . . . because the hardheaded teamster boss was going a little soft in the gut. . . . Hoffa will need all the exercise he can get."[60]

As court convened on January 22, Morris Shenker, a "veteran defense attorney from St. Louis, who was steadily rising in prominence in the hierarchy of the Teamsters Bar Association," joined the defense. The fifty-six-year-old Russian immigrant had represented several underworld figures during the Kefauver hearings in the early 1950s and defended Hoffa associate Benjamin Dranow before signing on to join the Hoffa defense in 1962. In the weeks preceding the Chattanooga trial, Shenker had reviewed newspaper and magazine articles about the trial for any prejudicial material. The tall, gray-headed lawyer would also track potential judicial errors so that the defense could appeal in the event of a conviction.[61]

Armed with Shenker's findings, Haggerty rose and held a section of newspaper in each hand. The first, he said, included articles charging that Hoffa had maintained two sets of books, one redacted and reserved for government investigators. The second sheaf of papers, titled "Union Official is Charged in Plot," linked labor representatives with criminal behavior. Due to these prejudicial articles, one of which he decried as a "scurrilous lie," Haggerty moved for a continuance. Judge Wilson overruled the motion but admitted the materials as exhibit six.[62]

Branstetter then unsuccessfully challenged the opinionated Elizabeth Gilliland for cause. Undaunted, he used his first peremptory challenge to remove her from the jury.[63]

A heavy quiet fell over the courtroom. "Gentlemen," Judge Wilson announced, "the court has reflected overnight upon the progress being made in the selection of the jury in this case." The eyes of the attorneys were trained eagerly upon the judge. "In two days we have not yet selected a single juror to try the case. We have completed the voir dire examination upon six prospective jurors. One of whom has been excused. At the rate we have been progressing, this would require approximately three weeks to select a jury." Wilson leaned forward. "I have, therefore, concluded . . . that the court should take over the voir dire examination. The examination of a single juror at a time will be discontinued."[64]

Although they had been warned of this possibility, the defense was distraught. Silets spoke. "I have come to a hospitable town but albeit an unknown town to me," he began. "I don't know the community that these prospective jurors live in, I know nothing about their background and I am confronted in the first instance with a name and an address turned over to me only on the morning of trial. I am confronted with the government sending out agents, apparently making a thorough investigation." He implored the judge to reconsider his decision, exclaiming, "This is a man's liberty, Your Honor." Branstetter, believing many of the jurors had a "burning desire" to serve, asked whether Judge Wilson might allow the government two minutes and the defense twelve minutes to question each juror. His proposal was also rejected.[65]

During the remainder of the morning session, Judge Wilson called one dozen jurors at a time for questioning. Compared to the rambling examinations of the prior two days, Wilson's questioning was brief, pointed, and straightforward. Some of his inquiries nevertheless drew criticism from the defense. Silets objected to the question "[Did] anyone contact you in a manner that would seek to influence you in this case in any way?"— he said it highlighted the accusations against the defendants. Silets also asked for a mistrial after the judge commented that it was *necessary* to sequester the jury, arguing that the statement created the impression that the jury *had* to be protected from the defendants. Defense attorneys were starting to believe they were being unfairly treated by not only the prosecution, but also the court itself.[66]

———

After the midday break, Schiffer took up another matter. Waving a newspaper article with an accompanying picture of Judge Wilson attending an FBI agent's retirement party, Schiffer asked for a thirty-day continuance to allow prejudicial publicity associated with the trial (and the photograph) to die down. As previously, the judge admitted the article into evidence while overruling the request for continuance.[67] Feeling that the defense's concerns had been repeatedly ignored, Schiffer fumed, "I think what the government wants is not a fair trial guaranteed under the Constitution. They want a drumhead court-martial kind of trial, or some similar proceeding." The attorney then raised an issue that would plague the remainder of the trial: "I so move, that Your Honor direct the law enforcement agencies here in this city . . . that they cease their surveillance on the . . . defense counsel, that they do the same concerning the defendants themselves."

As government attorneys looked to one another, questioning what he was talking about, Schiffer pointed at the courtroom marshals. "I can't even talk with a prospective witness for the defendant Parks without seeing people who are so obviously law enforcement agents," he complained. "I am convinced in my own mind now my own telephone wire is being tapped at the hotel, that I cannot talk to a prospective witness, I cannot talk with anybody else about this case. There is something wrong with the phone very suddenly. It started Monday night [the first night of trial], Your Honor."

Neal leapt to his feet. "The government states emphatically, categorically, without any reservation," he affirmed, "no phones are being tapped, no counsel is being surveilled, and no defendant is being surveilled by any agency of the federal government."

The ever-combative Schiffer cast a wry grin at the judge. "For my part, Your Honor," he sniffed, "I refuse to accept the assurance of Mr. Neal. I just don't believe it."

Berke stepped in to calm the mood. "I am willing to state that Mr. Neal is wrong, that he just doesn't have the right information." Neal was not lying, he explained; he was just naïve.[68]

Judge Wilson agreed to take the claims of surveillance under advisement, and the third day wound to a close. Thirteen potential jurors had been examined and, for the moment, accepted. Yet "despite the speed-up in questioning," the New York Times noted, "the third day of the trial ended without any jurors definitely selected." Considering that Hoffa told newsmen, "So far we haven't come across a juror I would want to sit in that box," the chance of a timely completion to the process appeared slim.[69]

Leaving the courthouse, the Hoffa entourage walked toward the Hotel Patten, a flock of reporters in his wake. Inside the low-slung brick buildings that sat across the street from the courthouse, onlookers watched the media spectacle drift by. FBI agents in vacant storefronts took photographs to determine if passersby had any untoward purpose for being there.[70] Hoffa groused that his team was "having a tough time" picking a jury because there was only "a bluestocking jury to choose from." "It seems to me," he explained, "that the number of college men and professional men on the panel is far out of proportion to the number of people in Chattanooga who have college degrees and are in professional occupations."

Despite his frustrations, Hoffa was ever conscious of opportunities for favorable publicity. He paused at the hotel door to buy a newspaper and tip the eleven-year-old paper boy, Joe Kirk Davis. Bulbs flashed, and the child beamed as Hoffa smiled and tousled his hair.

Reporters continued following the Teamster as he greeted a truck driver at a traffic light with "a handshake and a chat." On another occasion, he stopped to pose with the Hotel Patten doorman. If he could not control what happened in the courthouse, Hoffa would do all he could to influence media reports of his visit to Chattanooga.[71] Once inside the Hotel Patten, though, his camera-ready grins turned into scowls and critiques of the trial's trajectory. "This is a kangaroo court," William Bufalino warned. "Jimmy, they're framing you."

As the case progressed, the defense's feelings of persecution would only intensify.[72]

————

On the morning of January 23, Hoffa associate and surrogate son Chuckie O'Brien landed at the Chattanooga airport. FBI agents immediately initiated surveillance, following him to the Hotel Patten, where he joined the Hoffa team. "The surveillance was terminated at that point," Sheridan recounted, "and was not reinstituted." The defense would never believe it. Suspicions that Hoffa and his lawyers were followed, tailed, and surveilled would persist for decades after the trial.[73]

Otherwise, January 23 was somewhat quiet, especially as compared with the fiery day that preceded it. The court did little else besides continue the tedious questioning of jurors. After a flurry of peremptory challenges, the jury finally began to take shape. Ten potential jurors returned to the jury box at the beginning of the day. In addition to Baber, Haverty, Jones, and Vick, the panel included Irvin L. Huber, an electrical engineer employed by the Tennessee Valley Authority; Kendall Wood, another TVA employee (and a member of the Office Workers Employees Union); Ellis D. Case, a TVA unit operator and former IBEW member; Vallie Colvin Jones, a foreman at the Tennessee Products and Chemical Corporation (also a former union member); Mrs. Sam Oliver, a housewife; and Luke S. Liner, a farmer. Edsel W. Morrison, the deputy director of civil defense for the county and a former member of the United Mine Workers, and Joe Starnes, a non-union mechanic at the local Dupont factory, rounded out the potential jurors.[74]

Now the jury selection process became a whirlwind—jurors were removed from the panel and whisked out of the courtroom, then replaced by fresh jurors who might or might not be rejected minutes later. Hooker started things off by removing Vick, who was replaced by Irvin Morris Shipley, a supervisor at a local foundry; having barely sat down, Shipley was dismissed by Hoffa's attorneys. If the prosecution did not want union members on the jury, the defense certainly did not want corporate managers. John A. Kilgore, an electrician who had been a member of two different unions, replaced Shipley.[75]

After one of the first panel members, George Baber, was excused, he was replaced by Harry Winston Tyler, a non-union TVA employee. The defense dismissed another TVA employee, Irvin Huber, and Charles A. McCampbell, an accounts coordinator for the Tennessee Hospital Service, was seated in his place. Hoffa's counsel then rejected a second TVA employee (Wood), and hardware clerk William Link took his place. It was clear that the defense did not want federal employees on the jury after a third TVA employee was excused and replaced by Hoyle F. Albritton, an officer with the Cleveland Builders Supply Company who was adamant that he held no prejudice against unions. His declaration was not enough to keep him on the jury; the defense immediately dismissed him.[76]

By the end of the fourth day, the government had exercised three of its six challenges, and the defendants had utilized ten of their allotted twelve. Even if it was not imminent, the end was now in sight.[77]

———

The most interesting activity on January 23 did not occur in the courtroom, but in a banquet room at the Hotel Patten. During the lunchtime recess, Hoffa spoke to ninety members and guests of the Sertoma Club, a local business-men's group. Local 515 president George Hicks introduced Hoffa, labeling him "a friend of the little working man."[78] "Apparently trying to enlist public sympathy by convincing people that he is the innocent target of a vendetta by Attorney General Robert F. Kennedy," the *Chattanooga News-Free* Press reported, Hoffa charged the government with harassing him since his 1957 election as Teamsters president. Thirty-six grand juries had been convened against the Teamsters over the prior seven years. "There isn't a single business-man here if investigated as intently as the Teamsters Union has been, who wouldn't be in trouble if over nothing but his own expense account," Hoffa warned. He also turned his invective on the news industry, arguing that the media was more motivated by "profit than disseminating news," and that reporters manufactured conflict between unions and management "for the sole purpose of hate." On a sunnier note, Hoffa announced that Local 299 in Detroit would be endowing a million-dollar clinic to provide health care for union members. Funded by the new nationwide contract, the clinic would be a prototype for similar facilities throughout the country.[79]

"His remarks were received warmly," Sheridan recalled. Chattanoogans appeared to regard Hoffa with admiration, but it was unclear how much of this feeling stemmed from pro-Hoffa or anti-Kennedy bias. "It is difficult to assess just how much sentiment there is here [in Chattanooga] against Mr. Kennedy because of his leading role in the civil rights fight," the *New York Times* editorialized. "Conversations indicate that a substantial degree of animosity exists against the Attorney General among white citizens." Would Kennedy's vendetta against Hoffa backfire on the attorney general in the segregationist South? Whatever the cause for his warm reception, Hoffa was surely pleased.[80]

Later, while walking in front of the courthouse, Hoffa spied Neal in the midst of a television interview. As the government lawyer stood at attention, hands crossed before him, a grinning Hoffa called out, "the Marines are here," a sarcastic reference to Neal's rigid posture and rank as a captain in the Marine Corps Reserve. Neal paused, smirking as Hoffa passed.

The relationship between the two would soon find no place for such light-hearted shots.[81]

————

Friday, January 24, saw the recurrence of several themes that had developed during the week. Before the jury was brought in, Schiffer noted that media reports had emphasized the "over twenty marshals guarding the jury," arguing that jurors would thus believe they were being protected from the defendants. The court denied his motion to discharge the jury panel. Making a note onto a sheet of paper, Schiffer added this to the list of rulings that he would surely consider as grounds for appeal if the trial resulted in conviction.[82] Silets rose. "I will try to get to the lectern as quickly as I can," he remarked sardonically. "It's quite a long walk." Grousing that the defense had been placed farther from the jury than the government, Silets reiterated his request that the parties swap tables. Judge Wilson denied this proposal and remarked firmly that no changes would be made to the traditional arrangement of the courtroom.[83]

The remainder of the morning was taken up with the laborious process of questioning jurors. Then, after the lunchtime recess, Silets raised a new issue—the jury was being given newspapers with "gaping holes" in them. An exasperated Judge Wilson observed that the defense had demanded the newspapers be censored: "Haven't the defendants moved every day that we've been here in regard to publicity and the publicity that the jury might have read?.... Haven't you made a motion or hasn't some defendant made a motion and filed a newspaper every day that we've been here?" Silets offered that the jurors should not be given newspapers at all, as the redacted ones made "their imaginations run wild." Wilson, however, would not restrict the jury from reading newspapers or magazines throughout the duration of the trial.[84]

Once the potential jurors returned to the courtroom, the jury selection carousel began to spin. After the government struck farmer Luke Liner, Howard L. Clark, a purchasing agent for the non-union City Water Company, replaced him. The defense immediately removed Clark and replaced him with C. E. Rouse, a unit operator at the unionized Bowater plant who had lost a previous job after a labor strike. Before Rouse could take a seat, the government replaced him with Mrs. Oza L. Akers, a housewife whose husband owned a local service station.

The defense used its final peremptory challenge to strike former union member Vallie Jones,who was replaced by Mrs. Callie T. Key, a former nurse and the widow of a surgeon. Despite having challenges left, the government indicated satisfaction with the jury as it stood. The defense asked for additional challenges, but the court was not persuaded.[85]

The jury had been selected. The panel to decide the case—and the defendants' fate—included the following:

Patrick J. Haverty, life insurance supervisor
Ellis D. Case, TVA assistant unit operator
Mrs. Sam Oliver, life insurance agent
Edsel V. Morrison, deputy director, county civil defense unit
Joe Douglas Starnes, plant maintenance mechanic
John A. Kilgore, electrician
William Link, hardware clerk
Hal W. Bullen, retired sales consultant
Annie L. Guinn, housewife
Ray E. McConnell, retired welder, food store stockman

Emolene Akers, housewife
Callie T. Key, retired nurse

The "hard-earned" jury included eight men and four women. Only one member, Callie Key, was black, a fact most important to Campbell and Parks. The youngest juror (Case) was thirty-one years of age, the oldest (Bullen) was sixty-nine, and the average age was forty-eight. While only one of the jurors (Case) was a current member of a labor union, two others (Morrison, Kilgore) had been union members at some point. Two (Haverty, Oliver) had relatives with labor ties. Two jurors (Haverty, Morrison) were college graduates, and one (Guinn) had attended some college. Two, like defendant Allen Dorfman, were in the insurance business.[86]

These statistics did not ease the discomfort felt by the defense. Berke immediately moved for dismissal of the panel, pointing out that, of the seventy-two jurors submitted to the parties, twenty-seven—an unusually high number—had a college education. When Judge Wilson responded that only two of those individuals were on the jury, Berke replied that the defense had been forced to use its peremptory challenges to get to that point. "This is an industrial area, this is the second largest industrial city in the south next to Birmingham," Berke urged, "yet of the laboring class we see a very minimal percentage shown by the questionnaires."

As expected, the motion was denied. Even years later, Hoffa remained upset with the jury selected in Chattanooga. "What we faced," he described, "was a 'blue-ribbon' jury of upper-middle-class residents unlikely to be sympathetic to the cause of labor and we had no way of telling who to challenge for possible prejudice. They struck off anybody who might be friendly to unions."[87] New lawyer Marvin Berke, who assisted his father with the case, explained the situation as follows: "Hoffa was not the most popular person with the people that were on the jury, the type of people that made up the jury. It was a little higher [class] juror, and I don't think the jury was particularly fond of labor leaders of any type, much less Mr. Hoffa, who had a reputation in the newspapers before he came to Chattanooga." While he labeled it a "good cross-section, middle-class jury," Neal did concede that "it was better than average in terms of education and intelligence."[88] However, Patrick Haverty, the only one of the original twelve panel members to make the final cut, described the jurors as "a wide range of people." "I was definitely not an upper middle class person," he insisted.

Later that evening, Harold Brown, the attorney for Ewing King, received a call from a high school classmate who had been on the list of prospective jurors but had been struck for cause. "You know," the man complained, "I really wanted to serve on that trial, that jury. I'd of given anything to serve on that jury." The rejected fellow speculated that the government had struck him from the panel. Brown—who knew that both sides had asked for the man to be removed—cagily responded. "Yeah, I'm sure it was." The caller asked Brown whether he thought that the telephone might be tapped. Shrugging, Brown admitted that it was a possibility. "I thought it might," the man replied. "This," he hollered as he brought down the handset, "will be the last chance I have to tell them to kiss my ass."[89]

———

It still remained for the parties to select four *alternate* jurors. While those individuals would sit through the trial, they would not be involved in issuing a verdict; they would be called on only if one of the twelve regular jurors became ill, was unable to serve, or was removed due to some impropriety.

On Monday, January 27, the "weary panel of prospective panelists" returned to the courthouse for questioning. One prospective alternate, John E. Johns, revealed that he was a loyal member of Teamsters Local 515 who had gone to the airport to welcome Hoffa when he had arrived in town. "I wouldn't want to convict him of anything and me belong to the union and him our president. I don't think it would be right for me to do it and sit on a case and do it," he said. With little fanfare, Johns was excused from the proceedings.[90] Later, a TVA employee, Charles W. Trotter, was excused after reporting that he was biased due to his employment with the federal government. Haggerty then asked whether *all* TVA employees should be automatically excluded. Judge Wilson decided against such a broad rule.[91]

The process of selecting alternate jurors revealed a growing schism among the defendants. Each side was given a total of two peremptory strikes, which for the defense would have to be split among six separate defendants. Branstetter protested, stating, "We cannot agree among ourselves" as to how to exercise the two strikes. "It has been a cat fight so far as to who is going to excuse who," Harold Brown offered. The defendants had various interests, races, occupations, backgrounds, and public statuses. "It would take more than the wisdom of Solomon to divide those two among six," Silets chimed in.[92]

In his bombastic style, Schiffer leapt in waist-deep. "I can only appeal to Your Honor that in all fairness that this man [Parks] be afforded a fair trial within American principles," he asserted, "and if he is to be deprived of his free voice and choice of who sits among his peers then I say the government has succeeded in attempting and has actually at this point managed to secure a drumhead court-martial trial."[93] The usually quiet Dave Alexander then rose from his chair. "I am in a position of representing Mr. Nicholas Tweel who is a business man, whose background has been, if you please, anti-labor, not pro-labor. A man who never saw James R. Hoffa until the day that he was arraigned. A man who would want an entirely different type jury than possibly Mr. Hoffa would." Clearly, the defendants could not unanimously agree as to the proper use of their peremptory strikes.[94]

Given this disagreement, Judge Wilson recommended that the defendants use their challenges in the order that they were listed in the indictment. Of course, this would likely leave four defendants with no opportunity to strike an undesirable juror. The defense was dumbfounded, but the process plodded along nevertheless. Berke announced on Hoffa's behalf that he was striking Harold L. Seagle, an employee of the Chattanooga Manufacturers Association. Alexander protested because Seagle was the only juror active in labor-management relations. When Branstetter then struck retired service station employee W. L. Dickson, Schiffer objected because four of the defendants had no choice but to accept the panel without input or complaint. The court was unmoved.[95]

The four alternates were John D. Curbow, a TVA employee and member of the IBEW; Lemon R. Burrows, an employee of the local telephone company and former union member; Bryant Cramer, a member of the union at local Combustion Engineering who had once been on strike; and Stanley V. Bonner, the chief quality control engineer at the same company.[96] After these individuals had been seated, Branstetter reiterated his dissatisfaction with the seating arrangement in the courtroom, particularly the fact that the alternate jurors were situated quite close to the prosecution table. Asked if minor changes to the layout had improved his view, Branstetter grumbled, "I can see him [an alternate juror] only from the shoulder up."

Judge Wilson leaned forward in his chair. "Is there any other portion of the anatomy that it is necessary to see?"

Barely suppressed laughter trickled through the courtroom. Red-faced, Branstetter conceded that his view was better than it had been.[97]

The selection of the jury had taken "five grueling days of polemics and maneuvers." "You gentlemen are all able and very experienced lawyers," Wilson told the attorneys. "You are well aware that there are proper and improper subjects for argument in the presence of the jury. In this case, just as in any other case, for example, one subject upon which argument would be considered improper by the Court in the presence of the jury relates to the matter of the custody of the jury. The Court will neither expect nor permit any argument in the presence of the jury relating to this matter." Comments concerning the publicity given the case or the presence of federal marshals would likewise not be tolerated. "The Court will not expect to deal leniently with any such improper argument."[98] Almost reluctantly, the judge asked whether there were any final pretrial matters. A flurry of motions ensued, including Branstetter's renewed request to alter the courtroom's seating. Dispensing with the motions, Judge Wilson sent for the jury.[99]

A full week after the parties had entered the courthouse, the trial was about to begin.

SEVEN

"If the Nashville trial had been a circus,
the Chattanooga trial was a zoo."[1]

—"The People vs. Jimmy Hoffa (Part 2),"
Nashville Scene, April 4, 2002

THE 1964 JURY tampering trial is invariably referred to as the "Hoffa trial." Most people are surprised to learn that five others stood alongside Hoffa at the bar of justice. Throughout the proceedings, the spotlight was trained narrowly on the IBT president. Every morning, every afternoon, and during every break in the proceedings, dozens of reporters clustered around him, hoping for a colorful quip or, even better, a seething tirade about Kennedy and the Get Hoffa Squad. Meanwhile, five other men stood nearby, quietly smoking or conferring with their attorneys. "The others are often seen standing alone in the shadowy corridors of the federal building," the *New York Times* reported.

Referred to in news reports as the "5 Forgotten Men," Hoffa's codefendants were a trivial sideshow to the circus swirling around the IBT president. "The dominant image of bareknuckle Teamster President James R. Hoffa," the *Detroit News* declared, "dwarfs the five men who are standing trial with him here on charges they attempted to bribe a federal jury." "They were so insignificant as far as the publicity was concerned," Harry Mansfield said, "that they were hardly mentioned at all during the trial." Inside the courtroom during the early days of the trial, however, it was *Hoffa* who was hardly mentioned as the prosecution began weaving together the details of the various attempts to tamper with the Test Fleet jury.[2]

Ever since the trial's relocation to Chattanooga, an aura of anticipation had hung over the city. The tedium of jury selection had occupied the first week. Finally, on the afternoon of January 27, the trial began. At 2:40 p.m., the United States called its opening witness. The first step would be to show the removal of a juror or jurors during the Test Fleet trial. Jack Reddy called Andrew H. Mizell, the clerk for the federal court in Nashville, to the stand. Confirming that James Tippens, Gratin Fields, and Betty Paschal had been called to jury service in the 1962 case, Mizell testified that Tippens had been excused from the prospective jury, and that Fields and Paschal had been removed before a verdict was rendered. The government would now seek to link these jurors' removals to attempts to influence them.[3]

The prosecution had boiled the case down to "four major thrusts at the jury" during the Test Fleet case. Federal attorneys would begin with count two of the indictment, which accused Hoffa of conspiring with sandwich store owner Lawrence "Red" Medlin to offer Tippens $10,000 to influence the jury.[4] Because the case involved a number of separate counts, information relating to one accusation might not apply to every defendant. For example, evidence for count two might be connected to Hoffa, but it would be largely irrelevant to Campbell, Dorfman, King, Parks, or Tweel. Judge Wilson told the jury as much, but defense counsel repeatedly objected to testimony not related to their clients, demanding a mistrial due to the prejudice and confusion caused by such testimony. "Instead of having a jury," Harvey Silets muttered at one point, "we should have an IBM machine to keep straight which counts apply to what defendants and what evidence applies to which defendants."[5]

The first witness called to the stand on count two was Josephine Carlton, Tippens's personal secretary. At the outset of the Test Fleet trial, she said, she had taken a message for Tippens to return a call to Medlin. The note was introduced as an exhibit. On cross-examination, when James Haggerty questioned whether the note had been given to Tippens, Carlton pointed to a check mark on the message indicating that she had, in fact, given it to her boss.[6] Tippens was then called to the stand. Harry Berke raised a motion as to the order of proof in the case, and after the jury left the courtroom, he filibustered for one hour. Stating, "You can't prove the conspiracy by the statements themselves," Berke posited that testimony from a coconspira- tor—Medlin—was inadmissible until a conspiracy had been proven.[7]

Jim Neal responded that it was necessary to demonstrate what the princi- pal (Medlin) had done before showing that his actions stemmed from a con- spiracy with Hoffa. "A conspiracy does not spring full blown from the mind of Zeus," Neal explained. "It is shown by a collection of the circumstances. And you can't put on a conspiracy by just getting somebody on the stand and saying there is a conspiracy. You put on all acts and statements."[8] "The government does not want to take advantage of anyone," he continued. "If we do not prove that the Defendant Hoffa and the other defendants induced what we show was done then we will agree to a judgment of acquittal."

Taking the matter under advisement, Judge Wilson called a recess to re- view the relevant cases the parties had cited. A thin haze of cigarette smoke rose to the ceiling of the courtroom as spectators stood, stretching their legs for a brief break.[9] When he returned to the courtroom, Judge Wilson granted the motion. Before any statement of Medlin's could be admitted—and he was no longer even a party to the case—his conspiracy with Hoffa had to be es- tablished.[10] With Medlin 120 miles away in Nashville, it would be extremely difficult to prove his involvement in collusion. As one commentator opined, Medlin's absence "left a huge gap at the heart of the prosecution's case." Fed- eral attorneys would be forced to move on. They might return to the second count later . . . if and when additional evidence of conspiracy emerged.[11]

———

Unsuccessful with respect to count two, Neal turned to count three. The government sought to prove that Hoffa, Larry Campbell, and Thomas Ewing Parks had conspired to offer Carl Fields $5,000 for himself and $5,000 for his father (Gratin Fields) if his father would vote to acquit Hoffa.[12] Neal sum- moned James T. "Jack" Walker, a Nashville Metro policeman, as the central witness for count three. According to Walker, Parks, whom he had known for five or six years, had shown up at his house during the Test Fleet trial and asked "if [he] knew anything about the Hoffa case." Specifically, Parks wanted to know whether Walker knew Gratin Fields—the only black member of the Test Fleet jury. Parks then told Walker that "the big boys," whom he did not identify by name, "needed one other to hang the jury or for a mistrial." "If Mr. Fields could be contacted," he said, "they would be willing to pay up to at least $10,000 to talk to him."[13]

The defense peppered the government with objections while Walker spoke, interrupting his thoughts and hindering the effectiveness of his testimony. At one point, an exasperated Hooker pled with the court: "They have been objecting to every question."

"Whenever I feel it is improper I am going to object," Schiffer retorted.[14]

Walker continued, noting that Parks had resurfaced a couple of days after their first conversation. Though he had done nothing to follow up on their prior exchange, Walker informed Parks "that . . . a Carl Fields was in need of employment." When Walker confirmed that Carl Fields was the son of the Test Feet juror, Parks reportedly said, "Well, that is my man."[15] Walker introduced Parks to Carl Fields, but he did not remain in the room when they met and talked. Later that same day, Parks and Fields met again at Walker's printing office. Walker said he was not present for the discussion: "They went across the street from my place there and sat in a car and talked." Thus Walker had introduced the men but witnessed no illicit offer.[16]

Walker testified that Parks had asked him to follow up with Carl Fields about his proposition. When he did so, Walker learned that the younger Fields "was afraid to talk to his father and would not talk to him."[17] When he relayed that disappointing information, Walker was told that all Parks wanted to know was what kind of necktie Gratin Fields would wear to court. A hopeful Parks reported that he had given Carl Fields some money and thought "he will come through."[18] When nothing materialized, Parks asked Walker to introduce him to "the boss of the Fields family," and Walker told him that he needed to speak to Fields's sister, Mattie Leath. Leath, however, was similarly unwilling to help: "I don't want any part of the government or anything of that particular type," she responded. In addition, she vowed to go to the FBI or police if she was contacted again. The Fields family had proven to be a dead end.[19]

A torrent of objections and motions taken up in the jury's absence peppered Walker's testimony. Almost as soon as the jury returned to the courtroom, a new motion would require them to be excluded again. "It is an ordeal for judge and jury," editorialized the *Chattanooga Times*. "So many motions and protests that the jury box should be put on rollers so the veniremen could be wheeled in and out of the courtroom more easily." Indeed, the antagonism within the courtroom was growing. One newspaper called the proceedings a "tangled scene." Singly or together, defense attorneys lodged constant objections, and the trial soon devolved into "a bitter inch-by-inch struggle over every point of the lawsuit with neither side willing to concede a single point." Observers murmured that the defense appeared to be trying to grind the trial to a halt with a steady stream of objections, protestations, and motions. That tactic would become even more overt as the trial wore on.[20]

———

When court resumed on Tuesday, January 28, Haggerty filed a surprise motion to restrict Nashville marshal Elmer Disspayne's personal contact with the jury. Affidavits submitted with the motion were kept secret by the court, fostering a good deal of speculation as to the basis for the demand. Clearly, though, the conflict with Disspayne dated back to the Test Fleet trial. The *Detroit News* revealed that "Hoffa and Disspayne [had] once engaged in a physical tug of war over charts that the government sought to introduce as evidence." As Disspayne had made comments revealing an apparent prejudice against Hoffa, the defense asked that the marshal not assume a position where he could influence the jury. Judge Wilson ruled that Disspayne was not to serve as a custodian of the jury outside the limited confines of the courtroom. However, the judge denied a request for a mistrial.[21]

———

During cross-examination, Schiffer, Parks's attorney, focused on the fact that Walker, an officer of the law, *helped* Parks speak with the Fields family instead of arresting or even reporting him. Walker admitted that he had taken no steps to arrest Parks after learning that he sought to influence the Test Fleet jury. Moreover, when he emphasized that he had spoken with *federal* authorities in the spring of 1963, he was forced to admit that *they* had come to him first.[22]

Schiffer had torn a gaping hole in Walker's credibility; he did not stop there. For the next several hours, he relentlessly scrutinized Walker's testimony, sometimes focusing on seemingly minor points concerning which he had already grilled the witness. As the tortuous cross-examination dragged on, Hooker complained that Schiffer was "taking an undue length of time."

"Well, I am sorry if I vex Mr. Hooker," Schiffer sniffed.

"You haven't vexed me," Hooker muttered, rearing back, thumbs looped in his vest, "just worn me out."[23]

On redirect examination, Walker denied the defense's insinuation that government agents had threatened or coerced him; no one was behind the scenes directing his testimony. Walker had implicated one of the defendants (Parks) in a direct attempt to contact a juror during the Test Fleet trial, and money had changed hands for that purpose. On the other hand, it appeared that no one had actually approached the juror, Gratin Fields. Moreover, some of Walker's claims, like the allegation that Parks had simply wanted information about Fields's tie, seemed a bit implausible. Walker's credibility had also taken a hit from his admission that he had not reported the jury tampering.[24]

Walker would not be the only government witness who had engaged in shady activities before the trial.

———

The next witness was Carl Fields, the thirty-two-year-old subject of Parks's alleged bribe. Fields corroborated that Walker had contacted him, that he had met Parks at Walker's printing shop, and that the two men had spoken in Parks's car. In basic terms, then, his testimony tracked Walker's. Fields added an important piece of information: "[Parks] asked me was my father on the Hoffa jury . . . he asked me how close was me and my father and I told him just about as close as any son and father relationship goes." After saying, "You know Bobby Kennedy is out to get Mr. Hoffa," Parks had asked whether Fields might talk to his father about voting for acquittal. According to Fields, he had refused.[25] Undeterred, Parks stated, "If you could talk to your father about it that it would be five thousand in it apiece for you." He added that "it would help him a lot" if Fields could report what kind of suit or coat his father would be wearing to court. Again, Fields demurred: "I don't know what kind of clothes he would be wearing because I just—I didn't live with my father."

Carl Fields did admit that money had changed hands. Parks had placed five twenty-dollar bills on the car seat between them, offering Fields an additional hundred dollars to report his father's attire before nine o'clock that evening, when Parks had to make a call to Louisville. This was an important reference, as defendant Larry Campbell was staying in that city. Noting that Parks's wallet looked to be "fat," Fields had taken the money.[26] Later, though, he had telephoned Parks and reported that he just couldn't do it. Parks told him to keep the money anyway, "for [his] trouble." That was Fields's last conversation with Parks.[27]

The young man's testimony seemed to corroborate Walker's. Still, like the patrolman, Fields would face a hard-hitting cross-examination. He had made multiple statements about his involvement with Parks. He had spoken with defense attorney Tommy Osborn and also with FBI agents, including Bill Sheets, on more than one occasion. Fields's story, however, had changed over time. Anticipating an attack on Fields's credibility, Hooker had preemptively raised the topic, and Fields had admitted that his statement to Osborn was inaccurate. Nevertheless, Schiffer leapt on Fields during cross-examination. He pointed to an initial statement made to the FBI, in which Fields said that "he [Fields was] not acquainted with Thomas E. Parks" and "he [had] no information that anyone contacted or attempted to contact his father in an effort to influence his vote in the Hoffa trial." These assertions contradicted his current testimony.[28]

"You say today that you told him a pack of lies when you made that statement, isn't that right?" Schiffer asked, his voice rising.

Fields had no choice but to admit the falsehood. "That's right, sir."

In the end, it was shown that Fields had lied *twice*—once to Osborn, and a second time to the FBI. According to the chastened witness, he had done so because he did not want to get involved.[29] By the time Hooker established, on redirect, that Fields's second FBI statement set forth an honest account of events, the witness's credibility had suffered irreparable damage.[30]

———

Fields's meetings with FBI agents had become a key topic of interest. It was only natural, then, that the defense would want access to FBI agents' notes. However, Neal informed the court that no such records existed; the normal FBI practice was to destroy original handwritten notes after they had been transcribed. Schiffer immediately moved for a mistrial on the basis that the government had destroyed relevant evidence. In response, Neal cited *United States v. Greco*, a case that found no "legislative requirement that all notes shall be preserved after transcriptions have been made and checked for accuracy."[31] The government offered the testimony of FBI agent Bill Sheets, who explained that his original notes had been destroyed per routine procedure. In the end, defense suspicions proved insufficient to question the accuracy of the transcribed interviews. Walker's and Fields's testimony would not be excluded simply because their draft notes no longer existed.[32]

With the jury out of the courtroom, prosecutor Jack Reddy complained about derogatory references to the case by the defense—and particularly Schiffer—as a "plot and frame-up." Such outbursts, he pronounced firmly, were inappropriate and prejudicial. Schiffer, already disturbed by what he saw as the opportunistic destruction of FBI notes, punched back: "For the record, may I say, if Your Honor please, that this is the kind of a case that cannot be tried with silk gloves. When I find that my defendant whom I represent is being framed by the government with Mr. Neal and the Attorney General and all of those assisting them and even taking the stand here depriving me of evidence which would exculpate my defendant, I certainly am not going to still my tongue. I will raise it in protest."[33]

This would not prove to be an idle threat. Schiffer was only warming up.

———

Following Carl Fields to the stand was his sister, Mattie Leath. She confirmed that Walker approached her to discuss her father's role in the Test Fleet case. At the time, she said, a car resembling Parks's sat outside, idling. Leath corroborated Walker's request to "tell him what [her] father was wearing each morning when he went to court." Recalling, "This seemed to me that he was trying to jeopardize my father in some kind of way," she responded as follows: "I didn't mess with the government in any kind of way and if anyone should contact me concerning that that I would call the police." In all relevant respects, Leath's testimony closely tracked that of prior witnesses.[34]

A spirited exchange between Neal and Branstetter, the attorney for Larry Campbell, proved an amusing sideshow during Leath's testimony. A native of one of the poorest counties in Tennessee, Branstetter had attended college on a work-study program, taking classes during the day and milking cows morning and night. After graduating from Vanderbilt Law School, he served a single term in the Tennessee General Assembly, sponsoring legislation allowing women to serve on juries. By 1964, Branstetter was well-known as a champion for the working class. He had represented the Highlander Folk School in Monteagle, Tennessee, a training ground aligned with the labor and civil rights movements. In addition, he had represented Teamsters Local 515 business agent H. L. Boling during the Raulston Schoolfield impeachment trial in 1958. Well-respected and genial, he was one of the more prominent members of the defense team.[35]

Upset by Neal's use of leading questions to guide Leath,[36] Branstetter stood and cleared his throat. "I might, as an aside state that for a goodly number of years I have taught a bar review class in Nashville," he began, casting a wry glance across the aisle, "and Mr. Neal was in that course once and I thought that he understood the law of evidence better than he is trying to tell the court at the present time."

"Must have been a poor teacher," Neal retorted.

"I am not sure the teacher is the motive."

There was no real antagonism between the two. Even so, before concluding his examination Neal found it impossible to resist one last jab. "I hope
the court won't hold it against me that Mr. Branstetter was my instructor."

Even Branstetter grinned as Neal gathered his papers and resumed his
seat.[37]

Relatively little was obtained through the cross-examination of Leath,
a tough witness. At most, Schiffer obtained her admission that she did not
actually know Parks; *he* had never approached her. With the jury excused
from the room, though, Leath revealed that Walker had promised that money
would be paid to her father on Parks's behalf. However, no offer was made to
Gratin Fields, and his role on the jury had never been compromised. None
of that information was presented to the jury.[38]

Once again, Schiffer commenced a laborious cross-examination, revisit-
ing every detail of Leath's testimony, searching anywhere for admissions or
inconsistencies. He needed a knockout punch. Leath, though, was a firm witness, and Schiffer eventually pushed too far. During direct examination, the
defense had won a point when the court disallowed questions as to whether
the Fields family had discussed the bribe. On cross-examination, however,
Schiffer misstepped, asking, "Have you ever discussed this alleged matter with
your family?" With that, he unwittingly opened the door to questioning on
the topic. It was a major mistake. In the wake of this ill-advised question, a
frowning Haggerty handed Schiffer a folded piece of paper. On it were written
two words: "Sit down." After asking one or two more perfunctory questions,
the discombobulated lawyer did so.[39]

————

The next witness, Mattie Mix, almost derailed the trial's plodding progress.
Mix owned a rooming house in Nashville where Parks had taken his meals
during the Test Fleet trial. Described in newspapers as a reluctant witness,
she had earlier that morning handed a letter to government attorneys indicating her intent to take the Fifth Amendment if placed on the stand. Seated
in the witness box, Mix refused to take the oath administered by the court
clerk. Leaping to her defense, Schiffer claimed that Mix had "consulted with
[him] as an attorney concerning this case" and that she would take the Fifth
in response to any government questions.[40]

Neal was fuming—Schiffer had engineered the scheme. When Neal had
asked Mix about the newly-inked letter that morning, she had told him, "Mr.
Schiffer gave me the letter and asked me to sign it," then added, "They told me
you were going to embarrass me about prior associations and something that

happened a long time ago." After Neal explained that he had no such intentions, she had indicated that she was comfortable testifying. Hooker noted
gravely that this had happened "not less than an hour ago."[41] Questioned in
the jury's absence, Mix offered vaguely that she had engaged Schiffer "because [she] had read about him before." It was unlikely that a boardinghouse
operator from Nashville would have contacted a labor lawyer from New York
to assist her—even if she could have afforded him.

Confronted by a suspicious Neal on the point, she blanched. "I would
rather take the Fifth, I don't know what you are going to say to me."[42]

"This is an effort to obstruct justice," Neal said bitterly. "She testified freely
before the grand jury."

If Neal was looking for a fight, Schiffer was game. "I am her counsel and
I acted in the course of what she instructed me to do," he replied, casting
a wide, possum-like grin across the aisle, "and Mr. Neal, you just ain't big
enough to stop her."

Branstetter stepped in, advising the court that witness Ernestine Williams
had also been "irked by [Department of Justice attorney] Mr. Durkin and
frightened on her previous trip." This, he said, was part of a larger scheme
to harass witnesses into testifying for the government.

"Mr. Branstetter," Judge Wilson cautioned, "that has nothing to do with
this witness." Branstetter quietly resumed his seat.[43]

As for the recalcitrant Mattie Mix, the Fifth Amendment allows a witness to avoid self-incriminating testimony, but it does not prevent questioning simply because the witness is uncomfortable. With that in mind, Judge
Wilson ordered Mix to the stand. Asked about telephone calls made from
her Nashville residence in October and November 1962, she testified that she
had neither made nor received any long-distance calls in that time frame; she
was unsure whether Parks had made any such calls. This statement contradicted her grand jury testimony, in which she had reported that Parks had
made calls from her home.[44]

As Neal hinted at the inconsistencies in Mix's testimony, Schiffer protested
that the prosecutor's questions violated her constitutional rights. "He has
converted it in this small degree to a star chamber proceeding questioning of
a person who is an American citizen," Schiffer railed, "and I want to take my
rights under the Fifth Amendment." Judge Wilson asked Schiffer whether he
had any legal support for his somewhat novel position that he could halt the
questioning of the witness on the basis of *his own* Fifth Amendment rights.
"Yes, Your Honor," Schiffer snapped, "the Constitution of the United States."

"Obviously irritated," as one observer noted, Judge Wilson sternly addressed the combative defense attorney. "Mr. Schiffer, I do not want to hear

arguments in front of this witness. You are going to obey the instructions of the court, are you not?"

"Of course, Your Honor, but . . ."

"All right, then let's move on."[45]

Assurances notwithstanding, Schiffer made no attempt to limit his relentless interruptions. At one time, it was estimated that he had objected a remarkable fifty times in the course of one hour. "Am I to understand that the government is giving this witness immunity?" he asked as Neal continued his questioning. Neal responded that the witness did not appear to need immunity, observing, "She hasn't done anything." Nevertheless, Schiffer asked the court to assign a local attorney to advise Mix of her constitutional rights. The court dutifully explained to Mix her constitutional rights.[46]

Mix then testified that Parks took his meals at her house, had a key to the house, and (along with several other people) had access to her telephone "if he wanted to use it." She also confirmed that her November 1962 bill included a call to Louisville, but she added that Parks never said he had made the call. She maintained a rooming house—thus, any of her boarders could have conceivably called someone in Louisville. But she had had no boarders in October or November 1962. This information whittled down the list of possible callers, and jurors could reasonably deduce that Parks had probably made the call.[47]

———

After the fiasco of Mix's testimony, the government turned to a tedious series of witnesses to detail the telephone calls made during the attempt to influence Gratin Fields. The baffling patchwork of information would require the jury's close attention. Miles Kitchen, custodian of records for the Southern Bell Telephone and Telegraph Company, described a number of calls made on October 24, 1962, between Mix's home and a Louisville number (JU 3-9385) identified as that of the Brown Guest House in Louisville. On cross-examination, Kitchen acknowledged that there were no identifying names on the records. Conceivably, anyone could have made those calls.[48]

The next witness was Anna Brown, the operator of Brown's Guest House. According to Brown, Larry Campbell was a frequent guest in October and November 1962, during which time he made and received calls on the lobby phone. He also commented in November 1962 that he might go to Nashville one weekend. For the first time, another of the defendants was drawn into the case, and jurors could infer that Campbell was possibly in contact with Parks during the Test Fleet trial.[49]

Nurse Ernestine Williams testified that she had spent time with Campbell in Louisville. She identified a number of pay phone booths from which he had made calls in late 1962, including those at Joe's Palm Room and the Paradise Bar. She also identified calls made from her residence to the Mix home in Nashville. Campbell, a Local 299 official, had told her on one occasion that "his boss was in trouble," although she did not know who he was talking about at the time. Williams also accompanied Campbell to the airport, where he picked up Hoffa associate Chuckie O'Brien and went to Joe's Palm Room for a drink.[50]

When he cross-examined Williams, Branstetter immediately took up the topic of government coercion. She stated, "At one time Mr. Durkin mentioned that it might be necessary for myself and my family to get away for a while." The defense expressed outrage at the idea that government agents would threaten a witness, or even create the impression that she might be in peril. "It frightened me, sure," she admitted, but on redirect examination she said that she had not been *intimidated*. Williams insisted that she had not testified falsely.[51]

J. J. Isaacs, an employee of the Southern Bell Telephone and Telegraph Company, identified twelve telephone calls made to Mix's Nashville home in October and November 1962 from the Louisville telephone booths Ernestine Williams described. Isaacs also spoke of three calls made to Mix from Williams's Louisville residence on November 14, 1962.[52]

Mary K. Reeves, a nurse from Detroit, testified that her November 1962 telephone bill included calls made from her home to the Mix residence. Although she did not know whether Campbell made any of those calls, she assumed that he had done so, as he paid the bills. When she was summoned before the grand jury, she added, Campbell had told her that "it [the inquiry] might have something to do with the calls made from my number."[53] On cross-examination, Reeves observed that Campbell had a sister in a mental institution in Detroit. After Reeves had assisted in securing her release, the sister had been moved to Nashville. Campbell had remarked that he occasionally called his sister. Even if he had made telephone calls to Nashville, therefore, it was possible that they had nothing to do with the Test Fleet trial.[54]

Next, an accounting manager with the Michigan Bell Telephone Company, Arthur Schneider, listed a number of calls made from Detroit:

At 12:49 a.m. on October 22, 1962 (the first day of the Test Fleet trial), a call was made from a Detroit phone booth to one of the phone booths identified by Williams;

Two minutes later, a call was placed from a Detroit pay phone to Hoffa in his suite at the Andrew Jackson Hotel in Nashville. Although the caller asked for Hoffa, the Teamster boss was not available at the time;

On October 25, 1962, a similar pattern was followed, including a call from a Detroit pay phone to a phone booth in Louisville, followed shortly by a call to Hoffa at the Andrew Jackson Hotel. Each call was charged to a credit card registered to Teamsters Local 299 (Campbell's employer); and

Fifteen additional calls were made from Louisville phone booths to Campbell's home in Detroit.

On cross-examination, Schneider conceded that the Teamsters credit account was "a large account" and that anyone could have used the credit cards to make those calls.[55]

Finally, the government called DOJ attorney Jim Durkin to introduce a summary chart of the telephone calls. The defense immediately objected. "I point out there have been a number of records here," Neal responded, "and I heard Mr. Branstetter on television last night saying there had been quite an accumulation and something to the effect that he didn't understand the significance [of the information]. I think he may have been a little less than candid that he didn't understand its significance[,] but he did point out there had been an accumulation." A chart could help summarize the convoluted evidence for the jury. Nevertheless, it could also be used to steer the jury, hinting at inferences that did not necessarily exist otherwise. With that in mind, the court sustained the objection and removed the chart. The jurors would have to parse the telephonic evidence for themselves.[56]

Records of calls from telephone booths. Receipts. Hotel bills. Even the members of the prosecution team recognized that the intricate information set before the jury was "fairly boring." Even so, it was necessary. When examined as a whole, the government believed, this evidence would reveal an attempt by several of the defendants to corrupt the Test Fleet jury.[57] The prosecution had offered plausible evidence showing that two of the defendants, Parks and Campbell, had been in contact during the Test Fleet trial, and that Parks had made an ineffective attempt to bribe the family of juror Gratin Fields. But there was no smoking gun. No one could show that Gratin Fields had ever been compromised in any way. Several witnesses had also admitted to making false statements about the case. The jury would be required to make a few not-inconsiderable assumptions to conclude that Campbell had been in on any jury tampering plan. And perhaps most importantly—at least to the key defendant—no evidence had been offered to link Hoffa to any jury tampering scheme.

EIGHT

"You're telling the jury that no matter how many times
you lied before, you're telling the truth, is that right?"

—Harvey Silets

BY THE END of the second week, it had become clear that the case
would not be over any time soon. At the Read House, jurors settled into a
life of monotony. Existence as a juror, Pat Haverty recalled, was simply "boring." The hotel rooms had no telephones or televisions, and a US marshal
monitored the communal TV set, switching it off whenever a news item
flashed onto the screen. Reading materials were scrutinized, and any articles
related to the trial were snipped out, leaving gaping squares. Jurors occupied
themselves with simple activities. Haverty worked on a paint-by-number kit

his family sent him, and others got a little exercise by walking up and down the hallway.

Keen to avoid duplicating what she wore to court, juror Callie Key periodically called Pickett's, a local dress shop, and "they brought over rolling racks of clothes for her to look at and purchase."

US marshals were present at all times, even when jurors went to church or visited family members on the weekend. Conversations were monitored to ensure that no one was discussing the trial. Still, deputies went to great lengths to accommodate the jurors. When one asked to spend the night at home with his wife, Haverty recalled, the request was granted. "Now," Haverty said, "where the marshal stayed I have no idea."

Many jurors found the walk between the Read House and the courthouse the most exciting time of the day. It was virtually the only time that they were out and about in public. Some federal marshals flanked the double-file line of jurors, while others went ahead stopping traffic at the three intersections along the route. It was this five-minute walk—and what might happen along the way—that kept US marshal Harry Mansfield awake at night. "The thing that worried me most of all," he said, "[was] that somebody would catch them going across the street and run into them with a vehicle."[1]

———

At midmorning on Thursday, January 30, the prosecution turned its attention to count four of the indictment, alleging that defendants Hoffa, Nicholas Tweel, and Allen Dorfman had approached Nashville nightclub owner Dallas Hall to influence the Test Fleet jury. Again, the government would present much of its evidence through a series of minor witnesses whose testimony would fit together like the pieces of a complex puzzle.

At the outset, the prosecution would need to connect Tweel to Dallas Hall. "A number of attractive young women were brought before the jury" for that purpose, including Carol Pettijohn, who had played piano at the Surf Rider Lounge in the Andrew Jackson Hotel during the Test Fleet trial. According to Pettijohn, she and the lounge's hostess, Helen Rippey, had gone out on the town one night with Tweel and two other men. They had visited a number of local night spots, including the Sportsman's Lounge, where Rippey had introduced them to the proprietor. Pettijohn could not fully recall the man's name. "Dallas, that's all I knew," she said.

On cross-examination, Pettijohn asserted that Tweel had spent most of his time at the end of the bar talking to the owner. She did not hear the specifics of the conversation. She also noted that Tweel had talked to people at each of the spots they visited that evening.[2] Helen Rippey mirrored Pettijohn's story. In addition to visiting clubs such as the Black Poodle and the Carousel, the group had gone to the Sportsman's Lounge, where she had overheard the proprietor discussing horse racing—not jury tampering—with Tweel.[3]

———

Next, the government would seek to link Tweel to codefendant Allen Dorfman. That effort would prove explosive and contentious. Hazel Fulton was Tweel's secretary and business partner at Mayflower Distributors, a wholesale tobacco company in Huntington, West Virginia. The sole purpose of her testimony was to recount a late 1962 telephone conversation between Tweel and Dorfman. The second Fulton referenced her telephone calls to Dorfman and Hall, Dorfman's attorney, Harvey Silets, was on his feet, objecting. He protested that her testimony was based on inadmissible hearsay; she could not testify as to what another person might have said. Yet again, the jury was removed from the courtroom.

Silets argued that Fulton could not reliably identify the voice on the other end of the line—she had admittedly never even met Dorfman. Fulton countered that the person speaking to her had identified himself as Dorfman. However, the court considered this assertion inadequate. Anyone could have *said* that he was Dorfman. "I don't believe that I should at this time allow her to testify as to what anyone on the other end of the line may have said," Judge Wilson ruled. Neal and Hooker reluctantly withdrew Fulton as a witness. They would need to provide additional evidence that she had spoken to Dorfman.[4]

Changing course, the government called Mary Myers, the custodian of records for the Illinois Bell Telephone Company. After identifying Dorfman's telephone number in Dearfield, Illinois, Myers thumbed through a volume of records to find an emergency call placed from Dorfman's number to Nicholas Tweel's unpublished West Virginia number at 10:25 p.m. on October 21, 1962 (the day before the Test Fleet trial). She then identified calls made to Tweel from Nashville using Dorfman's credit card—which, according to the witness, only Dorfman was authorized to use—on November 27, 1962. One brief call was made at 7:57 p.m., and a second call, lasting eleven minutes and forty seconds, was made thirteen minutes later. By her testimony, Myers demonstrated that Dorfman had repeatedly telephoned Tweel, connecting the two and reopening the door to the testimony of Hazel Fulton.

Cross-examined by Silets, Myers had to concede that the telephone company did not verify the identity of the person using a credit card. "So then," Silets queried, "if Mr. Dorfman had authorized some of his seventy-five employees to use his credit card number the phone company wouldn't know the difference who used it, that's right?" Myers had no choice but to agree. The mere fact that *someone* had used his credit card was not enough to conclusively link Dorfman to those calls.

At one point Myers went to a nearby conference room to search for a specific entry among the phone records. As everyone waited quietly for her return, Judge Wilson leaned back, smiling. "This is so quiet and peaceful," he said, "I'm sort of enjoying it."[5] The respite would not last long. Harold Brown, the attorney for Ewing King, seized the opportunity to raise an issue that had been nagging him. Recommended by his close friend Cecil Branstetter, Brown had been a last-minute addition to the defense. After serving in World War II, he had worked for the Chattanooga police department and a number of trucking companies while attending the Chattanooga College of Law at night. Law license in hand, he then worked in the district attorney's office and in private practice. Considered "one of the principal labor lawyers in Tennessee and the Southeast," Brown had represented Teamsters Local 515 in Chattanooga, making him a natural fit for the Hoffa team. Though a "very good attorney," he was known less for his mastery of legal citations than his ability to connect to a jury—he "knew people" and what would move them.[6]

Rising to his feet, Brown waggled a finger at prosecutor Jim Durkin. "He has detracted completely three jurors by his conversation across the table with Mr. Neal in such a voice, in a voice so loud that the jurors are constantly watching the two and never watching the witness," Brown complained, "and we object to this procedure because, of course, Mr. Durkin which I assume by the grins and the laughs that he was making, was taking issue with the evidence being presented by the defendants, or making some comment on it." Durkin did not deny these accusations. Judge Wilson instructed the attorneys to avoid distracting the jury. Clearly, the enmity between the parties was increasing.[7]

The ninth day of the trial came to a close when Myers stepped down from the stand, and the wearied participants trudged back to their hotel rooms. As the day wound down for others, Hoffa simply shifted gears, keeping up a "collar-wilting pace" handling IBT business in the evenings. "A staff of secretaries are kept busy taking care of the heavy correspondence handled by Hoffa," the *Chattanooga News-Free Press* reported, "and phones ring incessantly from parties wanting to speak with the union president." Even after a long day of litigation, the chief defendant spent his evenings taking calls, writing letters, and advising Teamster affiliates throughout the country.[8]

On the evening of January 30, Hoffa ventured to the Old South Restaurant to present a rousing speech to thirty members of the Chattanooga Building Trades Council. There, he urged supporters to look past outdated geographical boundaries and to push national contracts in order to maximize their strength. Hoffa remained fiery and resolute while addressing the criminal charges against him. "When I leave this town," he announced, "I will have another victory and ... I will be able to continue representing people all over the United States."[9] Hoffa also announced that he would soon speak before a far larger gathering, the general meeting of the 1,700-member Teamsters Local 515 scheduled for February 9 at the local Tivoli Theater. With any luck, by that time the accusations of jury tampering would be in his rearview mirror, and he could focus on the future of the union.[10]

Friday, January 31. Day ten. In light of the telephone records introduced the prior day, Judge Wilson announced that he would allow Hazel Fulton's testimony. She reported answering two November 1962 telephone calls from a man identifying himself as Dorfman. Dorfman had given her a list of eighteen to twenty names, addresses, and occupations, which she transcribed. The addresses were located for the most part in small towns around Nashville, and, according to Fulton, one of the names was "Pashell, or something in that line"—similar to the uncommon name of Test Fleet juror Betty Paschal. After hanging up, Fulton had typed three copies of the list and given them to Tweel. At first, she had used Mayflower company letterhead; Tweel, though, asked her to redo the list "on a plain piece of paper, plain stationery." Papers in hand, Tweel then had asked her to place a call to Nashville nightclub owner Dallas Hall, with whom he would presumably be sharing the names.[11]

Anticipating a rough cross-examination, Hooker presented Fulton with a prior statement she had signed. In that document, Fulton had claimed that the telephone call had related to the organization of an insurance company (and not to any list of names). Once again, a government witness was shown to have altered her testimony. Admitting that her statement was untrue, Fulton explained that "Mr. Tweel [had] dictated the statement" and instructed her to sign it. Nevertheless, she quietly admitted that she had made *other* false statements about the telephone call, first when speaking with Tweel's attorney, and then when testifying before the grand jury. Fulton said that Tweel had instructed her to do so: "Under any circumstances I [should say that I] did not take down the names of anything." She was simply doing as she had been told, she insisted, and she had later reported the truth to the Huntington sheriff and the FBI.[12]

Silets was not placated. Observers described his examination of the red-haired witness as "blistering" and "withering." He hammered away, stressing that she had lied when signing her original statement, when meeting with Tweel's attorney, and when appearing before the grand jury. Fulton already had three strikes against her. She could not possibly be trusted. "You're telling the jury that no matter how many times you lied before, you're telling the truth," Silets baited, "is that right?"

"That's right," she nodded somberly. It was not a compelling answer.[13]

Silets then attacked Fulton's character, exposing the fact that she had been married three times (once when she was thirteen years old) and describing her as an unfit mother. Over Neal's feverish objection that the witness's family life was irrelevant to her credibility, the wound-up Silets announced, "I am going to show that this woman was denied custody of those children, she was declared an unfit mother, they were taken away from her and she tried to get them back, she couldn't get them back. This goes to what kind of woman we have here for this jury to believe her testimony." Fulton's protestation that her husband had obtained custody of her children simply because he "had the money [to hire counsel] and I did not" could not overcome the negative image Silets painted. The attack caused discomfort, not only for the witness, but also for those in the courtroom watching her cringe-inducing testimony.

A questionable personal history does not automatically make a witness a perjurer. Fulton attempted to explain her false statements by affirming, "Mr. Tweel was my employer and I didn't want to lose my job." But by then the damage was clearly done. As her testimony fizzled out, Fulton maintained that the government had not threatened, coerced, or paid her to alter her testimony. Although she adamantly denied receiving any money from the government, the jury surely noticed that she had become a half owner of Mayflower Distributors shortly after a trip to Washington—where it might be concluded that the government had paid her in exchange for a change of testimony. Fulton's admission that the government had paid her travel expenses connected with the case did not alleviate suspicions as to her motives. In the end, it was hard for the jury to overlook her multiple falsehoods, and she did not prove to be a particularly convincing witness.[14]

———

To get things back on track, the government called Dallas Hall, proprietor of the Sportsman's Lounge in Nashville, to testify. The young bar owner appeared unkempt as he entered the courtroom, his dark hair tousled and uncombed, his eyes tired. FBI agents had guarded him tightly, as his life had been threatened.[15] Hall confirmed that he had spoken with Tweel about racehorses one evening in Nashville. Three or four weeks later, Tweel called Hall and asked whether he would check into the list of potential jurors in the Test Fleet case. Hall responded that he might be willing to help out. Yet in reality, he said, "I wasn't interested in it." Of course, there was nothing unlawful about Tweel's asking a local resident for his thoughts about the jury pool, and Hall said he had not been asked to make contact with any juror.

Hall testified that Tweel had called him a second time. "Yeah, I will drive around and check on it for you," Hall had replied. Tweel rattled off a list of names—presumably reading the document Fulton had typed. According to Hall, he never wrote any of the names down, and he had no intention of checking into them. When Tweel called to check on his progress, Hall said, "I told him I hadn't [discovered anything] and that I drove all over the place and I couldn't find nothing that could help out any." By that time, Tweel was frustrated by Hall's ineffectual efforts. "Just forget it," he muttered. That was the last contact between the two.[16]

Handling the cross-examination, Dave Alexander worked to paint Hall as an undependable, unreliable witness. He focused on his extensive criminal background, including charges for whiskey possession, "loitering about a bawdy house," and possessing a gaming device. Unlike prior witnesses, however, Hall's story had not shifted over time. No real evidence was introduced to question his veracity.[17]

———

Richard Chichester, records custodian for the Chesapeake and Potomac Telephone Company in West Virginia, was the final witness called to address count four. The prosecution once again used telephone records to substantiate earlier testimony. Chichester identified a call made from Mayflower Distributors to Hall on November 27, 1962, lasting two minutes and forty-nine seconds. He also identified a subsequent series of calls to Hall on November 29, November 30, and December 6, each from Tweel's telephone or charged to his credit card. By all appearances, Tweel and Hall had engaged in more than a single instance of small talk about horses. That said, while the evidence indicated Tweel's curiosity about the Test Fleet jury, the government had not shown any effort to corrupt or rig that jury. Several questions were left hanging as the government wrapped up its evidence on count four.[18]

———

At midafternoon on January 28, a US marshal entered the Coulter Barber Shop in East Chattanooga, a few miles from downtown. There, he found barber Bill Knowles working for his father-in-law. Two of Knowles's normal customers had been selected as jurors in the trial and recommended his services for the other male jurors. Due to the trial schedule, they would have to come to the barbershop after normal business hours. "Just don't discuss the case," the marshal cautioned.

At 6:50 that evening, another marshal appeared at the shop. "You've been cleared for the job," he reported sternly before taking a newspaper from Knowles and telling him to turn off the television set. After they confiscated all reading materials, the deputies escorted five jurors into the barbershop and locked the door behind them. "They seemed jolly and very happy to be out of their routine," Knowles recalled. For the next five weeks, Knowles served as the official barber for the Hoffa jury. Security was always a concern. No one else was allowed to hang around while the jurors were in the shop, and when a juror's son brought his father fresh clothes, a marshal inspected the pockets of the garments before handing them over.

Despite the tight security, even the marshals relaxed in the Coulter Barber Shop, sitting around and telling stories while the barber worked. As Knowles later recounted, one marshal regaled them with a story about an unfortunate porter at the Read House who had walked unaccompanied onto the jurors' floor to deliver a set of coffee cups. A marshal stopped the porter and scared him so badly "that he dropped some of the cups, left the floor, and quit his job."

Finally, it was time to head back to the Read House. "Don't cut mine too short," one juror whispered. "I want to come back next week." As the last hairs were snipped, the men were reluctant to break up the party—the jurors most of all. [19]

NINE

"Each television station had a seat—except Mort Lloyd,
his was taken away from him."

—US Marshal Harry Mansfield

THOUGH TOMMY EASON remained friendly with Harry Mansfield, decades later he remained angry at the chief marshal's treatment of him during the 1964 trial. A cameraman for a local television station, the twenty-three-year-old Eason was assigned to capture footage in front of the federal courthouse. He had been covering local news stories since high school, when he started taking crime scene pictures for the local police. By 1957, Eason had taken a job with Channel 3 (WRGP-TV), the NBC affiliate in

Chattanooga. There, he worked closely with popular newsman Mort Lloyd, the "Flying Reporter," who had flown his twin-engine airplane back and forth between Chattanooga and Nashville to report daily on the Test Fleet trial. Throughout the Chattanooga trial, Eason worked the sidewalk in front of the courthouse, filming the comings and goings of the proceedings' participants.

Problems between Channel 3 and the US Marshals Service had begun before the trial. After it was announced that Hoffa was coming to Chattanooga, the station worked with local Teamsters officials to secure a live interview with the IBT president. The night before the trial, that extended interview aired, preempting scheduled programs. "That was just unheard of," Eason recalled. Not surprisingly, prosecutors complained about the prejudicial publicity this self-serving maneuver created, and the Marshals Service worried that the media hype Channel 3 had created would complicate jury selection.

Soon after the trial began, Mansfield walked up behind Eason while he was shooting film in front of the courthouse. He snatched a local newspaper from the cameraman's back pocket, snapping, "The jury don't need to see no newspapers." Although Mansfield later returned the paper, Eason was offended.

The final straw with respect to Channel 3 involved the transportation of jurors from the Read House to the federal building. Eason insisted that reporters were universally protective of the jurors. "I think we shot the feet of the jury as they went by," he explained. "I don't think we shot their faces, in fact I know we didn't shoot their faces. I didn't." That protection extended to ensuring that jurors were not exposed to newspaper headlines or other information about the trial. As juror Pat Haverty explained, "They formed us into a couple of lines, and there was a man in front and a man in back, and there was always a marshal close to a half a block ahead of us ... [he] would be running ahead of us, and they would throw the [newspaper] racks all down into the gutter, and we never saw the face of the newspaper the whole time during the trial."

According to Mansfield, however, as jurors were leaving the courthouse one day, Mort Lloyd instructed Eason to turn a newspaper rack around, displaying a sensational headline to the unwary jurors. "I ran down and grabbed the rack and turned it back around," Mansfield recalled, "and said, 'Tommy, you damned idiot, you.'"

Defending his cameraman, Lloyd asserted, "He's not a damned idiot."

Bristling, Mansfield turned to Lloyd. "Yes, and you are too," he said. "Furthermore, you don't have a reserved seat in the courtroom any more."

Eason asked Lloyd what was going on. "We don't have a seat," Lloyd said.

"I guess I'll sit in the audience. I guess I'll just get here early enough and sit in the audience." Each night thereafter, Lloyd informed Channel 3 viewers, "Although I'm barred from the courtroom, I'm still reporting on the Hoffa trial."

He was not barred from the courtroom, Mansfield maintained. Lloyd simply "had to get in line like everybody else did." Eventually, though, Mansfield relented and reissued Lloyd's press access. Nevertheless, Eason remained upset, feeling that he and Lloyd were unfairly victimized due to the hubris of the chief marshal.[1]

In the middle of the afternoon on Friday, January 31, the government turned to count five of the indictment, in which Hoffa allegedly conspired with Nashville Teamster Ewing King to offer patrolman James Paschal a promotion. In exchange, Paschal would influence his wife to vote in favor of acquittal in the Test Fleet case. Once again, the prosecution began by painstakingly compiling tiny "puzzle pieces" of evidence to reveal an attempt to influence the jury. *Nashville Banner* photographer Robert Ray identified an image he had made of King meeting with Hoffa upon his arrival in Nashville. After connecting King to Hoffa, the government introduced a parade of witnesses to detail King's activities during the Test Fleet trial. "There was a continual surveillance of Ewing King" during the trial, Sheridan noted. The first to testify was FBI special agent William M. Hobbs Jr., who observed King driving his Thunderbird to the home of a Teamster Local 327 member named Oscar Pitts on October 27, 1962. Who was Oscar Pitts, and what did he have to do with the Test Fleet jury? More pieces of the puzzle would be needed.[2]

Charlotte FBI agent J. Charles Still testified that on November 17, 1962, he saw King enter a restaurant outside of Nashville. After twelve to fifteen minutes, King emerged, climbed into a different vehicle—a blue 1959 Ford— and drove toward Woodbury, Tennessee, a small town an hour outside of Nashville. Another man, later identified as Teamster business agent George Broda, drove away in King's flashier, more recognizable Thunderbird. Federal agent Willis S. Turner of Murfreesboro, Tennessee, followed King as he drove the blue Ford to the home of Oscar Pitts in Woodbury. The same car then showed up at 1:07 a.m. "almost in front of the home of James Paschal," who was observed standing at the side of the car, talking to the driver. Francis W. Norwood, a Nashville agent, watched as the blue Ford bearing King and Pitts left Paschal's house around 1:30 a.m. Paschal followed behind. Thus, King had gone somewhere with Paschal, the husband of Test Fleet juror Betty Paschal, in the middle of the night.

Posted along the highway, twenty-three-year FBI veteran Warren L. Walsh watched as the same blue Ford, driven by King, sped by at 4:12 a.m. on its way back to Nashville. On cross-examination, the defense elicited admissions that Walsh wore bifocals and that the weather on November 18 was bad. Hoffa's counsel hinted that Walsh was in no position to identify King through the driver's window of a speeding car. Yet the agent remained steadfast in his identification. Finally, special agent Marvin Eubanks testified that he had strategically parked his car across the road with the hood up, as though it were broken down. When a blue 1959 Ford with license plate 1C-3705 pulled up, he walked over to say he would be out of the way in a minute, at which time he confirmed that King was the driver of the car. Through this series of well-placed witnesses, the prosecution had established a timeline of Ewing King's activities on November 17, 1962, the night that James Paschal was allegedly approached.

———

"Oscar Pitts."

Visibly uncomfortable in a tight black suit and skinny tie, the man was pointed to the witness stand. Labeled a "reluctant witness" in newspaper accounts, Pitts, nicknamed "Mutt," was a Nashville Teamster and an employee of the Dixie Ohio Express trucking company. His somewhat piggish appearance was augmented by fleshy cheeks and close-set eyes. Awkward and uneasy, Pitts was clearly in over his head, and his hesitant, often befuddled testimony would lead Hooker to remark during closing arguments that he felt sorry for "poor old Mutt."[3] Pitts confirmed that King had appeared at his house on October 27, 1962, to talk. The conversation had quickly turned to the topic of James Paschal, "a good boy" whose wife was "a woman who could stand on her two feet anywhere."[4] The discussion soon turned to money. "We were talking about what kind of shape Paschal was in," Pitts recalled. "Financial shape." Paschal was not interested in cash, Pitts offered, but he might want a promotion at the highway patrol. Seizing on the idea, King said that he "could get him [Paschal] a promotion." While no conditions were discussed, Pitts said, Paschal was expected to "talk to his wife, yeah." Nothing specific was mentioned about convincing Betty Paschal to vote for acquittal in the Test Fleet case.[5]

Once again, the government had offered evidence of a curious contact between a defendant and a relative of one of the Test Fleet jurors. Why would a Hoffa associate take a sudden interest in obtaining a promotion for a state highway patrol officer with whom he was not personally acquainted? Why do so when the man was not even a Teamster? And why help a man whose wife just happened to be on a jury deliberating Hoffa's innocence or guilt at the time?

————

After a brief, routine recess, Harry Berke rose to address the court. He would raise a momentous issue that would come to overshadow much of the remainder of the trial: "A matter of great concern to the defendants and should be of great concern to the government has come to our attention at ten o'clock this morning, at which time we immediately prepared motions and I would like to read the motion, a copy of which has been served on the government, if Your Honor please." A confused Pitts was escorted from the stand, and the judge cleared the courtroom. During the weekend, Berke said, the defense had obtained information indicating that the government was guilty of significant misconduct in obtaining the testimony it had presented to the court. The source of those allegations? Forty-two-year-old Fred Shobe, whom reporters described as a "four-time loser" with an extensive criminal record for burglary, armed robbery, and forgery.

Shobe claimed that he had worked for two years in Sheridan's special investigative unit as an "agent provocateur." He had agreed to work with the federal government, which employed him in a variety of clandestine activities, in order to avoid jail time for a probation violation. After fulfilling his obligations, Shobe had asked for a job as a computer operator. When government agents had tried to send him to Japan instead, an insulted Shobe had left and approached William Bufalino to share his story. On Saturday, February 1, Shobe had dictated a sworn statement to Bufalino in the presence of three Detroit police officers.[6] Based on this information, the defense made three allegations: first, that the government had fabricated Jack Walker's testimony; second, that the defendants and their attorneys were under surveillance, including the monitoring of telephone calls; and third, that unauthorized persons had improperly seen the grand jury minutes.[7]

Asked for a response, a frustrated Neal flipped through the document. "Well, Your Honor," he drawled, "I think this, I know since I've been in this matter in the Summer of 1962 there were allegations of wire taps. Mr. Haggerty filed a signed statement, not under oath, that somebody had told him that we had tapped telephones. The motion wasn't even argued. It has been made and made again. They have never been able to establish anything . . .

now, to my knowledge there has never been any wire tapping connected with this case at all, so I doubt that the motion will have any substance to it. I think at this time we should go on until the Court and the government is [*sic*] able to review the motion and review the supporting documents." As for the allegations of perjury, Neal responded, the claim was "downright untrue."[8]

Schiffer interposed, characterizing the prosecution's case as nothing more than an elaborate setup. "Your Honor," he bellowed, "the government indulged in black magic and tried to put on a hoax" by offering a witness such as Walker:

> We are helpless to a degree. We represent the defendants and as I look at Mr. Parks, who is he to fight in this courtroom? He can only sit there quietly and be the victim of a diabolical plan on the part of the government here using and preparing and conjuring up perjury. . . . Read the transcript, because from what it appears there this prosecution representing my government has already proved that it lacks not only integrity, it lacks the honesty with your Honor, and we appeal to your Honor to exercise your constitutional function in this case and dismiss the indictment when it is palpably and provably false what the government has adopted here as the most dastardly tactics adopted in any reported case that your Honor can find in any court in this country.[9]

Judge Wilson flipped through the Shobe affidavit. Remarking, "These are very, very serious charges," he retired to his chambers for a preliminary review of the papers.[10] However, if the defense felt that Shobe's claims would unravel the government's case, it would be sorely disappointed. After a brief review, Wilson returned to the courtroom and stated that Shobe's information appeared to be "quite a mixture of profanity and incoherence" in which he rattled on about "the government practicing voodoo" and other similar, astonishing claims. The judge would review the materials more deeply that evening and issue a final decision in the morning.[11] Ultimately, Wilson denied the defense request to quash the indictment. He offered no further explanation as to the reasoning for his decision. The defense was shocked.[12]

———

The bewildered Pitts, who had no idea why his testimony had been interrupted, returned to the stand. Questioned by Hooker, he described a code that informed King when to come to Woodbury to meet Paschal to discuss a promotion. On November 17, 1962, one month after their first meeting, Pitts telephoned King to report that his beagle hound had died—this was the signal that a meeting had been arranged.[13]

Later that evening, King picked Pitts up in a blue Ford—the same borrowed automobile federal agents had observed—and drove to Paschal's house. Arriving home after his evening shift, the patrolman pulled into his driveway to discover the blue Ford pulling in behind him. Cautiously, Paschal approached the open window of the vehicle. Pitts indicated that King wanted to speak to him, and Paschal suggested that they drive to a spring along a river road nearby. There, Pitts and King climbed into the patrol car. According to Pitts, Paschal said that "he had been on there [with the highway patrol] . . . twenty-something years and he knowed that he was going to retire from the state[,] and if he didn't get a promotion in it he wouldn't have no pension retirement from the state." King responded that he could get Paschal a promotion. "I think it was a Sergeant's rating," Pitts added.[14]

King then asked whether Paschal might talk to his wife. Pitts did not reveal the subject of this proposed discussion, but the subtext was clear. However, the patrolman demurred. Pitts stated that the husband and wife "wasn't getting along too good or something another like that and words like that." Resisting the request, Paschal added that his wife "went to church" and "was a lot better woman than he was a man."[15] The surreptitious meeting lasted about thirty minutes. Afterward, King and Pitts returned to Pitts's home, where they sat, drinking coffee and talking.

"Reckon that Paschal, reckon that he would talk to his wife?" King asked. Pitts shook his head. "No, I do not."

Finally, concluding that he could do nothing more to convince Paschal, a disappointed King left Woodbury around 2:10 a.m., returning to Nashville in the blue Ford.

So far, Pitts's testimony mirrored the sequence of events federal agents had offered.[16]

Following a lunchtime recess, Harold Brown began his cross-examination of the witness. Pitts claimed a personal interest in Paschal's promotion, as he had been responsible for Paschal's employment with the highway patrol. Because Pitts had backed the wrong candidate in the most recent gubernatorial election, however, he needed King's influence to secure the promotion. As such, *Pitts* had approached King about getting the promotion—not the other way around. Pitts also clarified that Paschal was not the only patrolman for whom he had sought a promotion. In fact, he said, he had gone to

King as early as 1960 to discuss a promotion for another individual, Aubrey Nichols.[17]

Taking up the examination, Haggerty showed Pitts a copy of an early steno-graphic statement in which Pitts had asserted that *Paschal* had brought up his wife's role on the Test Fleet jury. King had reportedly replied, "We ought not to say anything about that."[18] Why would Pitts change his testimony? The defense returned to a familiar allegation—the government had threatened him. "I'm scared to death," Pitts had already commented once from the wit-ness chair. Hooker had spoken with him earlier that morning to "refresh his recollection," he said, and FBI agent Bill Sheets had gone over his grand jury testimony that morning. It certainly appeared that the government wanted Pitts to get his testimony straight.

The defense contended that the government had once again used threats to manipulate a witness's testimony. Prior to his grand jury appearance, Pitts had met with three lawyers and Sheridan to discuss his account. "If you don't tell the truth," Sheridan had told him, "I will get you and your wife both in-dicted." FBI agents, Pitts added, had insisted that he was not telling the truth and wanted him to change his testimony. As a result, one reporter declared, "Pitts was obviously a harried witness," and his testimony was clouded by the threats against his job and his freedom.[19]

Approached by reporters asking about the allegation that his influence was sought on Paschal's behalf, Tennessee governor Frank Clement strongly asserted that "he had never been approached on such a matter, directly or indirectly, and knew of no member of his administration who had been."[20]

———

The next step in the chain of evidence for count five was James Paschal, the subject of the alleged approach. A fourteen-year veteran of the highway pa-trol, the sheepish witness explained that, after finishing his shift on Novem-ber 17, 1962, he had returned home at 1:00 a.m. to find Pitts pulling into his driveway. "Mutt said his boss [King] was up at his house and that he wanted to talk to me," he said. Pitts said King "wanted to see me about a promotion, helping me," Paschal recalled. Reluctant to meet with a stranger at an un-familiar place, Paschal suggested that they meet at a river spring along the highway.[21] There, King asked Paschal to get into his car, assuring him that it was not bugged. That suspicious comment only increased Paschal's anxiety. "I said that I wasn't going to get out of my car," he explained. "That I knew my car wasn't bugged." King yielded, climbing into the patrol vehicle.[22]

King advised Paschal that he could assist with a promotion. To Paschal, this strange offer came out of the blue—until King added, "He [Pitts] says your wife is on this jury." According to Paschal, then, *King* was the first to raise the topic of the Test Fleet trial, and he had done so immediately after offering to help Paschal obtain a promotion. Nevertheless, Paschal was reluctant to approach his wife: "I told him no[,] that I couldn't talk to her. That we weren't getting along too good."[23]

"You talk to her," King had insisted. "I will get you the promotion."

While he told King that he would try to talk to his wife, Paschal had no intention of doing so. "I didn't want to get involved in anything talking about it because I knew I wasn't supposed to," he explained.[24] What, if anything, did Paschal say to his wife? The only thing he had told her, Paschal replied, was to "take the evidence," stating, "You've got to live with yourself the rest of your life." Nothing was said to Betty Paschal about the inquiry made by King, and nothing had come of the effort to influence her in November 1962.[25]

———

The cross-examination of Paschal began the following morning. Once again, Harold Brown handled the questioning. Wasn't one o'clock in the morning an unusual time to discuss workplace promotions? "Well," Paschal shrugged, "it was kind of an odd hour [to meet]." Contrary to Pitts's claims, Paschal was adamant that he had never discussed a promotion before the meeting at the river spring. In fact, Paschal stated, he wasn't even on the civil service roster for a promotion. That testimony raised an important question—If the meeting had nothing to do with Paschal's career advancement, then what other purpose could there have been for it?[26]

Brown turned to *Paschal's* credibility. "During the conversation [with Ewing King]," Paschal had previously stated under oath, "no one mentioned the fact that my wife was serving on the jury in the trial of James R. Hoffa [, and] Neither Pitts nor King suggested that I talk to my wife." This statement, Paschal admitted, had been a falsehood, one that he had repeated several times. He had lied when he was summoned before Judge Miller on December 6, 1962; he had lied the next day when making a written statement; and he had lied when he told the same false story to the *Nashville Tennessean*. Once again, a prosecution witness had been caught in a series of conflicting and unreliable statements.[27]

Paschal explained feebly that he had simply wanted to avoid getting tangled up in the matter. "I was afraid that the Teamsters might cause me to lose my job and I did not want to embarrass my wife or get her involved." But why had that led him so far as to perjure himself? "I thought the Teamsters Union was a strong and powerful organization," he said. "I had heard they were a rough bunch, and I thought I might wind up floating in a river with a log chain tied around me if I told anyone about this contact." Ultimately, Paschal said, he had decided to tell the truth. Even so, his story did not actually change until a month later, on January 15, 1963, when he gave a new statement to the FBI and appeared before the grand jury.[28]

Brown wondered why Paschal would he change his story. "Well," the patrolman explained, "they [government agents] told me it was better to tell the truth than to go ahead and maybe lose, yes, lose my job, or get involved in something deeper." He had not been threatened, he insisted, but FBI agents had "told [him he] could get in trouble[,] maybe could get indicted." Once again, the government appeared to have made overt threats in order to influence a witness's testimony—even if simply insisting that he tell the truth.

As a state trooper, Brown observed, Paschal had surely testified in numerous courtrooms. Had he ever violated his oath of office in any of those cases? "Not until this happened," a subdued Paschal responded.[29]

"Are you still a state trooper?" Brown asked.

"Yes sir," Paschal replied quietly, "for the time being."[30]

On redirect, Paschal insisted that he had received no promises regarding his testimony. He had been told to tell the truth, and that was what he had done.

"So help you God?" Neal asked, an eye toward the listening jurors.

This unabashed baiting proved too much for Branstetter, who shot out of his seat. "I would assume that this witness has already said 'So help me God' many times," he announced, his words dripping with sarcasm. "He may need Him."

Judge Wilson was not amused. "Let's not make comments, gentlemen, outside of the record of each other. . . . That was highly improper, ladies and gentlemen. Disregard that comment. Let's not make such comments, Mr. Branstetter."

"I apologize," Branstetter responded.[31]

Once again, the government had offered a witness to corroborate that a Hoffa affiliate had tried to tamper with the Test Fleet jury. However, the defense had yet again raised significant questions as to the veracity and motivations of the witness.

———

Betty Paschal, the second of three jurors removed from the Test Fleet trial, still lives in the Woodbury, Tennessee home where she resided in 1962. Situated on a quiet street a few blocks from the main strip through the small town, the modest white frame house has a driveway off to the left—the same driveway where King and Pitts approached James Paschal to discuss his possible promotion. There was no reason to call Betty Paschal as a witness at the jury tampering trial; she was never contacted or offered anything in exchange for voting in favor of acquittal. She did, however, testify before the grand jury in early 1963. The questions thrown at her about the jury tampering allegations understandably puzzled her. "I didn't know what they were talking about," she explained. One day Betty Paschal was on the jury, listening to testimony about the ownership of trucking companies, and the next day she was inexplicably informed that she had been taken off of the jury. To this day, however, the implication that she and her husband might have been involved in accepting a bribe relating to Jimmy Hoffa's acquittal remains an open wound. It is something she does not wish to discuss.[32]

TEN

"The Hoffa case begins and ends with Edward Grady Partin."[1]

—Fred J. Cook, *Nation*, April 27, 1964

BARRELING THROUGH THE hallways of the Chattanooga courthouse on February 4, Hoffa felt confident. The government had failed in all of its prior attempts to "get" him, and things were looking good again. He had guided his counsel to what was shaping up to be a repeat performance. Recognizing his active role in managing his many lawyers, one reporter commented, "Hoffa himself has been the liveliest figure at the defense table, a crisp and taut quarterback to his team of legal talent."

There were sizable, obvious problems with the prosecution's evidence. The indictment's second count, charging that James Tippens had been offered $10,000 to vote for acquittal, had been shelved. No one had proven that the other two individuals removed from the Test Fleet jury, Betty Paschal and Gratin Fields, had actually been approached. And several witnesses—including Dallas Hall and James Paschal—had emphasized that they had never intended to discuss the case with any jury member. Serious questions hovered over the trial with respect to the character of the prosecution's witnesses and the tactics employed to obtain their testimony. Some witnesses admitted to presenting fabricated information on multiple occasions—often under oath. Others had sworn that the government had secured its proof through threats and intimidation. No smoking gun had been offered.

Most importantly, Jimmy Hoffa had barely been mentioned.

By February 4, it was apparent that the government was beginning to wind down its case-in-chief, and it appeared that it was going out with a whimper. The prosecution turned to a series of minor players, including two railroad employees who observed Hoffa at Nashville's Union Station during the Test Fleet trial, and a *Nashville Tennessean* photographer who identified an image of Hoffa's entourage leaving the Nashville courthouse. This curious, inconsequential information gave the distinct impression that the prosecution's case was slowly grinding to a halt.[2]

Hoffa had good reason to feel confident. Two weeks into the trial, and no witness had linked him to any effort to bribe a juror. The evidence had been a complex puzzle. "It was a mosaic," Neal explained. "It was a crossword puzzle thing. It was absolutely necessary, but it wasn't exciting." While Neal promised that a "solid chain of evidence" would soon be tightened around the chief defendant, such proof was at that point "conspicuous by its absence." Hoffa hoped that acquittal was imminent.[3]

———

February 4. A long pause. The courtroom was packed, the air thick with tension as the crowd quietly wondered who else would serve as a government witness. Hooker had hinted to reporters that something important was about to happen. Curious personnel who would have otherwise remained in the hallway had slipped into the courtroom, and visitors trained their attention on the double doors to the chamber. Judge Wilson asked the government to call its next witness. All was silent. Neal did not even call out a name. The courtroom doors opened. At that moment, the entire course of the trial was altered.[4]

The courtroom exploded as Edward Grady Partin, the Baton Rouge Teamster who had guarded the door to Hoffa's hotel suite throughout the Test Fleet trial, stepped to the witness stand. "It was like a bolt of lightning coming down on the defense table," Neal reflected. "You could hear them shout out, 'It's Partin!'" Mansfield echoed this reaction. "You could hear it all over the courthouse."[5]

Prior to that moment, the defense had had no clue that Partin would be a witness. Of course, lawyers suspected that someone had been feeding information to Sheridan and the Get Hoffa Squad. But the defense had had no idea who it was and presumed the information was obtained through a covert wiretap. After all, Partin had taken the Fifth Amendment before the grand jury, and there had never been any reason to suspect him as an informant. As it turned out, however, Partin had been working with the government the entire time.

The government had taken great care to keep Partin's role secret. Pretrial meetings had been held in remote locations where the sight of the big Louisianan would not arouse comment. Moreover, Partin had been holed up in a cabin on the side of nearby Lookout Mountain since the start of the trial. During the lunchtime recess on February 4, Sheridan drove him to the courthouse and sneaked him into the building through a rear loading dock.[6]

Partin was not naïve. He knew the impact of what he was doing, and he was certainly anxious as he waited to take the stand. He was also aware of what could happen to someone who testified against Hoffa. Yet Partin did not balk at the prospect of appearing in court, remaining calm as Sheridan ushered him into the building. Sheridan had approached Mansfield and explained, "We've got a witness going to go up on the stand in about an hour. He's in the courthouse. We want him brought up to the courtroom at a certain time, but we don't want him to be seen in the hallways or out there. Can you arrange that?"

"I said sure," Mansfield recalled, adding, "I didn't know who he was."

No one did.

On the third floor, Mansfield and Partin waited for a signal that the coast was clear before rushing to Jack Reddy's office. Partin would wait there for the afternoon session to begin. He was quietly escorted to the vestibule that led into the courtroom, where he buttoned his suit jacket and took a deep breath. The doors opened, and he entered the packed courtroom.[7] When the witness strode to the front of the courtroom, the color drained from a "visibly shaken" Hoffa's face. Most observers did not know who Partin was. Hoffa and the veteran members of his defense team, however, were very familiar with the man. The result was bedlam. As juror Pat Haverty recalled, "The table up front here, they just—they were all, one or two [attorneys] were standing up suddenly, looking at him, and the others were shuffling papers, turning to each other, and they were obviously in disarray when Partin came through the door." For jurors, the commotion was the most exciting thing that had happened during the trial.[8]

As the defense struggled to regain its composure, Partin was sworn in. After identifying himself as the secretary-treasurer and business manager of Teamsters Local 5 in Baton Rouge—a position that he had held for twelve years—Partin confirmed that he had been in Nashville during the Test Fleet case. He also identified himself in a photograph of the Hoffa entourage leaving the courthouse in Nashville. Partin explained that he had come to Nashville on October 22, 1962, after speaking with Hoffa. "Just come on down to Nashville," the IBT president had told him. This invitation (and how Partin had come to be in the city in the first place) would become a key issue in the case.[9]

The very night he arrived in Nashville, Partin said, he had met Nicholas Tweel at the Andrew Jackson Hotel, where he was informed about efforts to "get to the jury." As Partin began to reveal an apparently incriminating conversation with one of the defendants, a chorus of objections rang out. The jury was quickly ushered from the courtroom. Appalled, the defense demanded that Partin's testimony be suppressed because he was a government mole. "It's obvious from the testimony this far," James Haggerty said, "that this witness was planted for the purpose of undercover work on the Defendant Hoffa." Wouldn't that be tantamount to wiretapping the defendant?[10]

Other defense lawyers joined in. "This is a complete shock and surprise to all of us," Silets stammered. As Marvin Berke later recounted, "The defendants personally, when they saw Partin, *were* in shock, because they could not believe that this friend of Mr. Hoffa would come in and, first, betray him in the Test Fleet case, and then come in and testify against him in this case." Soft-spoken but forceful, Branstetter compared Partin's actions to Neal's dressing in costume and sneaking in to listen to defense lawyers' conversations. That would clearly be impermissible; how could the prosecution accomplish the same thing through a stooge like Partin?

The legal issues created by Partin's clandestine role during the Test Fleet trial needed to be examined. "May it please the Court," a clearly rattled Haggerty confessed, "I have been taken completely by surprise by this witness.

I ask before Your Honor makes a ruling I have an opportunity to check the law [on the issue]." Neal, reluctant to forfeit the advantage Partin's sudden entrance created, objected. Schiffer retorted, "While it may be very true that Mr. Neal wants to run very quick with a hatchet at the defendants, in the interests of the justice" additional time should be allowed for the defense to fully explore the legal issues that Partin's appearance created.[11]

Following a brief recess, Judge Wilson allowed a hearing outside of the presence of the jury on the motion to suppress Partin's testimony. The result was a bitter, four-and-one-half-hour "do-or-die" battle that became the fulcrum on which the case would rest. As Marvin Berke explained, it was a win-or-lose issue for the defense: "Without him [Partin], the government had no case." Attorneys for Hoffa and his associates prepared with this fact in mind.[12]

Partin's surprise appearance had brought "a mixture of concern, fury and contempt in the camp of the defendants." It also presented a tricky legal issue: Was it appropriate for the government to send an "undercover man" behind closed doors with a defendant and his counsel during the course of a criminal trial? Neal pointed to prior cases where courts had allowed somewhat similar tactics. In *Wellman, et al. v. United States,* a federal court had ruled that government informants could testify about what they had learned during undercover operations to infiltrate a Communist conspiracy. In *United States v. Thomas,* moreover, the use of a fictitious name on a return address was permissible in catching a postmaster guilty of stealing mail.

Nevertheless, some commentators questioned whether Partin tainted the trial with "a number of very troublesome questions of prosecutorial ethics." Did his presence interfere with Hoffa's constitutional right to confer freely with his lawyers? Did the government actually *prevent* the grand jury from obtaining all available evidence in instructing Partin to take the Fifth Amendment? The government had wrestled with these very questions at the outset while deciding whether to pursue the jury tampering indictment.[13] Three critical issues were raised during the Partin hearing. Why was Partin in Nashville in the first place? What had he heard while hanging around Hoffa's suite? And was he paid for his testimony?

The hearing began with a few cursory questions from Hooker as to whether Partin had been privy to any of the defense team's strategic conversations during the Test Fleet case. "Well," Partin drawled, "very little of what I had to say would be in the presence of lawyers, very little." Hooker then asked Partin if he was expected to relate any conversations with defense lawyers. "No sir," he replied firmly. "I would not."[14] Partin admitted that he had spoken with some of the attorneys during the Test Fleet trial, but he added, "I don't think they allowed anyone to sit inside when they were discussing it [the trial] . . . they would move you out." Silets asked how often he reported to Sheridan. "Only when it was evidence of jury tampering," Partin responded. He did note, however, that *he* was left to determine what met the definition of jury tampering.

As Branstetter took over the questioning, the defense lawyers' frustrations became clear, particularly as Partin's responses proved to be vague, elusive, and/or long-winded. Tensions rose as the lawyer and the witness began to cut one another off, muddling the record with fractured answers. Finally, perturbed by what he felt to be the evasiveness of the witness, Branstetter began to speak loudly over Partin and was cautioned by the court. "I apologize to the court," Branstetter said, "but I have done this because the witness has not been responding to the question."

"Well," Judge Wilson countered, "I don't know how you would know[,] because you have been interrupting him."[15]

Schiffer would take on the task of challenging Partin's personal character. "Mr. Partin, at the present time you have been charged with the crime of kidnapping, have you not?" Neal objected to the relevance of Partin's criminal background to the question of whether he could testify. "Are you trying to hide the truth?" Schiffer barked.

Judge Wilson sustained the objection. "We have spent more time in this lawsuit trying side issues than we have trying this lawsuit," he observed. "There must be some reasonable limitation."

At this stage, the only issue was whether Partin's presence at the Test Fleet trial was appropriate. His credibility could be examined later, *if* he was allowed to testify.

Schiffer asked Partin whether he had been paid for his cooperation. No, Partin replied, shaking his head. "I have never been promised anything by the government nor have I ever asked anything, sir." This unequivocal denial would soon evolve into a thorny issue for the key government witness.

Schiffer continued his questioning. At whose request did you go to Nashville? "Mr. Hoffa's," Partin readily responded. Did the government send you there? "No, sir, they did not."[16]

After having been grilled for the better part of the afternoon, Partin stepped down from the witness chair. The defense, hoping to render his testimony null and void, called a string of witnesses who had been present during the Test Fleet trial, each of whom detailed Partin's activities in Nashville. First came "fiery tempered and high strung" attorney William Bufalino, who asserted, "I had many discussions with Ed Partin regarding the actual strategy of the case." Asked whether he knew that Partin was informing the government, he shook his head. "Absolutely not. . . . I would not have helped him or permitted him in any way to be near the seventh floor or anywhere [if I had known of his role]."

According to Bufalino, Partin's observations had clearly assisted the government in 1962. The day after Partin had helped Bufalino staple and revise notes for the preparation of witnesses, Neal had confronted a defense witness on the stand, asking whether the witness had been supplied with questions and answers by the defense. Surely, Partin had told Neal about the notes; otherwise, Neal would not have known to accost the witness about them. On another occasion, Partin was present while the defense was preparing a witness for his testimony; the following day, as Bufalino began to question that witness, Neal leapt up to object. The problem? The objection was premature, before Neal could possibly have known what Bufalino would ask. Incredulous, Bufalino had turned to Neal. "How do you know what I'm going to ask, all I said was 1953?"

Neal responded sarcastically, "I'm psychic."

"Psychic or psycho?" Bufalino had retorted.

"If it was December of 1953," Neal had explained to the court, "I think I know the line of inquiry." To Bufalino, this was in no way convincing. Neal could not have anticipated the question merely because a certain month was mentioned. Someone had to be feeding him information.

Hooker asked Bufalino whether he had ever discussed jury tampering with Partin. "I had no discussions at all with Mr. Partin about any jury tampering," came the gritty reply. According to Bufalino, it had been *Partin* who, indicating that he knew one of the jurors, had tried to raise the issue with him: "I said, 'Look, I want absolutely nothing at all to do with any such discussion. Lay off that. We have a cinch case. This case is absolutely nothing . . . so far as I am concerned you just forget about anything like that.'" Finally, asked about his current understanding of Partin's role in Nashville, Bufalino sneered. "Well," he said, "he will never again help me staple papers, I will tell you that."[17]

James Haggerty, Hoffa's lead attorney, was next to the stand. While defense attorneys had debated strategy, discussed applicable law, and prepared for courtroom sessions during the Test Fleet case, he asserted, Partin had been present "on quite a number of these occasions." It was now abundantly clear that Partin had been sharing defense strategy with the prosecution. "I was of the opinion that the room where we held the conference was bugged,"

Haggerty said, "for the reason that on several occasions . . . something was designed to take the government by surprise, but it didn't work that way. The government seemed to be, this is the way it appeared to me, to have advance notice and they met it in stride."[18]

Daniel B. Maher, who had also assisted with the Test Fleet defense, informed the court that during the Nashville trial he had hung up the telephone in his room and immediately lifted the receiver to his ear to make another call. "That was Mayor [sic]," a voice on the line said.

"No," another voice corrected, "he's in [room] 926."

The first voice responded. "No, Haggerty is in 918. It was Haggerty."

There was no doubt in his mind, Maher said, that he was being surveilled by the government. He had tried to locate the bugs in his room, he said, but could not do so.

Maher added that at lunch one day he noticed an "FBI man" sitting in the booth next to several members of the defense team, giving him the impression that they were being watched. On cross-examination, however, Maher conceded that the agent had *already* been seated in the booth when they entered the restaurant. How could he anticipate that they would sit in an adjacent booth? "That is some surveillance, Mr. Maher," Neal said sarcastically.[19]

As a practical matter, Maher's anecdotes did not involve Partin and had nothing to do with the suppression of his testimony. Nevertheless, they highlighted the degree to which defense suspicions of surveillance had come to saturate the case. Since the start of the trial, the court had discounted the defense's concerns, and the press had labeled them as paranoid. Now, with the arrival of Partin, attorneys for Hoffa and his associates believed they finally had solid evidence of surveillance.

It was getting late in the afternoon. Dusky purple light drifted through the windows of the courtroom as Sheridan, Partin's primary contact throughout the Test Fleet trial, took the stand. The thirty-nine year old was Kennedy's aide-de-camp on the Get Hoffa Squad. A World War II veteran, he had attended Fordham University and taken a brief crack at law school before joining the FBI. Disillusioned, he left the agency, purportedly because "Hoover was more interested in guys who were Communists for 15 minutes in 1931 than he was in guys who were stealing New Jersey." In 1957, Sheridan was recruited to become a member of Kennedy's staff on the McClellan Committee. After assisting with the Kennedy campaign in 1960, he had joined the Get Hoffa Squad as a special assistant. Quiet and slight of frame, Sheridan was a meticulous investigator and tenacious in his desire to pin something on Hoffa that would stick. His role as Kennedy's chief "axe man" led critics to question his tactics, including the alleged use of threats and bribery—and wiretapping.[20]

Sheridan confirmed that he had instructed Partin to inform him if he discovered any evidence of jury tampering. Asked if he and Partin discussed any conversations with attorneys, Sheridan replied, "Oh, maybe very small bits, yes." He stressed, however, that Partin had made no recordings during the trial and that he had not been promised any payment. Sheridan said that everything he had written in his notes had related to jury tampering "or the comings and goings of people"—not to defense strategy.[21]

The hearing concluded at 6:40 p.m., well after the usual time for adjournment. While leaving the courthouse, a grim, exhausted Hoffa was asked about the shocking developments of the day. "I have nothing to say," he remarked. "You make your own evaluation of Mr. Partin."[22]

The following morning, the crowd waited anxiously to hear the critical ruling on which the case might turn. The proceedings had suddenly become more tense. Additional US marshals were posted in the courtroom; it was reported that Partin's life might be in danger. When asked how many marshals were guarding the surprise witness, an official for the Justice Department replied tersely, "Enough."[23] Judge Wilson "looked weary on the bench after a long night of studying law books to help him reach his decision." During the trial, the lifelong early riser had also stayed up into the early morning hours preparing for the next day. As his wife, Helen, explained, "he'd set right to work right after" a brief family dinner. Each evening, a courier would bring Wilson the transcript from the day's proceedings. "Sometimes it was midnight before they'd even get here with it," Ms. Wilson noted, "so he'd read on that until he went to bed." As a result, it was often three o'clock in the morning before he would retire to get a few hours of sleep before heading back to the courthouse.[24]

After a long moment, Judge Wilson cleared his throat and addressed the courtroom. Having fully evaluated the law on the issue, he explained evenly, Partin would be allowed to take the stand. There was no showing that he had interfered with the attorney-client relationship between Hoffa and his legal team. Moreover, the government did not plant Partin in the defense camp; rather, "he was knowingly and voluntarily placed in their midst by one of the defendants," i.e., Hoffa.

It was a decisive turning point. "The government won a major victory in the opening moments of today's session," the *Chattanooga News-Free Press* reported, "when Wilson permitted Partin to testify."[25]

Dressed in the same rumpled blue suit he had worn the previous day, Partin sat squarely in the witness chair, feet flat on the floor and hands in his lap, as the jury was returned to the courtroom after almost a full day's absence. In a slow, quiet drawl, Partin softly but deliberately drove a blade into the defendants' hearts.[26]

When he had contacted Hoffa in October 1962 to discuss union business, Partin said, Hoffa had invited him to Nashville for a discussion. He had not ingratiated himself into Hoffa's camp; he had been summoned. Only steps away, Hoffa chewed on a ballpoint pen and glared at the witness, fuming. He had been set up. In his view, Partin had invited himself to Nashville and "hung around like a leech the whole time." The Teamsters president had unwittingly allowed Partin to stick around and soak up information. By the end of the trial, in fact, Hoffa "had [Partin] guarding his door," giving him access to the comings and goings of the entire defense team.[27]

Once Partin was in Nashville, what were his instructions? "If I saw any evidence of jury tampering or other illegal acts," he said, "[I was to]contact Mr. Sheridan and I was given his phone number." Partin had made several such reports during the trial, "usually the same day they would happen." This information echoed Sheridan's testimony to the grand jury that information "was furnished to me, not on a daily basis but on an almost daily basis during the entire trial." "The voluminous information he [Partin] furnished, that which was subject to corroboration, was corroborated one hundred per cent," Sheridan explained. "We never found him to be wrong in any instance." Sheridan had added, "The pattern was followed without fail. He would tell me something was going to happen and it always happened, and it always happened just the way he said it would happen."[28]

Soon after Partin had arrived in Nashville on October 22, Dorfman had asked him to call Tweel and inquire about the status of efforts to get Nashville nightclub owner Dallas Hall to look at the list of jurors. Tweel said he needed the list. So, Partin said, "I told Mr. Hoffa that Mr. Tweel needed a jury list." Bufalino subsequently gave him one. Dorfman then called Tweel from a public phone, reading off the names. Days later, Tweel remarked that "things are hot down there [Nashville]" and urged his associates to lie low. The prosecution seemed to have inside information about every move they made.[29]

The color had drained from the defendants' faces. Even Hoffa could not mask his emotions as Partin related a series of attempts to bribe jurors in

the Test Fleet case. The Teamster glowered at the witness, barely able to restrain his anger. Despite his disdainful references to Partin as a "backbiting
bastard" and "the spy who came to dinner," Hoffa knew how damaging this
testimony was, especially coming from a charismatic witness who reportedly
"could charm a snake off a rock."[30]

Some commentators, however, found Partin's testimony to be utterly implausible and ridiculous. A cynical article in *Nation* noted, "He had hardly
set foot in the place [Nashville] before he discovered exactly what he had
been sent to discover . . . almost the first man he bumped into—a man whom
he had never known, at that—told him of Hoffa's plans to rig the jury." Why
would Hoffa employ a man from West Virginia to investigate a list of jurors
in Tennessee? And why would Tweel share that information with a man he
did not even know?[31]

As Hoffa glared across the room, drumming his fingers on the table, Partin
continued his astounding account, relating conversations with the Teamsters
president himself about tampering with the Test Fleet jury. For the first time,
Hoffa would be linked to each of the bribery attempts.

On October 22, Partin stated, "[Hoffa] told me he'd like for me to stick
around a day or two[,] that he might have one or two people he wanted me
to call. He said that they was going to get to one juror or try to get to a few
scattered jurors and take their chances." The following day, as he was preparing to leave town, Partin was called into Hoffa's hotel room. There, he
said, "[Hoffa] told me when I came back [to Nashville] he may want me to
pass something along for him. He put his hand behind his pocket like that
[indicating], and hit his rear pocket," where a wallet would be.[32]

After a brief trip to Baton Rouge, Partin returned to Nashville on October 25. "The dirty bastard went in and told the judge that his neighbor had
offered him $10,000," a livid Hoffa vented. "We are going to have to lay low
for a few days." Thus, Hoffa was implicated in the approach to Tippens. Asked
if anyone else had been present to hear these comments, Partin smiled. "Mr.
Hoffa never has anyone present when he says something."[33] On another occasion, Partin testified, he encountered an upset Hoffa who, gulping down
an Alka-Seltzer, muttered, "I would pay $15,000 or $20,000 . . . whatever it
cost to get to the jury."[34]

Then Partin dragged Ewing King into the plot, relating that on October 26
King had mentioned a highway patrolman whose wife was on the jury. "He
told me that the highway patrolman and his wife had money," Partin said,
"but they loved money and $10,000.00 was a lot of money." By early Novem-
ber, though, Hoffa had become displeased with King's lackadaisical efforts

to contact patrolman Paschal. "Mr. Hoffa said that he was raising cain at Mr. King[,] said he wasn't doing what he told him to do," Partin explained. "He keeps talking about it and fumbling around." King later confided to Partin that "Mr. Hoffa was on his rear end about not getting to the jury like he told him he would." Even a week later, Hoffa had remained upset with King's efforts and had "called Mr. King a stupid S.O.B. for thumbing around and not getting the job done."[35]

Finally, King had contacted the patrolman. A coded phrase that the jury had heard before—a beagle hound had dropped dead at ten o'clock—was the signal for a meeting. Partin described, step by step, the rendezvous between King and Paschal, mirroring the testimony previous witnesses had provided. Afterward, Partin recounted, Hoffa "was very upset because the Highway Patrolman didn't take the money. . . . He said if he had of taken the money it would have pinned him down and he couldn't have backed up." Of course, the prosecution had posited that Paschal had been offered a promotion, not cash, in exchange for assistance with the Test Fleet verdict. That not insubstantial mistake aside, Partin had directly implicated both King and Hoffa in a plan to bribe the patrolman in November 1962.[36]

Still, Partin said, the Hoffa camp was optimistic about juror Gratin Fields. As Partin was leaving Nashville on November 7, Hoffa remarked, "Don't worry about it too much," adding, "I have got the colored male juror in my hip pocket." The union boss explained that one of his business agents, a man named Campbell, "came into Nashville prior to the trial and took care of it."[37]

In the course of only a couple of hours, Partin had managed to implicate virtually all of the defendants—Tom Parks was the only exception—in the efforts to bribe jurors during the Nashville trial. While some onlookers felt that Partin's information was simply too tidy or didn't make practical sense, it did have a significant impact on the one group of observers who really mattered—the jury. Jurors had noticed Partin's dramatic impact on the defense from the moment he entered the courtroom. As juror Pat Haverty recalled, the reaction to Partin's entrance "said 'this is the person to listen to' . . . the first one to make Jimmy stand up . . . everybody noticed that." As a result, Haverty determined, "This is the one that knows what's going on and that they're scared of."

Partin's testimony only solidified that conclusion, at least in Haverty's eyes. "He gained my respect quickly, because he said exactly what he knew and no more . . . and he would say the same thing every time in a measured pace, it was like a machine," Haverty remembered. "He was the know-it-all, do-it-all, get the information for Hoffa . . . he knew everything that went on for him. He apparently was the man between Hoffa and the world." If he overstated Partin's actual importance, Partin's *apparent* significance in the eyes of the jury was critical. As Haverty concluded, "He was the key to the whole thing."[38]

———

Mercifully, Judge Wilson ordered a recess. As the jury filed out of the courtroom, Silets complained that an unknown individual had just "grabbed hold of the witness and . . . led him out of the courtroom right in front of these jurors," creating the impression that he was being protected from something (or someone). "Now," Silets waggled a finger, "that was the most prejudicial thing that happened in this, physically in this courtroom since the case started." The mysterious individual was identified as a US marshal. Judge Wilson admonished him not to interfere with the witness, and the parties filtered out into the hallway.[39]

Apoplectic, Hoffa stalked out of the courtroom and into a room set aside for the defense. "Roaring like a mortally wounded bear," he flung a heavy desk chair against a wall. "He's killing us with those asides to the jury," he hissed to his lawyers. "You've got to get him off that stand."[40] With that directive fresh on their minds, defense attorneys returned to the courtroom bent on curbing the impact of this damaging and, in their eyes, deceitful witness. When Hooker resumed his examination, he was met with "a continual barrage of defense objections and motions"—by one count, 168 during a period of three and one-half hours. As Hooker struggled to question the witness, four or five defense attorneys would contest virtually every question. In particular, Schiffer and Silets "seemed to work as a team in resisting, inch by inch, the effort of Hooker to get Partin's story in front of the jury." Judge Wilson was obviously frustrated with the glacial pace of the examination. "If the Court knew some way to keep attorneys from rising," he said, "I think perhaps we could move along." [41]

Such mind-numbing tactics placed the judge in a precarious position. Wilson was almost certainly annoyed, but an outburst on the part of the court could cause a mistrial, prejudicing the defense in the eyes of the jury. In the final analysis, Wilson proved particularly adept at performing his role in a patient, deliberate, and courteous manner. "He speaks calmly," the *Chattanooga Times* noted, "and never raises his voice." To each objection and demand for a mistrial he simply listened to the attorneys and then, very stoically and without sermonizing, issued his ruling, most often with a simple "sustained" or "overruled." In this manner, he compelled the trial forward despite a steady torrent of interruptions and objections.

Schiffer posed a sizable challenge. He had begun to push the envelope with his diatribes in an apparent strategy to compel the judge to blow his stack. As Mansfield concluded, "Mr. Schiffer was to be the bad guy, to aggravate the judge and the jury." In keeping with this role, Schiffer stood at the defense table on February 6, waving his arms and shouting over and over again that Partin was a "well-coached witness." This loud, vehement outburst "brought a rare display of irritation" from the otherwise calm judge, who ordered him to halt his argument. It would not deter Schiffer. Struggling to be heard over Schiffer's ranting, Judge Wilson was finally forced to raise his voice. "Did you hear me, Mr. Schiffer? Did you hear me, Mr. Schiffer?" This loud double warning did the trick, and Schiffer reluctantly took his seat.[42]

Despite the efforts of the defense to swamp the witness, Partin "testified with clarity and refused to be shaken by opposition lawyers who often in apparent anger, barked questions at him." As Hooker's examination continued, the allegations became even more intriguing. Partin revealed that on October 30, 1962, Hoffa had asked him to contact former Vanderbilt All-American football players Billy Wade (Chicago Bears) and Phil King (New York Giants) to see if they might drop in on the Test Fleet courtroom and "shake hands and mix it up with the defendants." Back in Louisiana, Partin had hired two former LSU standouts, Heisman Trophy winner Billy Cannon and All-American Jimmy Taylor, to serve as bodyguards. However, when he informed Hoffa, he was told that, because the trial was in Nashville, it would be better for him to push for the former Commodores. Partin then tried to telephone Wade, to no avail.[43]

This allegation seemed a bit farfetched. Hoffa surely had close connections in Nashville, Chicago, and New York who might have some direct association with Wade and/or King. Why would he instead ask Partin, from far-distant Baton Rouge, to track down those famous football stars? A critical observer could conclude that Partin was simply making the whole thing up. Nevertheless, the entire courtroom seemed to be hanging on every word issuing from Partin's lips.[44]

Finally, Judge Wilson adjourned court for the day, and the exhausted combatants filed out into the street. As Sheridan later summarized, "Partin's testimony had been accurate, thorough, and devastating. It clearly linked Hoffa with every phase of the activities of the other defendants." One of the defense attorneys ran into Sheridan in the hallway. "I have seen some great coups in my time," he remarked, "but that was the greatest coup I have ever seen." It would be one of the few courteous compliments to pass between the two sides during the case, and almost certainly the last.[45]

The following morning, Hooker almost reluctantly turned the witness over for questioning by the defense. Everyone expected a brutal cross-examination. The prior evening, one of Hoffa's lawyers had told reporters that the defense was prepared to "rip Partin to shreds." Even so, no one present could imagine how long the cross-examination would continue, or how tortuous the process would be.[46]

ELEVEN

"Tumult and drama have become hallmarks of the
James Riddle Hoffa trials. . . . It's a Hoffa trial all right."[1]

—*Detroit News*, February 9, 1964

DOUG PARTIN is the youngest brother of Edward Grady Partin. When his older brother founded a Teamsters local in Natchez, Mississippi, Doug joined the union, and in the mid-1950s, after serving in Korea, he joined Ed at Teamsters Local 5 in Baton Rouge as an assistant business agent. Later, when Ed stepped back from the leadership of the local, Doug became the business agent and trustee, running the organization until his retirement in 1994. If anyone was familiar with Ed Partin, it was his brother.

In his autobiography *From My Brother's Shadow,* Doug Partin details his brother's criminal history, a topic about which Ed Partin was notoriously ambiguous. Even as a youngster, Ed was involved in criminal activities, selling stolen BB guns throughout his neighborhood. Dishonorably discharged from the US Marines, by 1949 he had been arrested for grand larceny, robbery with the use of a firearm, and rape.

In 1962, Ed was indicted for manslaughter and leaving the scene of an accident, a charge that was hovering over him at the time of the Chattanooga trial. He had also been indicted for forgery, falsification of records, and embezzlement. September 1962 brought additional charges against Ed Partin for aggravated kidnapping. These emerged after he had given an associate, Billy Simpson, money and a car to take his children out of town after his wife was awarded legal custody.

In Doug Partin's telling, Ed was "a consummate liar." He was capable of telling a phony story so convincingly, Doug recounted, that a hoodwinked investigator would abandon further inquiry into a subject—and he was somehow able to fool a lie detector test, a skill that he reportedly employed on several occasions.

As Doug Partin summarized, "Ed was trouble."[2]

―――――

"I never personally felt that Partin was being truthful," attorney Marvin Berke asserted. Now the defense needed to make that point clear to the jury. Ever since the surprise witness had appeared, the defense had scrambled to assemble the information needed to attack his credibility. By the morning of February 6, the lawyers were well prepared. As Berke recalled, "By the next day [after his initial appearance] we had a lot of information on him."[3]

Partin was no angel; that much was clear from the beginning. Over Neal's objections, Judge Wilson allowed defense counsel to inquire about Partin's criminal background. The court would prove willing to allow the defense to go beyond the normal scope of cross-examination, asking about arrests that never resulted in convictions and other misconduct. Attorneys for Hoffa and his associates even brought up allegations dating back to when Partin was a minor.[4]

Partin, however, was extremely reluctant to go into any layers of detail. He calmly explained that he was not ashamed of his past, stating, "I believe that is what they build churches for, to repent of your sins, I believe so." The one time he had served a jail sentence for a felony charge, he added, "I had a full pardon in the eyes of God and in the eyes of the law, but evidently not in your [Harry Berke's] eyes." Partin could not deny that various accusations had been made against him, but he emphasized that most of the claims had come to nothing. As Neal remarked to the press, "The government does not contend that Mr. Partin has led a perfect life. The government does contend that he is telling the truth."[5]

Still, on cross-examination Partin proved to be a different witness from the steady, poised informant the jury had observed on direct. Then, he had been well prepared for the questions. Responding to Harry Berke, however, Partin was evasive and hostile at every turn. His memory was dissipated, his confidence vanished. As one commentator observed, the witness "instantly displayed a striking mental ambivalence." He could recite subtle details of the Test Fleet case, but he could recall nothing about his own multiple arrests and convictions. He aggravated the defense with his tendency to digress. Several times, Judge Wilson had to remind him to "just answer the questions and not volunteer information." This rambling evasiveness elicited a thin smile and often a chuckle from Hoffa, who "appeared to be in better spirits" after the Thursday session than he had been any time since Partin's arrival earlier that week.[6]

Even when pressed with specific details, Partin was unmoved, denying the allegations on the basis of a lack of memory. Asked whether he was arrested for robbery and auto theft in September 1941, Partin shook his head. "No, sir. You have your information wrong. Better check it again." After Partin similarly denied having been arrested for nonsupport of his wife in 1954, Berke even read off the number of the case—37,992—but Partin remained steadfast in his denial. Absent hard proof, he was not admitting anything.[7]

This thinly veiled blocking strategy failed to hinder Berke. To the contrary, Partin's evasiveness smelled like blood in the water. After playing around the fringes of the witness's criminal background, Berke slyly dropped a bombshell: "Weren't you charged with raping a colored girl in Mississippi?" In the civil rights–era South, this was a particularly explosive, prejudicial accusation.

Even before Neal could make the expected objection, Judge Wilson stepped in. "Now, gentlemen, if you have convictions of those matters I will allow you to ask about them," he warned. "The purpose of this is not to degrade anybody by making unsupported charges." For the first time, the court had established a boundary beyond which the defense could not attack the witness.[8]

It soon became evident that the defense did not possess tangible evidence to support the scandalous charge. Changing course, therefore, Berke addressed a series of *pending* charges against Partin. He had been under indictment since October 1961 for forgery of a union member's withdrawal card, but he had suspiciously not been brought to trial. The card had been signed with the approval of the local executive board and sanctioned by the International Union, Partin explained—so it was not a criminal act.

He was also asked about the kidnapping charge. "It was not a case of kidnapping for ransom and so forth," Partin asserted. "It was a case where my best friend was involved in a family dispute. The husband and wife separated. He took his children and went one place. She took another man and went another way. They live together. The charges were dropped." When Berke noted that the charges had been dismissed only weeks before his testimony against Hoffa, Partin responded that he did not know when they had been dismissed. On all of these points, Partin was combative and evasive. These revelations created intriguing questions about whether Partin's testimony was the quid pro quo for the dismissal of serious charges against him.[9]

Surely, Partin's questionable character was becoming clear. Even so, at least some of the jurors took the information with a grain of salt. Recalling the trial almost fifty years later, juror Pat Haverty was unmoved. "I didn't think like they had any real significance," he said of the criminal charges. "He was an honest man; he could not be shaken."

Berke, however, was not finished with Partin.[10] A series of questions as to when and where Partin had met with government agents resulted in an impromptu secret session, with jurors, reporters, and bystanders removed from the courtroom. The doors to the chamber were closed, with marshals posted at each one. The removal of the jury had become commonplace. As the *Detroit News* reported, "Much of what has gone on here has been kept from the ears of jurors." To Hoffa, this ritual had the result of distorting the evidence. "Wilson made a regular habit of sustaining government objections or, at best, ordering the jury from the courtroom so that he could hear privately some of our most pertinent evidence," he complained. "He did this to the point that 60 percent of our evidence was given in the jury's absence—and never was heard by the jury."

At the outset of the secret hearing, Neal voiced concern about the trajectory of Berke's questions. "If they go into prior meetings, if it's a prior meeting a week or two ahead of what [it is]and what it concerned," Neal explained, "then we are heading for trouble or the defendants are heading for trouble."

When the defense pushed him as to the curious topic he was dancing around, Neal sighed and bowed his head. "Very well. This man," he said, gesturing to Partin, "reported a threat by James Hoffa to kill the Attorney General. He took a lie detector test on it and passed the test with flying colors. Now, that's an FBI report, that is something I do not want to come out to this jury."

According to Partin, at Teamsters headquarters in the summer of 1962, Hoffa asked him whether he knew anything about plastic explosives. Incredibly, Hoffa also remarked that he knew where to get a silencer for a gun. "I've got to do something about that son of a bitch Bobby Kennedy," he had observed grimly. "He's got to go." According to Partin, Hoffa had also opined that the deed would be easy to pull off, as Kennedy had no security detail and drove to work in an open convertible.

The defense was surprisingly nonplussed. "We have no objection [to this allegation]," Berke chuckled. "We think it is so fantastic and so unbelievable as is some of his other testimony . . . we have no fear of it and know it is not true." In the defense's opinion, the allegation would backfire, showing that Partin was simply making up accusations. Nevertheless, finding the provocative topic irrelevant, Judge Wilson instructed Partin not to discuss any alleged attempt to assassinate Robert Kennedy.[11]

———

After the thirty-minute hearing, the jury returned, and Berke resumed his withering cross-examination. Immediately prior to the Test Fleet trial, he revealed, Partin had been under not only the kidnapping indictment but also a twenty-six-count indictment for theft, embezzlement, fraud, and failing to report union funds. Partin had also been charged with manslaughter after leaving the scene of an accident in which a service member had been killed. Frustrated, Partin refused to discuss the pending matters, remarking, "I am not going to answer that if I have a charge pending on me, sir. You can stand there all day. I have never admitted I was [involved in the accident], I'll put it that way." Partin was on the ropes. He stammered when Berke asked him whether he was also under investigation for attempting to smuggle guns to Fidel Castro.

Then Judge Wilson intervened. "Ladies and gentlemen, disregard that question and that answer. That has nothing to do with this case."

That was fine by the defense. It did not really matter whether Partin was allowed to respond; simply hinting that Partin was running guns to Cuba was enough to mar the witness's reputation.[12]

Partin was in trouble. He equivocated, digressed, and sidestepped direct questions. Frustrated by his rambling explanations, Silets stood to complain. Partin had no right to engage in long-winded justifications of his behavior, Silets implored. "That [justification] is for rebuttal purposes, the way your Honor has limited us on cross-examination."

Judge Wilson was astounded. If anything, he had been extremely permissive, allowing the defense to venture unfettered into topics with little real pertinence to the case. "Do you seriously feel the Court has limited the defendants in the cross-examination of this witness?"

"Yes, sir, I do," Silets replied.

"The Court has allowed the broadest possible, it seems to me, examination of the witness," Wilson chided.

In reality, it did appear that the defense had been provided with wide latitude in cross-examining Partin. The only significant limitations had been on questions about assassinating Kennedy, unsupported allegations of rape, and insinuations of gunrunning to Cuba. The fact that Silets could find fault with the scope of cross-examination shows the extent of the defense's very real sense of persecution.

Still, Neal could not resist shouldering in. Throughout the trial, he had taken special delight in jabbing at Silets, deliberately mispronouncing the Chicago attorney's name. Now he wanted to take a poke at what he viewed as Silets's silly complaint about the scope of cross-examination. "To show how unfair this cross examination is," he said, "when the Defendant Hoffa takes the stand we are precluded about asking him from any charges [not resulting in conviction] but yet no man probably has had more charges."

That last bit was more than Haggerty could stand. He had repeatedly shown impatience with Neal's bruising tactics, and he was not afraid to call him out. "Is this an alley fight or a courtroom?" he asked.

"Oh no," Neal responded, "I thought it was a courtroom."

"Well," Haggerty declared, "you don't show it at times."

Judge Wilson called for order.[13]

As the long afternoon session began to wind down, Silets saw his chance for payback. "Your Honor," he began, "I must indicate that I saw Mr. Neal indicate approval when the witness gives the right answer as Mr. Neal desires it[,] and in the presence of the jury." Neal had been nodding to Partin, trying to shore up the battered witness. "He knows that is improper."

Judge Wilson diffused the situation. "I sort of gather you gentlemen have chosen up sides in this lawsuit." This remark cooled down the rising tensions in the courtroom, prompting "restrained laughter" among not only the audience, but also the attorneys on both sides of the aisle.

The jocularity would not last for long.[14]

———

Friday, February 7, would be one of the most captivating and significant days of the trial. "The tension that had been building daily erupted into pandemonium" by the end of the day, and the embittered, volatile defense lawyers would turn their attacks on the judge himself. As the morning began, however, things were fairly quiet, with Berke wrapping up his cross-examination with a few final questions.[15] Though similar inquiries had been disallowed the previous day, Berke tried to sneak in a question about Partin's ties to Cuba, asking about a letter the witness had allegedly received from "a Cuban General working for Fidel Castro." Neal curtly objected. "This is the most offensive thing I have seen in my life," he declared. The objection was quickly sustained.[16]

Berke asked a particularly incisive question near the end of his examination. Focusing on Partin's claim that Larry Campbell had come to Nashville before the trial and "taken care of it," Berke inquired simply, "How could he fix the jury prior to the time when he didn't even know who was going to be on it?" The attorney astutely focused on a significant problem with Partin's testimony: Why would anyone take steps to bribe *prospective* jurors? Partin could provide no satisfactory answer.[17]

By the time Berke was finished, the prosecution's key witness was reeling. The brutal cross-examination had created a number of questions about Partin's character, background, and honesty. To anyone watching, the witness had been tremendously damaged. Then came a fateful decision: Would it be helpful to continue piling on a beaten and blemished witness? With the benefit of several decades of hindsight, those involved in the trial universally agree that Partin's cross-examination should have ceased at that point. "If they had quit after the first half-day of cross-examination, they might have been ahead," Sheridan wrote. Neal agreed. "He looked awful during the first day of cross-examination, and I had a juror tell me after the case was over that if they had stopped after the first day, it'd have been tough to get a conviction, because they literally tore him apart."

The defense, however, could not be certain of what might happen, and they could surely smell the blood in the water. "They were so angry that

they couldn't stop without trying to get another piece out of Edward Grady
Partin," Neal recalled. The result was probably the defense's most critical
strategic mistake. One by one, the other defense attorneys took their turns
swinging at Partin, unexpectedly shoring up his testimony and allowing him
to redeem himself. As Neal recalled, "The more they went at him, the more
he built himself back up, and after seven or eight days, this same juror said,
'I believed every word he said after that.'"

Neal was pleased. "If they'd let Harry Berke go with his cross-examination,"
he recounted, "we'd have had a much tougher time. Harry Berke was a good
lawyer. He had a good sense of timing, he knew when to start and when to
stop, and he had no particular animosity. The others were part of Hoffa's
crowd over the years, and they just couldn't stop getting after Edward Grady
Partin."[18]

———

The next lawyer to the podium was Silets. For the most part, the Chicago
attorney's examination re-trod ground Berke had plowed thoroughly over
the prior two days. When challenged on his repetitious examination, Silets
rationalized, "I want to test this man's memory. He has stated at great length
precise conversations which happened just a little more than a year ago and
he can't remember things that happened to him personally involving arrest,
detention, imprisonment."

"It is not appropriate," Judge Wilson cautioned, "to proceed over exactly
the same ground repeatedly on the theory of testing his memory."[19]

Partin's shifty testimonial tactics continually frustrated the defense. Finally,
Harold Brown could not control his disgust, remarking, "I wouldn't say he
wasn't rehearsed, but he is one of the best-informed witnesses on it until you
get him off of a certain step, when you take him off that beaten path then is
when he starts this extraneous matter," i.e., a long-winded diversion. "If he
is allowed to continue," he whispered, shaking his head, "we haven't got a
chance."

Branstetter echoed that complaint, arguing, "This witness here has not
responded to one question out of a hundred that has been asked him." Careful to note that he was not accusing the prosecution of coaching Partin, he
blamed the court for tolerating the witness's behavior. "It may have come
through the experience of this back alley man," he said, "but some way or
other this is one of the most cunning individuals that I have ever seen who

sat on the stand and then I feel strongly that the Court has protected him in that cunning."[20]

The prosecutors could not sit idly by and allow the defense to denigrate and smear their key witness. As usual, Neal would take up the banner. When Haggerty voiced his own criticisms, Neal interrupted him. "Can't you ever have manners?" a frustrated Haggerty chided. "Why don't you go back and learn a few manners?" Everyone, including the normally calm, mannered Haggerty, was beginning to wear his emotions on his sleeve.[21]

As Silets struggled to draw admissions from him, Partin slowly began to appear stronger on the stand. Rather than a struggling, evasive finger-pointer, observers were beginning to see a "square-jawed and apparently unshaken witness." Watching Partin redeem himself, defense attorneys became frustrated and frenetic. As one lawyer after another piled onto the witness, the trial took on the atmosphere of a street brawl.[22]

———

On the wall behind the judge's bench in the Chattanooga courthouse hangs a long, heavy broadsword. One of its two edges represents truth, the other reason. The symbolic blade hearkens back to the tale of the Sword of Damocles. After the naïve Damocles had prattled on about the fortune enjoyed by the tyrant Dionysius, the ruler let him sit on the throne. A sword was then suspended above Damocles's head by a single horsehair. Anxious and squirming, he begged to step down. Thus the story highlights the burdens borne by those in positions of authority.

The burden on a trial judge was nowhere more evident than in Chattanooga in 1964. The judge must carefully weigh every comment, avoiding any behavior that might be deemed prejudicial or erroneous. Each utterance, each ruling, is scrutinized, the unsuccessful party poring over the transcript in a search for some error justifying a reversal on appeal. Any appearance of favoritism or prejudice by the judge might lead to calls for a mistrial. As Partin returned to the stand day after day, it became evident that some members of the defense team had concluded that the best—or only—course of action left was to trigger such a mistrial. An outburst by the judge would accomplish this goal, and Judge Wilson would undergo an unprecedented ordeal as a result.

Aware of some of the attorneys' intentions, Wilson was obligated to remain dispassionate, stoic. He could never display a flash of anger. In handling the repeated, minute-by-minute objections of counsel, he would comment as little as possible, leaving no avenue for criticism or appeal. The frequent but simple refrain of "Let's have order in the courtroom" became an undercurrent to the proceedings. One newspaper complimented the "number of times Judge Frank Wilson retain[ed] his judicial temperament and composure during the sometimes hectic and heated sessions."

Still, the ordeal took a toll on the relatively new judge. "The animosity is thick," the *Detroit News* observed, describing the trial as "a daily test of judicial skill." Despite Judge Wilson's "remarkable restraint," however, he was under substantial pressure. "The strain is beginning to show," one reporter opined. As the only federal jurist in Chattanooga, Wilson held a solitary, isolated position—a "bottled up" and "confined" existence, according to his son, Randy, who was a grade schooler at the time. The judge had no one to whom he could confide, no source of advice, no one with whom he could chat about the trial or test his thoughts. At the courthouse, his only confidant was his law clerk, who was usually a "kid just out of law school for a year." Of course, Wilson did not take his concerns home to his wife and young children. "It was a trying time," Helen Wilson said. "The fact that he couldn't talk about it made it harder on him."

Craving a source of support, Judge Wilson sought the confidence of his minister, who would occasionally come to the judge's home in the evenings. Behind closed doors, the two men would talk and pray. In this manner, Wilson was able to obtain advice, express his frustrations, and maintain his sanity through what was becoming a tribulation.[23] Possibly as a result of these calming late-night sessions, Judge Wilson maintained his composure throughout the trial. Yet he could not allow the disruptive courtroom tactics to continue with impunity. "He's just about the finest man I've ever met," one old friend said. "And he is compassionate. But if you are wrong and have to go before him, you'd better watch out." For those members of the defense team bent on securing a mistrial at all costs, it would prove unwise to confuse Wilson's quiet self-discipline with weakness.[24]

––––––

Schiffer continued to voice the loudest, most strident accusations against Partin. As the examination dragged along, the lawyer became more and more incensed and exaggerated his conduct accordingly. Schiffer had long been associated with Hoffa, who in all likelihood hired him to assist with the trial. As a result, Schiffer's desire to do whatever he could to assist the Teamster boss would soon become uncontrollable.

"Hoffa had an assortment of lawyers, some good, and some bad," Gearhiser later recalled. "Jacques Schiffer would be an example of a bad lawyer. . . . He used intemperate language in the trial of the case." Looking back, Marvin Berke also found Schiffer's conduct to be regrettable. "Jacques Schiffer out of the courtroom was one of the nicest people you'll ever meet in your life," he remarked. "In the courtroom, he was a completely different person. He actually, he was belligerent, he . . . I think sometimes, some of these lawyers who came into town had been involved in representing the Teamster people and Mr. Hoffa and some of the others for such a long time, that they had gone through so much with Hoffa that they had their own chip on their shoulder."

"I believe he [Schiffer] was continually trying to get a mistrial," Mansfield explained. Seigenthaler agreed. "I can only conclude that from the minute Partin walked in and took the stand they knew they had to have a mistrial." From all appearances, that was the role assigned to Schiffer—to obtain a mistrial, whatever the cost.[25]

Over the several days of Partin's testimony, Schiffer's objections had become more and more animated and angry. On February 7, he would finally boil over. Repeatedly, he stood to demand a mistrial, objecting that the testimony had nothing to do with his client (Parks). Partin's account, Schiffer stated, "is becoming so highly prejudicial as far as Mr. Parks is concerned it is becoming a real Greek tragic comedy." When Judge Wilson accommodated this complaint by explaining that certain testimony related solely to Hoffa (and not the other defendants), Haggerty objected that the remark was prejudicial to Hoffa. The court could not satisfy all of the defendants.[26]

At times, Schiffer objected so frequently that it seemed as though he, and not Silets, was questioning the witness. Facing this continual barrage of often incomprehensible objections, Judge Wilson paused the proceedings at one point to ask Schiffer to explain an objection. "My objection," Schiffer responded shrilly, "is that this is a well-coached witness and they have no right to do this and give the man the testimony." The objection—in reality more of an argument—was overruled. Schiffer then asked the court to advise the jury not to think ill of his client "because of the zeal of his counsel in trying to . . . resist the phony charges put herein by the prosecution."[27]

Finally, Schiffer's wafer-thin patience reached its limit. In a speech that would occupy almost ten pages of trial transcript, he castigated Partin, the government, and the court. "This is the drumhead court martial they wanted and they're getting it," he shouted, slapping his hand down on the table. "They're getting it to the last vestige of the meaning of a drumhead court martial and they are getting a star chamber proceeding here." Warned to stop shouting and to be seated, Schiffer instead pounded on the defense table, bellowing, "They are not going to still my tongue if I have to drop dead at this trial!" When Neal attempted to interrupt, Schiffer waved his fist at him. "I'm not finished with you, Mr. Neal," he warned. "I don't want to listen to Mr. Neal. You subvert justice here!"

"Mr. Schiffer," Judge Wilson interrupted, "let's not be so loud. The Court can hear your remarks without being so loud. Just keep your voice down."

Schiffer could not be restrained. "I asked for instructions as to what I should do to protect the constitutional rights of my client," he continued, "but every time Your Honor sort of bawls me out the jury sees that." Referring to the jury, he declared that "they cannot help but feel that Schiffer, he's an obstructionist ... and that is why Mr. Parks cannot receive a fair trial here."[28]

Judge Wilson's restraint at that point was remarkable. As Seigenthaler opined, "There are moments [reviewing the trial transcript] when you really can't understand why Frank didn't explode."[29]

Finally, frustrated with what he considered the willful obfuscation of the witness, Schiffer shrugged his shoulders and motioned toward the judge. "May your Honor respectfully allow me to withdraw from the case," he asked, "so I can put this defendant of mine under the protection of the Court and let your Honor defend him because I am being prevented from defending him, but this is why, every time I rise for an objection your Honor takes it out on me in front of this jury and I think Mr. Parks is being deprived of—"

"Mr. Schiffer," Judge Wilson interposed, "I believe the record will reflect that you have had more opportunity to speak than any counsel in this record, and the Court has just requested that you state your objection and not be making repetitious argument on the same objection."

"I must make these objections and I find that now he doesn't need a lawyer any more in this case, your Honor," Schiffer said, "because the way this case is going with this witness[,] he has been permitted time and time again to make statements which are not responsive. He defies the order of the Court. But the Court idly does nothing with this witness and this is prejudicing my man."

"Do you have anything further?" an obviously irritated Judge Wilson asked.

Mopping his brow, Schiffer shook his head and sat down. Turning to the court reporter, Wilson issued what would prove to be a significant instruction, and a key moment in the case. "Just please make a note of this in the record. We will take it up at a later time." In the transcript Wilson reviewed that evening, a series of broad pencil strokes marked this exchange with Schiffer.[30]

———

A cloud of paranoia and suspicion hung over the trial in February 1964. Hoffa supporters would seize on one moment in particular as evidence of the court's anti-Hoffa bias. Upon hearing an improper question posed by Silets, Neal stood to object; before he could open his mouth, and sensing the objection that was coming, Judge Wilson stepped in. "Sustain the objection."

Silets turned to the bench. "I didn't hear one, Your Honor."

In practice, it is not uncommon for a judge to issue an anticipatory ruling where the objection is predictable and the ruling obvious. "Well," the judge explained casually, "counsel stood up."

Adding insult to injury, Neal could not resist commenting with a sardonic smile, "It was just so obviously objectionable you don't have to mention it."

To the defense, though, it was beginning to appear as though Judge Wilson was assisting the prosecution.[31]

Similar feelings of maltreatment arose when the defense raised the volatile question of whether witnesses had been paid for their testimony. Partin had been adamant that he had never asked for, or been offered, anything in exchange for his cooperation. Although Silets battered him on the topic, Partin insisted that he had not received anything, including leniency with respect to his criminal charges, for testifying against Hoffa.

Silets was undeterred.[32] "[I]s the government paying your wife?"

"No," came the expected reply.

At that, Silets introduced a thin slip of paper dated July 3, 1963, and addressed from Sheridan to S. A. Andretta, administrative assistant to the attorney general:

> Subject: Confidential Fund Item.
> In connection with the forthcoming trials in Nashville, Tenn., it is requested that a check in the amount of $300 be drawn against the confidential fund beginning July 8th, made payable to A. Frank Grimsley, Jr., Attorney in the Criminal Division. . . . He will cash the check and give the money to a confidential source.
> It is also requested that a check be drawn each month through November, 1963, made payable to Mr. Grimsley and mailed as above.

Four checks in the amounts of $300, $300, $150, and $150 were introduced. Partin scrambled to explain that the checks were paid to his estranged wife at his request. The money represented the reimbursement of *expenses* he had incurred in meeting with investigators to prepare for the trial. He added feebly that the government still owed him $300 to $600. Had Partin contradicted his repeated assertions that he was not paid for his testimony? As a purely technical matter, he insisted, *he* had never received anything; the amounts had been paid to his wife, from whom he was separated at the time. Moreover, he maintained that the reimbursement of expenses was very different from a payment in exchange for testimony. Still, Partin appeared to be playing a slick game with semantics.

Some observers questioned the lump-sum nature of the payments. The amounts seemed a little too tidy and rounded off. Where were the detailed expense vouchers showing the specific amounts? A bitter disagreement ensued as the defendants requested vouchers detailing the itemized expenses those checks represented. "I want to find out how much was paid this fellow to get him to perjure himself," Schiffer snapped. In response, the government labeled the charges of improper payments "an unmitigated lie." Prosecutors did admit that no itemized expense vouchers could be located, an explanation that seemed shaky.[33]

———

The quarrel over whether Partin had been paid would pale in comparison to the acrimony surrounding the issue of surveillance. Discussions of the 1964 Hoffa trial eventually turn to surveillance and wiretapping. Throughout the trial, the defense periodically protested that they were being monitored. As Marvin Berke maintained years later, "My phone behaved differently for the entire two months of the trial. Everywhere we went, we were followed." Hoffa himself groused, "Our rooms were bugged, our phones were tapped, and our lawyers' rooms were broken into and their files were stolen. We finally had to hire armed guards with pistols to be able to maintain our records. It was hard to believe we weren't in Russia."[34]

The government consistently responded that neither the defendants nor their legal counsel had been placed under surveillance. "I'm sure they thought they were wiretapped," Seigenthaler said. "I'm absolutely sure they were not." As Neal explained, "There were accusations emanating from the huge number of Hoffa's lawyers that the FBI was tapping their phones, getting information, pushing it on to me—not true. Just simply not true. I never got any information, anything like that, and as far as I'm concerned—and we looked into it—as far as I'm concerned, the FBI never tapped any phones."[35]

It is important to note the difference, in legal terms, between surveillance and wiretapping. Wiretapping is the covert monitoring of telephone conversations by a third party. Surveillance, on the other hand, is the observation of an individual in public. There is no question that the government placed certain specified individuals under surveillance during the trial. As FBI special agent Jim Cole recalled, "Chuck O'Brien, he was under surveillance by our group, and then there was several others that were, and we just assigned them numbers [and agent numbers and location/restaurant numbers] so we all had a long list of numbers we were trying to remember." But they were not following the defendants, he added, and there was no wiretapping at all.

One individual under observation was Bernard Spindel, a surveillance expert who had been affiliated with Hoffa since the McClellan hearings. On February 3, the evening before Partin took the stand, FBI agents learned that Spindel had flown into Nashville and was taking a car to Chattanooga. Skeptical as to why a known wiretapper and Hoffa associate happened to be visiting the city, government agents placed him under surveillance. Cole detailed the observations: "[A] surveillance was made of him from Detroit to here and we watched him unload all his recording equipment from the trunk of his car and into the Patten Hotel, and he went around town and bought some recording tapes at the old Violet Camera shop, and we knew he was recording our radio transmissions during this thing, which was pretty heavily coded, so they wouldn't know exactly what we was doing."

For the most part, Spindel remained hidden away inside the Hotel Patten during his stay in Chattanooga. All the while, *he* was surveilling government agents while *they* were surveilling him. As Marvin Berke recalled, "The amazing part of that was that the FBI was following us, but at the same time the defense through Mr. Spindel was wiretapping the FBI, was picking up their radio signals . . . it was an unusual situation."

The FBI suspected as much. "We knew or felt that Spindel was recording our transmissions," Cole said, "because he would have had no other reason for being here." There was no question that *mutual* surveillance was occurring during the trial. "Teamsters were behind our surveillers, surveilling our surveilling," Neal said. "The FBI surveyed Spindel while Spindel tried to surveil the FBI." Press corps cameraman Cecil Pearce recalled visiting the Hoffa suite and listening to FBI agents on Spindel's equipment. "They were joking with him and one thing or another that he was listening to everything they said," he recounted, "and of course they were listening to everything he said."

"He talked to them every night at about 8 o'clock when the clean-up people in the Federal Building were cleaning the building," deputy marshal Granville Sertel recalled, "and they were all in one place eating, the FBI would check all of our telephone terminals . . . he'd just say hello, just kind of aggravating them." Sertel's son, John, laughingly remembered that Spindel "ran circles around the federal people doing wiretaps of the phones in the federal building and the hotel . . . [he] would just kind of mock them."

"It was quite a show," Neal recalled. "But that doesn't mean there's wiretapping."[36] Hoffa strongly disagreed. "You don't think we were bugged? When Bernie got to Nashville he was met by two FBI agents. They followed him all the way to our hotel in Chattanooga, picking up a further escort of FBI agents by two-way radio as they came into town until Spindel was leading a regular parade."[37] Defense lawyers repeatedly complained that the government was surveilling *them* and impacting their representation of their clients. The prosecution responded that FBI agents observed only a handful of individuals, such as Spindel and O'Brien. Moreover, no surveillance had been made of the defendants or their legal counsel. The defense was unconvinced and suspicious.

At the end of the day on February 5, in the wake of Partin's shocking appearance, Haggerty had revisited the issue. As he did each time the subject was mentioned, Neal casually responded that no surveillance of the defendants had occurred.

"Evidently Mr. Neal is either forgetful or he hasn't the authority or the knowledge as to know if the surveillance is being carried on at the present time," Haggerty countered, "because I am reasonably certain that it is."

Joining in, Berke advised the court, "It is not a comfortable feeling to have cars following you everywhere you go[,] and I'm satisfied that I have been surveilled."[38]

On February 7, while the jury was absent from the courtroom, Haggerty once again raised the issue. This time, he was prepared to submit visual evidence to support his claims: "I say to your Honor we are prepared this afternoon to offer proof of the surveillance of the government of the Defendant Hoffa and of the defendants and of the attorneys and it's a very difficult thing to prove but we have photographs taken last night and we have photographs of an FBI agent by the name of Sheets and we will present that proof this afternoon and we think it's such an important question that your Honor should take up the matter promptly at 1:30 and render a decision because that surveillance is not casual, it's active, it's organized, and it hamstrings the defendants and the defendants' counsel."

Schiffer joined in the motion, stating that whenever he picked up his telephone at the Hotel Patten he heard a suspicious "double-noise" on the line. "I cannot defend Mr. Parks and I cannot interview witnesses," he complained. "I can't invite them to the Hotel Patten where I stay, I can't go out to see anybody, to visit anyone, to present the defense, because the prosecution is surveilling me." As Neal stood to respond, Schiffer turned toward him. "Despite what Mr. Neal will say to your Honor, I say my phone is being tapped by somebody." By this point, Schiffer was getting agitated. He charged, "Every time he [Neal] makes a representation to you or to another federal judge in another court you rely upon his integrity. I say he doesn't have it. I say the whole prosecution here doesn't have it at this table and everybody assisting them up to the Attorney General."

"I would expect," Neal said calmly as Schiffer took his seat, "the Court to hold Mr. Schiffer in contempt."

"For what?" Schiffer thundered, leaping back to his feet. "For telling the truth? That is the type tactic of the government, as soon as a defendant gets up and talks about the malfunctions of justice in this court by these prosecutors they run to the Court and they say, 'Throw Schiffer in jail, hold him in contempt, but leave us alone, Judge. We are the select fellows, we are the masters in this case. The Attorney General appointed us, he hates Hoffa and we will get Schiffer, too.'" Finally, out of words to hurl at the government, Schiffer fell back into his seat. Judge Wilson quietly overruled his motions for mistrial and severance.[39]

Berke then stood for one final comment. "I have not been able to talk with Mr. Hoffa," he declared, "unless I get out in a car at night and we went out the other night and we were followed[,] and we will show we were followed and we will show definite proof we were followed and I don't think that we can have a trial here, if your Honor please, under those circumstances." Judge Wilson asked Berke to file a written motion supporting his claims, at which time he would schedule a hearing on the issue. He would not, however, delay the trial for an immediate hearing.[40]

The issue of surveillance would not go away.

———

The news that Haggerty was preparing to offer hard evidence of surveillance caused a flurry of activity at the prosecution table. The government
would need to immediately subpoena Spindel to testify about the illicit means
by which he had obtained his information. Prosecutors had to act before
the defense could put the finishing touches on its purported proof. When
Haggerty remarked of surveillance, "It's casual, it's active," therefore, attorney
Jim Durkin dashed out of the courtroom.

To the defense, this act was a clear acknowledgment of the government's
guilt. Surely Durkin had sped off to cover the prosecutors' tracks. Branstetter
asked the court for an order preventing the prosecution from discussing
the issue with FBI agent Bill Sheets, one of the central figures in the fiasco.

"That wasn't the purpose I sent that man out," Neal explained. "The purpose I sent that man out was to get a subpoena to a well-known wire tapper
. . . who came into town the other day, Bernard Spindel."

When a stupefied Silets asked how he knew of Spindel's presense if he
wasn't surveilling the defendants, Neal held up his hands. "Your Honor," he
began, "the government has never said it would not surveil well-known wire
tappers who come into town. We will say and we will rebut any offer of proof
that we have surveyed the *defendants*."

"If Mr. Neal will put his law license on the line," Schiffer threatened, "I say
he [Durkin] went out to cover his tracks." In reality, Durkin had obtained a
subpoena, which he handed to controversial marshal Elmer Disspayne with
instructions to serve the noted wiretapper in Hoffa's suite at the Hotel Patten.
Accompanied by Sheridan, Disspayne went to the hotel and, while Sheridan
waited in the lobby, took the elevator to the ninth floor.[41]

Press corps photographer Cecil Pearce was accustomed to shooting film
of the Hoffa entourage as it shuttled between the courthouse and the hotel.
Walking backwards as the silent film whirred in the camera, he would crack
jokes with Hoffa and his attorneys. "Hoffa was joking with me one time there,
telling me 'watch out, you're gonna fall and . . . crack your butt,'" Pearce recalled. "I think he used different terms, though." As Pearce shouldered his
camera to get footage during the lunch recess on February 7, a conspiratorial
William Bufalino approached him. As Pearce explained, "We were leaving the
federal building to go back to the Patten Hotel and I was shooting some film
of Bufalino and Hoffa, and Bufalino said come on up to the seventh floor [it
was in reality the ninth floor]—said there's gonna be some fireworks up there.
So I hollered at my buddy that was working with me to get my light out of
the car so we could have some light up there." The photographer proceeded
to the elevator.[42]

Unbeknownst to Disspayne, he was walking into a trap—and a major propaganda coup for the defense. As he waited in the lobby, Sheridan saw Chuckie O'Brien enter the hotel with a man carrying a camera. At that point, Sheridan said, "I knew instinctively we had walked into a trap and I walked out the other entrance and back to the Federal Building." Meanwhile, on the ninth floor an unsuspecting Disspayne ran into attorney Daniel Maher. Advising Maher that he felt uncomfortable being alone on the hall where the defense was staying, he was accompanied to a room occupied by Tommy Osborn and several secretaries. Spindel, though, was not to be found. Disspayne asked to use the telephone; when he couldn't reach the marshals' office, he walked back to the elevator and punched the button. When the elevator door slid open, the marshal looked up to find Hoffa, Bufalino, and a passel of reporters anxious for a story.

In retrospect, Durkin could not have made a worse selection for the assignment than Disspayne, whose sour relationship with Hoffa stretched back to the Test Fleet trial. Hoffa detested the man. "Get the hell out of here!" Bufalino shouted as the group poured out of the elevator. As photographers feverishly snapped pictures, Hoffa flew into a rage that was almost certainly contrived for the press. "What are you doing up here?" he demanded. "Are you spying? You have got no business up here." When Disspayne responded that he had a subpoena to serve, Hoffa threw his briefcase and overcoat to the ground and shouted. "All right, let's have it out."

"You've got no business up here," Bufalino raged. "This is International Teamsters headquarters. We keep records and photostatic copies. What have you been doing, going through our records?" The next day's newspapers would run photographs of the furious defense team, accompanied by headlines such as "Hoffa Holds Back his Special Counsel" and "Hoffa Nearly Fights Marshal."

"It was pretty heated," recounted Pearce. "At one point this Disspayne pushed his coat back, put his hand on his revolver and his holster there, like he's fixing to do a quick draw or something, and I was kinda backing up a little then." "You pulled a gun on me," Hoffa was heard to remark, although newsmen in the dim hallway never saw a weapon, and Disspayne denied the accusation. Finally, Disspayne threw his hands up and implored Hoffa to back off. With little additional fanfare, the incident dissipated, and Disspayne returned to the courthouse.[43]

When he learned of the incident, Mansfield was apoplectic. Disspayne had already proven to be a disruption for the Marshals' Service, and now he was nearly getting into fistfights—or worse—in the chief defendant's hotel

suite. Mansfield recalled, "I heard about it from the news media, and imme-
diately—it shook me up, frankly—so I immediately went in and told Judge
Wilson that something had happened over there." The judge responded that
Disspayne should no longer have anything to do with the trial.[44]

———

The unfortunate Disspayne incident placed the prosecution in a difficult position, and the defense was quick to take advantage. As the parties returned to
the courtroom, a riled-up Schiffer, straining like a dog on a chain, claimed
that when he had returned to his hotel room during the break, "all of my
original documents, and the entire file which I have spent preparing for these
many months for this trial on behalf of the Defendant Parks[,] was missing."
What was more, both Sheridan and Disspayne had been seen lurking around
the ninth floor of the hotel during the lunch recess. "I don't know what to
do about the situation, your Honor," Schiffer muttered, "but I will say this,
it deprives Mr. Parks now of his whole defense in this case."

Judge Wilson instructed the prosecution to prepare a written response.
In that report, which would be filed the following Monday, government attorneys would "categorically and unequivocally" deny "that any agent of the
government . . . had anything to do with the alleged loss of papers which
allegedly were in the custody of Jacques Schiffer . . . [and did] not concede
that any such papers referred to by attorney Schiffer ever existed."[45]

Piling on, Silets informed the court that when Dorfman was seeking legal
counsel, Osborn had met with Hooker to discuss the case; confidential information about the defense had been disclosed during the meeting. Therefore,
Silets asked that the indictment against Dorfman be dismissed. "Of course,"
Hooker responded indignantly, "that is not true, if Your Honor please." Nevertheless, the court was once again forced to call for written motions on the
issue. The defense had forged a hint of hope to counter the desperate pes-
simism Partin had created.[46]

Finally, after hours of argument outside the presence of the jury, Partin
returned to the stand. Questioning the astonishing coincidence that the witness had obtained evidence of jury tampering from a complete stranger on
his first evening in Nashville, Silets brimmed over with disdain: "Wasn't it
a fact that you wanted to show the government your good faith in your assignment that you made up this story about Anthony Quinn [the alleged
nom de guerre of Nicholas Tweel] to give to Mr. Sheridan?"

"No, sir," Partin softly replied. There would be no sudden change of course or embarrassed admissions by the witness. In the end, Silets's questioning was intended more to plant questions in jurors' minds than to secure a confession from Partin.[47]

After a couple more hours of inconsequential interrogation, Judge Wilson signaled for a recess. The third week of the trial had ended. Both parties had crossed a sort of Rubicon. As Sheridan wrote, "A grimness and hatefulness had settled in and it would remain that way for the rest of the trial." Neal agreed. "From that point on," he said, "it was all-out, unmitigated warfare."[48]

"We will always be for Jo & Jimmy Hoffa." Waving signs and placards, a crowd of local Teamsters and well-wishers awaits Jimmy Hoffa's arrival at the Chattanooga airport in January 1964. Chattanooga Public Library and University of Tennessee at Chattanooga Special Collections.

Beginning in August 1957, Hoffa appeared before the McClellan Committee on four separate occasions, sparring with his chief antagonist, Robert F. Kennedy, before a live television audience on a variety of allegations of wrongdoing, including Hoffa's relationship to the Test Fleet corporation. The Test Fleet allegations would lead to Hoffa's 1962 trial in Nashville on misdemeanor criminal charges. Library of Congress.

Labeled by Hoffa as "one of the most vicious prosecutors who ever handled a criminal case for the Justice Department," Jim Neal prosecuted Hoffa in the Nashville and Chattanooga trials, during which time he was the target of one of the Teamster boss's most colorful stratagems—each and every day, when he looked in the direction of the defense, Neal would observe Hoffa giving him the finger under the table. Chattanooga Public Library and University of Tennessee at Chattanooga Special Collections.

Edward Grady Partin (right), the president of Teamsters Local 5 in Baton Rouge and the key government witness in the jury tampering case, talks with Baton Rouge district attorney Sargent Pitcher (left) and his administrative assistant, Billy Daniels, a few days after the verdict in the Chattanooga trial. Cross-examined for six days, the turncoat Teamster endured brutal questioning by the defense, which had been shocked and infuriated by his surprise appearance in Chattanooga on February 4. Library of Congress.

Confirmed as U.S. District Judge for the Eastern District of Tennessee in 1961, Frank W. Wilson was relatively new in his role when he presided over the 1964 jury tampering trial. One of the first significant rulings issued by Judge Wilson was the relocation of the trial from Nashville to Chattanooga. Throughout the trial, he would be subjected to a relentless torrent of abuse intended to provoke him into committing an emotional misstep requiring the granting of a mistrial in the case. Archives, U.S. District Court, Eastern District of Tennessee (Chattanooga).

The six-week jury tampering trial took place in the art deco Joel W. Solomon Federal Building (1933) in Chattanooga. The reflecting pool and fountain in this image were installed a decade after the trial; in 1964, a series of brick business buildings lined the street across from the courthouse. Library of Congress.

The ninth floor of the Hotel Patten (1908), situated two blocks from the federal courthouse, served as the command center for the defense team (and the de facto offices of the Teamsters president) throughout the jury tampering trial. Chattanooga Public Library.

Exiting the federal courthouse on January 9, Hoffa's lawyers make final preparations for trial. Accompanying lead counsel James Haggerty (left) is local
Chattanooga lawyer Harry Berke (center) and his son, Marvin (right), who
as a young lawyer assisted with the defense of the case. Chattanooga Public
Library and University of Tennessee at Chattanooga Special Collections.

Nashville sandwich shop owner
Lawrence "Red" Medlin was accused
of having offered $10,000 to pro-
spective juror James Tippens to vote
for acquittal in the Test Fleet case.
The allegations against Medlin would
be severed from the remainder of
the case, and he would be placed
on trial in Nashville in March 1964.
Chattanooga Public Library and
University of Tennessee at Chattanooga Special Collections.

"Miss Nellie" Kenyon, the indefatigable federal beat reporter for the *Nashville Tennessean* who covered each of the trials of Jimmy Hoffa in the early 1960s (Nashville, Chattanooga, Chicago). It is said that Hoffa referred to the ever-present Kenyon at times as "Nellie, dear," although she reportedly did not return the flattery. University of Tennessee Libraries, Special Collections.

Chattanoogans were inexhaustibly interested in the Hoffa trial. Each and every day throughout the trial, a line of hopeful onlookers waited in the courthouse hallways, eager at the prospect of securing a seat in the courtroom. Those lucky enough to make in into the courtroom were reluctant to step outside, even during breaks, for fear of losing their seats to other waiting bystanders. Chattanooga Public Library.

The six-week trial took place in the third-floor "ceremonial courtroom" of the federal courthouse in Chattanooga. Library of Congress.

Situated two blocks from the federal courthouse, the historic Read House hotel (1926) housed the sequestered jury throughout the six-week trial. Allegations of misconduct by jurors and US marshals at the hotel would become a source of controversy in the months following the conclusion of the trial. Chattanooga Public Library.

QUESTIONNAIRE AS TO QUALIFICATION FOR JURY SERVICE

1. Name (Please print) _PATRICK J. HAVERTY_

2. Home address _153 Bluff View, Chattanooga 3, Tenn._
   (Street)   (City)   (Zone)   (State)

3. Telephone: Business _266-2525_ Residence _267-4846_

4. How long have you resided there? _22_ Yrs. In this State? _32_ Yrs.

5. Married or single? _Single_ Age _32_ Sex _Male_

6. Place of birth _Chattanooga, Tenn._

7. Are you a citizen of the United States _Yes_

8. Can you read, write, speak, and understand the English language? _Yes_

9. If naturalized, state when _____ (Where) _____

10. What education have you had? _College Grad_

11. Are you employed at present? _Yes_ (Occupation) _Clerk_

12. Nature of business? _Life Insurance_

13. Employer's name _Provident Life and Accident Ins. Co._

14. Business address _Fountain Sq. Chattanooga, Tenn._

15. a. If you are married, give occupation of wife or

    husband _____

    b. If you are a married woman, give occupation before

    marriage _____

    c. If you are retired, or not working, give last occupation _____

16. Have you ever been convicted of a crime? _No_

    If so, state date, court and crime _____

17. Have you ever served as a juror? _Yes_ If so, in what Court? _Hamilton County_
    Circuit and when? _Fall 1962_

18. Have you any disability impairing your capacity to serve as a juror, including impaired eyesight
    or hearing? _No_ If so, state its nature and extent.
    (Yes or No)

    _____

19. Do you know any reason why you cannot serve as a juror? _No_
    If so state reason fully under remarks.
    Remarks: _____

    _____

    I certify that the foregoing statements are true
    to the best of my knowledge and belief.

Date: _13 Jan 1964_   xx _Patrick Haverty_
                                        Signature

No. 1 - Regular Panel

The jury questionnaire completed by Pat Haverty, juror number 193, who in later years would remain as the last-surviving member of the jury. National Archives.

At the Read House, jurors enjoyed spartan accommodations designed to shield them from news coverage of the trial. Telephones and television sets were removed from jurors' rooms, and reading materials were censored so that all references to the trial, Hoffa, or the Teamsters union were clipped out. Getty Images.

"Gymmy Hoffa" lifts weights at the local YMCA during the down time between court sessions. *Chattanooga Times.*

Eager for favorable publicity, Hoffa and Bufalino pose for a newspaper photograph with eleven-year-old newsboy Joe Kirk Davis after the close of proceedings on January 22. Smiling, Hoffa would tell reporters that "pictures made in the morning were free, [but] those made of him in the afternoon costs a penny apiece!" Chattanooga Public Library and University of Tennessee at Chattanooga Special Collections.

At the end of the day on January 22, Hoffa returns to the Hotel Patten along with his son, James P. Hoffa, co-defendant Allen Dorfman, and mob lawyer Frank Ragano, whose attempt to eavesdrop upon the jury during the latter part of the trial would earn him a stern reprimand from Judge Wilson. Chattanooga Public Library and University of Tennessee at Chattanooga Special Collections.

"The Marines are here!" Passing along the sidewalk in front of the federal courthouse on January 23, Hoffa calls out to prosecutor Jim Neal, a captain in the Marine Corps Reserve, while Neal attempts to give a television interview. Chattanooga Public Library and University of Tennessee at Chattanooga Special Collections.

Flanked by US marshals, jurors cross the street toward the Read House hotel in a ritual that would be repeated multiple times each day. To ensure that the members of the jury were not exposed to prejudicial headlines about the trial, one marshal ran ahead, turning magazine racks and newspaper boxes around as the jury passed by. Chattanooga Public Library and University of Tennessee at Chattanooga Special Collections.

The subject of an alleged effort to tamper with the Test Fleet jury, James Tippens arrives at the federal courthouse with his secretary, Josephine Carlton, on January 27. Chattanooga Public Library and University of Tennessee at Chattanooga Special Collections.

New York attorney Jacques Schiffer represented Hoffa co-defendant Thomas Ewing Parks in the 1964 trial. His provocative outbursts and diatribes accusing the court of a "drum head court martial," "star chamber proceedings," and "Stalinism, Hitlerism, Mussolinism and all kinds of isms"—which were probably purposefully intended to force a mistrial in the case—served as a daily challenge to Judge Frank Wilson. Library of Congress.

Carol Pettijohn, a piano player from Maitland, Florida, was performing at the Surf Rider Lounge in the Andrew Jackson Hotel during the Test Fleet trial in 1962. She accompanied Nicholas Tweel and two other men out on the town one night during the trial, during which time Tweel talked with bartender Dallas Hall. *Associated Press.*

Nashville nightclub owner Dallas Hall appeared at the Chattanooga trial on January 31 to testify that he had been asked by defendant Nicholas Tweel "to look around" and see what he could find out about the members of the Test Fleet jury. Chattanooga Public Library and University of Tennessee at Chattanooga Special Collections.

[*Facing top*] Accompanied by Jacques Schiffer, defense attorney Cecil Branstetter (left) walks along the sidewalk in front of the Hotel Patten. Well-known as a champion of the working class, Branstetter served as the lawyer for Local 299 business agent Larry Campbell throughout the jury-tampering case. Chattanooga Public Library and University of Tennessee at Chattanooga Special Collections.

[*Facing bottom*] Chattanooga attorney Harold E. Brown (right) stepped in as a last-minute replacement to represent Nashville Teamster Ewing King during the jury tampering case. In subsequent years, Brown's ties to organized labor—and Jimmy Hoffa—would obstruct his own political ambitions. Chattanooga Public Library.

Reporters wait on the sidewalk for the trial participants, particularly Hoffa, to emerge from the courthouse. A cluster of reporters hung around the courthouse throughout the trial, hoping to obtain footage of the notorious Teamster leader—and hopefully an inflammatory comment about his persecution at the hands of Bobby Kennedy and the Get Hoffa Squad. Chattanooga Public Library.

"Do I have the privilege not to testify?" Accompanied by her minister, Norma Jean Partin, the estranged wife of Ed Partin, arrives at the federal courthouse on January 31. Hoping for testimony as to dope addiction and extra-marital affairs on the part of the government's key witness, the defense was disappointed when Norma Jean Partin refused to testify, on the basis of spousal privilege. Chattanooga Public Library and University of Tennessee at Chattanooga Special Collections.

Nashville Teamster Oscar "Mutt" Pitts (left) and his wife depart the federal court-house on February 3. Labeled a "reluctant witness," Pitts was called by the prosecution to testify as to his role in arranging a meeting between defendant Ewing King (right) and Nashville patrolman James Paschal, the husband of a Test Fleet juror, during the Nashville trial. Chattanooga Public Library and University of Tennessee at Chattanooga Special Collections.

As he exits the federal courthouse, Hoffa is swarmed by reporters
seeking comment on the day's events. Chattanooga Public Library.

The interior of the third-floor courtroom as it looked during the 1964 trial. Above the judge's bench is the New Deal-era mural *Allegory of Chattanooga,* and behind the judge hangs a double-edged broadsword, one blade representing truth, the other reason. Library of Congress.

"Are you spying? You have no business up here." In one of the most confrontational episodes of the trial—and one almost certainly concocted for media coverage—US marshal Elmer Disspayne is confronted by Hoffa and Bufalino on February 7 while attempting to serve a subpoena in Hoffa's suite at the Hotel Patten. National Archives.

Two beneficiaries of the lengthy trial, court reporters Richard Smith and John E. Hamlin, pose with a stack of transcripts from the trial—nearly 4,000 pages in all. It was jokingly remarked that Smith purchased a new home in a trendy golf subdivision with his earnings from the Hoffa trial. Chattanooga Public Library and University of Tennessee at Chattanooga Special Collections.

On Sunday, February 9, Hoffa gave a rousing speech at the Tivoli Theater in Chattanooga. Despite the chance to hear Hoffa's customary harangue against Bobby Kennedy and the federal government, as well as the promise of meeting the IBT president in the flesh, the turnout for the speech was a disappointment, with empty seats throughout the theater. Chattanooga Public Library and University of Tennessee at Chattanooga Special Collections.

The West Side Urban Renewal District, a 403-acre "entirely desolate area" in the process of redevelopment as a new "Golden Gateway" into downtown Chattanooga in 1964. Defense attorneys would protest that on February 6, anxious to evade government surveillance of Hoffa and his attorneys, they piled into Marvin Berke's car and drove into this abandoned moonscape for a quiet, confidential discussion, only to be tailed by FBI agents. Chattanooga Public Library.

A "relaxed and cheerful" Hoffa holds his granddaughter as she dips her fingers into the icing on his birthday cake on February 14. Members of the defense team took a brief respite from the rigors of the trial to celebrate Hoffa's fiftieth birthday at the Pan-O-Ram Club on nearby Lookout Mountain. Chattanooga Public Library and University of Tennessee at Chattanooga Special Collections.

Hoffa and his legal team walk back to the Hotel Patten after another day of testimony in the lengthy trial. From left: William Bufalino; Hoffa; James Haggerty; and Harry Berke. *The Tennessean.*

Huntington, West Virginia, businessman Nicholas Tweel stood accused, along with Allen Dorfman, of attempting to persuade a Nashville bartender (Dallas Hall) to approach jurors in the Test Fleet case on behalf of Hoffa. *The* (Huntington, W.Va.) *Herald-Dispatch.*

A cold drizzle and a handful of reporters accompany Hoffa (left), son-in-law Robert Crancer (center), and Allen Dorfman as they leave the federal courthouse. Chattanooga Public Library and University of Tennessee at Chattanooga Special Collections.

Larry Campbell, the first black business agent for Teamsters Local 299 in Detroit. Count three of the jury tampering indictment accused Campbell and his uncle (Thomas Ewing Parks) of attempting to bribe juror Gratin Fields to vote in favor of acquittal in the Test Fleet case. Chattanooga Public Library and University of Tennessee at Chattanooga Special Collections.

Accompanied by an unidentified associate, Fred Shobe (right) walks to the federal courthouse to give his testimony on February 19. Shobe, who claimed to have been an "agent provocateur" hired by the federal government to help to "get Hoffa," told a fantastic tale of voodoo ceremonies and kidnapping plots that proved so incredible that Judge Wilson would not allow the majority of his testimony to be heard by the jury. *The Baltimore Sun.*

Members of the jury are escorted down the street between the courthouse and the Read House hotel. As the end of the trial neared, concerns over the safety of the jurors increased, and US marshals were under pressure to prevent any incident that might cause a mistrial in the case. Chattanooga Public Library and University of Tennessee at Chattanooga Special Collections.

With the anticipation that the case would be placed into the hands of the jury that day, a hopeful but tense Hoffa enters the federal courthouse on March 3. *The Baltimore Sun.*

IN THE UNITED STATES DISTRICT COURT FOR THE
EASTERN DISTRICT OF TENNESSEE,
SOUTHERN DIVISION

UNITED STATES OF AMERICA   +
                             +
              - vs. -   +   Criminal No. 11,989
                             +
                             +
JAMES R. HOFFA; THOMAS EWING +
PARKS; LARRY CAMPBELL; ALLEN +
DORFMAN; NICHOLAS J. TWEEL; +
and EWING KING   +

FILED
MAR 4 1964

VERDICT FORM

I - Third Count

(1) Thomas Ewing Parks: _Guilty_
                              (Guilty) or (Not Guilty)

(2) James R. Hoffa: _Guilty_
                              (Guilty) or (Not Guilty)

(3) Larry Campbell: _Guilty_
                              (Guilty) or (Not Guilty)

II - Fourth Count

(1) Nicholas J. Tweel: _Not Guilty_
                              (Guilty) or (Not Guilty)

(2) James R. Hoffa: _Not Guilty_
                              (Guilty) or (Not Guilty)

(3) Allen Dorfman: _Not Guilty_
                              (Guilty) or (Not Guilty)

III - Fifth Count

(1) Ewing King: _Guilty_
                              (Guilty) or (Not Guilty)

(2) James R. Hoffa: _Guilty_
                              (Guilty) or (Not Guilty)

Hal H. Bullen
Foreman

The verdict form in the jury tampering case, signed by
jury foreman Hal Bullen on March 4. National Archives.

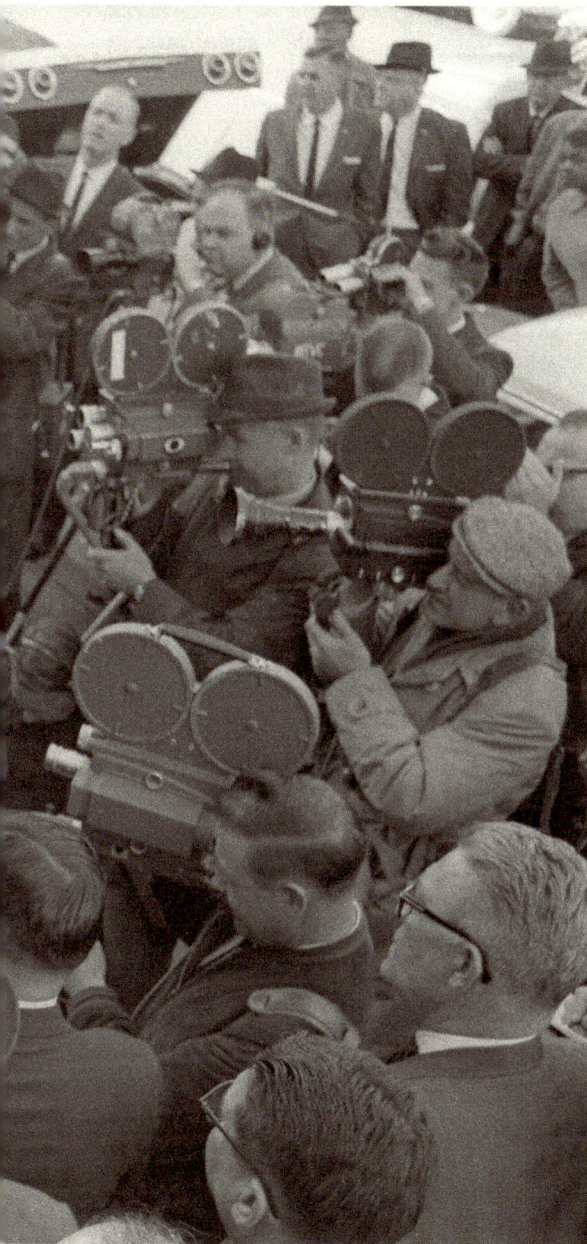

Hoffa is surrounded by a throng of reporters and curious onlookers as he leaves the federal court-house in Chattanooga. Library of Congress.

In this March 4 image, "Happy Prosecutors" (from left) Jim Neal, Jack Reddy, and Mr. and Mrs. John J. Hooker, Sr. depart the federal courthouse in Chattanooga after the announcement of the jury verdict in the jury tampering trial. Getty Images.

Holding the hands of his two small children, Ewing King makes the long, sad walk back to the Hotel Patten following his guilty verdict in the jury tampering case. Getty Images.

Members of the jury depart the federal courthouse on March 4, exuberant that their long period of isolation is over. To the right (front) is Callie Key, the sole black member of the jury, who would in subsequent days rebuff a $25,000 offer to sign a false affidavit alleging juror and government misconduct during the trial. Exiting the courthouse with his hand raised is juror Pat Haverty. Chattanooga Public Library and University of Tennessee at Chattanooga Special Collections.

Hoffa confers with notorious wiretapper Bernard Spindel in 1957. Spindel, a long-time Hoffa associate who had been summoned to Chattanooga by the defense to determine whether Hoffa and his attorneys had been placed under government surveillance during the jury tampering trial, would prove to be a key witness in a hearing held in the wake of the verdict to examine defense claims of wiretapping and surveillance by federal agents. Library of Congress.

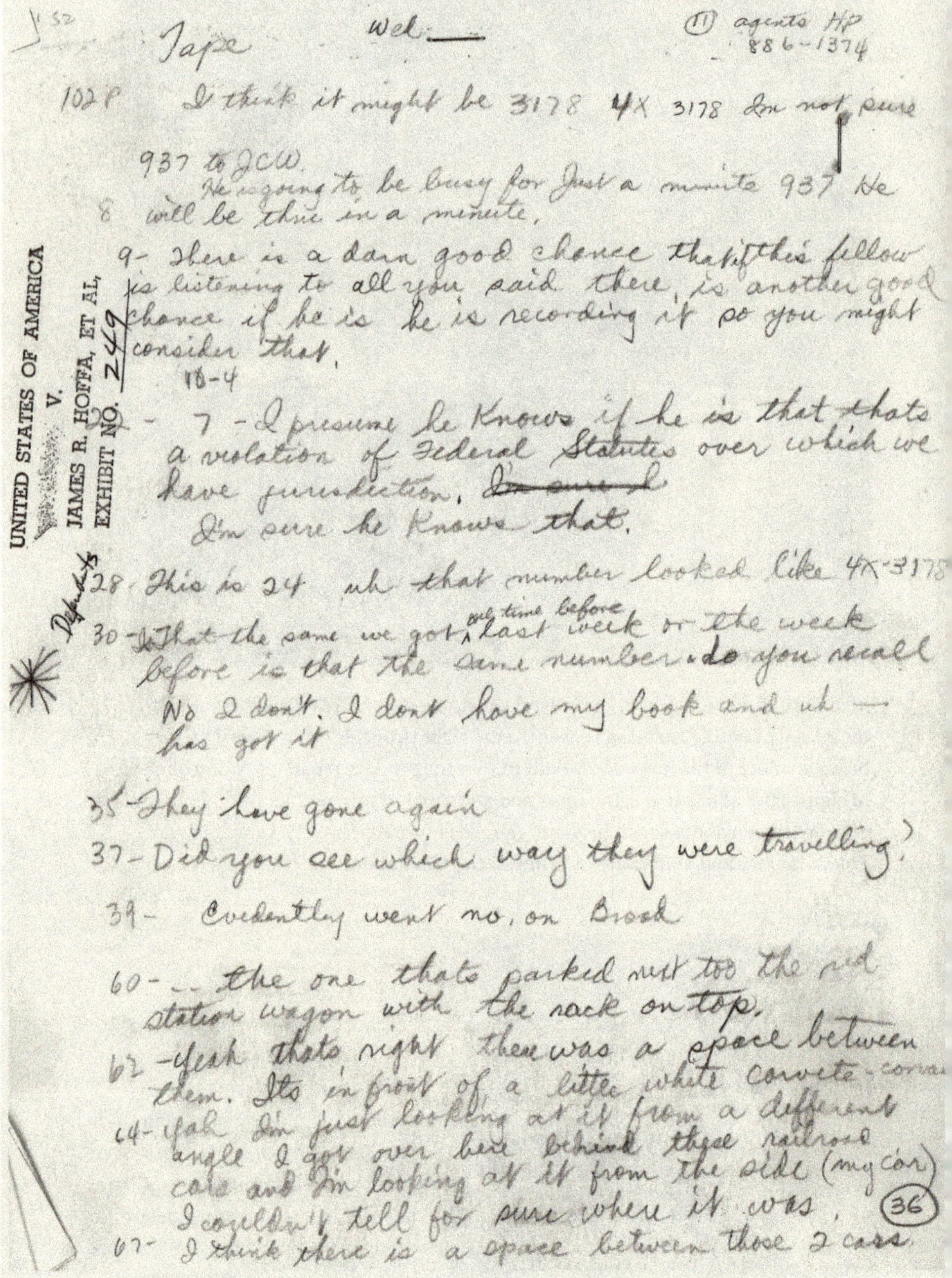

1:52

Tape Wel ___ (11) agents HP 886-1374

1028 I think it might be 3178 4X 3178 I'm not sure

937 to JCW.
He is going to be busy for just a minute 937 He
8 will be there in a minute.

9- There is a darn good chance that if this fellow is listening to all you said there, is another good chance if he is he is recording it so you might consider that.

10-4

2 - 7 - I presume he Knows if he is that thats a violation of Federal Statutes over which we have jurisdiction. ~~[illegible]~~
I'm sure he Knows that.

28 This is 24 uh that number looked like 4X 3178

30 - Is that the same we got one time before last week or the week before is that the same number. do you recall

No I don't. I dont have my book and uh — has got it

35 - They have gone again

37 - Did you see which way they were travelling?

39 - Evidently went no. on Brook

60 - .. the one thats parked next too the red station wagon with the rack on top.

62 - Yeah thats right there was a space between them. Its in front of a little white corvette - corvair

64 - Yeah I'm just looking at it from a different angle I got over here behind these railroad cars and I'm looking at it from the side (my car) I couldn't tell for sure where it was.

36

67 - I think there is a space between those 2 cars.

UNITED STATES OF AMERICA
V.
JAMES R. HOFFA, ET AL,
EXHIBIT NO. 249

Defendant's

"Hi ya Boin. Doing fine. Making lots of money working for 'Mr. H.' He is a good boy. Go home Bernard." Handwritten notes of comments made over two-way radios by FBI agents, apparently aware that their communications were being monitored by Bernard Spindel. National Archives.

New York Daily News truck drivers read headlines announcing the verdict in the jury tampering trial. Getty Images.

Cr. Form No. 25

United States District Court
FOR THE
EASTERN DISTRICT OF TENNESSEE, SOUTHERN DIVISION

United States of America

v.

JAMES R. HOFFA

No. 11,989

Judgment and commitment — March 12, 1964

On this 12th day of March , 1964 came the attorney for the government and the defendant appeared in person and¹ by counsel.

IT IS ADJUDGED that the defendant has been convicted upon his plea of² not guilty, and a jury verdict of guilty of the offenses of having aided and abetted in endeavoring to impede petit jurors in the discharge of their duties as such jurors, in violation of Title 18, United States Code, Sections 2 and 1503, as charged in Counts Three and Five of the indictment

=as charged=

and the court having asked the defendant whether he has anything to say why judgment should not be pronounced, and no sufficient cause to the contrary being shown or appearing to the Court,

IT IS ADJUDGED that the defendant is guilty as charged and convicted.

IT IS ADJUDGED that the defendant is hereby committed to the custody of the Attorney General or his authorized representative for imprisonment for a period of⁴ FOUR (4) YEARS and a fine of FIVE THOUSAND ($5,000.00) DOLLARS, in Count Three of the indictment; FOUR (4) YEARS and a fine of FIVE THOUSAND ($5,000.00) DOLLARS, in Count Five of the indictment; sentence imposed in Count Five to run consecutive to the sentence imposed in Count Three of the indictment.

IT IS ADJUDGED that⁵ defendant is to stand committed until payment of the fine imposed in both counts.

Filed 12 day of May 19 64
Ent'd Min Bk 22 P 223
KARL D. SAULPAW, JR., CLERK
By _____ Dep. Clerk

(CEILING IMPRESSIONE ONLY)

IT IS ORDERED that the Clerk deliver a certified copy of this judgment and commitment to the United States Marshal or other qualified officer and that the copy serve as the commitment of the defendant.

Frank W. Wilson
United States District Judge.

The Court recommends commitment to:⁶

KARL D. SAULPAW, JR.
Clerk.

¹Insert "by counsel" or "without counsel; the court advised the defendant of his right to counsel and asked him whether he desired to have counsel appointed by the court, and the defendant thereupon stated that he waived the right to the assistance of counsel." ²Insert (1) "guilty," (2) "not guilty, and a verdict of guilty," (3) "not guilty, and a finding of guilty," or (4) "nolo contendere," as the case may be. ³Insert "in count(s) number _____" if required. ⁴Enter (1) sentence or sentences, specifying counts if any; (2) whether sentences are to run concurrently or consecutively and, if consecutively, when each term is to begin with reference to termination of preceding term or to any other outstanding unserved sentence; (3) whether defendant is to be further imprisoned until payment of the fine or fine and costs, or until he is otherwise discharged as provided by law. ⁵Enter any order with respect to suspension and probation. ⁶For use of Court wishing to recommend a particular institution.

140

Signed by Judge Frank Wilson on March 12, this sentencing document details the punishment to be handed out to Hoffa following his guilty verdict. National Archives.

END OF THE TRAIL

"End of the Trail." This cartoon by Gib Crockett appeared in *The Washington Star* in conjunction with Hoffa's surrender to federal authorities and the beginning of his prison term in Lewisburg, Pennsylvania. Library of Congress.

A handcuffed Jimmy Hoffa leaves the federal courthouse in Chattanooga on August 25, 1969, after a five-day hearing in his continuing attempts to overturn his 1964 jury tampering conviction. *United Press International (UPI).*

Following the demolition of the old Hamilton County jail, this iron cell was salvaged and purchased by Chattanoogan John Holt. Identified as the cell which held Hoffa during his post-trial appearances in Chattanooga to protest his guilty verdict, the small chamber was exhibited at the 1976 Jaycees' Tri-State Fair along with a teapot and tea bags reputed to have been used by Hoffa during his post-verdict visits to the city. Chattanooga Public Library and University of Tennessee at Chattanooga Special Collections.

Josephine "Jo" Hoffa embraces her husband following his release from prison on December 23, 1971. "I can't believe it," she cried, "I just can't believe it." Standing in the background is an exuberant Barbara Crancer, Hoffa's daughter. *The Baltimore Sun.*

TWELVE

"It is Russia under Stalin in its darkest day
and that is what we are being subject to."

—James Haggerty

THE BIZARRE, hostile events of February 7 ratcheted up the vigilance of the Marshals Service. To observers, the defense appeared to be looking for a way to get a mistrial, and the FBI and the Marshals Service were clearly in the crosshairs. That evening, two jurors were scheduled to visit barber Bill Knowles's shop for a haircut. Knowles had visited the trial on one occasion; when a juror commented that he had not noticed him in the courtroom, Knowles confessed, "I was afraid to smile at him, as the 'secret eye' might swoop down on me."

At five o'clock, a marshal appeared at the barbershop, informing Knowles that the appointments had been canceled, as "something was up." Though Knowles would never be informed of the reason for the change, a juror later told him it had been a "cloak and dagger night." There is no doubt that the government was on high alert.[1]

The third week left everyone exhausted. While the defendants and their counsel retreated to their hotel suites to rest and prepare for the next week, jurors retired to their spartan accommodations at the Read House, where they would battle a now-familiar boredom. Marshals tried to keep the jury occupied, and a scenic bus tour of the Tennessee Valley was planned for the weekend. Nevertheless, jurors quipped sardonically that, with the trial dragging on so long, the out-of-town defense attorneys would soon be buying permanent homes in Chattanooga.

Indeed, the proceedings were so prolonged that court reporters Richard Smith and John E. Hamlin created nearly four thousand pages of transcripts. William Brown, the son of defense attorney Harold Brown, laughingly said, "Dick Smith built a house out at Valleybrook, which was kind of a fairly new subdivision at that time at the [Valleybrook] golf course, and they said that Dick Smith literally paid for his house out of the Hoffa trial transcripts."[2]

——————

The recuperative weekend of February 8–9 was not without incident. Newspapers announced that three Huntington, West Virginia, men—Herman Frazier, Alfred Paden, and Albert Cole—had been summoned to Nashville to answer charges that they had assisted with jury tampering efforts by making the "Allen from the *Banner*" calls during the Test Fleet trial. Also, Henry F. Bell, vice president of the International Longshoremen's Union, had been ordered to stand trial for "conspiring to offer one prospective juror $25,000 to vote to acquit Hoffa, and with offering $30,000 to a Nashville man to persuade two actual jurors to vote for acquittal" in the case.[3]

At 4:00 p.m. on Sunday, February 9, the Teamsters held a rally at the Tivoli Theater in downtown Chattanooga. Although there was no admission charge, and despite the promise of seeing Hoffa in the flesh, the event was a flop. Throughout the theater, seats were empty. Local newspapers reported that 400 supporters attended the rally, but Hoffa's own hometown newspaper, the *Detroit News*, set the figure more conservatively at 200, noting, "A fire department official, in a charitable mood, set the figure closer to 300, including a few babies in their mothers' arms. And a couple of Boy Scouts invited by their fathers."[4]

Despite the lackluster turnout, Hoffa did not disappoint. "Hundreds of federal agents are in Chattanooga," Hoffa told the crowd, "spying on our attorneys and stealing our records." He acknowledged his previous legal troubles yet declared, "Never have I faced what I have in Nashville and Chattanooga." Lingering surveillance suspicions plaguing him, Hoffa spent much of his thirty-minute speech attacking US marshals and FBI agents. "You of this All-America City now have a coverage of marshals and FBI agents that ranks second to none except the trial at Nuerenberg," he fumed, adding, "They are using paid stool pigeons as they did in the Russian Communist movement." The government, Hoffa declared, "is out to get a conviction by hook or crook."

In stark contrast to the enthusiastic crowd that had met Hoffa at the Chattanooga airport weeks earlier, the Tivoli crowd was listless and apathetic. As newspapers reported, there was "not a single burst of applause." Obviously displeased, Hoffa chided absent union members for their apathy. "I wonder if they realize these very vacant seats here today are what is wrong with labor," he complained. Because of the security and peace of mind the union provided, he said, "we have other things to do on a Sunday afternoon than to come to a meeting to find out what the threats to the labor movement are." As he concluded his remarks, Hoffa felt dejected and annoyed. He received no standing ovation, and attendees did not flock to the front of the theater for a handshake or autograph. "The audience just seemed to drift away," one reporter noted. In the end, the reception at the Tivoli was a far cry from the atmosphere only a couple of weeks earlier.[5]

That evening, shotgun blasts rang out at the Baton Rouge home of Teamster official (and Partin affiliate) Donice Bennett. As the perpetrators sped away from the shot-up house, it was evident, if unsurprising, that retribution was already being meted out for Partin's testimony.[6]

———

After an eventful weekend, the defendants, attorneys, courtroom officials, marshals, jurors, and interested observers filed back into the courtroom for the fourth week of the trial. The first matter to be taken up was the filing of the promised defense motion alleging government surveillance. It was accompanied by the affidavit of Harry Berke, who averred, "During this trial, I have been under surveillance by agents of the Federal Bureau of Investigation." This, he continued, "has impeded me in my representation of the accused, the consultations with other counselors, witnesses, and the defendant." As a result, he reported, meetings "have to be conducted in an atmosphere of apprehension and fear that our meetings were being watched and that our acts were under scrutiny."[7]

In his affidavit, Berke depicted a suspicious series of events occurring on February 6: "We had been trying to get a conference with Mr. Hoffa, but we were afraid to discuss the matter of defense and the evidence and so forth in either Mr. Haggerty's room or Mr. Hoffa's room or in fact any other rooms that are rented up there at the hotel. So I suggested that we go, that we just go out maybe and get a drink, a Coca-Cola, somewheres, and sit down and discuss the next day's proceedings." Hoffa, Berke, and Morris Shenker had piled into a two-tone Pontiac driven by Berke's son, Marvin. Convinced that they were being tailed, the group diverted their route and drove into the West Side Urban Renewal District, an "entirely desolate area" being redeveloped to create a new "Golden Gateway" into downtown Chattanooga. Within the 403-acre area, 1,158 structures had been removed, and 1,436 residents had been relocated. In the late winter of 1964, this bleak, muddied moonscape was the perfect place to have a private conversation.

Even so, a car had followed the men. When their car accelerated, so did the other vehicle; when they slowed to a snail's pace, it did as well. "We stopped when we got to the end of East Ninth Street before making the turn and this car stopped," Berke noted. When they turned back toward town, he said, "this car followed." Finally, as they reentered the downtown area, the mystery vehicle suddenly flew past them at a high speed. Without a doubt, Berke asserted, federal agents were stalking the chief defendant and his attorneys. The monitoring made it impossible for the defense to prepare or even discuss the case. "Where is [Hoffa] to consult with his lawyer," one cynical commentator asked, "in a soundproof vault?"[8]

According to Marvin Berke, this was not the only occasion when federal agents trailed the defense. One evening during the trial, a friend from law school asked him to grab a quick sandwich. Berke was working late on some legal research, and it was almost midnight when the two men met at Edmund's Restaurant, less than a block from the federal courthouse. While they were eating, Berke informed his friend, "Now, you're going to be followed when you leave me." Laughter met this warning. After dinner, the other man, relatively new to Chattanooga, turned the wrong way down a one-way street. A car followed him down the street "and . . . all the way [home]." An hour after Berke's friend arrived home, he looked out the window to see the same car sitting in the street.

To Berke, such abuse deeply damaged defense attorneys' ability to confidently plan for and litigate the case. "Attorneys cannot prepare the case properly, cannot talk to each other over the telephone, can't do many of the things that they want to do—can't go out and question witnesses," he explained. "If whoever they talk to is immediately singled out, it destroys the defendant's right to an attorney."[9]

In light of these challenges, Haggerty reiterated his request for an *immediate* hearing to investigate the alleged surveillance. While Judge Wilson granted the request, the defense was shocked and disappointed to find that "a hearing [would be] granted upon the motion *after submission of the case to the jury.*" In the eyes of the defense, the government would be allowed to continue to prejudice the case with impunity. Haggerty vigorously protested the decision. "Last evening," he explained, "a young man associated in my office here for no other purpose than research work, to give you an example, was followed by a car from the law library. The car pulled ahead of him. Then waited to get a good view of him. Then it followed him and someone else picked him up at the hotel and there were two men on surveillance out front of the Patten Hotel. This is 10:20 on a Sunday night." "Now, can we try a case under these Gestapo tactics?" Haggerty asked. "It is Russia under Stalin in its darkest day and that is what we are being subject to." Leaning hard upon the podium, Haggerty implored the court to hold an *immediate* hearing: "We need help and we need it now[,] not when the case is over, not when this surveillance continues to hamper us."

Absent court intervention, Harry Berke interposed, "we will just have to put the defendant on and ask him the questions cold because we haven't had a time to have a conference and we think that that certainly is a violation of due process of law." He continued, "Your Honor surely have [sic] enough evidence before your Honor now to know that this certainly must be going on in spite of Mr. Neal's protestations that it is not going on." Yet Judge Wilson was unmoved. The case had been plodding along slowly enough, with a sequestered jury removed from the courtroom for hours on end while lawyers debated and rehashed ancillary matters. Wilson would not create further delays. The issue of surveillance would have to wait until the end of the proof.[10]

———

Later in the afternoon, Schiffer finally had his chance to take up the cudgel against the government's star witness. The most interesting aspect of Schiffer's cross-examination might have been his stubborn refusal to address Partin by name, instead referring to him as "Witness" or "Mr. Witness." However, the

attorney revealed little new information in the course of his bitter, accusatory questioning. "The jury appeared bored and restless," the *Chattanooga
News-Free Press* reported, "as Atty. Schiffer trod over the familiar ground
of testimony on which Partin repeatedly has been cross-examined by the
contingent of defense attorneys."

At one point, when Partin paused before answering a question, Schiffer
pounced, charging that the witness had been looking to Neal for guidance.
Partin responded that he had paused because he saw Neal rising to object.
Undaunted, Schiffer pointed a finger at the witness. "I could tell by looking
in his eyes," he said. "I am watching you too, Neal."

Judge Wilson interrupted. "Mr. Schiffer, how many times have you heard
me this afternoon instruct attorneys not to direct remarks to other attorneys?"

"You are absolutely right," Schiffer replied nonsensically. "He is making
asides to me."

"How many times have you heard me give that instruction?" Judge Wilson
persisted.

"At least three times today, your Honor."

"All right," the judge sighed. "I don't want to repeat it."

Once again, Schiffer commented out of the side of his mouth that Neal
should be asked to stop making asides.

"May it please the Court," Neal sighed. "I never opened my mouth to Mr.
Schiffer. I may look at him in a certain manner but I can't avoid that." Those
observers who had come to regard Schiffer's antics with rolled eyes quickly
stifled their chuckles.[11]

After yet another day of cross-examination—interspersed with hours of
argument outside the jury's presence—Wilson mercifully ordered a recess.

––––––––

Tuesday, February 11, began as had the day before, with Haggerty renewing
his motion for an immediate hearing on defense allegations of surveillance.
"It's to a point now, Your Honor, where it is absolutely impossible to prepare
a defense in this case," he protested. "No matter where we go in this city they
are there." Calling the situation "ludicrous," Haggerty added, "As of yesterday
we were compelled to have armed guards stationed in the corridor at both
ends of it because there is a side entrance as well and we are now operating
with armed guards to guard our property and to keep eavesdroppers out of
our quarters where we have to live and have to work."

Schiffer joined in. "Your Honor may feel at times that I have been a bit
too loud," he offered, with no small degree of understatement, "but that has

been a direct result of this surveillance of the government where we cannot even prepare for the following day without this kind of observation." Judge Wilson reiterated that he would take up the issue of surveillance after the proof had been entered. The trial would continue forward.[12]

The court turned to another surveillance-related motion filed by Schiffer, this one accompanied by a mysterious, sealed Exhibit A. "I found out later," Marvin Berke recounted, "they had put all of these transcripts of what he [Bernard Spindel] recorded in a sealed envelope, and they filed a motion dealing with surveillance and attached this envelope to the motion." The document had been prepared by Spindel, who confirmed that he had been hired "to detect whether or not there is, or has been, surveillance of the defendants." If Judge Wilson would not hold an immediate hearing, Schiffer would nevertheless place the issue directly before the court.[13]

When asked to explain what he had filed, Schiffer admitted that he had never reviewed the envelope's contents. There was a practical justification for his purposeful ignorance. "Back then," Gearhiser explained, "the violation of the law was not wiretapping; it was making known what you had gotten by wiretapping." Section 605 of the Federal Communications Act deemed the disclosure of communications obtained by wire or radio a criminal offense. And so Schiffer filed the sealed document with the expectation that Judge Wilson would open it. By having the *judge* disclose the information, Spindel could avoid an accusation of wiretapping.[14]

When Wilson asked Schiffer how he could file a motion without knowing its contents, he received a rambling, unresponsive protestation. "They made an armed camp of Chattanooga," Schiffer railed. "This is a very peaceful and quiet city. . . . There seems to be more on the streets at least there are more marshals than residents of Chattanooga." The remaining lawyers listened bemusedly. "Your Honor is being used as a tool by the government," Schiffer shouted, "and I say that smacks of Stalinism and Hitlerism and Mussolini-ism and all these ism's that this country has spent all of its precious blood to keep away from our shores." As for the filing of the affidavit, Schiffer explained, "I did so with the understanding that all he [Spindel] would indicate to me was whether it was negative or positive as to his findings. If it was negative, he was to pack up and go home. If it was positive he was to collate all his information. Seal it. And deliver it to the Court."[15]

An unsuspecting Judge Wilson therefore opened the envelope and "made as a part of the record the affidavit and more than 20 pages of a handwritten transcription of government agent conversations which Spindel said he had intercepted."[16] Having addressed the mysterious Spindel affidavit, Wilson turned to one signed by Tommy Osborn, who claimed that to the "best of

[his] recollection" he had disclosed to Hooker secret information germane to the defense of the case. Of course, in light of his recent disbarment after lying to two federal judges, Osborn was not the most credible witness. "This is an unmitigated falsehood and I will take proper answer, take the witness stand or whatever is necessary at the proper time," an affronted Hooker shot back. Once again, the court tabled the motion; the case would proceed without further delay. Getting finished with Partin was the priority.[17]

By midafternoon, Partin returned to the stand, and the jury to the courtroom. During what would be only a brief session, Schiffer addressed the fact that Partin had taken the Fifth Amendment before the grand jury. Partin said that he had done so at the urging of Bufalino, who had given him a note to that effect. Schiffer asked whether he knew he was doing the wrong thing by taking the Fifth. "No," Partin cagily replied. "This has been a trademark of the Teamsters for years." Amid a flurry of objections, Judge Wilson instructed the jury to disregard the remark.[18]

Schiffer then addressed the curious payments made to Partin's wife. Why were the payments made through a *confidential* fund? Why all of the back-room maneuvers? A grim Neal explained to the court that "fear of terrorism"—epitomized by the shadowy shooting into the home of Donice Bennett—was the reason for the cloak-and-dagger tactics. The events of the prior weekend had provided the prosecution with a case in point for its decision to route the monies through Frank Grimsley.

"I say it's all stuffy nonsense," Haggerty sniffed, adding that Neal should be required to summon witnesses to substantiate his claims of terror in Baton Rouge. It was then revealed that Bennett had already been summoned to Chattanooga.[19]

Speaking of summoning witnesses, Judge Wilson asked about a subpoena that had been issued for the appearance of Partin's estranged wife, noting that he had received a call from a fellow federal judge in Baton Rouge on her behalf. "Gentlemen," he inquired, "what defense counsel issued a subpoena yesterday for Mrs. Partin? What defense counsel?" When Berke stepped forward, Wilson provided him with a lengthy lecture. "What possible occasion could you have had to subpoena her to be here at nine o'clock this morning?" he asked, referring to Mrs. Partin as "this lady with five children, [and] no way to take care of them."

When Berke responded gamely that the defense had no other option, as it had been unable to interview her in advance, an irritated Judge Wilson gazed at the passel of lawyers clustered around the defense table. "The other day there were six attorneys who are not participating in the trial who came

and took the witness stand," he chided. He also noted that any of those lawyers could have vetted potential witnesses before summoning them to Chattanooga. Berke objected to a suggestion that he notify the court in advance
when he wanted Mrs. Partin. He contended that doing so would equate to
giving away defense strategy. "Oh, well," Wilson scolded, "here was a woman
that obviously you never intended to use today, you couldn't possibly use
today, a woman with five children, looking after these five children and she
was subpoenaed in order to be up here and it didn't seem that was quite appropriate." Berke would receive no sympathy from the court.[20]

The reverses of the day, and the defense's failure to win any real ground, left
Hoffa in a foul humor as court recessed. As cross-examination droned on day
after day, he had "whispered in anger to counsels whose performance before
the Chattanooga judge and jury did not come up to his own high standards.
'Sit down!' or 'Cut it out!'" At times, "when the whispers were insufficiently
audible to achieve the desired result, he had handed the offending lawyers
notes expressing the same command in written form." There was no question
as to who was in charge of the defense. According to Marvin Berke, "with
the people that worked for him he [Hoffa] was tough, and he could let them
have it when he wanted to." Hoffa was not reluctant to let loose a barrage of
vitriol when disappointed. As Berke recalled, "when he was in his element,
he knew the four-letter words pretty well." On the afternoon of February 11,
he was more than willing to use them.

Hoffa reserved his greatest ire for Schiffer, whose hostile antics had neither
unearthed new revelations nor provoked a mistrial. He was asking ill-advised
questions without having any idea how the witness might respond, and he
was clearly unprepared. In an article entitled "Hoffa Blisters Defense Lawyer,"
the *Detroit News* recounted the IBT president's bitter explosion at the New
York attorney at the end of the day on February 11. Standing over Schiffer at
the defense table, Hoffa snarled, "Quit talking so much. And why don't you
read the transcript. I don't care if you have to stay up all night. Read it." "The
scolding continued" as the defense left the courtroom, despite the fact that
Schiffer was not technically Hoffa's attorney at all.[21]

Out on the sidewalk, Hoffa met a crowd of reporters who sensed he was
in a mood to give them a colorful comment. Flanked by Berke and Bufalino,
Hoffa shook a sheaf of papers in the air, asserting that he had evidence that
FBI agents were employing binoculars, television cameras, still cameras,

and stakeouts to watch the defendants and their lawyers. As a result, he had been forced to hire members of the sheriff's patrol to stand guard around the clock at his hotel suite. "This is the Gestapo method of Bobby Kennedy and Jim Neal," he said.

One of the reporters inquired about Hoffa's purported comment that he had the colored juror in his hip pocket. A flood of embittered vitriol issued forth in response. "If you would read the gobbledy-goop," Hoffa said disgustedly, "which you probably heard in the courtroom—it was so unintelligible language to distinguish what he was talking about—I denied it then, deny it now, and Partin was not there for any purpose of seeing that anything was being done illegal. He was there seeking the information that Neal and the other prosecutors wanted for the Justice Department and was an afterthought where they planned the paid script, a plot just like the movies do in Hollywood, to where he could say to the canned audience of the FBI and of the Justice Department and then report it like a parrot on the stand, a taped recording where they, through hypnosis in my opinion, instilled in his mind a complete lie that he reported and was allowed to ramble for three days on the witness stand—which has no substance in proof." Hoffa also accused the court of "trying to silence [his] voice" by delaying a hearing on the surveillance issue. It was all too much to stomach. "If this isn't grounds for a mistrial," he muttered, "there is no grounds for mistrial in America."

A dour, serious Berke stepped in front of the camera. All of the things that he could not say in court, he was going to provide to the press.

"At the time Mr. Partin agreed to perjure himself in this case," he said evenly, "he was under indictment for kidnapping, he was under investigation for smuggling arms to Cuba, he had killed a serviceman by manslaughter and had run off from the scene, he was under a 26-count indictment by the federal government, he had a perjury indictment that was coming up, he had so many charges against him, that it's easily understandable how the government can impose upon a weakling, a dope addict, which the proof shows he was, to get him to testify falsely against Mr. Hoffa. Now, any time you can get a man of that caliber to come in and testify on behalf of the United States government, I say it's a poor shame that the citizens of this country have to submit to persecution with a witness of that type."

Did the defense team believe that there was a deal between the government and Partin? "There is no doubt about it," Berke replied, noting the suspicious fact that none of the charges against Partin had been pursued to trial. "They have already dismissed the kidnapping charge, they have already dismissed the perjury charge, they have given him every consideration on the pending indictments, they have—they have postponed the 26-count indictment on four different occasions." What other reason could exist for such lenient treatment? With that question hanging in the air, the entourage marched off to the Hotel Patten.

The gathered reporters smiled and shook their heads. It had been the best outburst yet, and it would certainly translate into scintillating news—and newspaper sales. Then the reporters turned to Neal, who had been standing nearby listening to the tirade. Deliberately even-tempered, a counterpoint to the livid Hoffa, Neal downplayed the accusations as "a lot of baloney." The allegations of government wrongdoing were "aimed at diverting the attention from the courtroom," he said. "It will be exploded at the appropriate time. Hoffa is a master of hyperbole[,] and this is the master's work."[22]

————

February 12 saw the last of the defense attorneys take his shots at an exhausted Partin. During the barrage of objections, accusations, and motions for mistrial that had peppered the proceedings, Cecil Branstetter had for the most part remained seated quietly, purposefully leaving the mistrial-baiting tactics to others. As Seigenthaler opined, "I always thought that Cecil . . . emotionally separated himself from the antics." Now, stepping to the podium, the lawyer showed his deep disdain for Partin through a series of searing questions. During the course of his examination, Branstetter turned to the explosive topic of Fidel Castro, asking whether Partin had ever been to Cuba. The topic had been raised and barred twice already. Surprisingly, however, Neal's objection was overruled. Partin answered, "Yes, sir, I went to a good night club over there and had a good time for one night."

When Branstetter attempted to introduce a letter referencing gunrunning to Cuba, however, an impromptu hearing was held, once again outside the presence of the jury. Schiffer stated, "This man had committed and is committing treason against the United States of America by trafficking or attempting to traffic with Fidel Castro and ship him arms despite the public laws of the United States insofar as Cuba is concerned." Why not prosecute such treasonous activity?

Once again, Judge Wilson indicated that the defense would not be allowed to introduce extraneous, explosive topics. "We are not going to go off and try a half dozen other lawsuits in this lawsuit," he warned. "The only conclusion the Court can draw on this is you are seeking to degrade a witness by unsupported charges. If you have a conviction you can bring it in but we are not going into this case and try some alleged treason charges, as you say."

Schiffer could not restrain himself. "If that is not a reason to attack his credibility," he declared, "then I think the whole trial is a farce." Schiffer was treading on the edge of acceptable conduct. With admirable self-restraint and no additional comment, Wilson asked for the jury to be returned to the courtroom, and Branstetter resumed his questioning.

Nearing the end, and echoing the incriminating hint Berke had dangled on the sidewalk the prior afternoon, Branstetter asked Partin whether he had ever taken dope, or narcotics. No, Partin responded unequivocally. The court denied Haggerty's request that the witness undergo a drug test—there was no evidence to support it. With literally no unplowed ground left to cover with respect to the witness, at midmorning on February 12 the defense relinquished Partin. An exhausted Partin finally stepped down from the witness stand after seven days of testimony.[23]

THIRTEEN

"I'll hound you for the rest of your life, Neal."

—Jimmy Hoffa

"HOFFA TRIAL DEVELOPS Own Band of Devoted 'Fans,'" read the February 13 headline. The case was a hot ticket in Chattanooga, with spectators lining up in front of the federal courthouse an hour before it opened, hoping to get a seat inside. Local attorneys cracked that their time hanging around the courthouse was "costing [them] money," and one young lady attending business school lamented that the trial was ruining her attendance record. A school group from nearby South Pittsburg, Tennessee, came in to observe the trial one morning. As Harry Mansfield told the *Chattanooga*

News-Free Press, while it was impossible to set aside space for the children, all were admitted after waiting about an hour. Also among the "devoted fans" were "two attractive secretaries from Detroit" who attended the Hoffa proceedings while on vacation. Assuring reporters that they were taking "time out to shop," the two remarked, "We are enjoying it [the trial]."

Not all visitors came simply for the spectacle of the trial and its famous defendant. Mrs. Ora E. Modeland, identified as a "regular," said she cut short a vacation in Corpus Christi to attend the trial. "Not only is the trial itself interesting," she remarked, "but there is more at stake in this lawsuit than in any case in the history of Tennessee." She did not want to miss out on seeing history made before her eyes. As she gravely declared, "Our very judicial system is on trial here."[1]

———

The next witness called was Andrew Mizell, clerk of the federal court in Nashville. He confirmed that the list of prospective jurors in the Test Fleet case had been released on October 1 or 2, 1962, and that the jury had been selected on October 25. Mizell also identified Gratin Fields as the only black male chosen as a prospective juror, James Tippens as the twelfth juror listed, Betty Paschal as juror number four on the second list, and Fields as the sixth juror on list number three. Given the fact that prospective jurors in the Test Fleet case were called in numerical order (not randomly), the fact that those three were toward the top of the list made it plausible that they would be called as jurors in the Nashville case. Thus, approaching a *prospective* juror was not an unreasonable strategy in the Test Fleet case.[2]

The prosecution signaled its intent to call Tippens. The defense objected on the ground that the proffered evidence related to a principal defendant ("Red" Medlin) who was not on trial. Neal countered that Hoffa had already been linked to the attempt to bribe Tippens, commenting to Partin, "The dirty bastard went in and told the judge that his neighbor had offered him $10,000" and, as a result, "we are going to have to lay low for a few days." But, as the court pointed out, nothing had been offered to connect *Medlin* to any of the defendants—including Hoffa. A link was missing.

In light of Hoffa's various comments about paying jurors, Neal responded, the jury could infer that Hoffa had also aided and abetted those attempts. Witnesses such as Tippens would show that the attempts had been made. "We have to show the approach before we can show anyone aided and abetted," Neal argued. To resolve the situation, Judge Wilson suggested that Tippens be allowed to testify that he had spoken to Judge Miller. As a concession to the defense, however, the witness could not share the *content* of their discussion. That split victory established, the jury returned to the courtroom.[3]

Hooker called the Nashville businessman to the stand. Amid a constant flurry of objections, Tippens explained that he had spoken to Medlin by telephone on October 23, 1962, and had gone to Medlin's business, where the two men sat in a car and talked. The next day, Tippens said, he had approached Judge Miller: "I felt like that I could not serve under the conditions that existed in which were namely I had been. . . ." The court immediately cut him off. He tried again. "I told Judge Miller that I felt disequal to serve on the jury due to the fact that I had been offered a sum of money. . . ." The defense again objected; the objection was sustained. "I had a conversation with a neighbor that would prejudice my position and service." Again, an objection.

Hooker deliberately baited Tippens, disregarding the court's instruction. "Did you say anything to Judge Miller about whether any sum of money was offered to you?"

Before Tippens could even open his mouth, Silets shouted for a mistrial. "Once you have thrown a skunk into the jury box," he cried, "you cannot ask the jurors not to smell it." Judge Wilson denied the motion but instructed jurors to disregard the statement.[4]

Haggerty conducted a brief cross-examination. After Tippens acknowledged that *he* had never spoken to Hoffa, he was allowed to step down. The defense "appeared relieved to get him out of the courthouse," one newspaper noted. A respected, reputable member of the Nashville business community and a reliable observer, Tippens was labeled "the first key witness to be offered by the prosecution whose testimony had not been altered."

To some observers, it was ludicrous to believe that anyone would try to bribe a *prospective* juror who had not yet been selected. "An immediate effort to fix him, under the circumstances, seems so premature as to be almost idiotic," wrote one pro-Hoffa commentator. For his part, Hoffa insisted that the testimony did not link him to anything. "It's like asking a man on the witness stand how he got a black eye," he grumbled to reporters, "and having him say, 'I don't know, but Hoffa was the only other man in the room.'" It was clear that *someone* had attempted to bribe Tippens, but more evidence was needed to link Hoffa to that effort. In the end, though, who else had a motivation for doing so?[5]

———

After four relentless weeks, even Hoffa's nerves were starting to fray. During breaks in the testimony, he vented his frustrations on whomever he could find. "Constantly during the trial he was jumping on somebody," Mansfield recalled. Most often, Hoffa focused his ire on his own attorneys. During breaks, Hoffa would call out particular individuals for asking the wrong question, or failing to ask the right question, or asking too many questions or too few. News articles carried reports of harried attorneys bawled out on the sidewalk in front of the courthouse. When he felt that a lawyer was not well prepared, the union boss had no patience whatsoever. "Just get out of the courtroom," he would hiss, shoving the hapless lawyer. "You're not doing that right."[6]

Increasingly riled by his belief that the government was persecuting him, Hoffa also had choice words for US marshals and other government representatives, growling, "You fink" as he passed them in hallways. Mansfield witnessed many such incidents. Once, several marshals entered the courthouse wearing similar white raincoats. "He looked at me and the marshals," Mansfield recalled, "and said, 'you Gestapo SOBs.'" Hoffa reserved special disdain for Walter Sheridan, Kennedy's eyes and ears in Chattanooga. Whenever the two men crossed paths, Hoffa spat out venomous insults. Yet the greatest subject of Hoffa's ire was Jim Neal, who handled most of the questioning for the government. Hoffa often fixed Neal with a severe stare and offhandedly insulted him in the courthouse hallways. On one occasion, as Mansfield observed, Hoffa muttered to Neal, "I hope you die of cancer, you son of a bitch."

By the end of the day on February 13, Hoffa's feelings of persecution boiled over when discussing government telephone records. Grabbing one coded card out of a stack on a table, he remarked that only an expert could interpret them. The court clerk jumped in, remarking that the cards were under his control and should not have been grabbed. Hoffa began to shout at a nearby Neal, accusing him of hiding evidence. "I'll hound you for the rest of your life, Neal," he barked. "You won't be in the government forever."[7]

The trial had also been hard on Jo Hoffa, who was so distraught during the first few days of the proceedings that her husband had sent her back to Detroit. On February 13, however, she was at the Hotel Patten, along with their nine-month-old granddaughter. The following day (February 14) would be Hoffa's fifty-first birthday. That evening, family members and business associates gathered at the Pan-O-Ram Club on nearby Lookout Mountain to celebrate. Hoffa was described as "relaxed and cheerful," blowing out the three candles on his cake and laughing as his granddaughter dipped her fingers into the icing. "His usual toughness vanished" as he carried the child around the club on his shoulder. But the festivities did not last long. Departing early with his attorneys, Hoffa resumed his normal businesslike demeanor. "We've got a lot of work to do," he said as his car door clapped shut.[8]

———

The prosecution's final witness was Albert Gasdor, court reporter at the Test Fleet trial. He offered as exhibit 149 the transcript of the removal of Tippens from the Nashville jury list. Over strenuous defense objections, and in an abrupt about-face from the prior ruling that Tippens could not disclose the *content* of his meeting with Judge Miller, the transcript was read to the jury:

> He said after he left court yesterday he went to his office, and a person whom he has known for a long time, a next-door neighbor of his, and apparently a person with whom he had had some business dealings, as well as some social contacts, approached him, and told him that he would like for him to go out in the car, that he wanted to talk with him. He said he thought that was suspicious, but he went on out in the car with him, and this person said that he knew how he could pick up $10,000. Tippens said that he did not understand this, but thought he might be referring to the case.
>
> He said, "If it has anything to do with this case, I cannot discuss it with you."
>
> The person went ahead and said, "Well, it will be an easy way to pick up $10,000, and it will be paid in $100 bills, that you could get it in $100 bills."
>
> He said, "You are referring to my being a prospective juror in the case."
>
> The person said, "Yes," and he said, "I cannot talk to you any further about it."

To avoid any further revelations, the defense asked Gasdor no questions. At the very least, the defense could console itself with the fact that this information had not implicated Hoffa (or any other defendant) in any wrongdoing.[9]

———

With no other witnesses for the prosecution, Berke requested an immediate hearing on the issue of covert government recordings of Hoffa's telephone conversations. Federal officials had claimed that no recordings of Hoffa were ever made, Berke explained; however, recordings did exist, and the government was now refusing to turn them over. Judge Wilson said that he would take up the issue after the weekend. But Schiffer had to get in a final word, accusing the government of lying about the existence of recordings. Other attorneys joined in, such that the proceedings threatened to devolve into a back-alley scrap. "I am a Tennessean," an affronted Neal finally remarked. "I am not used to being called a liar and subornator of perjury. This man [Schiffer] has been doing it."

As the buzz in the courtroom petered out, all eyes turned to Wilson. The beleaguered judge set down the pencil with which he had scrawled notes throughout the trial. He sighed and gazed over the room. Calmly, and without sermonizing, he cautioned the parties to move along. He had made his ruling on the subject of telephone recordings.[10]

The government presented Hoffa with a welcome Valentine's Day (and birthday) gift at 11:10 a.m. by resting its case-in-chief. At that point, defense attorneys moved for dismissal of the indictments. His voice strained and hoarse, Branstetter moved for the dismissal of count three as it related to Larry Campbell. The only evidence against his client, he argued, included a number of telephone calls made from one station to another, and testimony that Campbell had at some point been seen in the vicinity of those telephones. There was "no evidence in this record to indicate the person called or the content [of any of the calls at issue]." Nor had any proof had been offered that Campbell had ever gone to Nashville. "The jury under no circumstances is permitted to speculate," Branstetter said. "The jury under no circumstances is entitled to consider suspicious circumstances." The motion to dismiss was quietly denied.[11]

Haggerty made a motion to strike the testimony of practically every witness who had testified on behalf of the government, largely because their accounts had not revealed any connection to Hoffa. The testimony of Hazel Fulton, James Walker, Carl Fields, and James Paschal, Haggerty continued, should be discarded because each of them "admitted and confessed in open court making false statements under oath and committing perjury." Haggerty further noted that Partin's testimony should be thrown out because of "the witness' evasive, non-responsive and highly improper answers, as well as the refusal to answer and the failure of the Court to properly direct the witness and reprimand him for his demeanor, evasiveness and equivocation on the stand." The court denied the motion except as to Josephine Carlton (Tippens's assistant), for whom it would reserve ruling.[12]

Silets moved for dismissal of the indictment against Dorfman, pointing out that Dallas Hall had never been requested to do anything corrupt with respect to the jury. Simply being asked to "find out about" the jurors was not a crime. "The government wants to go to the step saying that the mere communication, the mere talking to this man in itself constitutes an obstruction of justice," Silets said. "This is novel and far fetched." If the investigation of jurors was a crime, he contended, "every lawyer who has ever practiced law" would be guilty of a criminal act.[13]

It was then Dave Alexander's turn. The son of a political columnist for the Nashville Tennessean, Alexander had earned degrees from Vanderbilt University before serving in World War II. After the war, he served in the Tennessee House of Representatives and worked as the personal aide for two Tennessee governors. Alexander was one of the less vocal defense attorneys, and he focused on the lack of evidence that Tweel had fostered any approach to a Test Fleet juror.[14] Alexander echoed many of Silets's arguments. Even if Tweel had been interested in the trial—so interested that he had his secretary take down a list of jurors—he had never asked Dallas Hall to contact any juror. Without an overt act in furtherance of the conspiracy, Silets said, there was simply nothing illegal to prosecute.

Taking a sip of water as he completed his remarks, Alexander made a weak joke. "I am having to use some government water at this stage if it please the Court. It may stop me up but I will try to keep going."

"Your Honor," an unamused Neal interjected, "in view of some of the allegations made against the government, if they were sincere, if I were Mr. Alexander I wouldn't drink it."[15]

Next, spectators leaned forward in their seats as Schiffer stepped to the podium. Surely, he could be counted upon to inject some attention-grabbing turmoil into the courtroom. Somewhat surprisingly, however, Schiffer informed the court that, while he was filing a motion for the acquittal of Thomas Ewing Parks, he would not offer any oral argument. Others had already exhausted the topic.[16]

Speaking after Schiffer, Harold Brown made a brief argument for dismissal of the indictment against Ewing King. Because those witnesses offering testimony against King—Oscar Pitts, James Paschal, and Ed Partin—had given false statements, their allegations could not be taken as evidence at all.[17]

Finally, Harry Berke moved for dismissal of the indictment against Hoffa. If any of the prior motions were granted, he remarked, then the charge that

Hoffa had aided and abetted such effort should likewise be dismissed. The only witness who offered anything related to Hoffa himself was Partin, and his testimony was "so incredible and so unworthy of belief" that it could not support a conviction. Comments to the effect that "he is going to get one juror or scattered jurors," that "he would pay $15,000 or $20,000 to get to the jury," and that "Mr. King was supposed to have made some contact with a juror but that he is fumbling around," even if true, did not show that *Hoffa* had ever done anything. There was simply no link between Hoffa and any approach to a Test Fleet juror. The most that could be said was that Hoffa had been *aware* of certain efforts to contact Test Fleet jurors. Nowhere was it shown that Hoffa had encouraged those efforts, instructed anyone to carry them out, given anyone anything with which to approach a juror, or done anything unlawful himself. Without information proving criminal activity on his part, the indictment as it pertained to Hoffa should be dismissed.[18]

Neal offered the government's response, promising that his remarks would be short, unlike the defense counsel's. The brief arguments on behalf of Parks and King merited no response, he said, as those motions had "less than nothing" to support them. Focusing on count four, Neal stressed the tight timeline of events. After telephone calls were made from Dorfman to Tweel and then from Tweel to Dallas Hall, Tweel had contacted Partin to ask for a jury list "in order that he [might] contact Mr. Hall and read the jury off to him so that he could contact the people." Neal smacked his hand on the podium. "There is your evil motive, your Honor." One would have to be naïve, he said, to believe that Tweel had simply wanted to learn about the jury. After Dorfman had read the list of jurors and Hazel Fulton had recorded their names—on plain paper at Tweel's request—the list was read to Hall, who was asked if he knew anyone on the jury. Three calls were then made to Hall. Only after Hall had repeatedly indicated that he had discovered nothing did Tweel drop the matter. If Hall *had* known any of the jurors, Neal asserted, the next step would have been to approach them. It was not the success of the attempt, he declared, but rather the endeavor that established the crime.

Turning to Larry Campbell, Neal emphasized Hoffa's comments that Campbell had come to Nashville to take care of matters and that Hoffa "had the colored male juror in [his] pocket." The proof was "overwhelming," Neal asserted, that Parks had offered cash to Carl Fields to convince his father to vote for acquittal. How was Campbell linked to all of this? During the Test Fleet trial, a series of calls was confirmed from telephone booths used by Campbell in Louisville to the Nashville home of Mattie Mix, where Parks was the only boarder. Without a doubt, Campbell, a loyal member of IBT

Local 299, was in communication with the key instigator of the attempt to bribe juror Gratin Fields.

In regard to the IBT president, Neal read off the litany of comments Partin attributed to Hoffa. The attorney insisted those remarks were enough to show that Hoffa had aided and abetted the various attempts to influence jurors. Of course Hoffa would not simply admit, "I am an aider and abettor, counselor, producer, commander, procurer." Such direct evidence, Neal insisted, was never available. But Hoffa's numerous statements confirmed his role in the scheme.

Finally, he pointed to a few pieces of evidence that Berke had ignored. Rather than sitting idly by as his cronies tried to get to the jury, Hoffa had called King "a stupid so and so for fumbling around and not getting the job done." Hoffa had also commented, "It looks like our best bet is a hung jury unless we can get to the foreman of the jury," and he had said that he was disturbed because patrolman Paschal would not take the money offered to him. The jury could certainly infer, Neal concluded, that "Hoffa, the only man who stood to gain, the only man on trial, was aiding and abetting with respect to Counts 3, 4, and 5."

———

With oral arguments concluded, Neal filed the government's response to defense allegations of surveillance. Attached was the affidavit of Knoxville FBI agent Everett J. Ingram. Therein, Ingram averred that the only person surveilled after the start of the trial had been wiretapper Bernard Spindel, that agents had been specifically instructed not to surveil the defendants or their attorneys, and that the surveillance "did not involve any eavesdropping, wiretapping, microphonic installations, trespasses or any invasions of privacy." Separate affidavits from Bill Sheets and other FBI agents corroborated this information. The observation of Spindel, Neal wrote, occurred because there was reason to believe that he might be involved in unlawful electronic eavesdropping. Under those circumstances, surveillance had been "shown to have been entirely justified by the very documents which were submitted to the Court [through Schiffer]."

Of all of the photographs submitted by the defense, Neal indicated, only one depicted an FBI agent (Bill Sheets). The others featured private citizens going about their personal affairs. "The only illegal activity involved in the proceeding," Neal commented, "is the activity by this man Spindel in violation of Section 605 of the Federal Communications Act." Pausing, he lit the fuse.

"And perhaps by Mr. Schiffer, in aiding and abetting, counseling, procuring and inducing" such unlawful activity.

Predictably, Schiffer exploded. "You don't say that again unless you mean to back it up," he boomed. "I will meet you anywhere with anything. We will see who turns yellow first."

It took almost every bit of Judge Wilson's restraint to control himself. "Sir, we will not have that sort of conversation in this courtroom." He leveled a smoldering gaze at Schiffer. "Do you understand me?" A chastened Schiffer quietly slipped back into his seat.[19]

With that, another long week concluded. The court adjourned at 5:50 p.m. As the spectators filed out of the courtroom, Hoffa pounded the table and denounced the government's report on surveillance as "garbage." That weekend, the chief defendant, who usually left town on weekends, would remain in Chattanooga to work with his legal staff. The defense had a great amount of preparation to complete for its own case-in-chief.[20]

FOURTEEN

"I never asked him to do anything."

—Nicholas Tweel[1]

JUDGE WILSON DID everything he could to avoid dragging the mayhem of the Hoffa trial into his home. As law clerk Charlie Gearhiser recalled, "I know that Judge Wilson tried to conduct his life as though no trial was going on." Each night the family gathered for dinner, after which the judge would retire to begin the laborious process of reviewing trial transcripts.

However, creating the appearance of normalcy was not always easy. There were ongoing concerns about the safety of the judge and his family. "When the trial first started," Harry Mansfield explained, "Judge Wilson didn't want security on him." The judge's greatest safety concern was not himself, but his children, whom US marshals escorted to and from school for the duration of the proceedings. "[Frank] told the school not to let [the children] go with anybody else without a note from us, because of the people we were dealing with," recalled Helen Wilson, "so that made you apprehensive about what might take place." Yet for seven-year-old Randy Wilson, being chauffeured around by US marshals was a great adventure. "In my naïve age, it was pretty cool," he commented. "I didn't appreciate the potential danger [of kidnapping] . . . it was pretty cool to have all the marshals around the house."

One week into the trial, Mansfield insisted on dispatching guards to protect Judge Wilson himself, recalling, "His secretary told me he had received some phone calls that weren't exactly right." Each day thereafter, Wilson was driven to and from the courthouse. Local police were stationed at the home day and night, and marshals were posted in the woods and in a small travel trailer in a neighbor's driveway. Helen Wilson kept a large pot of coffee going twenty-four hours a day, "and the marshals would come and go and help themselves to coffee."

Delegated to oversee operations at the Wilsons' home, deputy marshal Granville Sertel occupied a guest room near the front corner of the house. Sertel's son explained his father's responsibilities: "He stayed with Judge Wilson every night guarding him, making sure there was nobody to harm him or try to get to him in any way, and so he stayed at their house during the whole trial." A World War II veteran who had served as a US marshal during the 1958 school integration crisis in Little Rock, Sertell was well liked and respected. Almost everyone referred to him as "Shirttail" or "Shirt" (nicknames which were plays on his last name), and Judge Wilson's children came to call him "Uncle Shirt." "My dad was the original G man," recalled Sertel's son, "and he lived, slept, [and] ate law enforcement and the federal marshal's office . . . he loved it."

One evening, long after midnight, a doorbell rang at the Wilson house. As Helen Wilson came downstairs to open the door, Sertel cautioned her to wait. Cracking open the door, he found a disheveled man in a fur coat on the front steps. As an alarmed Sertel moved to body tackle the fellow, the man mumbled that he wondered whether Judge Wilson needed any painting or yard work done. "They said he was the town drunk," Helen Wilson later recounted. "I didn't know we had one!"

Sertel aside, the marshals assigned to the Wilson home rotated periodically. "We would change crews about every week up there," Sertel explained.

When a fresh team arrived, he would gather them and go over their assignments, show them where they were to be stationed, and review the protocols
in place to ensure the safety of the judge and his family. "And I'd always tell
them when they got up there," Sertel said, "'Now, if the house catches on fire
or blows up . . . That guy in the bottom bedroom, right over there on the
right, get him out first.'"

"Oh," the newly assigned crew would reply, nodding in agreement. "That's
where the judge stays."

"No," Sertel grinned, "that's where I stay."[2]

Monday, February 17, began with a few minor housekeeping matters. Neal
conceded, "Since we were not permitted to prove the approach by Medlin to
Tippens we cannot go to the jury with respect to Hoffa's aiding and abetting,"
as required under count two. "I think that we would have to agree that the
government would have to take a judgment of acquittal as against Defendant
Hoffa on Count 2." Thus that charge was dismissed—a significant, if incom-
plete, victory for the defense.[3]

The remaining counts, Judge Wilson announced, would not be dismissed.
Silets reacted by requesting that Dorfman be severed from the case. Of the
forty to fifty witnesses who had testified, Silets argued, only two related to
Dorfman in any way. Lumping all of the defendants together was a misjoin-
der, he asserted, as "there is not one scintilla of evidence to establish that the
acts of each of these defendants arose from the same act or the same series of
transactions." Branstetter promptly joined in the motion on behalf of Larry
Campbell. Both motions were denied.[4]

Silets then asked the court to disallow any and all of Partin's tape recordings of Hoffa, contending that such activities constituted an illegal search
and seizure in violation of Hoffa's Fourth Amendment rights. Partin, Silets
explained, had represented that no recordings had been made of his conversations with Hoffa. Now, however, the defense had revealed an affidavit
from William R. Daniels, assistant to the Baton Rouge district attorney, in
which he stated that, on October 8 and 18, 1962, "I was authorized by Edward
Grady Partin to instruct him in the use of an attachment to his telephone
of a recording device on the occasion of his calls to James R. Hoffa." Partin
himself had signed an affidavit confirming that two conversations were recorded "by use of a device on [his] receiver given [to him] by William R.
Daniels." Labeling the testimony deceitful was a bit misleading. Partin had

been asked whether he had recorded Hoffa *during the Test Fleet trial*. However, the calls referenced in Daniels's affidavit were made before that trial began. Nevertheless, while technically accurate, Partin's denials might seem like cunning hairsplitting.

Two calls had been recorded. In the first, Partin asked, "Jimmy, I would like to get together with you and talk this thing [the twenty-six-count indictment] out." Hoffa responded that he would be glad to meet with Partin. Ten days later, a second call. "I need to talk to you, Jimmy," an exasperated Partin pleaded. "When can I see you? You said you'd be in Nashville on the 22nd [of October]. When would be the next day I could come up?" Hoffa replied that he was arriving for the trial on Sunday, October 21, and that they could get together on the following Monday or Tuesday. Clearly, a listener could conclude that Partin had invited *himself* to Nashville.[5] According to Haggerty, the disclosure of these tapes had the effect of "the release of a hydrogen bomb."[6] Previous motions to suppress Partin's testimony had been quickly denied. After an initial review of this volatile new material, though, Judge Wilson surprised everyone and granted a hearing on the motion to suppress Partin's testimony. Later, however, Wilson revisited the testimony and reversed his decision. The judge concluded that Partin had not dissembled; he had answered the question posed to him, which related to recordings made during—not before—the Nashville trial. What was surely anticipated as the best chance for a mistrial to date slipped from the feverish, grasping fingers of the defense.[7]

———

The defense proceeded with its case-in-chief. Speaking with reporters, one defense attorney had predicted that more than thirty witnesses would be called to testify. Therefore, the proof might take three weeks. In reality, though, the defense would complete its case quickly, within about a week.[8]

The court indicated that it would offer "wide discretion" concerning the order in which defense witnesses would be presented, with the one exception that a defendant should take the stand first. The first witness would be Nicholas Tweel, "a figure of mystery" to news reporters. He was rarely seen in the company of the other defendants, stayed at a different hotel from the others, and "often is observed taking his meals alone." Gray streaks flashing through his wiry black hair, the 49-year-old lowered himself into the witness chair and nodded slightly to the jury. His testimony, consistent with the strategy of his attorneys throughout the trial, would be soft-stated and low-key.[9]

After completing public school, Tweel explained to the jury, he had become an attendant at a Pure Oil Filling Station in Huntington, West Virginia,
served during World War II, married and had children, and worked in the
investment business.[10] Yes, he was acquainted with Dorfman. In 1962, the
two had been introduced by a mutual friend in New York. There had been
some difficulty in obtaining financing for Tweel's West Virginia Life Insurance
Company, and so Dorfman had agreed to meet him in New York to discuss
the matter. On October 20 (two days before the Test Fleet trial), however,
Dorfman had asked if they could instead meet in Nashville. According to
Tweel, this was the first time he had ever been to Nashville, and the trip had
nothing to do with Hoffa.[11]

After checking into the Andrew Jackson Hotel, Tweel had eaten dinner
alone. The next morning, he and Dorfman had walked to the Nashville courthouse, where the trial was taking place. Although he had possibly looked
over a list of jurors, Tweel said, "Naturally I never had any interest in it."
Returning to the hotel, the two men had talked business for thirty or forty-
five minutes. During their conversation, Tweel recalled, "a gentleman came
over and made himself acquainted or made himself known to Mr. Dorfman
as Mr. Partin[,] and Mr. Dorfman promptly introduced me to Mr. Partin."
This, the witness said, was the first and only time in his life he met Partin.
Tweel denied introducing himself by the curious nom de guerre "Anthony
Quinn."[12]

Later, Tweel had gone along as an "uninvited guest" with Helen Rippey,
Carol Pettijohn, and two men to the Black Poodle, some other lounge, and
eventually the Sportsman's Lounge, where they stayed for about forty-five
minutes. At that last stop, Tweel had discussed horse racing with Dallas Hall.
After he had mentioned some of his connections in the racing business, Hall
had asked him to get annual passes to Miles Park outside of Nashville, and he
had indicated interest in obtaining a stake in a Florida racecourse. According
to Tweel, he and Hall had not discussed the Hoffa case. Tweel had returned
to the hotel by 2:00 a.m., and the following morning he had left Nashville,
never to return.[13]

Although he had observed Hoffa in the hotel lobby and the courthouse,
Tweel had never personally met the man. "The next time I saw Mr. Hoffa," he
remarked matter-of-factly, "we were being arraigned together in Nashville,
Tennessee . . . and I didn't even meet him on that occasion."[14]

Mayflower Distributors, Tweel said, was his brother's business. When his
brother had become ill, he had stepped in to assist in selling the company.
Tweel insisted that he was never Hazel Fulton's employer. And while he had

spoken to Dorfman by telephone several times in late 1962, he stated, "We had no other business relationship other than the properties and the insurance company [with which they were both involved]." At no time, he added, did Dorfman read a list of jurors to him over the phone.[15]

On one occasion, Hall had called Tweel—Tweel had to admit to the call, in case the government had another surreptitious recording—but only to discuss horse racing. "I never asked him to do anything," he said. He had never read a list of jurors to Hall; moreover, had he wanted to get information about people in Nashville, Tweel knew others whom he could have asked. He would not have had to rely on a bartender whom he had met for only a few minutes on a single occasion.[16]

Tweel then leveled an incendiary accusation—government officials had threatened him. At the grand jury in Nashville, he had been ushered into Sheridan's office, where he received the following message: "If I would answer the questions in the Grand Jury right[,] I wouldn't have any trouble." Refusing to bow to intimidation, Tweel said softly to the jury, he had told the truth—just as he was doing in Chattanooga.[17]

———

Hooker took up Tweel's cross-examination. Thrusting out his belly, the Nashville lawyer ran his finger along his watch chain. "What did you think about him [Partin] asking you, a man from Huntington, West Virginia, about who you knew on a jury in Nashville in the Federal Court?"

"Well, I wouldn't think anything about it," Tweel responded coolly. "I don't see anything unusual about that, it's perfectly legal and proper to do a thing like that, isn't it?" There was nothing wrong with simply discussing a jury list.[18]

Had he gone to dinner with Herman Frazier in Nashville? Yes, Tweel responded, he had had dined with Frazier, whom he had known his entire life, along with Nelson Paden and Albert Cole, whom he met for the first time in Nashville. Tweel did not know why the three were in Nashville. They had mentioned the trial, but they had not discussed the jury. Of course, those three men—also from West Virginia—were awaiting trial in Nashville, having been accused of the "Allen from the *Banner*" calls to prospective jurors in October 1962.[19]

Did you ever speak to Partin about tampering with the jury? "No," Tweel said with a genial smile, "and I'm certain about what I have heard at this point from the courtroom if I had had any such conversation with Mr. Partin it would have been recorded."[20]

After Hooker completed his questioning, Silets conducted a brief, supportive examination, introducing a couple of letters confirming discussions between Tweel and Dorfman regarding properties in which they were interested.[21] Tweel once again leveled accusations against Neal: "[He had] threatened to indict me if I didn't change my testimony at the last meeting I had in Nashville, Tennessee." Though he was warned that his wife and children were in danger, Tweel added, he did not believe any such statement. This closing remark seemed to buttress defense arguments that witnesses who refused to perjure themselves—like Tweel—would be transformed into defendants.[22]

To support Tweel's testimony, the defense offered a series of minor witnesses. Vann A. Bagby, Tweel's accountant, testified that he had begun talking with Tweel in October 1962 about an "analysis of income and expenses dealing with two buildings of which Mr. Tweel was interested." Bagby had met Dorfman at the organizational meeting of the American Hemisphere Life Insurance Company on October 12, 1962. No mention had been made of Hoffa. Tweel's personal attorney and banker, moreover, confirmed that they had both worked with Tweel on the purchase of the properties with which Dorfman had also been involved.[23]

Tweel's amiable testimony did not do much to move the needle one way or the other with respect to count four of the indictment. He admitted that he was improbably in Nashville, a city that he never otherwise visited, at the beginning of the Test Fleet trial. There, he had met with Dorfman, Hall, and Partin as alleged—not to mention dining with the three men accused of making the "Allen from the *Banner*" calls. Tweel had reviewed a jury list. But he was adamant that all of the aforementioned interactions had related to legitimate business opportunities. Indeed, supporting witnesses had confirmed that those business dealings were very real. In the end, one did have to question why a man from West Virginia would be called on to help influence jurors in Tennessee.

———

Tweel's testimony occupied the entire first day of the week. The following day, a rainy Tuesday, February 18, it was Allen Dorfman's turn. The forty-one-year-old was the second-most prominent defendant after Hoffa. His stepfather, Paul "Red" Dorfman, was reputed to have been a Capone associate in Chicago, and his underworld ties ran deep throughout the Midwest. Despite his lack of prior experience in the insurance industry, by 1964 Dorfman presided over what *Reader's Digest* referred to as "a head-reeling complex of agencies and companies that cash in on Teamster welfare-fund insurance, on the required bonding of Teamster officials—and more." Over eight years, Dorfman received more than $3 million from his business with the union. To the general public, he served as an obvious link between Hoffa's Teamsters and organized crime.[24]

Those connections were never raised during Dorfman's brief examination by fellow Illinoisan Harvey Silets. Dorfman was a magnetic witness who exuded a calm credibility. "He is quiet and seldom smiles," the *Detroit News* commented. The University of Illinois graduate had served in the Marine Corps, where he rose to the rank of captain, receiving a Purple Heart after having been wounded at Iwo Jima. He had worked as a physical education instructor at his alma mater, before entering the insurance business.[25] Much of Dorfman's testimony mirrored Tweel's. He explained that he had met Tweel in early 1962 in connection with a company planning to produce a self-lighting cigarette; Dorfman hoped to obtain midwestern distribution rights for the product. In October 1962, he had planned to meet Tweel in New York to discuss some business properties and the possibility of Dorfman's company becoming the exclusive service agency for Tweel's American Hemisphere Life Insurance Company. Dorfman described the circumstances under which he moved this meeting to Nashville: "[I received a call from Hoffa] requesting that I have certain [insurance] documents brought down to Nashville in conjunction with his trial."[26]

In Nashville, Dorfman had spoken with Tweel about business matters. While he conceded that he might have looked over a jury list at the courthouse, he maintained, "I never discussed a jury list with Mr. Tweel." In addition, Dorfman insisted that he had never engaged in an effort to manipulate the jury. At the hotel, Dorfman had met Partin. "I introduced Mr. Partin to Mr. Tweel," he said, "and I left shortly thereafter because I had to get my plane." During a subsequent visit to Nashville, Dorfman had called Tweel from the Union Station to discuss business matters. Due to static on the line, he had tried the call again, ten to fifteen minutes later, from a phone booth down the street. All of their conversations had been strictly about business. He never read a jury list to anyone. He had never met Dallas Hall, and he had never spoken to Hazel Fulton. When asked if he had ever been charged with a crime, Dorfman responded that he never had been, adding neatly that he was also innocent of the charges pending before him in Chattanooga.[27]

After only fifteen minutes, Neal took over the examination. Under brisk questioning, Dorfman explained that he had met Hoffa in 1947 or 1948. Despite possessing only two years' experience in the insurance industry at the time, by 1950 Dorfman had been handed the Teamsters' sizable insurance business, and his income had increased "substantially"—possibly fivefold. He insisted, though, that he had obtained the business through competitive bidding. He had also invested with Hoffa in the Whispering Pines Ranch camp in Wisconsin, the Northwestern Oil Company, and the Jack-O-Lantern Lodge.

During a baffling, objection-riddled recitation of times, airline tickets, and telephone calls, Neal attempted to highlight Dorfman's association with the criminal underworld. Do you know Al Dirisio? he asked. When Dorfman denied familiarity with the man, Neal referenced the alias "Milwaukee Phil."

Silets objected. "I don't know Milwaukee Phil from One-Eyed Jack and neither does he," he argued. "Now, but to leave an inference with the jury about somebody called Milwaukee Phil or Gimpy Pete or something that has nothing to do with this lawsuit and he knows it." The objection was overruled. Reluctantly, Dorfman admitted that he did in fact know the notorious Chicago mobster and hit man.[28]

As Neal tried to work his way through the complex maze of telephone calls to and from Dorfman in 1962, Jacques Schiffer complained that telephone records being shown to the witness had not been disclosed to the defense. A surprised Judge Wilson cleared the courtroom. When he asked Schiffer to swear under oath that he had never received the records, Schiffer backtracked. "I can't say I have never seen these records."

Judge Wilson was beside himself. "You made the statement in the presence of the jury that you haven't," he responded tautly. Unless Schiffer could swear to that statement, it was time to return the jury and move forward.

Neal was incensed. "He questions a lawyer's integrity and said he didn't believe those had ever been turned over," he protested.

"What I am saying, Your Honor," Schiffer said, regaining his footing, "is very simple, I don't like, and I want the record to reflect that, Mr. Durkin came in here and surreptitiously pulled records out of his pocket. Now, let me say if those records had been shown to us he didn't have to come stealing into the courtroom like some thief of some kind and go to his pocket and hand these things up to Mr. Neal." By that time, though, Schiffer had squandered any latitude he might have had with the court. If there was no showing that the records had been improperly withheld, it was time to continue Dorfman's testimony.[29]

On redirect, Silets asked Dorfman whether he would ever be so foolish as to stand in an open phone booth while reading out a jury list, as accused by the prosecution. It was a softball question. "No, sir," Dorfman responded confidently, adding that the phone booth was across the street from the courthouse, where the FBI maintained its Nashville offices. He would have been crazy, he said, to choose such a location for an untoward purpose.[30]

After two hours of questioning, Dorfman stepped down. A series of supportive witnesses followed, corroborating his testimony about his business involvements with Tweel. An Illinois attorney, Alvin Baron, testified that he had reviewed brochures Dorfman had sent him for several available West Virginia properties. Sol Schwartz, Dorfman's insurance partner, confirmed that the insurance company was under consideration to become the exclusive agency for Tweel's American Hemisphere Insurance Company. Finally, the president of Dorfman's insurance company corroborated that Dorfman had called him on October 20, 1962, and asked him to gather some insurance-related documents Hoffa needed in Nashville.[31]

Not much could be gleaned from Dorfman's brief appearance. He had to admit that he had met with Tweel and Partin in Nashville and that he might have read over a jury list while visiting the Test Fleet trial. Certainly, he had an undeniable incentive to help his cash cow—Hoffa. Dorfman's explanation of his business dealings, however, made practical sense, and it was corroborated by the witnesses who testified in his wake.[32]

The defense was content with its handling of count four. No one could point to any actual attempt to bribe, influence, or even contact a juror by Tweel, Dorfman, or Hall. The explanation of how Dorfman and Tweel ended up in Nashville on the eve of the Test Fleet trial was reasonable, and a string of seemingly impartial witnesses had corroborated the defendants' legitimate business interests. The defense was well advised to quit while they were ahead. Attention was therefore turned to count three.

FIFTEEN

"Mr. Partin has testified that his troubles arose and were created by
his association with the Teamsters. We are prepared to show that
his troubles arose and were created basically by dope addiction
and too much female company, other than his wife."

—James Haggerty

FINISHED WITH COUNT FOUR, lawyers for the defendants
yet again took up the subject of government recordings. Neal responded that
the defense had alleged nothing *illegal*. A party to the phone calls (Partin)
had recorded them; that was not unlawful, and it was certainly not wiretapping. Silets objected to Neal's "play on words," arguing that he was "passing
himself upon the legality or illegality of the recordings." It was not Neal's
place to do so. Judge Wilson ordered the government to respond to the
charges in writing.[1]

With that issue left pending, the defense called William Hawk Daniels, the administrative assistant to Baton Rouge district attorney Sargent Pitcher. The fifty-year-old raconteur had worked as a spy for the Office of Strategic Service during World War II, and he had served with the counterintelligence corps in Korea. It had been Daniels whom Partin had first contacted to report his claims concerning Hoffa.[2] In September 1962, Daniels testified, Partin had asked for a meeting, and they had met in the warden's office of the East Baton Rouge Parish Jail, where the beefy Teamster was incarcerated. The two men spoke for an hour the next day at the district attorney's office, at which time Partin first mentioned Hoffa.

By October 6, Partin had been relocated to a Baton Rouge Holiday Inn, where Daniels also stayed in order to keep his eye on him. "He had long before given me to understand that he had to contact Mr. Hoffa," Daniels explained, and on October 8 Daniels listened in as Partin telephoned the IBT boss. Daniels confirmed that the call was recorded with an IBM battery-operated recorder the district attorney's office had provided.

A second call to Hoffa was tape-recorded on October 18. These were the *only two tapes made*, Daniels insisted; both were provided to the government. He conceded that there was no way for Hoffa to have known that the calls were being recorded.

On October 20 or 21, Daniels accompanied Partin to Atlanta. There, DOJ attorney Frank Grimsley asked Partin "would he keep his ears and eyes open and report any attempt at witness intimidation or tampering with the jury" while in Nashville. Partin agreed, and he was given a telephone number and instructed to report any incidents to Grimsley or Sheridan.[3] On cross-examination, Daniels was confronted with the accusation that Partin had been "excused from the jail house" in exchange for spying on behalf of the government. Daniels was adamant. "Positively not, sir." His office had no control over such decisions. He did admit, however, that on October 7 (conveniently, the day before his first call to Hoffa), a new bond was placed on Partin. It would be up to the jury to determine whether this tight sequence of events was more than a mere coincidence.[4]

———

The defense turned to count three, calling Thomas Ewing Parks to the stand. Reporters described the stoop-shouldered, sad-eyed witness as "reticent and dour." He cut a shabby figure as he walked quietly to and from the federal courthouse. Parks told the jury that he had been employed by a dry-cleaning business in 1962. While on his way home from Carlton's Cleaners one day in October, Nashville patrolman James Walker approached him and asked him to "come out to his place of business about 5 o'clock that same afternoon." Parks did as he was asked, and Walker then gave him some money. As Parks recalled, the patrolman "said he had an assignment from the government, the federal government, and he wanted me to help him out on a little detail that for the reasons of his own he wanted it did that way." Parks admitted he had passed the money on to Carl Fields, but only because a police officer had told him to do so.

Later that night, Walker called to see how the meeting had gone. When Parks reported that he had not heard back from Fields, he was told to telephone the young man. Fields, though, said that his mother had told him not to get involved. "Well, you know Mr. Walker is a policeman," Parks urged, "it wouldn't be anything illegal, I don't think." Still, Fields expressed unease. He offered to return the money, but Parks told him to give it back to Walker himself.[5]

As for the series of telephone calls between himself and Campbell, Parks said that three of his relatives in Louisville had passed away in late 1962, so it was not unusual that he would have spoken to relatives there during that time frame. Also, his family had been working to secure the release of his sister, Audrey, from the Northville Mental Institution in Michigan. In early 1963, they had succeeded, and she had been relocated to Nashville.

Well, Schiffer asked, if you were innocent as you now claim, why had you found it necessary to take the Fifth Amendment before the grand jury? Walker had told him to do so, Parks said, because he did not have a lawyer. Once again, he was simply following the advice of an officer of the law, who certainly knew better than he did.

As prior witnesses had done, Parks charged that government representatives had pressured him to testify against Hoffa. He had met with Sheridan, who "said he was as high as they go in the Justice Department." Sheridan had reminded him that he was facing a charge for not paying income tax one year; Sheridan, Parks recalled, "told me I wouldn't have to worry about that income tax indictment if I would just go along with the program that he had on" and offer information against Hoffa, Bufalino, and Campbell. "I could take my choice of any city in the United States with government protection," Parks said. "I could even change my name if I was scared." When Parks responded that he would not make up false accusations, Sheridan sweetened the offer, promising to overlook his nephew (Campbell) in any future indictment because "it was Mr. Hoffa he was interested in." Parks however, insisted that he would not lie.[6]

Hooker handled the cross-examination. Yes, Parks conceded, he had given $100 to Carl Fields and kept $25 for himself. Parks stressed the fact that he had been told to do so by a policeman, who surely would not ask him to do anything unlawful.

When asked whether he had ever told Carl Fields that he could earn $5,000 for himself and another $5,000 for his father if he would talk to his father about the Test Fleet trial, Parks misstepped a bit.

"Mr. Hooker," he replied, shaking his head, "I might tell you that any $5,000 that I am going to handle for anybody is going to be first my $5,000."

Hooker grinned. "In other words, you wanted at least part of that?" It certainly did Parks no favors for jurors to hear him remark, even sarcastically, that he would have wanted in on any kickbacks.

Hooker had Parks on the ropes. Schiffer remained uncharacteristically (and surprisingly) quiet while his putative client was battered by the veteran attorney. Why didn't Schiffer level his characteristic bombast on Hooker in support of his own client? "He doesn't look natural just sitting there," one observer quipped. Although it allowed Hooker to slice through his questioning quickly, Schiffer's unexpected passivity raised some questions as to where his real interests lay—with his longtime associate Hoffa, or with his nominal client Parks.

Parks's testimony did make some sense. Despite their somewhat suspicious timing, the flurry of calls between himself and Campbell during the Test Fleet trial had a decent explanation. One could also understand why he would go along with the demands of someone like Walker, simply presuming that a police officer would not be involved in any untoward activities. Even so, Parks's testimony raised some pesky issues. Like other defendants, he was forced to admit that at least some of the facts were true. He *had* met with Walker and Fields. Parks could not deny, moreover, that he had passed money to Carl Fields—and that he had kept some for himself.

———

The defense counsel remained haunted by Partin and felt that a more solid counterpunch was needed. To discredit the government's star witness, they would take the offense with incendiary witnesses of their own. The first was Sol Fox, who claimed he was involved in the real estate business in Puerto Rico. When Schiffer asked about a report Fox had made to the FBI regarding Partin, Neal objected. The jury was removed. What is the purpose of this testimony? Judge Wilson inquired.

"Ed Partin called Mr. Fox, this witness here, in Puerto Rico to endeavor to enlist his aid in securing ships to carry arms to Fidel Castro in the end of ... 1962 into 1963," Schiffer said confidently. "I want to be able to show that this type of evidence in and of itself is sufficient to discredit the credibility of the government's star witness, Ed Partin, as committing a treasonous act against the United States." The explosive Cuba issue had been addressed several times previously, but Schiffer would not give it up. Judge Wilson ruled that the parties could question Fox in the absence of the jury at the end of the day, but he would not allow the witness to testify in front of the jury that morning.[7]

As the day wound to a close, Fox reappeared. The jury was not in the courtroom. In November 1962, Fox offered, he had received a call from Partin about acquiring boats. When he asked what the boats would be carrying, Partin told Fox, "I have got a terrific connection in Cuba with people connected with Castro," adding, "We want to haul munitions, guns [and] war materials to Cuba."

"I told him that I was no God damned communist," Fox spat, "and that he could drop dead and I slammed the phone down and that was the last I heard from Mr. Partin."

Fox conceded that he had never actually met Partin; he had spoken to someone who claimed to be the man. Fox also admitted that he had first reported the situation only one week earlier, on February 14—more than a year after the alleged contact. He confessed that he was friends with several Hoffa associates. Was he close friends with Hoffa? "I couldn't say," he replied. "I like him as a gentleman."

Schiffer pleaded with the court to allow this provocative testimony, which would surely condemn Partin in the eyes of the jury. "It's about time the government took the position in this case where they indict their own witness for treason," Schiffer implored. "They are looking to protect him even when he commits treason." The information, however, was simply irrelevant. While it might arouse indignation toward Partin, and while it might create questions as to whether he had engaged in seditious acts in 1962, it had little to do with his credibility. Neal moved to exclude the testimony, and the court agreed.[8]

The next witness would be even more incendiary. The government had had its surprise star witness; so would the defense. Photographers clamored to take pictures as the mysterious man made his way to the courthouse. Trailed by a burly, anonymous associate, he paid no notice to the swarm of newsmen chasing after him; he stared straight ahead, jaw set, an unlit pipe jutting out of the corner of his mouth.

What is the purpose of this witness? Judge Wilson inquired. "The purpose is to show the whole frame-up against the Defendant Parks and everybody else connected with this case," Schiffer replied, "and the activities of the Department of Justice and certain members of it to frame each and every individual here standing before this Court." Out of an abundance of caution, Judge Wilson allowed the jury to hear from the witness.[9]

Fred Shobe took the stand. The court had previously concluded that his testimony was a rambling, irrelevant, inappropriate mess. Now, though, the jury would be allowed to hear his story. Shobe, whom newspaper accounts described as shifty, scared, and barely able to keep his eyes open, was an eccentric witness at the very least. He described himself as an agent provocateur who had worked for Sheridan. His role had been "to harass, embarrass in any way, with the cooperation of people from the Bureau of Labor Management Relations, Mr. Hoffa and the Teamsters Union." In June 1963, Shobe said, he had been sent to Louisville to frequent Brown's Tourist Home and Joe's Palm Room "with the view toward finding someone who would state that Campbell or Charles O'Brien had made incriminating comments about their interest in the Hoffa trial." Did he still work for the government? "That is a matter of doubt," Shobe replied. He had last heard from Sheridan approximately one month earlier, on January 15.

Indicating that the relevance of the witness's testimony was unclear, Judge Wilson removed the jury from the courtroom. Under further examination, Shobe claimed to be a member of the Get Hoffa Squad. While the government would prefer to find something that incriminated Hoffa directly, he said, "to get him by any means, fair or foul" was the ultimate objective. "If we had to resort to unfair tactics," Shobe declared, "well, that's where a person like myself comes in at."[10] To that end, Shobe had been assigned to tail Parks in Nashville. When Shobe contacted Bishop St. Psalm, a religious leader and magazine publisher in Nashville's black community, for help, he was told that "Mr. Hoffa hadn't done anything to him and the government hadn't ever done anything for the Negro." If, however, the government convinced someone to purchase advertising space in St. Psalm's magazine, he would see what he could do about Parks. Shobe then went to St. Psalm's home, where the bishop conducted a voodoo ceremony, lighting candles on a portable altar onto which he placed an item—"a darned pencil stub or some cleaning tags"—from Parks's cleaning business. The bishop assured Shobe that, in two or three days, "if someone suggested to [Parks] that he was a dog[,] . . .

he would get on his knees and bark." By this bizarre tactic, Shobe explained, Parks could be convinced to turn on Campbell, O'Brien, and possibly Hoffa himself.

Shobe had also met with "Good Jelly" Jones, a "Negro political figure" in Nashville. Jones had taken the witness to several political clubs, where he sermonized, "Inasmuch as Mr. Kennedy and his administration were laying, putting their necks on the line for the many Civil Rights demonstrations that were going on at that time," blacks should recognize their obligation to help fulfill the government's objective of getting Hoffa and his associates.[11]

Shobe then turned to a bizarre plan to kidnap Parks. "I had noticed that Mr. Parks sat out in from of Tom's Cleaners either on a milk crate or on a half a chair," he explained. "And I felt that it would be comparatively easy for myself and a couple of companions to pull up there and unostensibly [sic] arrest Mr. Parks and tell him that he was wanted downtown and someone wanted to talk to him." The would-be kidnappers would use this explanation so that Parks wouldn't struggle. Once inside the car, however, they would handcuff, blindfold, and gag Parks before driving him to a park in East Nashville, and his associates would then drag their captive into the woods, dig a grave, remove his blindfold, and tell him it was "just a rub-out"—that Hoffa had ordered him to be killed. With any luck, Parks would turn on Hoffa. If not, however, "officers would suddenly burst through the woods and we would flee and there would be a flurry of shots," which might make Parks grateful to the government for his rescue. "So you see this was a thing that had to be played by ear," Shobe stated, shrugging. Either way, Parks would turn against Hoffa.[12]

A pause in the proceedings. Clearly unimpressed with this rambling cascade of screwy allegations, Judge Wilson asked the defense, "Do you in good faith believe it is admissible [before the jury]?"

"We certainly think so," replied Schiffer assuredly.

Berke was not so confident, conceding, "I say that some of the evidence is not competent. . . . Some of the evidence we say is."

"It would appear to the Court," Wilson declared, frowning over his glasses, "that it was obvious to any competent attorney that a great bulk of this witness' testimony could not possibly be competent."

Branstetter could sense the direction in which things were drifting. "I don't want a statement by the court on the record that it is offered by all defendants on all parts," he said.

"Gentlemen," Judge Wilson said, "let's do this, let's proceed with the trial of this case in good faith with the Court and let the attorneys proceed in good faith and let's offer witnesses that we think in good faith have competent testimony to offer." Any further discussion of Shobe would be put on pause. The jury, which had been exposed to only a few abortive moments of Shobe's testimony, would be left to speculate as to his precise role in the case.

Obviously misconstruing the court's warning, Schiffer made a bold announcement: "We will call Mr. Sheridan."

Judge Wilson was finished with entertaining wild tales about the unfair tactics of the government. "Gentlemen," he sighed, "we are trying to try this lawsuit." It was time to move on from cloak-and-dagger accusations and focus on the claims of jury tampering.

A resigned Schiffer stated that he had no other witnesses on behalf of Parks and took his seat.[13]

——

The questioning was turned over to Branstetter, who called Larry Campbell to the stand. The witness was a flashy dresser, often pictured wearing shiny, thick-striped jackets and loud ties. Walking down the street during lunchtime breaks he sported dark shades. Campbell's graying hair was a counterpoint to his youthful, boyish face, and his fixed smile projected mild-mannered affability throughout the proceedings. Appointed to his post by Hoffa, Campbell had been the first black business agent at Detroit Local 299. "Teamsters officials invited him into the leadership circle," the *Detroit News* noted, "after he successfully organized parking lot attendants in Detroit." In 1959, during the McClellan Committee hearings, Campbell countered accusations of race discrimination on the part of the Teamsters. "These implications and accusations regarding discrimination against Negroes by Mr. Hoffa and Local 299 are false," he testified. "I know this to be true because I am a Negro member of Local 299 and I am proud to say that I am also a business representative for Local 299."[14]

Believing the circumstantial evidence against his client did not amount to much, Branstetter propelled Campbell through his testimony as quickly as possible. The thirty-nine-year-old testified that he had served in World War II, attaining the rank of sergeant. In 1953 or 1954 he had joined Local 299, serving as a business representative. In the fall of 1962, Campbell had been sent to Louisville to encourage minority employees to support the union during an organizational campaign.

Campbell said that he had made telephone calls to Detroit to update local 299 leadership as to the status of the Louisville labor campaign. He had placed some of the calls from Brown's Guest House, where he was staying, and others from Joe's Palm Room, one of the spots where he spoke with potential union supporters. Corroborating Parks's testimony, Campbell said that the remainder of his calls to Detroit and Nashville had related to efforts to get a family member released from a Michigan mental hospital. To back up that point, he identified a September 1, 1962, letter discussing that situation.

Campbell asserted that he had never even been in Tennessee in 1962. He had had nothing to do with the Test Fleet case. He had never met with anyone to discuss the case. "I don't know no Fields, period, myself," Campbell declared. Did he tamper with the jury in the Nashville case? "No, I did not."[15]

During a brief cross-examination, Campbell confirmed that he had used the telephone booths at Joe's Palm Room and Ernestine Williams's home. He also testified that he had known Hoffa for roughly a dozen years, and Dorfman for three or four. Had Campbell told Ernestine Williams that he was planning to travel to Nashville, where his boss was in trouble? No, he had never said that. Nevertheless, he conceded, "I certainly didn't want to see him [Hoffa] convicted."[16]

To substantiate Campbell's brief testimony, Branstetter called Frank Fitzsimmons, the president of Local 299 in Detroit. The "phlegmatic, pumpkin-faced 66-year old with a heavy belly" had quit school at age sixteen and gone to work after his father suffered a stroke. At Hoffa's insistence, he had been named international vice president of the union in 1961, after the death of Owen Bert Brennan. Ridiculed by some as "Hoffa's errand boy," Fitzsimmons was a Hoffa stalwart.[17] He testified that he had dispatched Campbell to assist with an organizing campaign in Louisville, which was not out of the ordinary. From time to time, Fitzsimmons had also sent him to Chicago, Nashville, and other cities.[18]

Neal cross-examined the witness, forcing him to agree that Louisville was not a "surrounding area" of Detroit. The General Electric plant in Louisville, moreover, was not even a Teamster facility, but rather was affiliated with the IBEW. Certainly, one could question why a Detroit Teamster would be needed to help out with an IBEW campaign in faraway Kentucky.[19]

As the lawyers clapped their briefcases shut at the end of the day on February 19, Harry Berke announced that Partin's estranged wife would be appearing at the courthouse the following day, accompanied by her pastor. "It appears that she is a deeply religious woman apparently," he said, "but the main thing that she is concerned about is fear at the hands of her husband." Judge Wilson instructed that arrangements would be made to ensure her security while in Chattanooga.

The following morning, Norma Jean Partin stepped to the stand. "Do I have the privilege not to testify?" she asked Judge Wilson. Once again, the jury was removed. Scanning a courtroom bench lined with local lawyers, Wilson asked attorney Ben Cash whether he would consult with Mrs. Partin. Cash agreed and led the reluctant witness out of the courtroom.

A displeased Judge Wilson looked to the defense for an explanation. "I have talked with her," Haggerty remarked, "and her testimony certainly is competent." He presented an offer of proof as to what Mrs. Partin would say. In 1960, she had learned that her husband was maintaining an extramarital affair with a so-called "hustler." Confronted with the situation, Partin had explained, "I am not responsible for the difficulties that I am in and the way I am acting. It is due to dope addiction." He had agreed to consult with a psychiatrist (Dr. Levin Magruder) as a condition of being allowed to return home. Ms. Partin would also testify that she had observed syringes and bottles, as well as puncture wounds and scabs on her husband's arms.

"Mr. Partin has testified that his troubles arose and were created by his association with the Teamsters," Haggerty asserted. "We are prepared to show that his troubles arose and were created basically by dope addiction and too much female company, other than his wife." Asked about the rule that a wife cannot be compelled to testify against her husband, Haggerty responded that the two were estranged. As Judge Wilson pointed out, however, no final order of divorce had been issued. The Partins were still married.

Returning to the courtroom, Norma Jean Partin informed the court unequivocally, "I do not wish to testify against E.G. Partin." With that, she was excused from the courtroom. Defense lawyers would have to find another way to attack Ed Partin.

In the coming days, they would unveil several.[20]

———

Thursday, February 20. Outside, temperatures were dropping, and flurries were expected. The final witness called on Campbell's behalf was Marion M. Winstead, the secretary-treasurer of IBT Local 89 in Louisville. Campbell had visited that city in 1962, he stated, "to assist us in contacting the Negro workers at the General Electric plant." The witness confirmed that an election petition was submitted to the National Labor Relations Board on October 25 of that year—the same time frame in which Campbell had assisted with the campaign.[21]

Taken as a whole, the brief testimony offered with respect to Campbell did not reveal much. Without a doubt, the ties between Campbell and the Test Fleet case were attenuated. There was no evidence that he had been in Nashville in 1962, or that he had ever spoken to a juror about anything. He had admittedly talked with Parks numerous times throughout the trial, but he had a colorable explanation for those calls. Still, the justification for Campbell's sojourn in Louisville seemed somewhat implausible, particularly given the fact that the organizing campaign he had purportedly assisted was in a remote state—and on behalf of a different union from the one to which he belonged.

SIXTEEN

"I feel like I am tired, and need a vacation."

—Jim Neal

TWO FIGURES SPRAWLED in the back seat of the cab as it passed through downtown Chattanooga late on Friday, February 21. Doug Partin, the brother of the government's key witness, was leaving for Baton Rouge. Sitting next to him was Billy Simpson, the twenty-two-year-old Teamster whose domestic problems had led to kidnapping charges against Ed Partin. The two smoked and chatted as they rolled toward the Farmers Curb Grill Café, where they planned to grab a bite to eat while waiting for their scheduled 1:55 a.m. departure from the Chattanooga bus station.[1] The defense would be glad to see them go. According to Hoffa, Doug Partin had interfered with witnesses during his stay in the town, telling one, "Take the Fifth or you will be in trouble." He had also accosted a witness who had criticized his brother, threatening, "We will take care of it when we get back to Baton Rouge."

Stepping from the cab, Partin and Simpson headed for the restaurant. At that late hour, no one was inside except a waitress. Just after they settled into a booth and ordered their drinks, a gang of men appeared, accusing Partin and Simpson of being "dirty, stinking feds" and angling for a fight. A wild brawl ensued. Simpson ran and found a pay phone. Doug Partin never made it. He was beaten with a pool cue, kicked in the face, and struck repeatedly until he lost consciousness. He suffered cuts, internal injuries, a broken nose, and several loosened teeth. He was, he recalled, hospitalized for weeks.[2]

Count five, the allegation that Ewing King had offered a promotion to patrolman James Paschal to influence his wife to vote for acquittal, was the final allegation of the indictment the defense addressed. Harold Brown stepped to the lectern and called King forward. The media pulled no punches in its assessment of the witness, calling him "expressionless," "gangling," and "a tall, blank-faced man with no chin." The former president of Teamsters Local 327 in Nashville had been born on "a poor hill farm" in Middle Tennessee. After a stint in the Civilian Conservation Corps, King had become a truck driver in Nashville and then, in 1953, a business agent for Local 327. Although King had been the president of the local during the Test Fleet trial, he had recently lost his bid for reelection.[3]

In his official capacity, King had been at the courthouse "almost every day" during the Test Fleet trial. He had known Oscar Pitts for nine or ten years, and on November 17, 1962, he had met with Pitts at his home. King denied that a "beagle" code signal had been created. In reality, he said, "[Pitts had] asked me if I could come down and talk to him about arranging to get some more beagle hounds for a hunt Thanksgiving because one of his dogs had died and he thought he knew where we could buy some dogs together." As for the automobile switch, King had traded cars with George Broda so that they could explore a possible trade.

King insisted that he was genuinely interested in getting a promotion for Paschal. Pitts, along with a number of other local truck drivers, had asked him "many times" to try to help the patrolman. To that end, Pitts had asked King to speak with Paschal on November 17. Although it was admittedly late, Pitts implored, "This will get him[Paschal] off of my back if he[King] will do it."

Asked where the three men had met, King replied, "We met him at the arranged place by the spring down there just off of the main road on a little side road just over the bank from the spring where they had set up to meet."

There, Paschal had brought up the Test Fleet case, asking, "What is going to happen to your boy Hoffa in Nashville?"

According to King, he had simply responded, "I do not believe anything will happen to him, Mr. Paschal, if he gets a fair trial."

When Paschal offered that his wife was on the jury, King had stopped him. "Now, look," he had scolded, "I don't want to discuss your wife if she is on the jury and I know she is as well as you do, we just better not discuss that." King's explanation was tidy, if a touch sanctimonious.[4]

After leaving Paschal, King had sipped a cup of coffee at Pitts's house and then returned home around 2:00 a.m. On his way home, he came upon a car parked across the road with its hood up. "We'll be out of your way in a min-ute," the occupants told him. According to King, he had been surveilled by "as much as four cars" throughout the Test Fleet trial. This disabled vehicle, he said, was clearly part of the ongoing FBI surveillance that had plagued him during the case.[5]

King reported that in January 1963 Sheridan and Neal had spoken with him at his home: "[They told me that] if I was willing to cooperate . . . to help them get Hoffa, that they felt that they could help me." Yet again, the defense asserted, illicit pressure had been placed on witnesses to turn on Hoffa and assist the government. After a brief, thirty-minute examination, Harold Brown announced that he was finished with the witness.[6]

———

An antagonistic and condescending Hooker conducted one of the most scath-ing cross-examinations of the trial. "Grinning like a possum," Hooker elicited King's admission that Hoffa had come to Nashville to stump for him during the Local 327 election, which occurred in the wake of the Test Fleet trial. There was no question that the two men were connected and that King owed a personal debt to his IBT boss.[7] At Martin's restaurant on the Murfreesboro Pike, King explained, he had traded his blue Thunderbird for George Broda's 1959 two-door sedan. Yes, it was the same night as his meeting with Paschal; it was somewhat suspicious timing, indeed. King had sat alone at Pitts's house while Mutt went out "after some Coca-Colas and cold drinks." As for the odd, rain-soaked location of the meeting, King commented, "You well know for us country people it's not uncommon to meet at a spring or around some hill or some place by the side of the road to have a meeting or discuss problems."

Hooker scoffed. "What kind of country people do you know that meet at springs on rainy nights after twelve o'clock?"

"In my opinion," King calmly replied, "the best people they are, Mr. Hooker, is this type people that will go out of their way to try to help someone."

Hooker's livid disdain for King was plain. He asked King whether he had approached Paschal to discuss Betty Paschal's role on the Test Fleet jury.

"Mr. Hooker," King replied, shaking his head, "do I look stupid enough—"

"Don't ask me that question," Hooker cut him off, eying the jury suggestively.[8]

Emboldened, Hooker turned to the proffered reason for King's improbable journey to Woodbury. The dead beagle story was true, King insisted. Hooker scorned the farfetched tale. You really want the jury to believe you went to Pitts's house on the night of November 17 to talk about buying coon dogs? he asked.

"Mr. Hooker," King sniggered, "you don't hunt rabbits with coon dogs."

Grinning, Hooker turned to the jury. It was a moment made for a seasoned trial attorney. "You wasn't hunting rabbits that night," he drawled, "you were hunting jurors, weren't you?" Harold Brown shot to his feet and demanded a mistrial. Judge Wilson denied the motion, but he instructed Hooker to refrain from extraneous commentary in front of the jury.[9]

Brown asked only a single question on redirect examination: "Mr. King, since you have arrived at this trial, have you been under surveillance constantly?"

"I have, sir," King responded solemnly. With that simple assertion hanging in the air, Brown and King returned to their seats.[10]

———

The defense offered a trio of character witnesses to vouch for King and confirm that he was known to frequently trade automobiles. As Brown moved to introduce a fourth such witness, Judge Wilson cut him off, noting a court rule limiting such bolstering to a total of three character witnesses.[11]

Next, the defense offered Paschal's best friend, who said that he had asked King to try to get Paschal a promotion. A second witness testified that he had asked King to help his son get a promotion on the Nashville police force. Thus, it was not strange for King to try to assist officers seeking advancement within the police department.

Throughout the trial, the primary battlefront for the defense involved government allegations of jury tampering. Over time, though, excluding or dis-
crediting the damning testimony of the government's chief witness became
equally important. To that end, the defense turned once again to Partin,
and Branstetter undertook a "grueling questioning" of DOJ attorney
Frank Grimsley. On two or three occasions in September or October 1962,
Grimsley said, he had met with Partin in Baton Rouge. He had been made
aware of two tapes of conversations between Partin and Hoffa. These were
the surreptitious recordings that seemed to confirm the federal government's
inappropriate surveillance *and* Partin's perjurious testimony that no recordings had been made.

As Branstetter began to probe into the surveillance of Hoffa, though, Judge
Wilson interrupted. Was the defense attempting to ignore his instruction
that the topic of surveillance would be taken up at a later date? It was not
a surveillance issue, Branstetter insisted. "I am seeking to impeach Partin
and show that he lied from the witness stand when he said he knew nothing
about telephone recordation."

Convinced that the court was willfully ignoring evidence that might wreck
the credibility of the government's lynchpin witness, a fervent Schiffer leapt
in. He directed his indignation toward not only the government, but also
the court itself. "I say the prosecution succeeded in making Your Honor an
assistant prosecutor in this case and is using this court," he charged, "in an
attempt, without knowledge of the defendants, to make this court an adjunct
of the prosecutor without informing the defendants of that."

Schiffer was dancing on the end of a brittle limb, but he did not stop. The
court, he noted, had never advised the defense that it had been aware of the
two recordings, which the prosecution filed on February 10. Instead, the court
had ordered the records sealed. "Now, then," Schiffer argued, "how can the
Court—, I beg of Your Honor—, how can the Court be used as an adjunct
to the prosecutor to hide evidence and no where [*sic*] in the record disclose
that these are recordings?"

"Mr. Schiffer," Judge Wilson leveled, "are you accusing the Court of hiding
evidence?"

Schiffer skidded to a halt. "I say the prosecution used the Court for that
purpose the way they did it with you, Judge, they didn't make a full and clean
disclosure to you. They hid the information from you and they hid it from
us." He banged a hand on the podium. "This is chicanery, not law."

In his copy of the transcript, Wilson once again made a series of pencil marks in the margin next to Schiffer's words, highlighting a topic to which he would return.[12]

———

Still on the stand, Grimsley's attention turned to the series of $300 checks that had been sent to Norma Jean Partin in July–October 1963. As Grimsley related, the checks were sent to her because Ed Partin had "wanted his wife and kids to have money. He said he could take care of himself." The checks represented reimbursement for expenses in the amount of $1,200. Although some additional expenses were due to Partin, Grimsley offered, the payments had ceased after October 1963. Grimsley admitted that the outlays were equivalent to support payments due from Partin to his wife, a fact that appeared suspicious to objective observers.

"Was any promise of any payments ever made to Mr. Partin?" Branstetter inquired.

"None whatsoever."

"Was any promise of any sort of relief ever made to Mr. Partin?"

"None."

"Was Mr. Partin ever promised anything with respect to any action by anybody with the federal government so far as you know of?"

"As far as I know none has ever been."[13]

Silets, referring to the round figures as "highly irregular," remarked to the media, "This isn't the way books are kept in the government."

Hoffa was livid. The government had claimed—with a straight face—that no money had been paid to Partin. Yet here was a witness admitting that suspicious lump sums had been siphoned off, sent through obscure channels, and paid to the man's family in the months following the Test Fleet trial. During a recess, Hoffa undertook an extended rant, smearing marshals as "informers" and "stool pigeons" and confronting Neal, whom he called a "Tennessee liar." He was still hot when court adjourned. Luckily, the outburst occurred after the jury had left; only reporters, marshals, and attorneys heard his comments. "I say it here in public flatly," the IBT president barked to reporters looking for an incendiary quote, that Kennedy had "absconded with $600,000 in federal funds. He falsely and illegally spent the funds. . . . He has made no accounting of it. It's a violation of his oath of office. Neal probably handled half of it to handle cases against me—to get paid stool pigeons and perjurers." To an apoplectic Hoffa, he had clearly been set up.[14]

———

Friday, February 21, began with Fred Shobe's encore appearance before the jury. Judge Wilson announced that Shobe would be allowed to testify only with respect to his conversations with patrolman James Walker. By this ruling, the court essentially defanged the witness before he even took the stand. Journalists covering the trial did not treat Shobe with great admiration, referring to him as "a 250-pound Negro ex-convict." The *Chattanooga News-Free Press* reported that he was "somewhat groggy at times and frequently blinking his eyes." Shobe explained that the Justice Department had sent him to Nashville in advance of the 1962 trial "to stir up anti-Hoffa sentiment in Nashville's Negro community." Sheridan had asked him to investigate Carl Fields, to see "what kind of guy he was, if he was going to stand up." Shobe's testimony was "weird" and "incoherent," and the *Chattanooga Times* labeled it "a long, rambling, and often disconnected story . . . a conglomerate mass of eerie cloak-and-dagger episodes, mixed with a smidgen of voodooism and accounts of ordinary surveillance work."

Schiffer handled Shobe's questioning. While Judge Wilson had already specifically limited the scope of the witness's testimony, Schiffer felt strongly that the jury should know the depth of the government's corruption, and he therefore needed to question Shobe about Tom Parks. One way or another, he had to get Sheridan's bizarre kidnapping scheme in front of the jury; when he sensed an appropriate moment, therefore, the impetuous Schiffer brought up the plan in which, as he put it to Shobe, "you [were] going to abduct Mr. Parks."

"The question is highly inappropriate, ladies and gentlemen," Wilson interposed. "It has nothing to do with this lawsuit and Mr. Schiffer has been instructed that it does not."

Schiffer demanded a mistrial on the basis that he was being prevented from putting on his witnesses. "We claim that the government has framed up this case against the Defendant Parks," he bellowed.

"I have given you instructions very clear and very explicitly yesterday in regard to this matter," an obviously irritated Wilson replied.

Frustrated by the constraints placed upon his questioning, Schiffer stepped back from the lectern. "I don't feel that the prosecution wants the facts to come out in this case and I will retire."

Neal was incensed. "This man has been permitted all over during a month of this trial to continue to make insulting and unjustified, untruthful remarks," he vented, "and we object to it." An exasperated Wilson repeated his instruction for the jury to disregard Schiffer's comments.[15]

The trial was wearing on everyone.

Neal returned to his seat. "I feel like I am tired," he sighed, "and need a vacation."[16]

Reporters covering the trial universally criticized Shobe and his demeanor on the witness stand. His testimony's potential damage to the prosecution, however, was undeniable. As fanciful as parts of Shobe's story appeared, no government witness was offered to refute his assertion that he had been on the inside of the Get Hoffa Squad. Shobe's testimony also stood a chance of confirming the tactics Sheridan and his operatives allegedly utilized to obtain favorable testimony. In turn, these tactics might call into question the government's entire case.

———

Birmingham Teamster William J. Reynolds was the next witness to the stand. As he began to recount a meeting between himself and Partin in 1963, though, the prosecution requested a private examination of the witness. Federal counself wanted to ensure that his testimony, unlike Shobe's, was relevant and admissible. The jury was once again removed.

"I strongly resent this procedure adopted by the Court," Haggerty complained. The only two reasons for a voir dire examination of a witness are to evaluate claims of privilege or the mental competency of the witness, he explained, and not to go on a "fishing expedition." "Any time the government has requested during the defense for a *voir dire* Your Honor has granted it without any underlying basic reason for it."

"Well, now, gentlemen," Judge Wilson sighed, "here is the problem we face. The defense the day before yesterday offered and represented that it would be competent testimony of a Mr. Fox. Now, it was abundantly obvious when that testimony was brought in that it was not competent, could not possibly be competent or relevant. The defense offered and represented unto this Court the testimony of Mr. Shobe would be competent. The great bulk of that testimony obviously was not and could not possibly be relevant or competent. We have now a question here as to whether this conversation is or is not relevant and I know of no way in the world to determine it without the Court having some idea on what the conversation is."

Neal found it a good moment to pile on. "A man who has finished his first semester of law school knows [Sol Fox's testimony] would not be competent."

"I went to night school," Schiffer remarked sarcastically from his seat at the defense table. Judge Wilson paid no attention to this aside and asked for details as to the purpose of the witness. Six months earlier, it was said, Partin had appeared in Birmingham to convince Reynolds to claim that Hoffa had offered $10,000 for Partin to get to a juror in the Test Fleet case. Reynolds would also say that the government had offered to drop criminal charges against him if he would testify against Hoffa, but that he had refused to lie in order to save himself. According to Reynolds, Partin had commented, "It is either Jimmy's neck or my neck[,] and it ain't going to be my neck." Despite the lure of substantial sums of money, however, Reynolds had rebuffed Partin, told him that he was a disgrace, and instructed him not to call again. Judge Wilson indicated that he would evaluate whether the jury could hear Reynolds's account. For the time being, though, he asked the defense to proceed with other testimony.[17]

———

Hoffa's attorneys again took up the cudgel against Partin. With the jury still outside the courtroom, Berke called Otis Tynes to the witness stand. Describing himself as a farmer and cattleman from Ethel, Louisiana, the thirty-seven-year-old testified that he had worked for seven brief months in 1960 as an organizer for Teamsters Local 5. In that role, he had become a close friend of Partin's. Over Neal's vigorous objections, Berke inquired whether Partin was addicted to narcotics. "Positively," Tynes replied. "Yes."

However, Judge Wilson disallowed Berke's follow-ups as to whether Partin was a good family man and whether he had engaged in extramarital affairs. "We are not trying a domestic relations lawsuit here in this court," Wilson stated.

Berke tried a different tack. "Do you know whether or not Mr. Partin handled guns?"

"This is getting ridiculous," Neal protested.

The judge disallowed the question, saying, "We will be here this time several years from now" without reasonable limitations on the examination of witnesses.

What was Partin's reputation in the community? Berke asked. "Bad," Tynes replied. "Very bad."[18]

On cross-examination, it was revealed that Tynes had only seen Partin twice since 1960. How could his testimony be relevant to 1964? Neal objected to the entirety of Tynes's testimony on the ground that his observations were stale; no information indicated that Partin had used narcotics during the Test

Fleet trial or while testifying in Chattanooga. Silets argued that Partin was an *habitual* addict; for that reason, observations of his drug dependence at other times were relevant. Neal countered that he had a report showing that Partin had not been addicted to narcotics at any time. All right, Silets said, if such a report exists, then the government should turn it over to the court.[19]

While the court considered Tynes's testimony, the defense continued its relentless efforts to discredit Partin through a parade of minor witnesses. Lester Bloomenstiel, who had co-owned a truck stop with Partin, testified that they owed the government $9,700 in taxes on diesel fuel that Partin had not declared on their tax returns. Although he had paid his portion, Bloomenstiel said, Partin had never paid his own. Instead, he declared, the IRS "told me that they had received orders from New Orleans not to pursue Mr. Partin any further." Bloomenstiel understood that Partin's debts were to be forgiven in exchange for some assistance provided to the government. "Evidently they are going to use Mr. Partin for something a whole lot larger, bigger."[20]

Ann Smith, who had worked as Partin's personal secretary, lambasted her former boss. "I know that he is a professional liar and that he couldn't be trusted," she offered. She also addressed his use of illicit drugs: "I saw him take the pills but I haven't seen him take the needle. I have just seen the needle and the syringe." Partin, who took little white pills that he referred to as "bennies to give him energy," had reportedly handed Smith drug paraphernalia to be locked in the safe at Local 5. Other contentions that Partin owned guns and that he had told Smith to falsify union records were disallowed. On cross-examination, Neal elicited Smith's admission that Partin had terminated her, thereby fostering the impression that she might maintain some bias against him.[21]

J. D. Lewis, director of operations for a Dallas motor freight line, declared that "[Partin's] reputation was not good in Baton Rouge." Similarly, Hoyt Tillman testified, "I am not very proud of it, but that [Partin] is my first cousin." Schiffer asked Tillman whether Partin had ever asked him to perjure himself; when the court sustained an objection to the question, Schiffer simply repeated the inquiry. Judge Wilson halted the questioning. "Mr. Schiffer," he asked, "how many times do I have to sustain the objection to the same question?"

"I am trying to attack the credibility of the government's big, star witness, Your Honor," the pugnacious lawyer responded. "I don't know how else to attack his credibility." Wilson instructed him to move on to another topic.[22]

Unemployed Teamsters Edwin Stevick and Debbie George offered that on January 17, 1964, after Hoffa had instructed Partin to remove a picket line in Louisiana, an angry Partin had confronted the union boss. If Hoffa pulled the picket line, Partin had hollered, he "would come to Chattanooga and testify against him."[23]

Several witnesses were heard in the absence of the jury. Rena Mai Booth, a nurse who had at one time worked at the truck stop Partin owned, testified that Partin had engaged in numerous sexual affairs in Alabama and Mississippi—one with a fourteen-year-old girl. Judge Wilson was obviously frustrated. "Now, Mr. Berke," he rebuked, "you offer that sort of proof and then you wonder why or ask the reason why the Court excludes the jury. How could any lawyer think that that is competent, including that testimony?" Berke took exception to the insinuation that he had offered evidence in bad faith. "Perhaps the Court," a cautious Wilson backtracked, "was over-stating the situation." The judge's frustrated criticism of Berke was perhaps the closest he came to losing control of his temper and creating an opportunity for a mistrial.

In the end, the only testimony that Booth was allowed to present to the jury related to Partin's reputation. "To me, it's bad," she said.[24]

Truck mechanic J. D. Albin and truck driver Prentice Moak echoed accounts of Partin's bad reputation. Schiffer's follow-up attempts to sneak in questions about Partin's activities in Cuba, however, were expectedly stifled. "It cannot be that you do not know that the Court has ruled upon the matter," Judge Wilson castigated. On cross, Albin did admit that he was one of the "dissidents" within Local 5. He had been "trying to remove a dictator from this local union," he said, "and that is the reason it were run with an iron hand and a bunch of goons."[25] For his part, Moak said, "[Partin] is very unruly and very double-crossing in his statements." He also claimed that Partin kept firearms in his car and that he had threatened others with fistfights. Finding his account "obviously not admissible," Wilson excluded Moak's testimony.[26]

After a lengthy review, Wilson also ruled that the disparaging testimony of Tynes, Albin, and Booth would not be aired before the jury. In any event, enough information about Partin's reputation had been submitted, and extraneous claims about the man's illicit or immoral behavior were simply irrelevant. The court ruled that no further witnesses would be allowed to testify on the subject.[27]

Pivoting, the defense would delve more deeply into the accusation that Partin was a drug addict. To that end, Baton Rouge psychiatrist Dr. Levin

Magruder took the stand. The defense counsel were hopeful; they had previously referred to Magruder as the person who would prove Partin an incompetent witness. Partin was his patient, the psychiatrist acknowledged,
and had consulted with Magruder on four occasions in August 1960. In his
opinion, Partin exhibited "some anxiety, quite a bit of anxiety and depression,"
because "he felt he was under too much pressure in his job." Partin therefore took an off-market "Excitum" type of drug that was interfering with his
sleep. Magruder prescribed the patient a tranquilizer (Librium), Dramamine
for dizziness, and an antidepressant (Nardil). These were not narcotics, he
explained, and there was no evidence that Partin had ever taken narcotics.
After only a few appointments, Partin had reported that he was doing better
and discontinued his visits. Magruder had not met with him since 1960.[28]
Thus the defense's decision to call Magruder had backfired. If anything, his
testimony had dispelled the inference that Partin was a "dope addict."

A handful of witnesses were introduced to address lingering questions about
the status of the criminal charges hanging over Partin. Peter Duffy, former
assistant US attorney, testified that his busy workload had led him to seek a
continuance of the twenty-six-count indictment against Partin. The US attorney in New Orleans, Lewis C. Lacour, confirmed that the matter was still
pending. It had not been continued indefinitely; in fact, it was not even the
oldest case on the docket in that office. It had been continued twice at Partin's
request, and four times due to the priority of other matters within the office.
Had it ever been taken off of the active calendar? No, he said.[29]

The third witness on that front was Sargent Pitcher, the Baton Rouge district attorney. Pitcher confirmed that Partin had been in a Baton Rouge jail
facing charges of kidnapping when they had first met. Pitcher had advised
Partin that, if he could see to it that the "kidnapped" children were returned
to their mother, he could also reduce Partin's bail. A day or two after the
children's return, Partin had been released on a $5,000 bond. When the
mother asked that the charges be dropped, Pitcher had acquiesced. There
was no agreement to reduce Partin's bond in exchange for cooperation with
the government. Did you grant Partin immunity from prosecution? Schiffer
asked. "No, sir, I did not," came the firm reply.

On cross-examination, Pitcher verified that the alleged kidnapping was
a domestic affair. "What are we trying to justify in this action, right here,

Your Honor?" Schiffer broke in. "That it's legal now to kidnap children?" To emphasize his disgust, he tossed his pen down onto the defense table, where it skittered across the papers strewn before the attorneys and their clients. "Let's end this farce now," he muttered.[30]

In the end, the attempts to disparage Partin achieved mixed results. Although several witnesses called his reputation into question, attempts to paint him as a drug addict had fallen flat. Furthermore, much of the damning testimony was heard outside the presence of the jury. The defense would need to search for another way to defang the government's star witness.

SEVENTEEN

"My life depends on this verdict."

—Jimmy Hoffa

"MR. HOFFA AND I had an interesting relationship," Jim Neal recollected afterward, "although later on, after all these trials were over, he called me the most vicious prosecutor that ever lived." Neal never understood why Hoffa made that comment. To his recollection, and despite Hoffa's occasional impassioned outbursts toward him, Neal always felt that they had a "jocular, interesting relationship."

During the Chattanooga trial, Hoffa approached the government prosecutor daily and stuck out his chest. "Mr. Neal, we're wasting a lot of taxpayers' money on these things. Let's you and I go down to the gym and settle this."

"I never did," Neal grinned. Throughout the proceedings, though, the brash Teamster boss tried to rattle the young prosecutor. "Every day during the three-month trial in Nashville, and during the three-month trial in Chattanooga—every day," Neal said, "when I would look over at Jimmy Hoffa he'd be giving me the finger under the table." He added, "So you can imagine how hard it is to keep your eyes off of that when you know it's over there waiting for you."[1]

————

Over the several weeks of the trial, some reporters had drifted away from Chattanooga, going home "to await 'hotter' developments in the case." Anticipating that Hoffa would soon take the stand in his own defense, however, journalists from many of the nation's largest newspapers poured back into Chattanooga during the weekend of February 22–23. Everyone recognized the significance of what was coming. "With Hoffa himself likely to take the stand this week," *Time* reported, "the trial seemed to be boiling down to his word against Partin's."[2]

At 10:58 on the morning of February 25, Hoffa strode confidently to the witness stand. He sported a crisp, dark blue suit and a fresh haircut. The courtroom was as tightly packed as it had been at any time during the trial. Although hopeful onlookers filled the corridor outside of the courtroom, few gained the chance for a seat; those lucky enough to gain admittance were unwilling to step outside and lose their place.[3]

The courtroom was silent with anticipation. Leaning upon the lectern, Harry Berke cleared his throat and commenced the examination of his famous client. From the beginning, it was obvious that a great deal of time had been spent preparing Hoffa. "He never lacked for words," one newspaper offered. In his clipped, rapid-fire style, he laid out a condensed version of his background:

> I was born in Brazil, Indiana, February 14, 1913. My father died at
> an early age. My mother moved us into another small town and
> at about the age of eight or nine I moved to Detroit, Michigan,
> with my mother, two sisters and a brother. Went to school until I
> was seven years old. My mother worked in a factory. When I left
> school at the seventh grade I went to work in a department store
> as a stock boy. Stayed there a very short time. Went to work in a

warehouse. Worked in the warehouse for the Kroger Grocery and
Baking Company.

Organized that concern in an independent union. Moved that
into a federal union of the AFL. And moved from there into the
Teamsters Union. And I've been an organizer or officer since that
time, the year 1932 or 1933, up to the present date, sir. Officer of
a local union, Joint Council, State Conference, Area Conference,
Vice-President, Trustee. Now General President of the International Union.[4]

Dispensing with the preliminaries, Berke turned to Hoffa's relationship
with his codefendants. No, Hoffa said, he had not known Parks at all before
the Chattanooga trial. He had known Campbell, a Detroit Teamster, for
about ten years. What about Tweel? "I never met the gentleman until we
were indicted and at this trial," the IBT president replied. He was familiar
with King, he said, especially during the last few years, when King had served
as president of Teamsters Local 327. What about Dorfman? "Yes sir," Hoffa
responded, "very well." He and Dorfman had constant telephone discussions
about business matters. Still, Hoffa insisted, "we do no business directly with
Allen Dorfman's office." The business was held by Dr. Leo Perlman's Union
Casualty Company, he explained, for which Dorfman simply served as the
broker.[5]

While en route to Nashville in October 1962, Hoffa testified, he had telephoned Dorfman, asking him to bring insurance records concerning the Test
Fleet Corporation as "rapidly as possible." Hoffa's team had worked fifteen to
sixteen hours per day during the Nashville trial, laboring late into the night,
"trying to put together this intricate financial relationship that was involved
with this trial so we could properly present it intelligently to the jury to where
they could understand that it was not a million-dollar operation as has been
suggested." Dorfman's records had been necessary for that purpose.

Dorfman had come to Nashville on several occasions during the trial
to attend to business matters. Every year, Hoffa explained, they would sit
down and make plans for the next year's health and welfare program. The
Teamsters president had also encouraged Dorfman to work with some two
hundred doctors to develop a comprehensive plan for providing dental and
eye care insurance to Teamsters and retirees. Despite the distraction of the
Test Fleet trial, therefore, it had been necessary for them to get those plans
in place before union meetings scheduled for February 1963.[6]

In answering Berke's questions, Hoffa portrayed a deep thoughtfulness,
pausing while gazing up to the ceiling, his brow furrowed, before making

a response. His charisma could not be denied. Nor could his deep disdain for the government or the legal troubles diverting his attention from union business. Asked whether he had imported help from the IBT international office during the Nashville case, Hoffa responded, with a mild swipe at his legal counsel, "More so in Chattanooga than in Nashville because I was able to get competent legal help in Nashville to carry out the necessary work of the attorneys in coordinating the lawsuit."

Pursing his lips, Berke turned to the topic everyone was waiting for. "Mr. Hoffa, did you know Mr. Edward Partin?"

The witness's eyes narrowed. Yes, Hoffa answered. He said he had known Partin since 1957 or so, but he questioned "whether or not prior to the Nashville trial I had saw [sic] Partin more than ten or twelve times in my life." Faced with the two telephone recordings the government had disclosed, he had to admit that he had spoken to Partin on October 8 and 18, 1962. Did you invite him to Nashville? Berke asked. "No, sir," came the quick response. Was there any reason you needed him in Nashville? "Ed Partin knew nothing of the details of my lawsuit in Nashville, Tennessee," Hoffa replied. "I had no need for Partin to assist me whatsoever." Partin, he insisted, had come to Nashville to discuss his own legal troubles.

Later, after it had been determined that someone had ransacked the IBT offices in Nashville, Partin had perched near the door, allegedly to make sure that no unauthorized persons were admitted into the area. "Now I understand why he was there," Hoffa said pointedly.

Partin had hung around, pestering Hoffa for a meeting, and near the end of the trial Hoffa and Bufalino had finally agreed to sit down with him. "I never heard such a story in my life," Hoffa remarked, turning to the jury. Partin had rambled on and on, almost incoherently, about his criminal problems until Hoffa began to wonder whether he was physically ill or needed some form of treatment. The IBT president used the opportunity to insert an aside related to the previously forbidden topic of Cuba. "Listen, Ed, I want to ask you a question," he had asked. "Are you involved in smuggling arms into Cuba?" He warned Partin that he was going to investigate the allegation and take action if it was true. Although Partin pleaded for another chance, Hoffa had been firm. "It blew up," Hoffa said, and Partin stormed out of the room.[7]

The remainder of Berke's examination allowed Hoffa to adamantly deny each of the damning comments Partin had attributed to him. Asked whether he ever said that Tweel was in Nashville to help him, Hoffa responded, "I made no such statement and it is ridiculous on its face." As for his supposed remark that they were going to try to get to a few scattered jurors and take their chances, Hoffa was adamant: "I say I did not make the statement and I flatly deny it." Did he tell Partin that he might get him to pass something for him? "That is a ridiculous statement," he replied. "I never made the statement and the way it is couched I don't even know what it means frankly." Finally, Partin had also cited Hoffa's remark that since "the dirty bastards" had reported the Tippens bribe to Judge Miller, they therefore needed to lie low for a few days. Hoffa insisted that the comment made no sense, as Tippens wasn't even a juror at the time.

Had Hoffa encouraged Partin to contact any football players about appearing at the Nashville trial? The concept, the Teamster responded, made no practical sense. "Why anybody would get ahold of a football player for a trial is a mystery to me," he said. Hoffa also pointed out that he did not even know who Phil King was, adding, "I have never been to a professional football game, as ashamed as I am to say it."

Hoffa denied commenting that he would pay "fifteen or twenty thousand, whatever it cost to get to the jury." He denied grumbling that Ewing King was fumbling around in getting to Paschal, and he flatly denied saying that he had a colored male juror in his pocket. Had Hoffa opined that their best bet was a hung jury unless they could get to the foreman? Not at all, he responded. No one was chosen as foreman until the jury retired to deliberate. How could you even know who would be chosen?

Had Campbell come to Nashville before the trial to take care of the colored male juror? "Who would you come down to see?" Hoffa replied incredulously. How could you approach jurors before the trial even began? he asked. "Stop everybody on the street and ask them are you going to be a juror?" Asked if he had referred to Ewing King as a "stupid SOB" for failing to win over patrolman Paschal, Hoffa answered, "No sir." He added the self-serving (and inaccurate) observation: "I don't talk to my associates that way."[8]

For the most part, Hoffa's testimony was concise and self-assured. He denied each and every allegation, as expected. He did not miss an opportunity to take a jab at Partin or the government. Perhaps his best point related to the key issue of whether he had invited Partin to Nashville. As Hoffa adeptly explained, there was no reason that he would need or want Partin's assistance in Nashville. No, it had been *Partin* who had insinuated himself into the defense team; it was clear that he had been planted there to spy on Hoffa and his lawyers.

———

Loud, aggressive, and accusatory, veteran courtroom lawyer John J. Hooker handled the cross-examination. Just as the defense had the goal of provoking an outburst by Judge Wilson, Hooker doubtless sought to get the combustible witness to explode. Hoffa, however, was exceedingly careful. Outwardly, he professed that the government had manufactured the evidence against him. "It would not surprise me to see the government come up in this particular case with a manufactured tape corroborating Mr. Partin as they had a script," he vented to reporters staked out in front of the courthouse, "because I'm convinced under hypnosis they played a tape to this man to where he could repeat verbatim word after word, paragraph after paragraph, no matter how many times you talked to him, which is absolutely against the mentality of any individual in this country who is not under hypnosis."[9]

Privately, however, Hoffa was apprehensive, convinced that the government had bugged his hotel suite. At least two recordings had been made of his conversations with Partin, and there could be others. He equivocated, offering testimony that was careful, unsure, and tentative. Neal had already taken advantage of Hoffa's paranoia, connecting several old metal boxes with multicolored wires, attaching knobs and a wire resembling an antenna, and putting the contraption onto a cart. Jim Durkin waited until Hoffa and his entourage were in the hallway, then quickly rolled the cart past them. Not unreasonably, Hoffa concluded that the apparatus was some sort of recording machine.[10]

Hoffa and Hooker stared at one another for a long moment. Hooker took a deep breath. Did Partin tell you that he was going to testify in Chattanooga? he asked. "Are you kidding?" Hoffa responded. "Of course not." Then he caught himself. Did the government have some other recording they might roll out? "Not to my knowledge," he added curtly.

He was forced into the same corner when asked whether he had spoken to Partin by telephone in January 1963. "As I say, I have no recollection of any conversation in January, if it took place I cannot recall it taking place, it may have." Well, did you visit with Partin on February 6 of that year, before his grand jury appearance? "I may have," he equivocated. "I know he said he visited Bufalino there. He may have dropped in and seen me. I have no recollection of it. I would not either confirm or deny. I don't know." Hoffa was clearly nervous.[11]

Throughout his cross-examination, Hooker labored to antagonize the witness, his voice rising, dripping with contempt. Finally, Hoffa counterpunched. While he was careful not to take the bait and fly into a rage, he would not be intimidated by Hooker's aggressive grilling. He was combative, but controlled. "Now, Mr. Hooker, I can't hear you when you holler. If you will just go a little slower and not holler, I will answer you. I cannot hear you the way you holler."

"Is there something wrong with your hearing?" boomed Hooker.

"No, it's just I am not used to people hollering at me."

"You are used to doing the hollering yourself at people?"

"You are not going to holler at me, now, quiet down," Hoffa directed, jabbing his finger toward the overbearing prosecutor.[12]

Hooker asked what Hoffa had done with the list of prospective jurors at the Test Fleet trial. As was normal, Hoffa said, they had investigated the backgrounds of the various individuals on the list, "as we would like to have did with this one." Hoffa admitted that he had spoken with Dorfman numerous times on the telephone; however, none of those calls had related to the Test Fleet jury. Still, the IBT president knew the government might also have a tape recording of a conversation with Dorfman. Thus he conceded that he might have discussed the jury in some way. "I discussed the jury every single night with my attorneys in Nashville, Tennessee," he explained. "I discussed this jury every night in the Hotel Patten here in Chattanooga every night. It would be ridiculous if I didn't. My life depends on this verdict."[13] Did you see Dorfman and Tweel in the Nashville courtroom on November 22, 1962? Hooker asked. "I did not," came the reply. "I was very busy taking care of Hoffa, as I am trying to do here."[14]

Hoffa remained adamant that he had never made any of the comments Partin attributed to him. He had never called anyone a dirty bastard or patted his back pocket to insinuate that Partin might pass some cash for him. "I don't have any money in my rear pocket, it's right here," he said, gesturing to his breast pocket, "and I never hit my hand on my back pocket to my recollection and I say positively I never made the statement."[15]

When Hooker announced that he had no more questions, Hoffa offered a short, conciliatory statement. "Mr. Hooker," he said, "may I apologize to you if I was too aggressive or too loud in my debate. It is my natural habit. If I offended you, I apologize."

"You don't owe me any apologies," Hooker responded, smiling warmly. "I think you talk about as loud as I do, Mr. Hoffa."

Berke then rose to ask a handful of follow-up questions to soften the combative witness in the eyes of the jury. Are you aggressive in representing Teamsters workers? "In my business unfortunately if you are not aggressive with the individuals we deal with," Hoffa replied solemnly, "we would have no business hours or work conditions. We consistently must be aggressive."[16]

Hoffa did need to downplay his connection to Dorfman, with whom he clearly had considerable, ongoing contact. On cross-examination, Hooker had pointed out that Dorfman handled $35–50 million of the Teamsters' business. To the typical juror, that amount was remarkable, enough to foster deep loyalty on the part of the beneficiary. But was that amount a large portion of the union's insurance business? "No, sir," Hoffa explained. "I would say from maybe 15 per cent to 17 per cent of the entire International Union insurance is carried by Dorfman. No more." While that amount may not have been significant from the Teamsters' perspective, Hoffa's explanation did not dispel the inference that Dorfman benefited deeply from his relationship with the IBT.[17]

After three and one-half hours, Hoffa stepped jauntily from the witness chair.[18] Speaking with reporters on the sidewalk, he commented on the give-and-take between himself and Hooker. "Well," he said matter-of-factly, "it became rather, uh—heated in the discussing between he and I, and after all, he's not making this a personal issue I'm sure, and I certainly don't want to make it one, even though it's my life that's at stake, and I did not want anybody to believe I was trying to abuse him."[19]

No grand admissions came from Hooker's cross-examination. With a couple of exceptions, moreover, there were no outbursts, as might have been anticipated. Suspicious that he was being monitored and recorded, Hoffa could not be his normal, combative self. The result was a mostly mild-mannered performance—at least by Hoffa standards.

———

For onlookers, the final few defense witnesses carried a sense of anticlimax. Bufalino, who had been photographed glad-handing with "old friends" in Chattanooga, returned to the stand. The *Chattanooga Times* described his reunion with Isadore Kitchen, the proprietor of the Grand Loan Office at 918 Market Street, one afternoon while Bufalino was on his way to a dentist's office. While in the military, the two men had been stationed together.

"I would have been up to see him, but thought he would have been too busy," Kitchen explained for the cameras.

"I'm never too busy to see an old friend," Bufalino beamed, shaking his friend's hand.[20]

On the witness stand, Bufalino confirmed that he had observed Partin fifteen to thirty times in Nashville, where he had sat at a little table in the hotel hallway fooling around with a deck of cards. "Yes, he was a self-appointed watchman, so far as I was concerned," Bufalino remarked gravely, adding, "I now know why he was stationed there."[21] According to Bufalino, Partin had come to Nashville to discuss several "run-ins that he had with the law." When they had discussed the situation, Hoffa had instructed Partin to "stop running around chasing around all over the country with women, squandering the union funds. . . . And he told him to settle down and fly right and if he didn't straighten that local union out he was going to straighten it out himself by putting it into receivership or trusteeship." In response, Partin had stormed out of the room.[22] While hanging around in Nashville, Partin had also assisted with assembling documents for the trial, and he had been present when attorneys prepared witnesses.[23]

Bufalino averred that *Partin* had made most of the questionable suggestions during the Test Fleet trial. At one time, Partin had offered to contact several football players whom he knew, including Billy Wade, Jimmy Taylor, and Billy Cannon, and invite them to shake hands with Hoffa in front of the jury. According to Bufalino, he had commanded Partin not to do anything like that. Later, Partin had said he knew a military officer who was familiar with one of the Test Fleet jurors, and that he might try to get him to come to Nashville. "I had no desire nor any inclination to do anything like it," Bufalino insisted, "and I suggested to him that he should dispell [*sic*] the thought from his mind."[24] Well, Neal followed up, was Partin the one who suggested that you bring in Joe Louis to shake hands with Hoffa in a prior case? Before Bufalino could answer, the court sustained a flurry of defense objections.[25]

———

It was the end of a long and eventful February 25. Judge Wilson once again took up a series of motions and extended discussions, many dealing with surveillance. As defense attorneys proposed to file yet another reply on the subject, Wilson sighed. "I wonder," Neal inquired, sensing an opportunity for a bit of levity, "if Your Honor has ever read the book by Charles Dickens called 'Bleak House?'" He was referring to the Victorian novel about a never-ending, generations-long legal case that ultimately devoured the inheritance over which it was fought.

Wilson smiled. "Yes, sir," he replied grimly, "I read that every night."[26]

Defense lawyers asked if the prosecution would allow a Department of Justice representative to speak with them privately. Put him on the stand, Neal advised. But the government was not about to allow the private probing of the DOJ. "No, I don't want him on the stand," Haggerty retorted. "If he is going to be on the stand, let him be in the presence of the jury."

"May I state that we should like to examine the witness in front of the jury," Schiffer interposed. "It's about time we had a jury trial here, not the kind of a trial Mr. Neal wants and so far as his past remarks about high officials, there is no sanctification in this country, this is not a kingdom, there is nobody above a subpoena."

"In other words," a frustrated Judge Wilson answered, "you think you have a right to come before this jury with just unlimited numbers of witnesses about which you have no knowledge what they will testify and explore before the jury whether or not there is anything conceivable that they can add to the case?" Such an abusive process would cause the trial to go on forever. The court would not allow the parties to blindly vet witnesses before the jury.

The judge took a deep breath. "I suggest we read Chapter 20 in the 'Bleak House' tonight and adjourn court," Wilson said. Robe trailing behind him, he strode past the American flag and into his chambers.[27]

––––––

The defense offered its final witness on February 26. Once again, Lester Bloomenstiel testified that he had paid Partin's portion of a tax bill on the truck stop that the two men co-owned. Questioned as to why the government had not charged Partin, he was told, "We have been given orders from New Orleans not to pursue Mr. Partin."[28]

At 11:35 a.m., the defense reported that it had no further witnesses to call. Silets then read to the jury a series of excerpts from the Louisiana case *United States v. Edward Grady Partin,* Criminal Action No. 1452. Following the initial indictment on June 22, 1962, Silets revealed, the case had been continued several times at the request of both the defendant and the government. After an entry on March 29, 1963, no action had been taken on the case. The implication was clear: once Partin had agreed to help the government, he was rewarded with the suspension of pending criminal charges against him.[29]

The jury was excused for lunch. Things began moving quickly. The court rejected a series of now-routine motions—for severance of the defendants, to address government surveillance, and for dismissal of the indictment. Silets renewed his request that the entirety of Partin's testimony be suppressed, stating, "It is clearly and palpably false that this was a placing of Mr. Partin in the midst of the defense by Mr. Hoffa."

"I believe that should be overruled," Judge Wilson determined. A recess was ordered, with rebuttal testimony to be offered afterward by the
government.[30]

———

Officer Jack Walker was recalled on rebuttal. Contrary to defense allegations,
he said that he had never had an assignment from Sheridan. Even more significantly, Walker confirmed that he had never spoken with any man named
Shobe, who was then ushered into the courtroom. Are you familiar with this
man? Hooker asked. "I have never seen him before in my life," the witness
replied. Schiffer repeatedly asked whether Walker had spoken with Shobe,
eliciting repeated denials. Judge Wilson asked Walker whether he had given
money for Parks to pass to Carl Fields. "No, sir," came the terse reply. The
reverse had been true; Parks was the one who had raised the topic of offering money to Fields.[31]

The prosecution then called a series of witnesses to bolster Partin's character. Frank Jumonville, the owner of an equipment-rental business near
Baton Rouge, offered, "His reputation is very good." Donice Bennett, the
president of Teamsters Local 5 whose house had been shotgunned days earlier, reappeared to address Partin's reputation for honesty, and Victor Bussie,
the president of the Louisiana AFL-CIO, echoed that Partin's reputation was
"extremely good, sir."

Berke's cross-examination of Bussie resulted in one of the most heated
moments in the trial. One by one, Berke reviewed the criminal allegations
Partin faced. Yes, Bussie responded, he had read about some of that in the
newspaper, but he knew nothing personally. Had Bussie made negative public
statements about Hoffa? Yes, came the reply, and also against Partin. After
all, the IBT had been ejected from the AFL-CIO.

When Berke tried to raise the repeatedly barred topic of Mississippi rape
charges, the court instructed him to avoid the subject. And then Berke barreled into the allegation that Partin had smuggled arms into Cuba. Glaring
and irritated, Judge Wilson leaned over the bench and shook his finger at the
attorney. "Mr. Berke, there is absolutely no basis in the record for that." The
only purpose for such a question, the judge remarked, "was to get at . . . Mr.
Partin," and not to examine the witness on the stand. He instructed the jury
to disregard the question, then told Berke, "Counsel will not just willfully
disobey the orders and instructions of the Court."[32]

Later that morning, after the jury had been excused for lunch, several offended defense attorneys turned their displeasure on Wilson. The result, referred to as "the bitterest attack yet on the usually quiet-spoken federal judge," was unprecedented. Silets moved for a mistrial. "The Court," he brayed, "was not only loud and angered of counsel, but if it could be characterized I would say vicious."[33]

"This Court has absolutely no bias, no prejudice against any party to this lawsuit," a dumbfounded Wilson rejoined. "The attorneys in this lawsuit have made it difficult for the Court throughout the trial of this case . . . but this Court had attempted to be just as fair and just impartial as it could possibly be." He would not allow any attorney on either side, he added, to willfully disregard the court's repeated instructions.[34]

As for the recurring attempt to inject Cuban arms smuggling into the trial, Berke insisted that he was trying to address Partin's credibility. Wilson smiled. He was not buying it. "This Court, nor do I believe any court, can be so naïve as to doubt what the purpose of your examination was, Mr. Berke."[35]

Though he was not even involved in the discussion, Schiffer would yet again ramp up the dialogue. "I am now accused here with the other counsel of not being fair and honest with this Court and I must state, with full respect to the United States District Court, I resent it." His voice ever rising, Schiffer pounded on the lectern. "Why does it suddenly emerge in this Court? Why is the Court offended because I called Partin what he is, an outright perjurer? Whenever I stand to object, the court glares at me. What is my client to do? Lay his head down on the chopping block to satisfy the government here? The government has taken the position that we are charlatans—"

"Sir," Judge Wilson interrupted, "you make that characterization, the Court does not make that characterization."

"Am I to be accused," Schiffer barreled forward, "because Mr. Partin tried to trade with a dictator Castro, acknowledge to be accused of bad faith with this Court when I want to expose a traitor?" If he could not take steps to expose such a treasonous deal, Schiffer concluded, "justice is finished in America." Listening, Judge Wilson again made a few careful marks in his notebook.[36]

Haggerty asked the court to take up another issue in chambers, where it would not be heard by the courtroom audience. In Wilson's wood-paneled office, Haggerty explained the situation. "Your Honor," he began, "we have been informed that the marshals not only have been wining and dining this jury, but they took them to a concert by Liberace. They took those who wanted to go to the Tivoli Theater to a fight." The prosecutor in the case was the US government, he explained. The marshals were government employees; allowing them to treat jurors to extravagant meals, concerts, and sporting events was prejudicial to the defense.[37]

Of course, the jurors had been severely restricted in their comings and goings for more than a month. Under such circumstances, it was neither surprising nor novel that they would be provided with some outings and entertainment. On February 19, the jury had attended a Liberace concert at the Memorial Auditorium. "Almost before it was over, while [Liberace] was bowing," juror Pat Haverty recalled, "we were out of there. In the hallway, they had blocked off an area, and we used a side door. It was tight as a tick." The next evening, they were taken to a local bowling alley "for a little exercise." On February 25, they went to the Tivoli Theater to view a live feed of the Cassius Clay–Sonny Liston heavyweight boxing match.[38]

The current *Reader's Digest* magazine, Haggerty persisted, contained an article with detrimental comments about Hoffa (and Dorfman), and it was for sale in the lobby of the Read House, where the jury was staying. The article in question, by Lester Velie, noted, "Hoffa, at 52, is a man halfway up a mountain peak. The footing is treacherous, and below yawns a double abyss." Velie went on to posit that the Chattanooga trial would determine his future. "For Hoffa," Velie wrote, "this is the year of decision. And the decision, read in the courts and in the union halls, will be one that affects all Americans." To protect jurors from this prejudicial information, the defense had bought all thirty copies at the hotel. Some, though, Haggerty noted, had already been sold.[39]

Haggerty also asserted, "Marshals in charge of the jury have permitted them [jurors] to attend . . . a motion picture entitled 'Trial by Jury,' which has to do with the very subject matter that the jury is performing here."

Judge Wilson was stunned. "'Trial by Jury' is a motion picture of this lawsuit?"

"No," Haggerty shook his head, "but it is a motion picture of a jury in the trial of a criminal case." Without making any immediate decision, Wilson took the matter under advisement. In the end, nothing would come of defense objections to jurors' after-hours field trips during the trial.[40]

———

Undaunted, the defense took up yet another issue involving the jury, arguing that, this time, there was evidence that some members of the *jury* were biased against the defendants and their counsel. During Schiffer's boisterous argument minutes earlier, Haggerty explained, one of Hoffa's legal team, Frank Ragano, had overhead an objectionable comment by a juror. Why was he in a position where he could hear jurors' comments? Jack Reddy asked. The jury had been out of the courtroom at the time. "Mr. Branstetter and I were listening to the argument and we commented on the fact that it might be overheard by the jury," Silets offered. "I called Mr. Ragano over and asked him if he would please step around the other side [of the hallway]."

"Why was it not suggested that counsel be a little more temperate in their argument?" Judge Wilson asked. Schiffer was shouting "to the rafters ringing," the judge said, so that it could be heard blocks away.

"Well, Judge," an ill-advised Schiffer remarked, "for the record I wasn't shouting. I can really shout."

Sidestepping that tone-deaf statement, Silets offered that *he* had sent Ragano out into the hallway. "It seems to me," Reddy noted shrewdly, "that this is a matter of sending an attorney for the defendants around there to spy on the jury to see what the jury is thinking about this matter."[41]

After mulling over the matter, Judge Wilson called for Ragano, who made his first appearance in the case. The son of Sicilian immigrants, the forty-one-year old had been awarded the Bronze Star during World War II. He had also come to represent several influential underworld bosses, including Santo Trafficante (Tampa) and Carlos Marcello (New Orleans). In 1961, Trafficante had recommended Ragano to Hoffa; Ragano would have a long association with both Hoffa and the mob.[42]

After entering the hallway, Ragano explained, he had opened a door leading into a corridor where a few jurors were standing. A marshal had allowed him to put his ear up to the door leading to the courtroom, and he could hear Schiffer but not distinguish what he was saying. At that time, one of the alternate jurors, John Curbow, had commented that "he had always heard some statement to the effect that the weaker the case the louder you holler." Some of the regular jurors were standing around when he made the remark. Certainly, this demonstrated prejudice by at least one of the jurors.

Judge Wilson set his glasses down on his desk and rubbed his eyes. "Mr. Ragano," he asked, "were you conducting surveillance of the jury? Were you eavesdropping on the jury?"

"No, sir," came the nervous response. "I wasn't eavesdropping on the jury. I was attempting to ascertain whether or not—"

Wilson cut him short. "Were you or [were you] not in the area where the jury is kept when it is outside of the courtroom?"

"I have stated it, Your Honor."

Who sent you? the judge asked. No one, Ragano responded. A thick "X" would be penciled in the judge's copy of the transcript that evening. It was another topic to which he would return at a later date.[43]

————

Eager to counter the portrayal of Partin as a narcotics fiend, the government called Dr. Robert W. Rasor, the medical director for the US Public Health Service Hospital in Lexington, Kentucky. He had examined Partin a few days earlier (February 21), Rasor testified, and he had found no evidence to show that the man had ever taken narcotics. On cross-examination, Silets obtained the doctor's admission that the February 21 tests would not have revealed anything about Partin's condition *at some other time*. Rasor also conceded that the symptoms of addiction fade away about one month after quitting; by implication, then, Partin could have recently stopped taking narcotics.[44]

Next came Dr. Harry Isbell, professor of medicine at the University of Kentucky Medical Center, who corroborated the test results. He had found no evidence that Partin was under the influence of any drugs, that he had used hypodermic needles in the past, or that he had exhibited any symptoms of drug withdrawal. "As a matter of opinion," Isbell concluded, "I found no evidence whatsoever that Mr. Partin ever had been an addict." Yes, he conceded to Silets, Partin did have scars on his arms—but they were not narcotic scars. This evidence seemed to support Levin Magruder's earlier testimony that Partin was not a "dope addict," as the defense maintained. Whatever else the jury might think about Partin, claims about his use of illicit drugs seemed to fall flat.

————

Jurors were basically given the day off on Friday, February 28, as proceedings were held in their absence. Outside, it was bitterly cold, with snow flurries. Frank Grimsley was recalled to address the recordings of Partin's conversations with Hoffa in October 1962. The two tapes of Partin and Hoffa were the only ones that had been provided to him, Grimsley promised. And he had no tapes of any conversations between himself and Partin. Grimsley denied that Partin's indictment was ever suppressed; he also denied requesting postponement of the kidnapping charges against Partin. There was no quid pro quo for Partin's testimony, Grimsley insisted.[45]

Grimsley did confirm that the assassination plot Partin had referenced did not involve John F. Kennedy. During a recess, Hoffa branded the alleged "assassination plot" a fabrication: "I deny it. It's a lie and it never happened. There was nothing in the conversation concerning anything but union business." "This follows in the same pattern of the lies and perjury that has poured out of the lips of the government's star witness," Bufalino added. "It's strictly a get-Hoffa campaign."[46]

The defense pushed for access to copies of *all* tapes made of Partin between October 6 and 18, 1962. But Judge Wilson, who had listened to the same recordings and found they had nothing to do with the present case, denied the request. Of the forty to fifty tapes made, Daniels indicated, only two involved Hoffa and Partin.[47]

Walter Sheridan was brought into the courtroom. Did he know that recordings were to be made of Partin and Hoffa? No, he responded. He did not know about the tapes until after they had been made. He had never even heard the tapes in 1962. Had he encouraged Partin to go to Nashville? No, sir, he replied. Yet Sheridan admitted, "I was glad that he was there when he was there. In fact, he left many times when I wished he could have stayed there." Did you not encourage him to call Hoffa to create a pretext for going to Nashville? "No, sir."

With that simple denial, the government concluded its rebuttal case.[48] All testimony had been entered in the jury tampering trial.

———

The defense once again requested that Partin's testimony be stricken, as he had only gone to Nashville because of the unlawful recordings he had made when talking with Hoffa. That request was again denied.[49] At long last, Judge Wilson entered his ruling with respect to the Hoffa-Partin recordings. The tapes, he found, were made lawfully and with Partin's consent, then introduced by the defendants themselves.[50]

The defense was dejected by Wilson's ruling that surreptitious recordings were to be allowed as evidence. Various motions for mistrial and the exclusion of Partin's testimony had gone nowhere. Therefore, Hoffa determined to rely on others besides his apparently snakebitten attorneys. Teamsters legislative counsel Sid Zagri would join Senate minority leader Everett Dirksen (R-IL) in demanding that the House and Senate Judiciary Committees send observers to the Chattanooga trial. These individuals would supply reports for an anticipated "full-scale investigation of the Gestapo tactics" used by the government. Senator Hiram Fong (R-HI), who entered Zagri's letter into the *Congressional Record*, opined that it "raised questions of the possibility of the infringement of the constitutional rights of a defendant." But Representative Emanuel Celler (D-NY) threw cold water on this strategy, pointing out, "It has been the practice of the Judiciary Committee not to intervene in any case pending or in the process of trial."

Still, Hoffa and his codefendants held their collective breath, hoping that Congress might come to their assistance, even if the court in Chattanooga would not.[51]

EIGHTEEN

"I have heard things come from this witness stand
that I would never have believed would happen
in the United States of America. Never."

—Harold Brown

"Chattanooga after more than a hundred years,
has survived a Chickamauga and a Missionary Ridge,
but Chattanooga can never survive the acquittal of those who
have been proven to be guilty of contaminating, tampering with,
and fixing a jury in the courts of justice in this state."

—John J. Hooker Sr.

"THE TRIAL PROBABLY set many records," wrote a *Chattanooga Times* reporter. One was for the length of the proceedings. The 1964 trial was one of the longest, if not the longest, court case ever held in Chattanooga, and the transcript reflected it. "The record," the *Times* reported, "contains 8,249 pages, divided into 30 volumes. . . . Nearly 750,000 words are in the voluminous transcript." Over the course of the trial, 254 exhibits would be introduced. It had also been a remarkably combative experience. "One record," the *Times* related, "was the number of motions made by the defense for a mistrial." Day after day, the distrust and bitterness between the parties had intensified. Closing arguments would do nothing to temper the acrimony hanging over the courtroom.[1]

———

As February gave way to March, the end of the trial was in sight. Jurors made their final visit to Bill Knowles's barbershop on March 2. "The jurors will not visit the shop again," a US marshal informed the young barber. When Knowles commented that everyone might be glad when it was over, "the marshal emphatically said that *he* would."[2]

As the parties prepared for closing arguments, the magnitude of the case— and the possible impact of the looming verdict—settled heavily on all present. Yet another acquittal would reinforce Hoffa's hold on the IBT and potentially doom further efforts to get Hoffa. By contrast, the *Chattanooga Times* opined, if convicted Hoffa "will almost certainly be finished as the iron-handed leader of the largest union in the world."[3]

———

At the end of the day on Tuesday, February 25, the parties discussed how to handle closing arguments, given the large number of defendants (and lawyers). Hooker proposed that each defendant be given one hour to argue the case, and the prosecution a total of three hours. Berke responded that Hoffa's lawyers would probably need ninety minutes for themselves alone; Schiffer calculated that he would need at least two hours himself.

The government also asked to present a chart summarizing the intricate telephone call records presented in evidence. The defense considered it the jury's responsibility to determine the significance of those records; it was not appropriate for the prosecution to steer jurors in any particular direction by interpreting the documents for them. Certainly, the telephone records were confusing, and the defense was happy to leave them that way. "If there is [*sic*] going to be charts," Haggerty said, "we'd just like to know it because we intend to bring in one of Walt Disney's cartoonists in here to make our charts. . . . We'd like a drawing to show at the inception of this thing that Mr. Partin was incarcerated in jail. We intend to make charts of the telephone over in Louisville of Joe's Palm Room, of the FBI man snooping around and of the telephone man, Shobe, and Campbell in there."

284EIGHTEEN

"Well," Judge Wilson declared, "I'm inclined to think, gentlemen, that you better plan your argument without the use of charts."[4]

Monday, March 2, the thirty-first day of the trial. At 9:00 a.m., the attorneys once again converged on the courthouse, this time for final arguments. Informed that five hours would be allocated to the defense, Berke requested one additional hour. No, Judge Wilson replied. "Out of this entire record not more than twenty percent of the record is devoted to testimony of witnesses before the jury, over eighty percent of this entire record is devoted to argument, to objections and to matters heard out of the presence of the jury," he said. "Last evening the Court timed itself and in a period of two hours the Court read the testimony of all of the witnesses, or its notes and the summary of the testimony of all of the witnesses who have testified before the jury and in the presence of the jury." No additional time would be necessary to summarize the case.[5]

Did the court intend to assign each attorney a specific amount of time? Branstetter inquired. "No, sir," Wilson replied. The attorneys should determine an equitable arrangement.[6] The prosecution would go first, followed by each defense attorney. Some time would be reserved at the end for final comments by the government.

Jim Neal would make the first argument, providing a comprehensive, detailed summary of the evidence amassed against the defendants and answering some of the defense attorneys' questions. After thanking the jurors for their service, he spent a few minutes discussing the jury system, which he described as a "delicate instrument" that needed to be protected. "For one who would obstruct justice, for one who would attempt to influence jurors improperly is not hurting merely one individual," Neal observed. "He is making a thrust at the very foundation of justice in America."[7] Local schoolteacher Etta Williams, who visited the courtroom throughout the trial, was particularly impressed with Neal's demeanor during his closing remarks. He had "the steeliest eyes I ever saw in my life," she said. "He never cracked a smile. He didn't yell, he just talked in [a] normal tone. . . . He stood there like a stone statue, and everybody listened."

"Consider the people who converged on Nashville in October 62," Neal reflected. Hoffa had flown in through Cincinnati, summoning Dorfman, who had then made an emergency call for Tweel to meet him in Nashville as well. In the same time frame, Campbell had come to Louisville and initiated a series of calls to Parks who, along with King, was already in Nashville. At that point, Neal remarked, "the stage was set and the actors had arrived for one of the greatest attacks on the jury system this country has ever known and we hope will ever have to survive."[8]

The key to the case, the one who drew together these various figures, was Partin. His testimony confirmed the involvement of each defendant. The defense had slandered Partin for days on end, Neal reminded the jury. And in the end, what had they shown with respect to his criminal record? Neal provided the answer: "His record in fact is that he was convicted once in his life when he was 19 years old."[9] Despite the flurry of accusations against the man, Neal stressed, Partin had been a *Hoffa confidante*. When he called Hoffa on October 18, 1962, he was told, "[Hoffa] is not taking any calls." Partin, though, was able to immediately get through to the IBT president, one of the most important men in the country. "He was Hoffa's man during the trial in Nashville," Neal said, jabbing a finger upon the podium. "He was their man." It came as no surprise, then, that Hoffa would confide in Partin about the various attempts to influence the jury.[10]

Everything that Partin had predicted had happened. He had reported that King intended to approach patrolman Paschal; subsequent surveillance proved this assertion true. Partin had also indicated that Campbell was to make contact with the sole black juror in the case, whom Hoffa had said was "in his hip pocket." Subsequently, Parks, who had also constantly communicated with Campbell, approached the Fields family. What had happened after Partin reported that Dorfman and Tweel wanted to convince bartender Dallas Hall to communicate with the jury? "The government checks and finds it to be true," Neal said. Based on all of these events, Neal pointed out, "all he [Partin] said was happening, was happening; and what he said was going to happen, did in fact happen."[11]

The defense had repeatedly questioned why anyone would attempt to contact *prospective* jurors. "In Nashville the jurors were called to the box in order," Neal explained. Tippens, Fields, and Paschal had been among the first thirty-five names on the list, making it especially likely that they would be chosen. Approaching them, then, was simply a calculated gamble.[12]

Neal then trudged through the various accusations leveled against the government's main witness. Partin was not a paid informer, he insisted, and "the government had promised him nothing." In fact, Neal added, "the government had not even paid all of his expenses."

Other defense strategies, like calling Dr. Levin Magruder to testify about Partin's alleged narcotics use, had failed miserably. Attempts at slander had similarly failed: "They brought some young girls here from Baton Rouge and some disgruntled members of his union and you saw how flat they fell."[13]

Even though defense attorneys had harangued Partin on the stand for six days, Neal said, they could not shake him. Had he not been telling the truth, he never could have endured such a barrage. "You can rest assured no man can maintain a pack of lies through six days of cross examination as the witness Partin went through on that stand."[14] "Now, the government does not contend that Mr. Partin has led a perfect life," Neal conceded, "but consider the fact that it's only because of his background that Hoffa, Dorfman, King, and Tweel would confide in him." Partin was one of them.[15]

Neal turned to defense questions as to why anyone would give Carl Fields money simply to report what tie his father would be wearing to court. As the only black juror in the Test Fleet case, the defense attorneys said, Gratin Fields should have been readily recognizable. Neal clarified that the question about the tie was to demonstrate to Hoffa that progress was being made in influencing Fields. If Hoffa had been told that Fields would be wearing a green suit or a red-striped tie, and then he actually showed up in that attire, Hoffa would know that contact had been made.[16]

The story as to why Campbell had been in Louisville did not hold up. It was simply not believable that a union member from Detroit would be needed to quell labor issues in Louisville. Ernestine Williams, who had spent "practically every day" with Campbell, testified that she had never heard about any work he was doing in Louisville. And while Campbell now claimed that he had never been to Nashville, he had told Anna Brown that he was going to the city. Moreover, Campbell had reported to Williams that his boss—Hoffa—was in trouble there. It was not hard to fit all of the pieces of the puzzle together.[17]

Neal then focused on the chief defendant. Hoffa's contention that he did not know what was going on was ludicrous on its face: "Yet you have seen Hoffa in this courtroom, the Defendant Hoffa every day for six weeks directing his own counsel in every detail of the case. You have seen him pass questions up to his attorneys. You have seen him review the documents that come in here in evidence. In short, you have seen him in complete control of this case, and you have heard him testify that he was in complete control of the Nashville case. You have heard him testify that he was closeted on many occasions with his attorneys in Nashville, that he was reading every page of the transcript. Yet in the Nashville case the approach was made to a member of the family of a juror in the trial in which the Defendant Hoffa was the only Defendant on trial in that case." Hoffa's own remarks had indicated his knowledge of these contacts. He had said that he had "the negro male juror in [his] hip pocket" and that Campbell had handled the matter for him. It was clear that Hoffa—and Hoffa alone—had masterminded the scheme.[18]

Turning to the attempt to pressure Dallas Hall, Neal recounted Tweel's comments to Hall: "Do you know anyone on the jury? . . . It will be worth your while if you could help us." Neal conceded that the plan to influence the jury was not stated explicitly. "But people engaged in this kind of activity," he offered, "seldom spell out this sort of things. They don't have to." When Tweel discussed the jury with Hall, the jury had already been chosen. There was no longer any need to investigate them. Why would anyone need to know anything about any of the jurors at that time—unless he was intending to make an inappropriate approach to one of them? While Tweel said that Hall had been calling him to talk about horses, Neal noted that no telephone record had been introduced to show a call from Hall to Tweel. All of the calls were *from* Tweel *to* Hall. The mere fact that Hall had not gone through with the plan could not save Tweel and Dorfman, who "had taken every step that they had to take to effect this approach to the jury."[19]

The sequence of the calls only confirmed their shady purpose. When Dorfman called Tweel, Tweel *immediately* called Hall. "More than mere coincidence," Neal remarked.[20]

At this point, Neal addressed the attempt to influence juror Betty Paschal. Remember, Neal said, Ewing King was "one of Hoffa's closest associates." He had met Hoffa at the airport at the beginning of the Test Fleet trial, he had escorted Hoffa to his hotel room, and he had been present "practically every day" of the trial.[21] Indisputably, King had made a strange night-time excursion to meet with James Paschal, swapping cars with George Broda on the way. Neal offered that King was not simply trying out the other man's automobile, stating, "It is an obvious effort to leave the FBI and apparently was successful." Had it been an innocent switching of cars, he added, "you can rest assured that Mr. Broda would have been on the stand here to testify it was innocent." At no time had Broda appeared to corroborate King's version of events. Why not? His absence only reinforced questions as to King's story.[22]

Concluding his remarks, Neal cited the lessons of the Holy Bible:

> I am reminded of the biblical story of Jacob and Esau, in which Jacob sought to steal his brother's Esau's birthright by covering his hands with goat's hair so that his near-blind father would think it was Esau. And you remember the statement of the Bible, the only part of the story that is appropriate here, that the hands were the hands of Esau but the voice was voice of Jacob.

> Here, ladies and gentlemen, the hands were the hands of Parks,
> Campbell, Dorfman, Tweel, King, but the voice was the voice of
> Hoffa, the one man who stood to gain by all of their activities on
> his behalf.

After a little more than an hour, Neal returned to his seat. He had been meticulous and thorough. In his stern, low-key manner, he had marched through the evidence piece by piece, tying together all of the tiny pieces of evidence while addressing many of the questions that had been posed by the defense. Following Neal's remarks, a brief morning recess was taken at 10:40 a.m.[23]

———

Jack Reddy was next to the podium. Whereas Neal had walked through the facts of the case point by point to demonstrate the defendants' guilt, Reddy intended to respond squarely to the contention that the trial was the product of anti-Hoffa persecution. "This is just another lawsuit for the government," Reddy contended. "It was handled in the same manner and is being handled in the same manner as any other criminal case that might come before you ladies and gentlemen." None of the defendants had been singled out for prosecution because of his name or notoriety. "They were brought here before the Court merely and solely upon the evidence of their illegal acts."[24]

Reddy also stressed the importance of the jury system. "Now," he remarked, "if right of a trial by jury is to mean anything it means that the jury's verdict shall not be corruptly influenced." The evidence showed that the defendants had attempted to influence the jury, and a guilty verdict was therefore appropriate. "In so doing," Reddy assured the jurors, "you will sound a pronouncement for equal justice under the law and also prove in this year of 1964 and for all times to come the law of this country still prevails and will be enforced against those who violate it." After only twenty minutes, Reddy thanked the jury and concluded his remarks.[25]

———

Hoffa's personal attorneys would bookend the defense arguments. First was the tired, thin Haggerty, whose speech was "polished[,] and its phrases bristled with logic." Partin would be the focus of Haggerty's remarks. "No Adjectives Wasted by Defense Counsel Attacking Partin," the next day's headline would read in Chattanooga. "May it please the Court, ladies and gentlemen

of the jury," he began, "inscribed on a tablet revealed by God to Moses included in the basic concept and belief of Christians throughout the world
and those who follow the Jewish faith, is inscribed, 'Thou shall not bear false
witness against thy neighbor.'" Partin had violated that sacred covenant.[26]
"The hardest case to defend," the venerable attorney assured the jury, "is
when your client has been framed. . . . Why? I will tell you. The persons
doing the framing have plenty of time for the plotting and scheming. Your
client is indicted, but you do not know of the frame until sometime during
trial when the scheme is disclosed."[27]

There was no evidence of any actual criminal influence on the Test Fleet
jury, Haggerty said. The prosecution did not call a single Test Fleet juror
to testify that he or she had been bribed (Tippens had testified at the trial,
although his testimony was significantly limited). Instead, a government
plant fabricated all the accusations. The defense was not provided with the
recordings revealing how Partin had maneuvered his way to Nashville until
February 25, toward the end of the trial. "I say to you," Haggerty pointed at
the jury, "whatever Partin may call himself, he was planted by the government as an informer in Nashville for the reason that the government had no
confidence in the ridiculous charges made against Mr. Hoffa in the Nashville
case."[28]

The story began in a lonely Baton Rouge jail cell, where Partin had sat,
accused of aggravated kidnapping and ineligible for bond. Charged with a
twenty-six-count indictment, he faced up to seventy-eight years in prison.
"His position is hopeless," Haggerty recounted, "but in his cunning and criminal mind there comes a thought, 'I have merchandise to sell or trade. Perhaps
the Department of Justice will pay a price. They may restore my life and I
can deliver the life of James R. Hoffa.'" In this manner, Haggerty continued,
a "foul, filthy frame was born."[29]

Haggerty addressed Partin's character: "Married but not living with his
wife and children, as a matter of fact arrested for non-support of his children,
and it always rather occurred to me that if a man was at all capable and is
earning wages or has an income his first duty is the support of the little ones
that he was responsible for bringing into the world. A philanderer. Other
women were his avocation. A convicted felon, a man accused of betraying
his trust, a man of violence, kidnapping, a man whose word was not worthy
of belief, as evidenced by his general reputation in the community in which
he resides." Would you ever believe a thing Partin said? Haggerty asked. "Or
would you reject him as unstable, [an] untrustworthy liar, doesn't the man
his antecedents and his proven character rate at least a reasonable doubt in

your mind?"[30] "Yes, I say [to] you, Edward Partin," Haggerty's voice quavered, "thou shall not bear false witness against thy neighbor."[31]

The attorney then set his sights on the secondary subject of his ire, "the architect of this diabolical plot, the servant of his master Robert Kennedy, Attorney General of the United States, Walter Sheridan." Why hadn't Sheridan testified? Sheridan had threatened King, Pitts, and Paschal with indictment unless they changed their stories. Those who had played along with Sheridan—like Carl Fields and James Walker—were protected; those who had not were sitting in the courtroom as defendants. No, Sheridan could not have risked being put under oath. He would have had to tell the truth.[32]

As further evidence of Sheridan's mendacity, Haggerty noted, when Shobe claimed to be a secret government informant, "Walter Sheridan did not take the stand and contradict him." Why not? Sheridan's silence, Haggerty insisted, was damning.[33] By contrast, Hoffa *had* taken the stand. No evidence had been introduced of any past misdeeds on his part. "He denied categorically every statement made by Partin concerning him and his alleged knowledge of jury tampering." On the witness stand, Hoffa was intelligent, straightforward, honest, and "hostile towards wrong and evil." Yes, he was aggressive, Haggerty remarked. "Would you not be aggressive and hostile if you were unjustly accused of a crime, of a plot against you engineered for the benefit of an enemy, in this instance Robert Kennedy?"[34]

Haggerty smiled warmly toward the jurors, coming only slightly short of daring them to find against his client. "I say that this jury should not serve the Attorney General's desire for personal revenge against Hoffa in order to further his own political ambitions but render a true and just verdict of not guilty against all Defendants in order that the myth, and it is a myth, that a southern jury will not render justice in a just case be dispelled forever."

Haggerty remained soft-spoken but intense during his summation. Exhorting jurors to examine the evidence with a critical, logical eye, he raised very real questions as to the testimony that, for one reason or another, had *not* been offered by the government. After Haggerty relinquished the podium, a lunch break was taken at 12:15.[35]

———

Following lunch, Dave Alexander addressed the jury on behalf of Nicholas Tweel. For the most part, Alexander had hovered quietly behind the scenes throughout the trial, likely part of an overall strategy to keep Tweel under the radar—and separated from some of the more aggressive antics of the defense. Now, Alexander wanted jurors to be able to relate to Tweel, who had only briefly appeared on the stand. "I say to you ladies and gentlemen of the jury," he began, "that the Defendant Tweel is not merely a name or a number on an indictment. He is a human being. He has all of the fears, he has all of the feelings that you would have were you at his place in the prisoner's dock with the other Defendants."[36]

What corrupt action had there been on Tweel's part? When asked whether Tweel had ever compelled him to contact anyone on the Test Fleet jury, Dallas Hall himself had responded, "No, he didn't." Well, then, what had Tweel asked him to do? "Just find out what I could about them," Hall had replied. There was nothing unlawful about that. Every lawyer, Alexander explained, does his best to find out what he can about the individuals sitting on the jury. "I say to you," he added, "if the testimony produced by Dallas Hall was an indictable offense every lawyer within the sound of my voice, including Judge Wilson, would have been in the penitentiary a long time before now according to the theory of the government's case[,] and I defy them to say that is not true."[37]

Alexander also addressed Hazel Fulton, the "poor creature" who had admittedly lied on three separate occasions, including when questioned by the grand jury. What was the chance that she would also lie in Chattanooga? "The trouble with a liar, ladies and gentlemen," he said, "is that you never know when to believe them."[38]

Like the other defense attorneys, Alexander could not resist taking a poke at the government's chief witness. "Now, my memory is far from infallible," he said. "And I can't remember what happened 7 or 8 weeks ago. I'm not like Mr. Partin, who could take this witness stand and say to you that on one occasion a year and a half previously he had called Nicholas Tweel at the Hampshire House in New York City and that the number was Circle 7-2345, or whatever it was. And yet, who couldn't remember on cross examination the date of his marriage. I couldn't possibly remember as did Mr. Partin that James Hoffa took an Alka-Seltzer in the bathroom of his suite at the Andrew Jackson Hotel, as he testified, and yet who could not remember when Mr. Berke cross examined him of running over a soldier and killing him."[39]

The allegations against Tweel, Alexander said, were simply implausible. Why would a man such as Tweel have traveled 1,000 miles to a city he had never visited in his life to influence a juror for the benefit of a man whom he had never met? It simply did not make sense. "Is this the kind of testimony with which a Defendant will be sent to the penitentiary?"[40]

Alexander looked squarely at the jurors. "I have tried a lot of lawsuits in almost 25 years of practice and I believe that if all of the evil of all of the witnesses which I have ever examined in a court of justice were all rolled into one that they couldn't touch Edward Grady Partin topside nor bottom," he asserted. "I don't think that I've ever seen and I don't think that you will ever see if you sit on juries for the next 50 years such a witness as this."

The allegations against his client were absurd, he remarked. "If you think that the Defendant Tweel took this man of 5 minutes acquaintanceship to his room and told him all of these intimate facts about his life," Alexander insisted, "if you believe that, then you send the Defendant Tweel away, but don't send him to the penitentiary, send him to the asylum and I will change his plea from not guilty to insanity."[41]

Concluding with a saccharine sentiment, Alexander claimed he was re-lieved to shift the burden of the case onto the jury. "It is getting to where I dread going out into the hallway and having those two little girls of his, who are sitting over here against the wall with their mother, now 16 and 18 years old, look me in the eyes with those dark eyes and say, 'Please don't let them send my daddy to the penitentiary.'" Telling the jurors to "Do unto others as you would have them do unto you," Alexander shook hands with his client and sat down.[42]

———

Harold Brown took to the podium on behalf of Ewing King, offering witty, homespun remarks. All of the evidence against King, he began, had come from three witnesses, each of whom had admitted to lying on repeated oc-casions. How could they be believed now?[43]

Much had been made about the curious meeting among King, Pitts, and Paschal along a river road. "It's hard for these Washington attorneys to un-derstand how people in the country live," Brown drawled, "because they attach intrigue to everything, and I'd say rightly so from where they are from. I guess there's more intrigue in the shadows of a [Washington] cocktail lounge every day than there is in the state of Tennessee in the history of the country." *Of course* they had not met at Paschal's house. "Well, what would they have said if he [King] had gone up to Mr. Paschal's house and his wife on the jury?" Brown asked. They had met elsewhere for the express purpose of avoiding suspicious appearances.[44]

The "most absurd" thing about the whole story, Brown continued, was the idea that King would climb into a car "with a 2-way radio with a high-way patrolman in full dress with a pistol" and remark to him, "I want you to talk to your wife to get her to hang a jury." If such a story could be believed,

Brown said (echoing Alexander), "I would have made a motion to this Court on the first day to get him psychiatric help."[45]

Paschal had been told that if anyone approached him about his wife, he should inform his supervisor. Yet he had failed to do so after speaking with King. Why? When asked about the meeting, Paschal had said, "I never attached any importance to it." Of course he didn't, Brown observed. He was being honest; no approach was made to him.[46] Furthermore, why would Paschal change his testimony? FBI influence, Brown asserted, shaking his head sadly. "Never underestimate the power of the Federal Government," he declared. "I have heard things come from this witness stand that I would never have believed would happen in the United States of America. Never."[47]

As for Partin, Brown said, "I think we all will agree with the government on that point that he is the main attraction." On four different occasions, Partin had met with government lawyers to prepare his testimony. "Mr. Partin answered questions on that witness stand like reciting Mary Had A Little Lamb," Brown said, smiling. "Never missed a one. Yet when it came time for his cross-examination, he never answered a single, simple question yes or no. It is a slam at the intelligence of this jury to produce the likes of this witness and tell you to swallow it." Partin, Brown continued, "couldn't remember that he had disgraced the uniform of this country, he couldn't remember that he had served time in the penitentiary for burglary and highway robbery while he was in serving in the Armed Forces or rather in the Marines, he couldn't tell you the incident that happened in Mississippi."[48] The attorney concluded, "You are one of the most important juries in this country. You are like the little boy in Holland with his finger in the dike. If you hold tight, we can stop this sort of thing."[49]

———

Courtroom observers leaned forward in their seats as Jacques Schiffer collected his papers and prepared for his summation. The crowd would not be disappointed in its expectation of histrionics on the part of the excitable Schiffer. Schiffer spoke for thirty-five minutes—far from the two hours he had insisted he would need. As he bounced from one topic to another, he "barked out his tirade at the prosecution like a machinegun."

At the outset, Schiffer wanted to answer a question that had presented itself to many observers. "How does it happen," he asked, "that a poor man like Tom Parks, a fellow who barely earns $1500 a year gets this New York lawyer down here and defends Parks?" "Well," he answered, "as the government wire taps will show, because I can't make a call out of my office or receive a call out of my office—they know the truth—Larry Campbell called me, I have known Larry for many years, he asked me would I defend his uncle." It was as simple as that. Schiffer did not explain how he would be paid for six weeks of trial and related expenses.[50]

Schiffer employed two time-honored tactics for relating to a jury. He emphasized the simple, rural nature of his upbringing, and he quoted liberally from the Bible. His attempts to identify with southern jurors seem silly and overreaching. He grew up on a farm, he explained, "five generations on the same farm." Schiffer continued, "I went to the same little red schoolhouse you went to. I was brought up on grits. I don't know whether these Washington prosecutors like it, but there's many a time when I grew up there was only grits to eat for the whole family." He was a simple man, he insisted.[51]

Pivoting, he railed that Kennedy had sent his "chief axman" (Sheridan) to Chattanooga to finish the job he had started in Nashville. "It is a shame, isn't it," Schiffer blasted, "people feed on our tax money, people who are servants suddenly become our public masters or at least they so attempt and use our money to defeat us. At times you wonder in the course of this trial with these Washington prosecutors was Nazism really licked? Are the Russians or Stalin really stopped? Is Mussolini dead? Is there [sic] brand of ism really over?"[52]

In what the Chattanooga Times called "the most unrestrained attack" on Partin, Schiffer catalogued the various criminal convictions the government witness faced. Rather than convict the man, however, the government had made a deal with him. "And if Partin tomorrow goes out and shoots a man at a gas station and kills him," Schiffer hollered, "he has got a license. These Washington prosecutors gave him a license. . . . They gave him immunity. He can do anything he wants. . . . This is the man who is going to testify against the man the Attorney General selected to be his foe." He thrust a finger at the jury, asking, "Does that sit right with you?"[53]

Notwithstanding these unfathomable attempts to miscarry justice, Schiffer continued, "the jury could not be misled by Ed Partin." "In my old farm days," he mused, "I remember the preacher always saying remember, truth crushed to the ground, trampled in the mud, when the full rays of the sun dispels the myths, the truth will rise."

"The truth is now rising in this case," he reassured the jury.[54]

Schiffer paused before pointing to Sheridan, who had slipped into the back of the courtroom. "Sheridan slithers in and out of the courtroom for seven weeks," he stated. "Did you ever see the prosecution put him on the stand to

tell you what he did here?" Sheridan could have easily refuted Shobe's testimony, but he never even took the stand. "He was hiding from you," Schiffer
asserted. Sheridan had not denied that he had offered Parks a deal to change
his story and testify against Hoffa. Thus, the defense attorney told jurors, "He
hid from you." When testimony showed that Jack Walker had worked for
the Get Hoffa Squad, Sheridan never appeared to deny the allegation. "He
didn't want to be cross examined, didn't want the whole shoddy, dirty, filthy
story brought out, so he hid himself and the government prosecutors from
Washington swept him under the rug," Schiffer said, smacking the lectern.[55]

Schiffer held out a hand toward his client, stoop-shouldered in his seat.
Unlike Partin, he boomed, Parks had a clean record and character. "Little
Tom Parks here rich or poor, powerful or weak, doctor, lawyer, Indian chief,
everybody is entitled to justice according to the rules of law . . . is he to be
deprived and called a convict because Walter Sheridan concealed from you
and wouldn't take the witness stand even when he was the active participant
and in the frame-up because he is a government official?" He pounded upon
the lectern. "Is this what America has sunk to?"[56]

Then came one of the more bizarre moments of the trial. Schiffer reminded jurors that a great debt was owed to the men and women who had
died protecting American liberties in recent wars. His voice rising even further, he hollered, "The prosecutors and investigators and everybody who
lends a hand to the destruction of American justice to that extent, has sold
them out." Schiffer pulled his fist from his pocket. "And in their name and
in my own," he declared, "I say to these Washington prosecutors, including
Mr. Sheridan, take the 30 pieces of silver." Schiffer then flung a pocketful of
change toward the prosecution table, stating, "You have earned it. Share it."
A gasp filled the courtroom. "Everybody," juror Pat Haverty recalled, "was
sort of shocked."

With his customary self-restraint and lack of comment, Judge Wilson announced a brief recess. Crawling on their hands and knees, reporters gathered
the change, which totaled $2.45. There were, the *Chattanooga News-Free Press*
noted, only twenty-four—not thirty—coins.[57]

––––––

Branstetter's measured argument was an anticlimax. Throughout the trial,
the genial, mannered lawyer had remained, probably purposefully, above
the hijinks some of the defense counsel displayed. In that same vein, his
summation would be simple and brief. Branstetter asserted that he had not

anticipated making a closing argument because he had never imagined the case against his client would go so far. "Had I been in the government's position," he said, "at the conclusion of this case I would have arose and said, if your Honor please, I move that Larry Campbell's case be dismissed."[58]

The prosecution, however, had subverted justice in its rabid attempt to secure a conviction. "You know," Branstetter remarked, smiling and gazing toward the ceiling, "when I grew up out in the country we had a pretty big old sow . . . that wallowed in the spring occasionally and when she did the water all below that spring became muddy." He leveled his gaze on the jury. "Let me tell you[,] if the well spring of justice is wallowed in by anyone it can become very muddy indeed and its total source and outlet will be muddy." Muddy insinuations were all that the prosecution had been able to throw at Campbell, he said, and the actual evidence against his client was "indeed small."[59]

Branstetter asked the jury to focus on a single question: "What evidence is there in this record that Larry Campbell committed any act whatsoever to encourage, to aid, to abet, or counsel or command anyone to do anything about any juror?"[60] He had placed some telephone calls, but no one had unearthed anything corrupt about them. In fact, it was undisputed that the calls had been made to a family member. The government's case was built from "whole cloth" and based on "flimsy testimony." There was no evidence to convict Campbell of anything.[61]

The attorney then turned to the government's key witness. Unlike prior defense smears, though, he took a different (if sarcastic) tack, which reporters referred to as the "mildest attack" on the big Louisianan. "I feel for Partin and I'm not going to criticize him," Branstetter said, shaking his head sadly. "Partin didn't ask to be born . . . he had nothing to do with the brain that he had when he came into this world at all. Since then he has had something to do with it, but I would suggest to you this that whatever you did yesterday controls in some measure what you will do today and what you do today will control at large measure what you do tomorrow." Given his debauched nature, poor, immoral Partin couldn't control himself. However, Branstetter said in a tremulous voice, "when we reach a point in this country to where you can send men to jail and take them from their families and deprive them of their freedom on the unsupported testimony of one individual of that character, then we are no longer free."[62]

Finally, and with deep gravamen, Branstetter reminded jurors of their responsibility. "This whole life, the totality of your life is just a procession to the grave," he said. "I would suggest this, that wrong decisions sincerely made where the liberty of the fellow human being is concerned is one that will march right down that road with you to the graveyard." With this solemn instruction, he quietly gathered his papers, patted his client on the shoulder, and sat.[63]

———

The final argument of the day would fall to Harvey Silets. At the outset, he detailed Allen Dorfman's experiences as a World War II veteran and respected businessman. Like Branstetter, Silets focused on the lack of evidence against his client. "You have heard scores, you see before you transcripts, thousands and thousands of pages of transcripts," he said to the jury. "In all of those thousands and thousands of pages of transcripts, what is the evidence? Only two witnesses have mentioned [Dorfman's] name, Edward Grady Partin and Hazel Fulton." In the end, the evidence showed nothing more than a legitimate business arrangement between Dorfman and Tweel.[64]

Partin had sidled up to Tweel and Dorfman at the Andrew Jackson Hotel and started up a conversation. What had his motive been? "Ladies and gentlemen," Silets suggested, "it is simple. The answer is freedom. He said, 'it's my life or his.' What he meant to say was, 'it's my freedom or theirs.'" The evidence of Partin's calumny became clear when he testified that Dorfman had asked *him* for Tweel's telephone number. Why would Dorfman, who had been engaged in business with Tweel for a considerable period of time, ask Partin—who had barely met the man—for his telephone number? "Does that give you any reason to doubt this story?" asked Silets.[65]

As for the alleged call from Dorfman to Tweel at the Union Station, Silets offered, if a man had wanted to discuss jury tampering over the telephone, would he really have done so in a crowded railroad station across the street from the local FBI office? "Wouldn't he do it in a dark, secluded street?" inquired Silets. And would he have used a credit card identifying him as the caller? "No, if a man were trying to hide something, wouldn't he drop coins in a box?" It was ridiculous on its face.[66]

Silets pointed to the heavy broadsword hanging above the judge's bench. "You see that sword of justice there?" he asked the jurors. "That sword of justice is in your hands. It is up to you to do with it as you wish. You can use it to destroy, destroy that man and those children and that woman with a child-to-be, or you can defend the very system by which we live, the very system by which that man gave part of his body and part of his blood to preserve." With that, Silets returned to his seat.[67]

After an exciting day of argument, intrigue, and accusations, Judge Wilson adjourned court at 4:40 p.m.

———

On the morning of March 3, Hoffa treated reporters to a "blistering sidewalk press conference" denouncing the government and the methods used to harass him. As he spoke, Hoffa observed the jurors arriving at the courthouse, flanked by US marshals. Trailing the marshals into the building, he accosted them about the number of men guarding the jury, which gave the impression that the jurors needed to be protected from the defendants. He lambasted federal agents, calling them "bums" and "trenchcoat stormtroopers." Yet, as the *Chattanooga Times* reported, they simply turned and silently walked away.[68]

As court convened, Haggerty echoed Hoffa's protests, stating, "The handling of the jury by the marshals is more fitting to a Russian spy or traitor trial than it is to the handling of a jury in a [*sic*] American court of justice." Their presence was proving detrimental to the defense, he insisted, and he asked the court to "break up this military display." Silets added that eleven marshals had been present during his closing argument the prior day. "[E]ach time I turned to the back of the room there," Silets said, "I see these handsome, huge men with folded arms." There was no way such a display did not intimidate the jury.[69]

"I attended some of the war crimes trials," Branstetter intoned, "and I never saw a display of this sort of thing. In a free country . . . justice cannot be dispensed under that type of surveillance."[70]

Schiffer suggested the marshals were part of a federal plot: "The government is attempting by some means, psychotic, call it whatever you will, but they are attempting to the very last moment to influence this jury on the side of the government." It was unfair to have the jury supervised by representatives of the very same government that was persecuting the defendants. Schiffer yet again drew a comparison to dictatorial Europe and Russia: "Now, what happened today with a trench coat scene and all the rest of it certainly happened in Nazi Germany and the Russia of old and the new regime. It happened in Italy under Mussolini." "We are not in a court of justice," he boomed. "We are not dealing with cattle. . . . I want a fair trial."

"Mr. Schiffer, Mr. Schiffer," Judge Wilson sighed, "throughout this trial the Court has asked you if you would please just be more logical and not so loud in your argument. There is nothing served in arguing these matters so terribly loud." Deaf to the court's exhortations, the strident New Yorker continued, targeting the court itself:

I have asked Your Honor a hundred times on this record to do
something about it to protect us here and make sure that we get
due process and in not a single instance has Your Honor said anything to the prosecution and cut it out and stopped it[,] stop this
interfering with the judicial processes.

Not once has your Honor done anything but say to the prosecution, I expect they will obey the law. Well, your Honor, every
time they have disobeyed it, we have brought it to the attention of
the Court but again nothing happens. What are we supposed to
do, counsel in the case when we look for due process? We can only
look to your Honor, so your Honor is the only one with the power
to correct the situation, but the Court refuses to do it.

Now, what happened today is precisely what my co-counsel,
Mr. Branstetter, said, these are the things that were exposed at
Nuremburg. These were the things exposed about the Russian sys-
tem and the Mussolini system[.]

Judge Wilson held up his hand. "All right." In the transcript of the day's
proceedings, the judge would scratch a heavy pencil mark, underlining the
words "Nuremburg" and "Mussolini." By training his invective on the court,
Schiffer had crossed into a perilous new country.[71]

Wilson ruled that four marshals would be sufficient to maintain order in
the courtroom. He then turned to Hoffa and informed him that his hollering could be heard throughout the building. "There has been this extremely
loud shouting and comments and statements made out in the halls and in
the corridors during every recess and at the beginning of court and at the
end of court." He continued, "[Upon hearing the disruption,] I called the
marshal to find out what the difficulty was and the marshal advised me that
Mr. Hoffa was complaining very bitterly about the marshals attending the
jury." Wilson exhorted everyone present to "discontinue these extremely loud
arguments, both in the Court and outside of the Court."

Hoffa nodded silently. He would reserve his comments for reporters on
the sidewalks.[72]

———

As the jurors settled into their seats, Harry Berke rose to address the twelve
men and women who would determine the fate of the defendants. He spoke
slowly and deliberately, "emphasizing each word" as he debunked the evidence offered against his client. "We're not trying a man because the attorney
general of the United States doesn't like him," he stressed.[73] As might have

been expected, Berke directed a "blistering attack" on the government's star witness. He reminded the jury of the litany of criminal charges hanging over Partin's head in 1962 and 1963. None of these cases had been prosecuted to judgment. Why not? Berke left the question hanging.

There were recordings of Hoffa, but it had been the defense—not the government—who had fought for their disclosure. "If they wanted this jury to know everything about this case," Berke remarked, "why didn't you bring them in here instead of hiding them for weeks[?]"[74] And why did Partin take the Fifth Amendment before the grand jury? Why not share his damning testimony at that point? "They couldn't afford to have Mr. Partin come in and tell a story that early in the procedure," Berke explained. The government had not yet finished threatening Paschal, Pitts, Walker, and Fulton with indictment. They needed more time. "What was happening for three whole months this grand jury was meeting?" he implored. "They were threatening these people hoping they could get somebody, someone to testify against them."[75]

The only evidence against Hoffa, Berke reminded the jury, had come from Partin. Conveniently, the damning comments attributed to the IBT president were said to have been made when *no one else* was present. As a result, no defense witness could be called to deflate Partin's bold fabrications.[76]

In addition, both Walker and Paschal were admitted perjurers who had not been prosecuted. Walker was "still wearing a police uniform," Berke stated, and "Paschal [is] riding around in this patrol car." Clearly, they were being protected in exchange for their fabricated testimony. "They have saved their lives," Berke insisted, "they have saved their jobs. Now they want to save the life of Mr. Partin and put his [Hoffa's] head on a chopping block for you to chop off."[77]

Berke turned to one of the original questions that had plagued the case. Why would Hoffa commit a felony to obtain acquittal in a small misdemeanor matter such as the Test Fleet case? "Would you think that a man with his intelligence would risk his whole future, would risk his life, would risk his reputation and his family's reputation to try to tamper with a jury which is a major offense?" Berke held up his hands in supplication. "Do you think that Mr. Hoffa would spend $100 to fix a $1 parking ticket? That is what it amounts to."[78]

Closing his remarks, Berke addressed Schiffer's disruptive antics. "If during the course of this trial, any attorney has been overzealous and at times it appears that Mr. Schiffer might have been," Berke reflected, the blame should not be attributed to the defendants. "This is not an ordinary case," he said. "Here we have got the power and the might and the wealth and the desire and the urge of the government to convict Mr. Hoffa. Why does Mr. Neal then criticize Mr. Hoffa for his zeal and determination to defend himself, to defend himself against the type of evidence that you have heard here displayed day after day. Is it any wonder that the attorneys at times become overwrought?"[79]

Despite the government's corruption and Partin's mendacity, Berke professed faith that the jury would reach the proper result: "You are on trial just like these defendants are on trial because the whole world wants to see if in spite of what the government has done in this case if we still have a jury, a jury that is fearless, a jury that can go ahead and determine that regardless of what the United States Government wants, regardless of how bad they want Mr. Hoffa, that our American jurisprudence, our American system of trial by jury is more important."

Mopping his brow, Berke walked to the defense table, where he sat and nodded to his client. The defense had completed its case. At 10:42 a.m., the judge ordered a brief recess, after which the prosecution would offer its rebuttal.

———

As the last of the jurors exited the courtroom, Hooker spoke up. While defense attorneys had lambasted Sheridan for not taking the stand, the government had actually been prohibited from calling him on rebuttal. The basis for this prohibition was that Sheridan's testimony should have been offered during the government's case-in-chief, if at all. Now the defense was taking advantage of that fact by creating an unfair, false inference in the minds of jurors. The government attorneys, Hooker reasoned, should be allowed to inform jurors that they had attempted to present Sheridan.

The defense met this request with howls of protest. The prosecutors had committed a strategic misstep in failing to call Sheridan to testify; why should they be allowed to profit from their mistake? In any event, Branstetter pointed out, Sheridan had sat in the courtroom during much of the testimony in the case. Witnesses were not permitted in the courtroom prior to their testimony, and so it had been proper to exclude Sheridan.

After a brief recess, Judge Wilson held that "the defendants having objected to the production of the testimony of the Witness Sheridan, and then having argued upon the fact that his testimony was not produced . . . the government would be permitted to respond to the fact that he was not produced to the extent that that [was] reflected in the record." The prosecution would be allowed to point out that the government was not hiding Sheridan.[80]

———

The jury returned to the courtroom. Hooker would offer the final argument in the case, but the defense would not make it easy. In an effort to disrupt his pacing and flow, defense attorneys tossed out a multitude of objections. In particular, Schiffer repeatedly objected on the ground that Hooker was inaccurately stating the facts. For the most part, those objections were quietly overruled. Hooker remained unfazed. A seasoned trial attorney, he had a particular capacity for getting under the defense attorneys' skin. "He was great to watch," Gearhiser reminisced. "One of my fondest memories was John J. Hooker, Sr. was making a bombastic argument at the podium, and all the defense lawyers almost in unison and were objecting and objecting, and John J. Hooker never flinched a muscle. He just said something like, 'I love it. I know I'm getting to them when they do that.'"[81]

At the outset, Hooker asked whether anything could have been done to tamper with the Test Fleet jury without the chief defendant's knowledge. It simply was not believable. Everyone in the courtroom had observed Hoffa's domineering presence throughout the trial. "I say it in all good humor," Hooker continued, "and with friendliness toward my adversaries here that I think it's pretty apparent here that nobody that sits in this table would dare eat a meal unless they ate what Mr. Hoffa told them they should eat at that particular meal."[82]

Hooker turned to the evidence. Did the jury really believe that James Walker, a policeman and "substantial citizen there in Nashville," had worked with Shobe as a government agent? "Did you ever see anything like that in your life?" Hooker asked, chuckling.[83]

As for the explanation that Dorfman and Tweel had simply been negotiating a business deal in October 1962, Hooker countered, it was certainly a "strange circumstance" that two men had taken private jets "in the wee, small hours of the night" to fly to Nashville for a meeting—coincidentally, on the day that the Test Fleet trial had begun. And wasn't it a little unusual that on the day of this important business meeting Dorfman and Tweel had found themselves at the courthouse watching the trial? Hooker asserted, "I wouldn't have thought that the commencement of the selection of the jury and whatever motions that they had there about it would have been very interesting to a man from Huntington, West Virginia that didn't even know [Hoffa]."[84]

During the trial, Dorfman had telephoned Tweel from Nashville to read off a list of jurors. Why? "Could there be any reason," Hooker boomed, "except that there was something corrupt about it?"[85] Poor Hazel Fulton had corroborated that testimony, stating that she had taken down a list of jurors' names on plain white stationery. How did the defense respond to her account? By attacking her character, grilling her about her marriage at age sixteen, and calling her an unfit mother. "I say to you, ladies and gentlemen," Hooker leveled, "what the original Henry Grady said in the *Atlanta Constitution*, that anyone who would attack the virtues of a woman in a court of justice, whether she be a virgin or a harlot, ought to be in hell."

"Your Honor," Schiffer said, "I want to object to the misquotation. Mr. Grady spoke of a lady, not the kind of woman here depicted by Mr. Hooker."

Hooker glanced disdainfully toward the defense table. "That is just the reply that I would expect Mr. Schiffer to make."

Judge Wilson urged him to move on, but Hooker had his blood up:

> Yes. From the man that makes the objections, the same man that hurls thirty pieces of silver on the table here, the purse that was paid for the life of our Lord, and he would have the audacity in a court of justice to throw money down in that fashion and in the manner which he did.
>
> Oh, it takes a strong man. It takes a brave, courageous man to have a lady get on the witness stand and then to deride and defame and abuse her, and I don't believe that juries in Tennessee—I have been standing before them for long, many years. I don't believe that they appreciate that sort of thing.[86]

Hooker paused for effect before asking what motive Dorfman might have had to help Hoffa. Noting that Dorfman admittedly received $35–50 million in insurance business annually from the Teamsters, the prosecutor added, "I would be willing to risk a wager that there is not an insurance agent in Tennessee that handles that much in premiums in a year's time." [87]

Turning to the fifth count, Hooker shook his head. "In all of the time that I have been watching around the courts," he said, "I have never seen anything quite like this." You don't hunt rabbits with hound dogs, King had suggested. "I never did know before that you hunted jurors with beagle hounds," Hooker observed, returning to his earlier quip.[88] King had met with Paschal at one o'clock in the morning, in the dark, along a deserted river road. Amazingly, King described these circumstances as "a country way of doing it." Hooker rocked back onto his heels. "Well," he remarked, "I live on a farm myself and was born and raised in the country. I didn't, my younger days I didn't know of many meetings that my father and anybody else had at twelve or one or two o'clock in the morning on a dark, rainy night. The kind of people that lived in the country where I lived didn't operate that way."[89]

King would also have the jury believe that he had just been talking to Paschal about getting a promotion. "Is there anybody on the jury that is gullible enough to believe any such story as that?" the prosecutor asked. And could the jury really believe that Hoffa had no knowledge of what was going on? King was a close Hoffa associate. He had picked Hoffa up at the airport in Nashville; he had been at the trial practically every day; and he had been in the hotel suite every evening. Then he had gone to Woodbury and met with the husband of a woman sitting on the jury. "Do you believe he told Mr. Hoffa about it?" Hooker questioned rhetorically.[90] Chattanooga jurors, Hooker offered, were in a similar situation to that of Betty Paschal. How would they feel if someone involved in the trial had visited their homes and spoken with their spouses? "Would you resent it?" he asked. "Would you know that somebody was making an effort to corrupt you and to ruin your good name?" That is exactly what King had tried to do.[91]

Turning to "Mutt" Pitts, Hooker shook his head and chuckled. "Poor old Mutt. I kind of felt sorry for Mutt. . . . I don't believe Mutt was very used to being in the jury fix. I got the impression that he wasn't very experienced at it."[92]

Of course, it was necessary to address defense attacks on Partin. The defense had made a "terrible assault" on Partin, Hooker said gravely. "They went way beyond what I thought was the rule in asking a great many things about collateral matters," he remarked, yet the only conviction the defense had been able to prove was a robbery charge when Partin was nineteen years old. Lacking credible evidence, defense counsel had resorted to baseless accusations of rape, treason, and drug addiction. As Hooker observed, "They brought the charge which was, to my way of thinking, one of the most serious charges that you can make against a man. I don't know of anything that is more horrible in life than to be addicted to dope, morphine or heroin or some derivative of opium." And what came of that allegation? Dr. Magruder and two other experts testified that Partin had never been addicted. Hooker called this information the "one fact in the record that has been conclusively established."[93]

He acknowledged that Partin's record was not unblemished. "Oh, you may say, I don't think Partin is an entirely exemplary character," Hooker mused. His eyes met those of the jury. "I say so, too." But in a case such as this, he added, one that involved tampering with a jury, "you are not going to find any elders and deacons and stewards and people in the church around." Partin was a close associate of Hoffa's. He had been present throughout the Test Fleet trial, even guarding Hoffa's suite. "He has told you about things that he couldn't possibly have known unless he had been up there in that suite and heard them," Hooker maintained. Partin's character flaws allowed him to fit in as a validated member of Hoffa's crew.[94]

"This is a case," Hooker declared, "the record of which will extend throughout the State of Tennessee and probably throughout the United States." Rising up to his full height, he stared intently at the members of the jury. "Mr. Hoffa is the head of the largest labor union in the world, but that don't give him a license to fix a jury, and I say to you with all the sincerity at my command, that Chattanooga after more than a hundred years, has survived a Chickamauga and a Missionary Ridge, but Chattanooga can never survive the acquittal of those who have been proven to be guilty of contaminating, tampering with, and fixing a jury in the courts of justice in this state."

As Hooker gathered his papers, observers shifted in their seats, waiting to see what would happen next. Closing arguments were complete.

———

After the court dispensed with a flurry of motions for mistrial, Judge Wilson spent two hours laboriously reading the jury their instructions for deliberations. "In any case, not only are the parties to the suit on trial, but the judicial process itself is on trial," he informed the jury. "Remember, that our system of justice is itself on trial in every lawsuit. . . . Each time you apply your best and your finest faculties in ascertaining the truth in accordance with the evidence, and in accordance with the instructions of the court, justice will prevail and justice is the only condition under which freedom can survive."[95] At 7:30 p.m., jurors retired to a room nearby to deliberate. Wilson fielded a series of objections to the jury instructions, denying each of them in turn after yet another brief recess.

Judge Wilson then called the four alternate jurors (Curbow, Burrows, Cramer, and Bonner) into the courtroom to thank them for their service. "There are no medals that I could give you for such dedicated and essential service," he commented. "Nor are there any material awards that can be given to you." In sitting patiently through weeks of trial on the off chance that they might be needed, Wilson remarked, those individuals had performed "one of the highest duties of citizenship." Now that deliberations had begun, however, they could go home. "You can, therefore, rest assured that your services were not only deeply appreciated but that they were absolutely necessary," the judge said in closing.[96]

As the jury began to deliberate, most of the defendants and their lawyers waited at the Hotel Patten. Hoffa and his attorneys, however, chose to remain in and around the courthouse. For the most part, the scene was calm, with a heavy atmosphere of anticipation. At one point, though, observing Sheridan in the courthouse, Hoffa could not restrain his disgust. Hearkening back to the allegation that Sheridan had hidden out to avoid testifying, the IBT president barked at him, "You don't have an ounce of guts in your body."[97]

While the jury considered the evidence entered in the case, Judge Wilson summoned legal counsel for both sides to address Frank Ragano's recent effort to listen in on the jury:

> One defense counsel, Mr. Schiffer, arose to address the Court at
> the time in a very loud argument[,] unquestionably the loudest argument that the Court had heard in this case. At the same another
> attorney for the defense privately left the courtroom and went to
> the private area where the jury is kept allegedly to see if the argument was coming through to the jury.
>
> Now, it is an odd procedure to say the least, where if a defense
> counsel is thought by another defense counsel to be arguing too
> loudly that they would resort to this circuitous method of sending
> another attorney privately to the jury room rather than merely
> suggesting that the defense counsel arguing tone down his remarks
> . . . the defendants cannot create such a situation as this and then
> seek to take advantage of their own actions.

When Haggerty rose to comment, Judge Wilson held up his hand. "Mr. Haggerty," he said, "I believe it would be best if you will just file a written reply if you desire to reply to it. File any written reply that you wish." It had been a long day, and the judge was disinclined to hear any further arguments.[98]

With that matter addressed, the court adjourned at the late hour of 10:05 p.m. Jury deliberations would continue the following morning.

NINETEEN

"They are trying to take me out of circulation."

—Jimmy Hoffa

AFTER SIX WEEKS of silence, cautioned to never share their opinions, isolated from media coverage, and subject to marshals hovering over their shoulders, the twelve men and women of the jury were anxious to discuss the case. They occupied a tight room dominated by a wooden table around which were clustered a dozen chairs. The jurors were expected to distill weeks of testimony, exhibits, and evidence into a tidy, neat decision as quickly as possible.

By the end of the proof, Pat Haverty felt that he had made up his mind about the case. Not everyone agreed, however. "We all started talking at once, and we were all exchanging conversations in little groups of one or two or three," Haverty recalled, "but it wasn't a whole table working together at first." Slowly, the jury progressed toward a consensus. "At first, there was some doubt in a lot of people's minds," he said, "and then toward the end there was no doubt, everybody was in agreement." In Haverty's opinion, the key to the deliberations was a simple question: "Do you believe Partin?"[1]

Around the courthouse, federal agents were on high alert. It was a jury tampering case, after all, and the jurors were hidden away, mulling the possibility of criminal convictions against six men, one of whom was one of the more powerful persons in the country. Before the jury was shepherded away, Judge Wilson had asked Mansfield to ensure that the room was devoid of bugs or other listening devices. "So I went to the FBI, and asked the FBI would they de-bug the jury room," Mansfield said, "[and] so they debugged the jury room, and it was clean." The concerns about jury interference were not necessarily without basis. The tiny windows of the jury room faced the nearby Hotel Patten, where the Hoffa team was staying. The trial had been drenched in claims of surveillance. As jurors traded their opinions about the weight of the evidence, no one could know whether anyone might make one last bold attempt to sway the outcome of the case.

Such attempts plagued Mansfield's thoughts until the very last moment of the trial. "I was up on the roof one day with some glasses, looking toward the Hotel Patten to see if they happened to be trying to bug the jury room with electronic surveillance," he observed, "and when I was up there looking at them, they was looking down watching me." Similarly, US marshal Granville Sertel recalled noticing a window open at the Hotel Patten on a particularly cold day. Surveying the spot with binoculars, he was surprised to see a telescope looking back at him, monitoring the federal building.[2] With those experiences fresh on their minds, federal agents felt keen pressure to protect the jurors' deliberations from any outside influence.

———

Wednesday, March 4. As they had done for thirty-two days, the parties gathered in the third-floor courtroom to begin the day. No one said much; everyone was worn out. Smoke curled in the folds of the brown drapes lining the sides of the room. A few stifled coughs broke the silence as spectators shifted on the wooden benches of the courtroom. Outside, a heavy rain lashed the windows, distant thunder a backdrop to the shuffling of papers and creaking of chairs.

As usual, the proceedings began at nine o'clock. The jury was hidden away in the small room where they sifted through their impressions from the past six weeks. While waiting for a verdict—which could be delivered at any moment, or be delayed indefinitely—the court would take up other matters. At long last—and far too late, in the eyes of defense counsel—the court would hear the allegation that the government had surveilled the defendants and their lawyers throughout the trial. Anxious to keep the hearing focused (and to prevent it from spiraling out of control), Judge Wilson announced that he would only allow testimony addressing surveillance during the Chattanooga proceedings. Nothing else was admissible.[3]

Schiffer kicked off the hearing with an unexpected revelation. He announced that he had filed "a sealed envelope containing certain information," including a twenty-nine-page handwritten affidavit signed by surveillance expert Bernard Spindel. Only Spindel had seen the contents of the envelope, Schiffer added carefully.[4] Judge Wilson was hesitant. How could Schiffer file something without knowing what it was? "The Court is just not familiar with the practice of a stranger to a lawsuit filing a sealed document in which no attorney or party alleges to have any knowledge whatsoever," he said. "I am just not familiar with that sort of practice, gentlemen."

Schiffer snapped back with a biting pronouncement that would earn him a few more underscored scribblings in the judge's notebook. "It has been the practice in this court in this very case," he bellowed, "for the government, and I say surreptitiously, to take papers and put them into a sealed envelope and give them to the Court. We get no copies of what is in the sealed envelope and that has been permitted by the Court in exhibit after exhibit . . . the Court nevertheless kept it from the defendants in its sealed state."

Judge Wilson inquired whether anyone—a nonparty, in particular—had submitted a sealed document about which he admittedly knew nothing. "I just am totally unfamiliar with that sort of procedure," he added. "If that were the case then I suppose that everyone across the United States that has anything that they think the Court ought to look at could seal it up and send it in here and the Court would have to read it and consider that." He returned the envelope to Schiffer. If the attorney wanted to open the envelope and submit the document himself, he was welcome to do so.[5]

Schiffer retorted that he had provided Spindel with specific instructions. "When you come to Chattanooga and find there is no surveillance," he had advised, "you pack up and go home. If you find that there is surveillance there is only one party I want you to report to by a sealed document that is to the Judge presiding in this very trial." The fact that Spindel had prepared a sealed document, then, served as apparent confirmation of such surveillance.[6]

Relenting, Judge Wilson indicated that he would permit Schiffer to submit the envelope. Hooker, though, was having none of it. "If it is not going to be read," he interjected, "it ought not be filed."

The judge wavered. Would he not be setting a dangerous precedent by allowing a nonparty to submit whatever he wanted the court to review? "If I have to read all that material, I take it you could file the Library of Congress and seal it and require the Court to read the Library of Congress." Wilson leveled a withering gaze upon Schiffer. "Why are you unwilling to examine it yourself and determine whether it has any relevancy and if it does then submit it to the Court?"

The answer involved Section 605 of the Federal Communications Act. Under federal law, it was not a crime simply to engage in wiretapping; the crime occurred when the information from wiretapping was *divulged*. Schiffer, therefore, could submit Spindel's findings, but he could not review or disclose the information himself. He was unwilling to be tricked into committing a criminal offense. "They will never see me in that position," he announced.[7]

In his reserved, controlled manner, Judge Wilson was incensed. "If you think it's a violation of law to open the envelope," he told Schiffer, "then don't ask the Court to do something for you that you think would be a violation of law for yourself to do."[8]

———

The long-awaited surveillance hearing was at long last under way. The first witness was Everett J. Ingram, special agent in charge of the Knoxville FBI office. He explained that a total of twenty-five agents had been assigned to Chattanooga during the trial. On January 16, four days before the trial began, they had been dispatched to observe the former president of Teamsters Local 515, William Test. Current Local 515 president George Hicks and Washington Teamster John Cleveland were added to the list a few days later. Ingram had observed no one else. After reviewing a handful of investigative notes Ingram had brought with him, Judge Wilson confirmed that the documents contained no mention of any of the defendants or their attorneys.

Silets asked whether the agents had ever observed Hoffa. "I am sure they saw him on one or two occasions," Ingram responded. It was difficult *not* to notice Jimmy Hoffa; however, he had not been placed under surveillance.

Yes, photographs had been taken, at both the courthouse and the Hotel Pat-ten. These were reviewed "to see if they showed individuals present in and around the courthouse building, people who might be here for some ulterior motive." Photographers had not been instructed to focus on any particular individual. Of the 723 photographs FBI agents had taken, Hoffa appeared in fourteen, and the other defendants and their attorneys in a handful. No photographs had been taken after January 23.

Silets leaned on the podium. He was not convinced by the claim that he had not been tailed throughout the trial. Wasn't it true that agents had been assigned to follow him? "You have not been under surveillance at any time before or during the trial," Ingram replied coolly. Wasn't it true that the FBI pored over long-distance calls made to and from the Hotel Patten, monitoring defense communications? "That is not true," Ingram shot back. Nor had there been any surveillance of post office records or "mail watch." Likewise, there had been no surveillance of the Read House, where the jury was sequestered. During a second surveillance conducted between Febru-ary 3 and 6, Ingram reported, Bernard Spindel was the only individual who had been followed. The comings and goings of the defendants and their legal counsel were not observed. Since that time, no surveillance had taken place.[9]

At that moment, a deputy US marshal from Nashville, Charles Kemp, knocked on the courtroom door and handed a staffer a folded piece of paper, which was then passed on to Judge Wilson. The room fell to a hush. After inspecting the note, the judge informed the anxious spectators that the jury had reached a verdict. Ingram was ushered from the witness stand.[10] At 1:58 p.m., the jury filed silently into the courtroom and stood in a semicircle facing Wilson. The crowd outside the courtroom spilled out into the street.

Wilson looked over the jurors. Had they reached a verdict? The foreman, thick-set Hal Bullen, his wiry gray hair a bit disheveled, cleared his throat. "Yes, your Honor."[11] Hoffa leaned forward, muscles tensed, his elbows on the defense table. To prevent any possible disturbance, Mansfield stood behind him.

"On the third count what is your verdict with regard to Thomas Ewing Parks?"

"Guilty," Bullen said.

An audible gasp snapped the silence of the courtroom. Chairs creaked as the startled defendants turned to their lawyers, to one another, to their families scattered throughout the courtroom. Parks hung his head. In the meantime, the jury also found Larry Campbell guilty of attempting to influence Test Fleet juror Gratin Fields. For Hoffa, though, there was still a chance; the jury might have found that, whatever Parks and Campbell had done, he had not been involved. He took a deep breath and waited.

"What is your verdict on the Defendant James R. Hoffa on the third count?" Wilson asked Bullen.

"Guilty."

The color drained from Hoffa's face. For a long moment he "stared grimly in apparent disbelief" at the backs of the jurors. Seated behind him, daughter Barbara Crancer burst into tears. Hoffa silently reached back to reassure her.

Turning to the fourth count, Bullen announced that Hoffa, Dorfman, and Tweel had been found not guilty. Perhaps jurors had been convinced that a legitimate business relationship existed between Dorfman and Tweel. Perhaps the fact that no actual approach was made to any juror had moved them. Whatever the basis for the decision, Dorfman and Tweel could sit back in their chairs with quiet relief.

If Ewing King found a faint source of hope in the verdict on count four, it was short lived. "Guilty," Bullen reported when Judge Wilson asked for the decision of the jury on count five. Hoffa was also found guilty of conspiring to influence Betty Paschal by offering to obtain a promotion for her husband. Sitting on a second-row bench with her four small children, Margaret King began to cry. Chuckie O'Brien comforted her.[12]

Their service completed, the exhausted jurors were doubtless ready to go home. Judge Wilson would waste no time discharging them, though he first said, "It is men and women such as you yourselves who are willing to serve as you have served that assure the preservation of freedom in this country ... You have performed outstanding service and I wish to commend you." As the jurors left the courthouse, reporters scrambled to call in the judgment, which would make for attention-grabbing headlines in newspapers and on newscasts that very afternoon. Throughout the country, front-page photographs showed Teamsters snapping up the latest editions carrying headlines about the verdict: "Hoffa, 3 Others Guilty," "Hoffa Guilty of Jury Fix," and the like.[13]

As the room cleared, Dave Alexander stood to address the court. Would Dorfman and Tweel be needed any further? "Mr. Tweel and Mr. Dorfman are free to go," Judge Wilson replied. The two men walked away, their loved ones accompanying them. Wilson then set the remaining defendants' bonds, amounts paid to ensure their appearance before the court when summoned.

Hoffa would be required to post a bond of $75,000, King and Parks $20,000, and Campbell $25,000.[14]

At 2:25 p.m., Wilson called a recess—the shaken defendants needed time to collect themselves, talk with their families, and make plans to post bond. Accompanying Hoffa into the hallway, Harry Berke and Harold Brown asked to use Mansfield's office for a moment. The IBT president needed to call his wife to inform her of the verdict, and he had to call Teamsters headquarters to have cash money sent to post his bond. "I was all for him making bond that day," Mansfield later confessed. "I didn't want him in custody." The marshal waved the men into his office, where two deputy marshals had been posted at the door. Hoffa, though, objected to the officers' presence. "No, no, no, no," he barked, "you all get the hell out of here."

"Mr. Hoffa, you don't understand," Mansfield interposed. Hoffa was in custody, and he had not yet posted bond.

Standing up, Hoffa came around from behind the desk and confronted Mansfield. He wanted privacy. "Young man," he declared hotly, "you'll be in the penitentiary before I will."

"Yes sir, Mr. Hoffa," Mansfield responded, matter-of-factly. "I may be. But right now you're in my custody, and this is my office, and you've got two damn choices. One of them is you can sit down and use that telephone, or you can go in the lockup. Whichever one you want to do . . . but the deputies are staying in this office."

Grudgingly, Hoffa returned to his seat and dialed the number for his Detroit home.[15]

The hallway outside the courtroom was abuzz. Racing to the office he had maintained throughout the trial, Sheridan telephoned Kennedy. "We made it!" he shouted into the receiver.

While he was certainly gratified and relieved to receive the news, the attorney general's response was surprisingly understated: "Nice work." When reporters approached him for comment as he left a meeting concerning a new John F. Kennedy memorial library, Kennedy was similarly low-key. "I congratulate Mr. Hooker and Mr. Sheridan and Mr. Neal for their handling of the prosecution," he remarked.[16]

The prosecution team, though, was rightfully pleased. "Happy Prosecutors," read the caption for a photograph of the government lawyers leaving the courthouse. Mrs. John J. Hooker, slipping her gloved hands into the arms of her husband and Jack Reddy, beamed with pride. Neal walked a few feet ahead, his tan trenchcoat flapping behind him, lit cigar in hand. "I think justice has been done," Neal informed reporters, adding, "I am certain there is no reversible error in the record." Journalists asked how he felt about the dismissal of the charges against Dorfman and Tweel. The steely-eyed Neal took a draw from his cigar. "I suppose if I had to pick out the count in the indictment I considered the weakest," he responded, "it would have been that one."[17]

A few minutes later, the doors to the courthouse burst open, and Hoffa stepped down to the sidewalk. A barrage of reporters scrambled for footage of the newly convicted Teamster leader. Escorted by a helmeted motorcycle policeman, Hoffa shoved his way through the throng while the other defendants and their lawyers hung back. He wanted to meet the crowd alone—he had actually told one person near him, "I don't want you in the pictures." Swamped with questions, Hoffa responded tersely, "No comment whatsoever." Before reaching the street corner, though, he turned and looked over the teeming crowd. Then, after a long, tense moment, he denounced the trial and its result. Hoffa did not mention Kennedy, Sheridan, or government prosecutors—a departure from his familiar script. Nor did he lay the verdict at the feet of a massive government conspiracy. "A black fury marking his demeanor," one news report stated, Hoffa "was temporarily reduced to one frustrating weapon, a barrage of blistering denunciation."

"We did not get a fair trial," he said flatly. He declared that the court itself had doomed the defense: "A jury has returned its verdict, and in my opinion the verdict that was returned was returned because of the confusion that was created in this courtroom by sixty percent of the evidence being tried outside of the jury's presence, and the hamstringing of our defense by the federal government of deliberately holding back information and doing everything that is unjustified to do in a federal court trial in the United States, and if this is to be the turn of events of justice in the United States, then I pity those who do not have the funds to be able to carry on a fight to the appeals courts of the United States, because this is a railroad job in my opinion." Concluding with the observation "They are trying to take me out of circulation," Hoffa declined to take questions, then began to inch his way through the jostling crowd once again.

Several feet behind Hoffa, at the rear of the procession, a somber Ewing King walked quietly toward the Hotel Patten, holding the hands of his small children. When a reporter asked Margaret King if she had any comment, a truculent O'Brien shoved him away. Stooping down, King pulled a handkerchief from his pocket and wiped the eyes of his youngest child before resuming his long, sad walk.[18]

Back at the hotel, Hoffa took off his coat and looked around the suite, where a handful of his advisors were scattered about, sprawled in chairs, exhausted and shocked. He pointed at an unfamiliar face, snapping, "Who is that?" The interloper was escorted away. As the initial shock of the verdict wore off, Hoffa grew calmer. He sat for a brief interview in which he once again denounced the amount of evidence heard outside the jury's presence, as well as the decision to confine jurors to a hotel for an extended period of time. "I listened to the judge talk about justice," he said, "and I wondered if he really realized what justice is when he lets the jury know his personal feelings . . . even in his charge." He took a deep breath and rubbed his forehead. "I am confident that somebody will say, 'this is not American justice, this constant surveillance and harassment which is unparalleled in American history.'" Looking up, he noticed the dazed and dour faces that filled the room. There was no use wallowing in despair. There was still work to do. Drawing on the vigorous charisma that had enabled his rise to the presidency of the international union, Hoffa leapt up from his chair. "All right," he announced, clapping his hands. "Let's get started. Let's have the lawyers in here."[19]

———

After a break to allow everyone to digest the verdict, the court reconvened. It seemed anticlimactic, but the parties were still in the middle of a surveillance hearing. For Hoffa and his three remaining codefendants, that hearing might prove their only lifeline. The decision had been, as *Time* magazine announced, "A Jolt for Jimmy." After the break, however, he had "bounced back." With his normal magnetic charm he stood beside the defense table, talking and joking with reporters and exuding confidence that everything would work out in the end. As court was resumed, he smiled at one of his attorneys and commented, "Here we go again."[20]

FBI agent Everett Ingram returned to the stand. Silets, who had been conducting the examination, found himself in a curious position. His client had been dismissed from the case. Technically, he had no further role to play. Salvaging the situation, Silets announced that Campbell had retained him for a limited appearance—Hoffa, the attorney added, had not wanted him.

Silets resumed his questioning. Where were FBI agents posted to take photographs of visitors to the trial? One building, labeled B-1, stood across the street from the courthouse, and the other, B-2, was across from the Hotel

Patten. According to Ingram, all surveillance had ceased after February 6. No further transcriptions of conversations had been made; the surveillance had been purely visual.[21] Judge Wilson asked the witness one question. "Do I understand that you were checking Spindel and Spindel was checking you," he asked, "is that it?"

"That's correct, Your Honor," Ingram responded.

Berke, who felt strongly that he had been followed during the trial, wanted to ask a few questions of his own. Where in Chattanooga do FBI agents keep their official cars? he inquired. Ingram explained that the Volunteer Garage across the street from the courthouse had housed those vehicles for many years. Did you know that I also park in that garage? Berke asked. "I didn't know it until recently," Ingram replied.

"And did you know," Berke continued, leaning toward the witness and narrowing his eyes, "that some agents had followed me over into North Chattanooga and the area of my home?"

"I know that they did not," Ingram responded firmly. "I am positive."

"Was my son's car ever surveilled?"

"No, sir."[22]

Why, then, would FBI agents rattle off Marvin Berke's license tag number, as recorded by Spindel? The agents were not following anyone, Ingram replied, including Marvin Berke. They were sitting in a stationary vehicle. "The car kept passing our car," Ingram explained. "The agents took note of it and mentioned that it was a car with license number so and so." They had not followed the car, he insisted. "That car was coming by us."[23]

Was Hoffa surveilled? No, answered Ingram. If he had even been observed, it would have been incidentally as he interacted with one of the individuals under surveillance. Well, Berke continued, if you did not follow Hoffa, why do the transcripts include the comment "Mr. H and three others getting into a white Pontiac which is parked on the street up from Market Street?"

"That Mr. H," Ingram replied coolly, "was Mr. [George] Hix [sic]." Berke was confusing two separate incidents, Ingram explained. Hoffa had been observed getting into *Spindel's* rental car, a beige Chevrolet; Hicks was the individual who had been in Marvin Berke's white Pontiac. If Hoffa had ridden around in Berke's car on some other occasion, it was not during the incident reflected in the transcript. This information, of course, did not square with Berke's recollection of the events that had occurred in the abandoned West Side.[24]

After an unsatisfied Berke resumed his seat, Branstetter took the podium. Ingram informed him that FBI agents did not have two-way radio conversations with Spindel. Agents had spoken to Spindel over the radio—with the assumption that he was listening to their transmissions—but there had been no communications with him.[25]

As Ingram stepped down from the stand, Judge Wilson addressed the attorneys. Should they cut to the chase and put Spindel on the stand? Silets contended that they needed to hear first from other FBI agents. "This has been solely a fishing expedition attempt to make a discovery," the judge responded. "So far the record of this witness is that there was no surveillance whatsoever of any defendant or any defense counsel." Wilson did, however, allow the defense to call additional FBI agents.[26]

The next witness was Knoxville special agent Carl N. Barrett. Echoing earlier testimony, he explained that agents were initially assigned to observe only William A. Test. But the list of individuals under observation later expanded to include George E. Hicks, John Cleveland, Chuckie O'Brien, and Bernard Spindel. The surveillance had taken place between January 16 and 20, and then from February 3 to 6. According to Barrett, no defendants, defense attorneys, or witnesses had been surveilled. Nor had Barrett received any photographs of the defendants or their counsel. The agent understood that the five individuals under surveillance were rarely in Hoffa's presence. Once, when Test had driven to the Chattanooga airport to pick up the IBT president, Barrett had pulled off into a parking lot and ceased tracking the vehicle.

As the questioning dragged along with no new revelations, Judge Wilson implored Silets to speed things up. "Even though this Court reasonably expects to sit upon this bench the rest of his life," he drawled, "I don't expect to sit here the rest of my life on this case." After a couple of additional perfunctory questions, Silets relinquished the podium.

Neal asked one question: "Did you ever surveil the defendants or their counsel?"

"No, sir," Barrett replied.

"That is all." Neal resumed his seat.[27]

All in all, four FBI agents testified that there had been no surveillance of Hoffa or his attorneys during the trial.

Next to the stand was the obvious star of the surveillance hearing, self-professed wiretapper Bernard Spindel. The "6-foot, 210-pound sack of a man" was noticeably nervous. When asked to state his occupation, he mumbled and had to be told to speak up. "I'm an electronics technician," he repeated. "I specialize in eavesdropping devices. The detection of the devices. Methods. Equipment. And the design, development, and the manufacture of special-ized equipment for eavesdropping and detection." Are you an expert in this field? Silets asked. Yes, he responded.

On February 1, Spindel reported, Schiffer had asked him to come to Chat-tanooga to determine whether the defendants or their counsel were being surveilled. His instructions were simple. "He said that if my report showed that it was negative," Spindel explained, "I was to pack up my equipment and return to New York and bill him for my services; if it was positive I was not to divulge to anyone other than to indicate the results of my—that the results of my examination were positive and I was to make my report as an aide to the Court and seal my information and present it to the Court."

Spindel had arrived in Chattanooga on February 3, at which time he had conducted an impromptu examination of the ninth floor of the Hotel Pat-ten. He inspected the telephones, appliances, walls, air ducts, and furniture in each room. He also examined the hotel switchboard and the telephone cable and terminal box in the hotel basement. What was Spindel looking for? Microphones wired directly into the telephone lines, as well as hidden radio transmitters.[28]

Using binoculars to survey the area around the hotel, Spindel had imme-diately detected FBI agents stationed across the street, in a vehicle in front of the Greyhound bus terminal. He had also observed an agent with an earpiece, which signaled that he and his colleagues were using two-way walkie-talkie radios. In addition, Spindel's listening equipment detected "exceptionally strong and exceptionally clear signals indicating that the sources were nearby." The signals, he concluded, were coming from FBI agents stationed around the hotel. Spindel had then borrowed dictation equipment from one of the hotel's secretarial offices. "I decided to make actual recordings of the trans-missions so that I may have a record and also for future identification," he explained. He had also notified Schiffer that yes, he did feel that the defense was being watched.

After Tuesday, February 4, Spindel did not leave the hotel again until Feb-ruary 10. During that time, he had stayed hidden away in room 803, listening in to see what he could learn about the extent of the surveillance. "Did you ever intercept any telephone communications?" Silets asked.

"No."[29]

At that point, based on Spindel's testimony, Silets announced that the de-fense would not need to call any of the remaining FBI agents who had been summoned to Chattanooga. Judge Wilson had been upset by the defense practice of summoning far-flung witnesses without any commitment to call those persons to testify. "It does appear that the subpoena power has been abused in this case," he commented. "Anyone who has abused such subpoena powers will certainly be called upon to account." Feeling vulnerable, Silets sought to explain himself. The agents had been summoned in good faith, he said; ensuing testimony had simply made their presence unnecessary. "I don't want the Court to imply that I have abused the Court's process," the attorney maintained. Without further comment, Wilson urged Silets to focus on examining the witness.[30]

Turning back to Spindel, Silets took up the topic of the sealed envelope Schiffer had filed. Its contents included a partly handwritten, partly type-written transcript of FBI radio transmissions intercepted by Spindel. The wiretap specialist said he had recorded the conversations as accurately as possible. He had not otherwise divulged the details to anyone. "Is there any information in there," Silets asked, "which indicates that some observation or surveillance was being conducted of Mr. Hoffa or Mr. Berke?"

"Yes."

Judge Wilson leveled his stern gaze on the witness, asking whether he knew exhibit 249 was being filed with the court. Yes, Spindel replied, shifting un-comfortably in his seat. "Did you intend for it to remain a sealed envelope?" Wilson inquired. Spindel had no choice but to admit that he had expected the judge to open and review it.[31] Recognizing the legal risk involved with opening the envelope, however, Judge Wilson announced that he would not do so.

Berke was disconsolate, protesting, "It is the active duty of the Court to . . . see if there is anything in there that caused this defendant to have his con-stitutional rights violated." In fact, he added, the judge had previously done so, opening a sealed envelope submitted to the court.

Wilson corrected Berke, asserting that he had had no idea what he was opening on that prior occasion. Schiffer had filed a sealed document, and "the Court opened the document thinking all the time that this was a docu-ment that everyone knew about, . . . The Court now understands that there was some attempt to put something over on the Court in regard to delivering a sealed document in that manner."[32]

At that point, when it was probably wise to remain silent, Schiffer decided to address his prior filing. "I was flabbergasted at the Court as Mr. Neal," he shrugged, "when the Court took the contents of that [previous] sealed en-velope and made it a part of the court files for the Court's perusal."

Judge Wilson was incensed. "Do you mean to say that the Court can take these documents that you had filed as an exhibit to your motion . . . [a]nd not make them a part of the record, withhold them from the record?" he sputtered.

"Your Honor," Schiffer stammered, casting about for a reasonable response, "suppose the document contained things concerning national security."

"The documents did not contain national security matters," Wilson remonstrated, his patience exhausted.

Exhibit 249 did contain information to help the court address a violation of the defendants' constitutional rights, Schiffer offered. In such case, Judge Wilson responded icily, you submit the evidence as with any other piece of evidence. Do not "ask the Court to do the work that you yourself are unwilling to do because you believe it to be a violation of law."[33]

Schiffer was in a tough spot. "There is no other way to give it to your Honor," he replied. He could not disclose the information without violating Section 605 of the Federal Communications Act. That was the reason he had submitted the document under seal. The frustrating conundrum set Schiffer off on one of his characteristic outbursts:

> Well, your Honor, may I state for the record that I personally most respectfully resent the imputation of doing something by devious means that I have practiced in good faith with this Court from the very beginning of this case, that at no time have I attempted in any fashion to do anything with this Court which an officer of the court should not do. I have certainly strenuously objected to the Court being used by the prosecution at their behest and every objection they have made to what would help the defendant, it is much their obligation to help the defendant as to prosecute them honestly, I have resisted the attempts of the government in every instance to use the Court against the defendants. That is my oath, that is my obligation, but it has been done with good faith with your Honor.

By that point, however, Judge Wilson was not buying any of Schiffer's justifications. Schiffer could not convince him that the plan was not intentionally devious. The court was not going to open a sealed envelope, but either Schiffer or Spindel could do so if he wanted to. Absolutely not, Spindel responded.[34]

Ultimately, Spindel described a handful of the FBI communications he had recorded. He focused on the evening on which a suspicious car had followed Berke and three others as they drove into the deserted West Side area. FBI agents had noted that one of the four individuals who got into the car was a slight fellow with a bald spot, "sort of like a monk with a crown." Spindel had such a bald spot, one of the agents had opined.

"Just for the record," Silets inquired, "Mr. Spindel[,] do you have a bald spot on the top of your head?"

"Not that I know of," Spindel replied. The defense pointed out that the individual to whom FBI agents were referring was likely Harry Berke, who did have a bald spot.[35] Spindel also confirmed that FBI agents had made comments directly to him over the radio. He read some of those remarks into the record: "Hi ya, Boin. Doing fine. Making lots of money working for Mr. 'H'? He is a good boy. Go home Bernard."[36]

Neal cross-examined Spindel, summoning a string of biting inquiries that provoked the latter to insist that he had engaged in no unlawful efforts during his brief sojourn in Chattanooga. The wiretapper's longtime connections to Hoffa and the Teamsters were a key focus of Neal's aggressive questioning. Yes, Spindel admitted, about eleven years earlier he had done some work for Local 299 in Detroit. Neal referenced Spindel's indictment—along with Hoffa—for illegal wiretapping in 1957. Silets immediately objected. "I don't know how anybody can be expected to remember a thing that happened in 1957," he declared. That weak disclaimer, of course, ran counter to the defense's fierce recriminations when Partin had failed to remember his own past criminal accusations. The court overruled the objection, allowing as much latitude with respect to Spindel as had been granted with regard to Partin.

Instructed to answer the question, Spindel asked to confer with counsel. He stepped out of the courtroom for a few long moments, after which he returned and announced, "I decline to answer that question and assert my privilege under the Fifth Amendment." Spindel would proceed to take the Fifth in response to twenty-five separate questions posed by Neal. Forced to change direction, Neal asked how much information Spindel had provided to Schiffer about the FBI communications he had intercepted. The wiretap specialist insisted that he had only told Schiffer that his findings were positive. No further details had been provided.[37]

As his testimony drew to a close, the witness acknowledged that the photographs proffered by the defense did not actually depict FBI agents. One of the cars was a Volkswagen, another a Lincoln—models government agents did not use. In his opinion, Spindel said, the photographs featured a grand total of one FBI vehicle.[38]

———

On the heels of Spindel, Harry Berke took the witness stand. Even before the trial had begun, he explained, Haggerty, the veteran of several prior Hoffa trials, had warned him about possible surveillance. He had been on guard, then, when he first noticed that he was being watched. The surveillance started on January 9, almost immediately after Berke was announced as Hoffa's local counsel. When Berke left the office that evening, a service truck at the Volunteer Garage had blocked him in. As he waited for the exit to clear, he saw FBI agent Bill Sheets walk by his vehicle. Then, as Berke pulled out of the garage, a car began to follow him. When he turned, so did the trailing vehicle; when he slowed to ten miles per hour, so did the other car. "A lot of cars started passing me but this car didn't," he said. When he stopped for gas, the vehicle pulled over, turning off its headlights. Then, when he began driving again, the lights came on and the car resumed following him. The car even trailed Berke when he purposefully went the wrong way down a one-way street. Only when he pulled into a driveway—not his own, he noted—did the car speed past.

Berke noticed continued surveillance throughout the trial. The most rattling incident had occurred on February 6. "We had been trying to get a conference with Mr. Hoffa but we were afraid to discuss the matter of defense and the evidence and so forth in either Mr. Haggerty's room or Mr. Hoffa's room or in fact any other rooms that are rented up there at the hotel," he explained. Therefore, he, Hoffa, and attorney Morris Shenker had climbed into Marvin Berke's car to "just go to a restaurant or somewhere and try to talk a little bit about this case." Almost immediately, the men had noticed they were being followed. To try to shake the vehicle, Berke suggested that they go into the vacant West Side. "Now the West Side Urban Renewal District it is entirely desolate," he explained. "There are no street lights out there now. There are no houses. They have all been torn down." Nevertheless, the car continued to follow them, matching their speed. After about fifteen minutes, as they reentered the main downtown area, Berke recalled, "this car passed us at a high rate of speed."

Harry Berke's son's car was the same white Pontiac with license tag 4U-8888 that had been referenced in intercepted FBI communications. And, like the person described in those transmissions, Berke said, he was slightly built, with a bald spot on the top of his head.

Berke also noted that he had heard strange noises and "disturbances" on his telephone line since the beginning of the trial. He could not definitively say whether his phone was tapped. However, some unnamed individuals had told him that they were afraid to share information with him over the phone, and that reluctance had impacted his ability to prepare for trial.[39]

On cross-examination, Neal would imply that Berke was paranoid, imagining FBI agents around every corner. When Bill Sheets had walked by his car in the Volunteer Garage, he had niether spoken to nor looked at Berke. For his part, Berke admitted that Sheets could not possibly have been behind the wheel of the car that had followed him.

Speaking of cars, Neal said, did you ever get the license plates of *any* of the cars that allegedly followed you? No, Berke replied. It was dark, and the cars had been behind them. Nor had he identified the drivers of the vehicles. "You cannot say that was an FBI car at all?" Neal asked.

"I can't say who it was," Berke said. "That's right."[40]

Marvin Berke, who had been practicing law in Chattanooga for three years, followed his father to the witness stand. He echoed his father's testimony as to surveillance during the first week of the trial. When Harry and Marvin Berke walked into the Volunteer Garage, Marvin had noticed two men sitting in a running car inside the building. When his father pulled out of the garage, the other car had slipped in behind him. Although the younger Berke had tried to follow the suspicious vehicle, he had been unable to do so.

On another occasion, Marvin Berke had successfully pursued the trailing vehicle and written down its license number. However, the number did not match the car that had been following his father; while the license was registered to a Ford, he said, the actual car had been a Plymouth or Oldsmobile. At some point, therefore, Berke had thrown away the piece of paper on which he had written the number.

What impact did this have on you? Branstetter asked. "When this first started," Berke explained, "I thought it was rather funny, but after a while it got to be a sort of a harassment, every place I would go there would be somebody behind me."

Branstetter then addressed the incident in the West Side. Yes, a car had definitely been following them, Marvin Berke said. None of the five purported targets of FBI surveillance were in or around his vehicle, he noted, and there should have been no reason for his car to have been tracked or followed.[41]

On cross-examination, Berke confirmed that he had not noticed anyone following him since February 6. He could not, moreover, identify any of the agents who had tailed him. Could you think of any possible reason that anyone would follow you? Neal asked. "No, sir," the youthful lawyer responded. "I never thought this would happen in a free country."[42]

———

The following morning, local FBI agent Jay Hawkins, who would prove to be the final witness in the six-week case, was recalled for a handful of desultory questions. After he stepped down, Judge Wilson addressed the courtroom. "All right, is there anything further in the case from either side at this time?" The attorneys announced that they were at long last finished. "The Court understands then that all matters have now been completed in the case and that ... the Court is now to rule upon the motion before the Court," Wilson said.

First, the judge addressed the lingering motion to dismiss the case based on Fred Shobe's testimony, announcing, "The Court was unable to find any merit in that motion or in those motions." Shobe's tale of shady government schemes, voodoo ceremonies, and kidnapping plots, the judge determined, had been contrived. Stating that "The witness is without credence," Wilson denied the motion.

Turning to the crucial motion to address government surveillance, Judge Wilson concluded that the FBI had not surveilled the defendants, their attorneys, or witnesses. "The Court finds that there was no interference by the government in any way with the defendants' right to counsel or with any constitutional right of the defendants in this respect," he said. With little fanfare, that motion was also denied.

With no other matters to take up, the court announced that sentencing would be held in six days. The defendants and their lawyers were instructed to report to the courthouse at nine o'clock on the morning of March 12.[43]

———

Despite the dismissal of the surveillance motion, the FBI was humiliated that agents had been unwittingly monitored while making unprofessional comments to Spindel, thereby risking a mistrial. They would face repercussions. After the trial, a 3,500-page report was prepared and sent to FBI headquarters for review. As special agent Jim Cole remarked dismissively, "Surely it was heavy enough to pass inspection when it got back to Washington."

In the end, a handful of agents were reprimanded for their sloppy fieldwork. Cole was not impressed with the quality of the investigation. "We knew we were in trouble," he explained, "when the fellow reviewing the transcript in Washington apparently had little or no field experience because he called down and wanted to know what this '10-4' meant all the time." Cole himself was reprimanded for giving out the position of his FBI car over the radio while helping another agent to find him. Other agents were scolded for making comments to Spindel, such as "Hi ya, Boin" and "Go home, Bernard." Cole shrugged the matter off. "Petty stuff," he commented.[44]

———

With little to be done in Chattanooga until sentencing, the exhausted trial participants staggered out of the city. Haggerty was so worn out that he had become ill; although he had been present for the verdict, he had skipped the surveillance hearing and been confined to his bed at the Hotel Patten. He did not comment publicly on the verdict. However, Hoffa would later write that Haggerty had remarked to him, "I have never seen such an exhibition. It leaves me clearly puzzled and somewhat disgusted." The lawyer would subsequently fly back to Detroit to consult with his physician.

Silets, informed that his father was in critical condition, quickly caught a plane to Chicago. Other defense lawyers filled a large laundry hamper with notes, memoranda, and other scraps and burned them. Harry Berke disparaged the verdict as "a miscarriage of justice."

Buoyed by the verdict, Hooker and his wife departed Chattanooga, bound for their farm outside of Nashville. Neal flew out to join his family for a much-needed respite.

Rather than heading home to Detroit, Hoffa flew to Washington to attend to union business. He did not know that Walter Sheridan was on the same plane.[45]

TWENTY

"In its way, the courtroom on the third floor of the
Federal Building here is as important a battlefield as any
in our history-laden area. Chattanooga has been rigorously
tested and has been equal to the test. The rest is up to the
appellate courts—and the Teamsters' collective conscience."

—*Chattanooga Times*, March 13, 1964

THROUGHOUT THE TRIAL, cameraman Tommy Eason had been among the small group of reporters outside the federal building waiting to film Hoffa and his team as they walked to and from their hotel. Over time, he had developed a comfortable rapport with the chief defendant. On March 8, however, Eason was absent. Hoffa asked one of the other reporters where he was and learned that Eason's wife had given birth to a child. That afternoon, several members of the Hoffa team, including William Bufalino and James P. Hoffa, surprised the cameraman at the hospital. "They come and brought flowers and a little outfit," Eason recalled.

When Eason returned to work a few days later, Hoffa patted him on the back. "Congratulations," he said. "I hear you've got you a . . ."

"I got a girl," Eason beamed, smiling at the Teamster president.[1]

————

Following the verdict, reporters sought quotes from jurors, who had remained silent throughout the trial and were only now available for comment. On March 5, the *Chattanooga Times* published a lengthy article containing interviews with all the jury members except for Pat Haverty and Joe Starnes. For the most part, they shared only superficial information about the trial, focusing on their relief that it was over and their appreciation for the US marshals' considerate treatment.

William Link smiled and admitted that he was "happy to be back home." Edsel Morrison insisted, "The hardship [of jury duty] came on our families, rather than us." Emolene Akers reported that she was looking forward to simple things, like cleaning her house, and that her husband was glad to have his wife home for some "home cooking." Morrison commented that "the marshals did an outstanding job." Asked whether he had been intimidated or influenced by the deputies' presence, Link was indignant. "Definitely not," he said. "I couldn't ask for any better treatment. The marshals treated us like kings; that's the best bunch of nicest fellows I've ever met."

Perhaps surprisingly, the arduous, belligerent trial did not sour the jurors on the judicial process. "I was very much encouraged and impressed," Morrison said, "and my faith in the jury system was cemented by the experience." Although he admitted that "No one likes to be pinned down or confined in any manner that they're not accustomed to," Ellis Case added that the experience was interesting enough to overcome his feelings of restriction.

In the end, the members of the jury were unanimous in their relief that the long ordeal was over. They were ready to move on and put the Hoffa trial, and its swirling media circus, behind them. When describing her feelings about the case, Annie Guinn may have best expressed the fundamental sentiment of the jury: "I want to forget this thing as soon as I can."[2]

————

Thursday, March 12. After almost a week away from the courthouse, during which time they had quietly contemplated the impact of the verdicts, the defendants and their attorneys reconvened for sentencing. Judge Wilson's peculiar order requiring all defendants *"and their counsel"* to be present had some of the attorneys on edge. In and out of the courtroom, US marshals had also been on high alert. "We really beefed up the security after the verdict," said Granville Sertel. "After the guilty plea [verdict] we had a crew of four marshals that came in and stayed around the [judge's] house all the time." On March 12, moreover, marshals surrounded the courthouse to ensure that the hearing would not become disorderly.[3]

As usual, the sidewalks outside the courthouse were a fascinating sideshow to the formal courtroom proceedings. Squads of newsmen jostled against loyal Hoffa backers, fervent Hoffa detractors, and the idle curious—all seeking a clear sight line to the doors from which the IBT president (and the others) would emerge after the sentencing. In the street, supportive truck drivers "made a circle around the block and kept going and stalled traffic considerably during that period of time." The occasional squawk of police sirens punctuated the low rumble of diesel engines and the honking of horns as traffic ground to a halt in front of the courthouse.[4]

In contrast to the scene outside, the courtroom was calm. Spectators sat quietly. At nine o'clock, Judge Wilson entered the courtroom for a hearing that would last a little less than an hour. Hoffa was the first defendant called. When he rose and faced Wilson, Mansfield and Sertel stood behind him, ready to prevent any outburst or disruption.

Hoffa had the opportunity to comment before the sentence was passed. Journalist Clark Mollenhoff, who years earlier had pushed Kennedy to investigate the Teamsters Union, noted the "sullen defiance" of Hoffa's remarks:

> Judge, I stand here today a convicted man by a jury. However, on May 10, 1963, I stated that I was innocent in front of Judge Gray in Nashville, Tennessee. I stand here today and state that I am innocent of the charge and that ultimately when the evidence has been sifted calmly, coolly, and collectively and a review of the record and the evidence finally substantiating what I know is the truth, that I did not at any time attempt to tamper with any jury anywhere in the United States, that I will be found innocent, and whatever the verdict may be of this Court, I have lived my life, 51 years, servicing my fellow man, servicing the members of the International Union, and whatever may happen, nobody can say that I have betrayed my trust because the record speaks for itself, regarding wages, hours, conditions and the fringe benefits, the

pensions, welfare that has never before been attained in the history
of this country, and I stand here today accepting the verdict of this
Court subject to appeal to the highest court of America so that
the working people will know, who I have the privilege and the
pleasure of being their General President, that I have not betrayed
their trust and I am not guilty and I so stand here in front of you.[5]

With no additional commentary or deliberation, Judge Wilson read from
his prepared notes the judgment of the court:

Mr. Hoffa, it is the opinion of the Court that the verdict of the jury
in this case is clearly supported by the evidence. It is the opinion
of the Court that those matters of which you stand convicted, that
you did knowingly and that you did corruptly, after the trial judge
had reported to you his information with regard to an alleged attempt to bribe a juror.

Now, it is difficult for the Court to imagine under those circumstances a more willful violation of the law. Most defendants
that stand before this Court for sentencing, and certainly sentencing is the most distressing duty that this Court ever has to per-
form, most defendants that stand before this Court for sentencing
have either violated the property rights of other individuals or
have violated the personal rights of other individuals.

You stand here convicted of seeking to corrupt the administration of justice itself. You stand here convicted of having tampered,
really, with the very soul of this nation. You stand here convicted
of having struck at the very foundation upon which everything
else in this nation depends, the very basis of civilization itself,
and that is the administration of justice, because without a fair,
proper and a lawful administration of justice, nothing else would
be possible in this country, the administration of labor unions, the
administration of business, the carrying on of occupations, the
carrying on of recreation, the administration of health services,
everything that we call civilization depends ultimately upon the
proper administration of justice itself.

Now, if a conviction of such an offense were to go unpunished
and this type of conduct and this type of offense permitted to pass
without action by the Court, it would surely destroy this country
more quickly and more surely than any combination of foreign
foes that we could ever possibly have.

Grim-faced, Hoffa stood at the podium as the judge read the statement.
"The two stared intently at each other during the exchange," one newspaper
reported. After a solemn pause, Wilson continued: "I say it is most distressing

for the Court to pass sentence upon any individual, upon an individual that holds the responsibility which you hold." He then read the sentence. Each of counts three and five would carry a prison sentence and a fine, to be served consecutively. Hoffa would be required to serve eight years and pay $10,000. "Do you understand the sentence of the Court?" Wilson asked.

"I understand the sentence perfectly and I will take my appeals," Hoffa replied evenly.

Observers lauded Wilson's eloquent statement on the fragility of justice. "Long after the details of the teamster leader's activities have faded," the *New York Times* opined, "United States District Judge Frank W. Wilson's affirmation of justice will be part of the literature of the law." It was speculated that the court's unwillingness to assign Hoffa the maximum sentence for each count—five years—was the product of Wilson's desire to bend over backward in the interest of fairness and justice toward the defendants.[6]

Amid an air of deflated denouement, Larry Campbell was the next defendant called. His attorney, Cecil Branstetter, would speak on his behalf: "I would like to state to this Court that I grew up in a system respecting the law . . . I have tried this case as best I know. I will conceive very readily that my idealism gets shook from time to time from all sources in the courtroom, both sides of the table and from the bench, and I want to say this on behalf of Larry Campbell if a man can have his freedom taken in this country on the proof in this record as far as Larry Campbell is concerned my idealism has been shook some more."

Judge Wilson announced that Campbell would be required to serve three years. Nodding that he understood the sentence, Campbell quietly sat down.[7]

Next came Thomas Ewing Parks. Jacques Schiffer read a prepared statement:

> From the day of arraignment in this case, your Honor, the defendant has pleaded innocent. He has taken the position that no man in this country could be convicted on the evidence which was presented before this Court. He feels, and I agree with him, that the prosecution in this case had been engineered in such a fashion that in any real sense it deprived him of any such thing as a constitutional right as we lawyers know it in our own profession.
>
> He still feels innocent. He knows he has done nothing illegal. He had nothing whatever to do with this case. He never knew Mr. Hoffa until the date of arraignment or shortly thereafterwards on this very case and, therefore, I would respectfully urge that insofar as this defendant is concerned that any judgment imposed by this

Court should be vacated as far as the conviction is concerned and
the verdict of this jury.

Asked if he had anything to add, Parks quietly declined. Like Campbell,
he was issued a three-year prison sentence.[8]

Ewing King was the final defendant called before the court. Harold Brown
asked to say a few words on his behalf: "Since I represented this boy I have
grown to really know him. He's been an honor to the organized labor. He has,
from all of my investigation, been one of the finest boys that has come from
Tennessee anywhere. He was raised in the country, never been in any trouble
in his life, and that impressed me more as to the charges in this case would
be completely alien or foreign to a man of his character and background."

An emotional King opted to add a few comments. "I would just like to say
that I am not guilty of the crime that I am to be sentenced for here today," he
said haltingly. "I told the truth to the best of my ability the way I remembered
it. At no time did I have conversation[s] with Hoffa about the State Highway
Patrol, and I hope that we will be vindicated somewhere along the line."

Judge Wilson nodded with compassion as he regarded King. "The Court
is a human being," he said, "and feels sympathy for each defendant here
and feels sympathy for the family of each defendant here." It was necessary,
however, for the court to do its duty. As expected, the judge announced a
three-year prison sentence for King as well.[9]

Though the sentencing was completed, Judge Wilson was not yet done.
He announced that he was prepared to read something into the record. Everyone looked around expectantly, wondering what was left to address. The
result was a moment a long time in coming, and one that many observers
had predicted. It would occupy sixteen pages of trial transcript, more than
the sentencing of all four defendants.

Wilson read a citation for contempt against Jacques Schiffer stemming
from his over-the-top mistrial baiting throughout the proceedings. Scribbling fiercely on a legal pad, Schiffer never once looked up as the judge read
the statement into the record: "I find that the acts, statements, and conduct
of Jacques M. Schiffer, the defendant in this contempt petition, hereinafter
specified, constitutes, first, a deliberate and willful attack upon the administration of justice. Second, an attempt to prevent by improper means the
functioning of this Court. Third, an attempt to degrade and debase this Court;
and Fourth, such misconduct by an attorney at law in the practice before
this Court as would be calculated to destroy all respect for this Court, both
by attorneys at law in the practice before this Court and by members of the

general public if such misconduct went unnoticed and unpunished by this Court."

Wilson recited a list of seventeen incidents in which Schiffer attempted to provoke the court into an outburst or error that might justify a mistrial. His references to a "drum head court martial" and "star chamber proceedings," as well as his claims of "Stalinism, Hitlerism, Mussolinism and all kinds of isms" were recounted, as were his repeated allegations that the court was assisting the government in fostering and concealing perjury. Nor did Wilson overlook Schiffer's attempts to file sealed wiretapping affidavits for the court to publish. The thorough and meticulous contempt certificate had clearly taken substantial effort to prepare; it reflected each of the marks made in the judge's copy of the transcript. "By reason of his misconduct," Wilson concluded, "the task of maintaining order and proceeding with a proper and a fair trial was rendered extremely difficult."

Did Schiffer wish to respond? Gathering his papers, Schiffer asked for a hearing before a different judge. The request was summarily denied. "May I say, your Honor," Schiffer said softly, a departure from his trial demeanor, "in connection with everything in this certificate, your Honor has taken everything in the worst light imaginable where I am concerned[,] and I certainly never had an intention to mislead this Court or to do anything but to protect my client and I believe with what violations of due process in this court, instituted by the government, I believe that any Court in the country up above, when it reads the entire record, will find that there has been an illegal encouragement of his rights. . . . There never was any intention, certainly on my part where the Court is concerned, to do anything against the dignity of this Court."

Judge Wilson was not moved. He had endured Schiffer's baiting tirades almost every day for weeks. There was no question that securing a mistrial had been Schiffer's objective. Wilson explained that he realized the pressure placed on attorneys in a case such as this. He also understood how in the heat of the moment lawyers might make remarks that "in the calm light of later reflection they would not have said." Schiffer's relentless tirades, however, were different. "The Court cannot possibly but conclude other than that they were a part of a deliberate and studied plan over the entire period of the trial." Schiffer would serve sixty days in jail and pay a fine of $1,000. "I have never in my life performed anything which caused me greater sadness than to have to prepare and file this contempt certificate," Wilson advised Schiffer, "but I feel that, and I have felt that it was necessary if I were going to attempt to continue to perform my duties here and if I were going to attempt to continue to function as a presiding judge upon this bench."

No one was particularly surprised. "Mr. Schiffer's conduct, which seemed quite deliberate, was an affront to traditional and carefully derived standards of courtroom conduct," read an editorial published in the *Chattanooga Times*.

Gearhiser subsequently made a surprising revelation. "I remember working on another one [contempt citation] that we decided not to do," he recalled. "The lawyer is extremely lucky, because in my judgment, it would have held up." Gearhiser did not reveal the name of the lawyer who had narrowly dodged this second contempt citation. Ragano? Silets? The answer is unclear. As Gearhiser added, though, "He was a good lawyer, and maybe he deserved a better fate."[10]

At 9:55 a.m., after less than an hour, Judge Wilson announced that the hearing was concluded. The Chattanooga trial was officially over.[11]

Following the sentencing, Robert F. Kennedy sent a US Customs plane to Chattanooga to fly the victorious prosecution team to his home for a celebration. Not everyone attended the gathering. FBI agents Bill Sheets and Ed Steele declined their invitations "because they would have to explain to J. Edgar Hoover what they were doing at Bob Kennedy's house." Mansfield likewise stayed in Chattanooga, going so far as to hide from Walter Sheridan, who was insistent that he travel to Washington. "Somebody had to stay here and mind the store," Mansfield explained.

Granville Sertel, who had stayed with the Wilson family throughout the trial, also declined, feeling that it would be inappropriate to attend. Hearing that, Judge Wilson summoned Sertel to his chambers. "Don't worry, Judge," Sertel assured him, "I'm not gonna go."

"You are going, too," the judge replied. "I want you to go."

At Kennedy's Hickory Hill home, Sertel stood among the crowd, picking at his buffet dinner. Joking, one of the guests pointed out that Sertel was a Republican. Ethel Kennedy put her arm around him. "We love Republicans, too," she said, smiling.

Members of Kennedy's legal team were presented with leather-bound copies of the verdict. Such merriment infuriated Hoffa. "The Get-Hoffa Squad presented Kennedy with a leather wallet embossed with the words the jury foreman said when he announced the guilty verdict," he wrote in his autobiography. "They should have put a bill inside for the $12 million his hatred had cost the government in the nine years it took him to 'get' me."[12]

———

The day after the sentencing, at a luncheon at the Hotel Patten, the president of the Chattanooga Rotary Club called for a resolution:

> Today this club is compelled by pride and gratitude to pay tribute to judge Frank Wilson. His conduct throughout the Hoffa trial has done more than bring honor to himself. It has brought honor to all of us in this community. But more than that, his conduct under assault and even abuse has given us who watched a new pride, a new understanding and a new respect for the American judicial system. Judge, you have justified so well and made real to us all the concept of American Justice as expressed by the late Oliver Wendell Holmes when he said: no nation can long survive upon the face of the earth through whose national existence there does not run the Golden thread of equal justice for all.
>
> So, we of the Rotary club say to you that your conduct under the pressures that we have seen in the last few weeks has given us a new faith and a new pride in our system of American Justice, and your conduct as a judge has brought honor to the judicial system which you represent. To those of us who have watched, the words "equal justice under law" have been given a new meaning. Therefore, we, as fellow Rotarians, for ourselves and for this community, pause, in all sincerity, to honor you as you have honored us. Thank you for a job well done.

For several minutes, applause rang out. A Rotary member himself, Frank Wilson was called forward and presented with a copy of the resolution. With a slight, shy smile, he shook hands with the president and returned quietly to his seat in the back of the room.[13]

TWENTY-ONE

"Will the Law Ever Get Hoffa?"

—Saturday Evening Post, March 30, 1963

AFTER THE SENTENCING HEARING, the main phase of the jury tampering trial was complete. But there was still a long way to go— and Hoffa would not be going without a fight. The Chattanooga trial had not tackled all of the claims arising from the Test Fleet case. On March 30, Lawrence "Red" Medlin was tried in Nashville for attempting to bribe James Tippens to vote for acquittal in the Test Fleet trial. Unlike in Chattanooga, presiding judge Frank Wilson permitted Tippens to testify about his conversations with Medlin, who admitted to meeting Tippens and mentioning the bribe. However, Medlin conveniently (and somewhat nonsensically) claimed that *Tippens* had offered *him* $10,000. According to Medlin, Tippins had commented, "We have a chance to make a lot of money. No one will know where it came from. It will only take one vote, maybe not even that." After only three hours of deliberation, the jury voted to convict the ready-made sandwich shop owner. He was sentenced to eighteen months in prison, and subsequent appeals proved fruitless.[1]

Also in April 1964, Henry F. "Buster" Bell was found guilty of offering $30,000 to a bartender and numbers operator, Nathan Bellamy, to tamper with Test Fleet jurors Gratin Fields and Mrs. Matthew Walker. The "burly, baldish" defendant was proclaimed innocent of two other charges. "Well, we won two out of three," Bell told reporters. "The main bout goes 20 rounds. We've gone only one round and have 19 to go." He faced a $5,000 fine and five years' imprisonment. Bell's subsequent appeal on the grounds of unfavorable publicity, judicial bias, and Bellamy's undisclosed extensive (but irrelevant) criminal history was denied. In the court's opinion, Bell's additional claim that Judge Gray was "incompetent to hear and try this cause" was "in poor taste" and should be rejected.[2]

The final trio on trial in association with the Test Fleet trial included Herman Frazier (the chief of detectives in Huntington, West Virginia, and vice president of the national Fraternal Order of Police), Alfred Paden (a Huntington police detective and surveillance specialist), and Albert Cole (an insurance investigator). The three were accused of making the "Allen from the *Banner*" calls. On October 20, 1962—the day before the Test Fleet trial—the men had flown to Nashville and taken rooms at the Noel Hotel, a few blocks from Hoffa's hotel. The aforementioned phone calls were traced to Frazier's, Paden's, and Cole's hotel rooms and to pay phones near their hotel. Frazier explained that they had been recruited to conduct background investigations into prospective jurors. A man whom he had never met had come to the hotel and made a sample call, identifying himself as "Allen from the *Banner*"—thus the tracing of the calls to Frazier's hotel room. After the man left, Frazier, Paden, and Cole had second-guessed the calls' propriety, Frazier insisted, and they had never made any calls themselves.

After it was determined that one of the jurors at the 1964 trial had also been on the jury list for the Test Fleet trial, the case ended in a mistrial. Then, on January 7, 1965, a jury found that there simply was not enough evidence to show an illicit attempt to influence the jury. A second charge against Cole for perjury, on the basis that he had lied when FBI agents interviewed him, was subsequently dismissed due to a technical mistake in the date written on the indictment.[3]

On April 19, 1964, the *Nashville Tennessean* reported that the Tennessee Bar Association had initiated proceedings to prohibit the mercurial Jacques Schiffer from ever again practicing law in the state. Noting that "Schiffer's conduct at the Chattanooga trial was repugnant and his intemperate remarks toward the court were both abusive and deliberate," the newspaper expressed the hope that the American Bar Association would adopt a similar ban.

Judge Wilson rejected Schiffer's request for a new trial, noting that the lawyer's conduct had "prejudiced the expeditious, orderly and dispassionate conduct of the trial." Represented by Harvey Silets, Schiffer appealed his contempt sanction to the Sixth Circuit Court of Appeals, which found that "the remarks [he had made] were contemptuous per se." The fact that Schiffer had made all but one of his incendiary comments outside the jury's presence was immaterial. "They were calculated to provoke and to bring undue pressure upon the Court in the making of various rulings in the course of the trial," the court held, also stating, "We do not have an isolated outburst in the heat of the trial, but rather deliberate, continuous and repeated acts, extending throughout the trial, which were wholly unwarranted . . . Schiffer not only resisted rulings, but he repeatedly insulted the Court."

While it was admittedly "a bitterly contested trial charged with emotions," Schiffer's "deliberate, continuous and repeated acts" insulted the court and the administration of justice. The Sixth Circuit noted Judge Wilson's "infinite patience." "He did his utmost to preserve order and decorum," despite the New York attorney's relentless efforts to derail the case. The Sixth Circut also found that Schiffer's furtive attempt to file a second sealed affidavit was "trifling with the Court and making its processes a mockery." On September 9, 1965, therefore, the Sixth Circuit affirmed Criminal Contempt Citation No. 12010—although it did strike the $1,000 fine. Schiffer would be sent to the minimum-security Maxwell Air Force Base in Montgomery, Alabama, to serve his sixty-day sentence.[4]

On April 27, 1964, Hoffa and seven codefendants stood trial in Chicago for pension fraud. Hoffa had allegedly made loans out of the $200 million Central States Pension Fund in exchange for kickbacks, some of which were then used to extricate him from the failed Sun Valley scheme. All in all, 114 witnesses and 20,000 documents were introduced during the course of the ten-week trial. After 441 ballots, the Chicago jury rendered a second guilty verdict, this time for conspiracy and mail and wire fraud. Hoffa was sentenced to an additional five years in prison and ordered to pay a $10,000 fine. "This court is one that believes that the sound of the clanging jailhouse door has a salutary effect on the defendant and the community," the judge declared at the sentencing hearing.

Hoffa appealed, arguing that the proof had not demonstrated any unlawful conduct by him. He also contended that he was unfairly prejudiced by the scheduling of the trial only six weeks after his conviction in Chattanooga. On January 11, 1971, the Supreme Court denied a petition for review, exhausting Hoffa's appeals in the case.[5]

———

With two guilty verdicts tallied, observers began to question whether the rank and file might abandon the embattled IBT president. Hoffa raced to quell any doubts as to his status. As early as March 7, 1964, newspapers had published staged photographs of a cheery Hoffa flanked by Teamster drivers offering their encouragement. It was also announced that the union had received 400,000 telegrams from members voicing their unflagging support.[6]

The *Chattanooga News-Free Press* related a call received from a North Carolina IBT member whose "voice cracked with emotion as he deplored the [Chattanooga] conviction and as he declared that Hoffa to him was the greatest man alive." He had been provided with higher pay because of Hoffa, and he therefore opposed the verdict. "We received no calls yesterday," the newspaper jabbed, "from rank and file Americans who have been victimized by gangsterism and dynamiting and beatings in the Teamster Union's battle for and exercise for power."[7]

On July 4, 1966, Hoffa was reelected as IBT president and his salary raised to $100,000. To many observers, it seemed apparent that he would "retain his post without serious challenge." Some influential Teamsters felt that it would be unfair to challenge him while he was battling for his freedom; other more practical rivals feared provoking a wounded, embattled Hoffa. "Anyone who openly challenged the Teamster boss," it was predicted, "would lay his own job on the line without any guarantee of success." Despite his legal obstacles, therefore, Hoffa remained confident that his hegemony was secure.[8] Yet as the *New York Times* editorialized, "if Hoffa goes to jail, his foes will be considerably bolder."[9]

———

Back in Chattanooga, the defense filed a motion for a new trial, claiming that the court had committed ninety-four errors. Accompanying the anticipated challenges to jury selection, the failure to delay the trial, the litany of overruled objections, the failure of the FBI to provide investigative notes, the decision to allow Tippens to testify, the refusal to reveal Partin's Cuban gunrunning activities, and the indications of government surveillance were surprise allegations concerning the behavior of the *jury* during the trial. These accusations would prove some of the most salacious ones in a case chock full of scandal.

Chuckie O'Brien had remained in Chattanooga after the verdict, trolling around for anyone willing to accept cash in exchange for an affidavit indicating that Hoffa had been railroaded. Not surprisingly, he unearthed several willing collaborators. Their affidavits would accompany a motion charging that "United States marshals supplied intoxicating liquors in large quantities to the jurors during the time the jurors were in custody of said marshals during the trial." Another charge indicated that the same marshals had spent their time drinking and fraternizing with jurors.

The documents were signed by bellmen, maids, and an elevator operator at the Read House. Bellman Ezeil Evrons reported that he had delivered a pint of Old Hickory whiskey to the tenth floor of the hotel, stating, "Almost every night I would take chasers, ice, glasses and things for mixing drinks." "On several occasions," bellman Seymour Ball echoed, "I have seen persons that were intoxicated going up to the 10th floor, accompanied by a person I thought to be a marshal." He also reported that martini mix, glasses, and beer had been sent to jurors, and he claimed to have assisted a loud, intoxicated juror stumbling to the elevator on one occasion. Johnny Brown, an elevator operator, remarked that he had heard jurors "having a gay time" in the hallways on several occasions, adding that Hoffa was mentioned one time in the elevator.

An offended Hal Bullen adamantly denied the claims. "I am flabbergasted," the jury foreman informed one reporter. "It is ridiculous. We were most circumspect, because we realized the importance of our assignment. That is terrible—just terrible. I am willing to testify at any time, if anyone in authority considers it should be done." Jurors Edsel Morrison, John Curbow, Emolene Akers, and Mrs. Sam Oliver joined Bullen in filing affidavits to categorically deny any misbehavior on the part of the jury. Mansfield filed an affidavit stating that no government funds had been used to purchase alcohol during the trial. In addition, Read House bellman Anthony Charles Bradford revealed that he had declined Seymour Ball's promise of $500 to offer a false statement.

Another affidavit was signed by a Dorothy Vaughn, who said that her neighbor, Margaret Daves, had rented a room to a US marshal during the trial. On February 21, she said, she had visited her neighbor and observed gifts stacked on the kitchen table. When she inquired whom the gifts were for, the marshal replied, "my jurors." Vaughn said she had seen sixteen gifts—enough for each of the twelve jurors and the four alternates. After the packages were wrapped, a marshal came to retrieve them. "That little imped son-of-a-bitch, that cocky bastard," the marshal had remarked about Hoffa, striking the table so hard that he toppled a glass. "We're doing everything in our power to convict him. We're going to convict him one way or another. We know he's guilty, and we're going to convict him."

The deputy marshal accused of anti-Hoffa bias, Jack Irwin, filed his own affidavit explaining that a fellow marshal had proposed to give the jurors small trinket mirrors with "nominal value and appropriate for use as an automobile accessory." However, Irwin had disallowed the suggested gifts. Thirteen of the mirrors, he added, were still in his possession, and none had been given to a juror. He also denied making the combustible statements Vaughn attributed to him.

Reached by telephone, alternate juror John Curbow took "sharp issue" with an affidavit in which Frank Ragano claimed to have heard him remark, "When a lawyer has a weak case he talks loud, and also that a person with a weak hand in a card game tries to bluff others in the game." It was "a complete misunderstanding," Curbow said; he had been talking about a card game from the prior evening. As for the jury, Curbow stated, "I never saw a better behaved group of men and women. . . . I was really surprised that a group of men and women could be so compatible for such an extended length of time. . . . The marshals were all gentlemen and they behaved commendably. There was no misconduct on anyone's part. The marshals treated us courteously and made no effort to exercise any sort of influence upon any of us."

Responding to the bombshell claims, the prosecution filed affidavits from other Read House bellmen who claimed that they had been approached about signing false affidavits. One said that he had been shown a briefcase full of cash and told that the more helpful information he provided, the more money he could have. So long as it was helpful to Hoffa, they were told, it did not matter whether their stories were true or false.

On March 12 (the day of the sentencing hearing), Judge Wilson addressed each of the ninety-four assignments of error in detail, denying them all. He concluded that the incendiary affidavits were not persuasive. Noting that he had "made careful and individual observations of each juror many times a day, each day the jury was in the court room," Wilson believed that the jury had performed its duties faithfully.[10]

Ragano, moreover, had evidently pushed the envelope a bit too far with Wilson. On March 18, he received a written reprimand due to his improper observation of jurors. In the words of the court, Ragano, in "knowingly and intentionally going into the private area reserved by the jury and observing and eavesdropping and conducting surveillance upon the jury," had exhibited "a willful disregard of the orders and instructions of this court."[11]

An embarrassed Read House quickly discharged the employees who had signed the affidavits. "They immediately obtained jobs at the Atlanta Cabana Motor Hotel in Atlanta, Georgia," Sheridan reported, "which had been built with loans from the Teamsters Pension Fund."[12] On April 2, O'Brien, who had led the push to secure the affidavits, was indicted by a special grand jury in Chattanooga for attempting to bribe juror Callie Key, having offered her $25,000 for her signature on a false affidavit supporting claims of juror and government misconduct. Refusing the offer, Key had reported O'Brien to the court.[13]

———

As this post-trial sideshow played out, Hoffa prepared for the formal appeal process. With a long-shot chance of overturning the verdict, however, he wanted to explore alternate options, including a sweeping plea for members of Congress to condemn the verdict. The Hoffa public relations campaign was handled by IBT vice president for community relations Sid Zagri. Hard-hitting and intimidating, Zagri aggressively lobbied legislators in Washington. By March 24 it was announced that a subcommittee of the House Judiciary Committee had been charged with reviewing the trial transcript to determine if Hoffa had been railroaded. A potential inquest in his sights, Zagri penned a flurry of letters encouraging rank-and-file Teamsters to flood their representatives with petitions on Hoffa's behalf. By August 1964, Zagri had taken his claims to the Republican and Democratic National Conventions, securing a plank at the former calling for the investigation of the Department of Justice. Zagri's efforts continued into early 1967, when he convinced a handful of senators to call for an "in-depth investigation into bugging and wiretapping by the government."[14]

One sympathetic elected official was Senator Edward Long (D-MO), who in early 1965 initiated an investigation into government surveillance. "Folksy and affable," Long was also biased, having previously stumped for Hoffa. "I told that crowd and told you that you delight your friends, and you amaze your enemies," Long had gushed, "and to keep on fighting them, Jimmy." Long was lambasted after *Life* magazine revealed that Hoffa attorney Morris Shenker had paid him $160,000 for "legal work" during the investigation— despite the fact that he had not practiced law since the mid-1950s. Although he denied the allegations, Long was discredited, losing his bid for reelection in 1968. In the end, the legislative campaign to reverse the Hoffa verdict quietly fizzled.[15]

———

While public relations efforts plowed forward, the defense evaluated the best avenue(s) by which to appeal the Chattanooga verdict. Lacking a guarantee that a court of appeals would overturn the verdict, though, the Hoffa team also needed to determine whether they might be able to *change* the proof— or at least call it into serious question. In early 1965, therefore, Hoffa filed a second motion for new trial. This time, his counsel alleged that Robert Vick had interfered with Hoffa's rights under the Sixth Amendment by causing him to lose the legal services of Tommy Osborn. The motion also claimed that, while supposedly working for Osborn, Vick had been quietly sharing information with Sheridan. On February 26, the government responded to the motion, attaching an affidavit from Sheridan denying the accusations.

Simply making the allegation might be enough to create some doubt on the part of the court. However, if the defense could convince Vick to actually *recant* his testimony, it might have a very good chance of changing the trial result. Vick, though, proved to be a hard sell. In exchange for a statement supporting Hoffa, IBT executive assistant James Harding offered Vick a lump-sum payment of $25,000 and an $18,000-a-year job in "a place in the sun." He rejected the offer. After Vick refused to name his price, former Local 327 business agent Red Vaughn warned him, "Some cold night they [may] drag your body out of the river." Still, the attempt to secure a disavowal from Vick went nowhere, and Judge Wilson denied the second motion for a new trial on April 15, 1965. Though efforts to influence Vick would continue into 1966, he would prove to be a dead end.[16]

Other Nashville Teamsters were pressured to convince Vick to recant. In August 1966, two officials with Local 327, Don Vestal and Earl Wingo, filed affidavits claiming that Hoffa had offered to "set them up for life" if they could help to secure Vick's cooperation. In particular, Wingo said that he had been offered $25,000 in cash, a $10,000-a-year union job, and an $8,000 expense account in exchange for his assistance in getting a new trial for Hoffa. Five other Nashville Teamsters claimed that the IBT was "harassing and interfering with Local 327" to make Vick alter his testimony.[17]

Similar efforts were made to secure new information from other witnesses. Quite astoundingly, affiliates of New Orleans crime boss Carlos Marcello approached Baton Rouge district attorney Sargent Pitcher and Billy Daniels (by that time a judge) in June 1965. Marcello's associates told Pitcher and Daniels that "money was no object" if they would be willing to share tape recordings or other evidence that might help exonerate Hoffa. As might have been expected, the offer was rejected. Later, Pitcher was offered a sizable reelection contribution if he would agree to help Hoffa. When he rejected that proposal, Hoffa and Morris Shenker were said to have directed a $50,000 payment to Pitcher's opponent in the election.[18]

———

The key testimony linking Hoffa to the Test Fleet jury had come from a single witness—Edward Grady Partin. If Partin would disavow his damaging account, Hoffa supporters believed, the entire case would crumble. Efforts to cajole, bribe, and threaten the big Louisiana Teamster would persist for years.

Returning to Louisiana in March 1964, Partin called for a show of support from Teamsters Local 5 and received "a full vote of confidence." At the so-called "Hoffa Hall" in Baton Rouge, the photograph of Hoffa that had hung in a prominent place was removed and discarded.[19]

Soon, though, Partin began to receive overtures testing his willingness to change his stance. The prominence of some of the persuaders—lawyers, politicians, mobsters, judges, and even a war hero-turned movie star—was astounding. Aubrey Young, the administrative assistant to Louisiana governor John McKeithen, brokered a meeting between Partin and D'Alton Smith, the son-in-law of New Orleans crime boss Carlos Marcello. If he would provide information to help Hoffa, Partin was assured, "the sky's the limit. It's worth at least a million bucks." Smith also promised to help Partin resolve his own criminal entanglements, and he hinted that Marcello could protect him from contracts that had purportedly been placed on his head.

After Partin agreed to meet, a roadside rendezvous was scheduled outside of New Orleans. Who appeared? Jacques Schiffer, who asked Partin to strip down to confirm that he was not wearing a recording device. "All I'm wearing is a gun," a grim Partin replied, "which I intend to use if I have to." Rattled,

Schiffer proposed that they move the meeting to a hotel room, where they could verify that Partin was not hiding anything. "As long as I hold the gun," Partin said, "I'll strip down as much as you like."

Schiffer presented Partin with a four-page typewritten statement providing that Sheridan had coached Partin on his testimony and that the government had wiretapped the defense. "These are nothing but lies," Partin said, tossing the papers aside. He refused to sign. Though he was willing to help Hoffa, he insisted, "This statement is a lie. There was no wiretapping." Attorney Harold Brown was dispatched to Baton Rouge to convince Partin to sign a revised statement averring simply that Sheridan had coached Partin. Partin met with Brown, New Orleans Parish judge Malcolm O'Hara, and James "Buddy" Gill, an associate of Senator Russell Long. After reviewing the statement, Partin again refused to sign it. After O'Hara quietly slipped out of the room, Partin was offered a $1 million sweetener to reconsider. He refused. Gill then approached Sargent Pitcher to ask if he might convince Partin to help Hoffa. Pitcher replied that he wanted nothing to do with the effort.[20]

After repeated offers of payoffs failed to flip Partin, Hoffa's agents adopted a different strategy. If the carrot would not work, they would try the stick. As Sheridan characterized the effort, "The stage was set for what was to become an all-out effort to destroy Ed Partin." "Do anything but kill him," one operative instructed. "He has to be alive to testify that he committed perjury in Chattanooga."

The attacks against Partin came from all directions. An indictment was brought for conspiracy to commit extortion and restrain trade within the Baton Rouge concrete industry. Rivals were sent to Baton Rouge to poach members of Local 5. A commission investigating labor strife in Louisiana drew a bead on Partin's local. Newspaper articles questioned why he had not yet been prosecuted on pending indictments. Plans were hatched to sabotage industrial equipment and blame it on Partin, and also to plant drugs or machine guns on him. The specter of his old criminal charges raised its head again, and in May 1970 the twenty-six-count indictment against Partin was reactivated. All the while, he received gentle reminders that the pressures on him could be removed if he would only cooperate and help Hoffa.

When New Orleans district attorney Jim Garrison initiated an investigation into the Kennedy assassination, he hinted, "We know that Jack Ruby and Lee Harvey Oswald were in New Orleans several times . . . there was a third man driving them and we are checking the possibility it was Partin." Soon thereafter, Partin revealed, "Frank Ragano called me, and he said he could get Garrison off my back. In return he wanted a signed affidavit saying that I lied in Hoffa's trial." "Naturally, I didn't sign," he added.[21]

When Partin scheduled a press conference at the offices of Local 5, it appeared as though he had finally caved to pressure. At the last minute, though, he sent everyone home and placed a note on the door of the local claiming (falsely) that his mother had passed away. Partin even posted the supposed details of the nonexistent funeral.[22]

Probably the most fascinating effort to pressure Partin involved decorated World War II hero Audie Murphy, who had become a Hollywood movie star after his service. Murphy's acting star had since fallen, and several business failures had led him to file bankruptcy. At the same time, he was trying to raise funds to finish a new film. Through his own associations with Louisiana mobster D'Alton Smith, Murphy was persuaded to approach Partin. He told the Teamster that Hoffa was coming before the parole board on March 31, 1970, and that a Partin affidavit might be particularly useful. He also reminded Partin that he would be paid handsomely for helping Hoffa. The IBT president would even forgive him for testifying at the Chattanooga trial—and presumably call off the dogs nipping at Partin's heels.

Pressured by Murphy, anxious to be left alone, and likely feeling uncharitable toward the federal government (which had turned its back on him), Partin finally agreed to meet in Los Angeles. On March 27, 1971, he gave a rambling deposition transcribed into a thirty-one-page affidavit. The document was not signed or notarized. "I gave 'em nothing," Partin later explained. "Sure, I said some words, and they wrote them down. But they were accusing me of doing everything, including being involved in the Kennedy assassination. So I just told them what they wanted to hear and refused to sign anything." Ultimately, Hoffa's attorneys chose not to use the worthless document.

On May 28, 1971, Murphy and three others boarded a flight from Atlanta to Martinsville, Virginia, to inspect a potential investment opportunity. Though scheduled to accompany them, Partin backed out at the last minute, claiming that his wife was ill. The airplane crashed into the side of a mountain during a thunderstorm, killing everyone onboard.[23] For four years, Partin had been hounded relentlessly to renounce his Chattanooga testimony. Despite the cruel turn in his fortunes, Partin stood firm. He never recanted or signed any of the numerous statements placed before him.

———

Hoffa tried everything to overturn the Chattanooga verdict. Pricey per-plate dinners defrayed the cost of the appeals process, as the IBT could not pay his legal fees. In a two-page letter to Teamsters supporters, Hoffa reported, "The best legal minds in the country are certain that the record is filled with error." By revealing "the police state and vendetta methods of the Justice Department," he assured his followers, the defense would see to it that "this foul conspiracy to jail a labor leader is reversed."[24]

The resulting appeal included sixteen challenges, divided into thirty-six parts, attacking the government, the court, and the jury. The arguments were familiar to those who had been following the trial since its beginning— with one exception. For the first time, the transcript of the "secret session," in which it was alleged that Hoffa and Partin had discussed assassinating Kennedy, was revealed to the public. Hoffa labeled the allegation "stupid nonsense" and remarked, "I may not like him very much, but I certainly would not plot to kill him."

On July 29, 1965, the Sixth Circuit addressed the appeal, snubbing the majority of the claims with little discussion. The court explained that Hoffa's own counsel had created much of the newspaper publicity on his behalf. In addition, the number of plainclothes marshals who had attended the trial was within the discretion of the court—and had been reduced at the request of the defense. The joinder of the defendants was appropriate, as the various charges had related to the same trial, time, and place. "It seems to us," the court concluded, "that the acts of the defendants were certainly connected."

As for the claim that the defense had been limited in its cross-examination of witnesses, a skeptical Chief Judge Paul C. Weick wrote, "Almost every question which the ingenuity of counsel could think of, was raised in the trial court." Similarly, the court rejected claims that the trial court had erred by overlooking the destruction of FBI notes and by failing to force Norma Jean Partin to testify against her husband.

What about the claim that Partin had been planted in Nashville? Even if Hoffa had not invited him to Nashville at first, the court ruled, Partin had remained there at Hoffa's request or with his consent. This circumstance rendered Partin's presence there appropriate in the eyes of the law. No matter how he came to be in Nashville, moreover, the conversations Partin relayed to the government had occurred in the absence of counsel. Thus there had been no violation of the defendants' constitutional rights.

What about government surveillance? "The trouble is that the claim is not supported by the evidence," the court stated. A two-day, two-hundred-page hearing had been held on the topic. The result? The pretrial observation of four individuals not involved in the trial, and the surveillance of Bernard Spindel, "a person having a reputation in the field of telephonic and electronic interceptions." There was simply no showing that anyone had surveilled Hoffa or his attorneys.

The appellate court concentrated on the fact that Hoffa was the main individual who stood to gain from efforts to corrupt the Test Fleet jury. "We think," Judge Weick announced, "that the jury could reasonably have concluded from the evidence that the large scale endeavors at jury tampering were not brought about by spontaneous action of the other participants, who derived no benefit therefrom and were risking criminal prosecution; and that the endeavors resulted from the instigation, careful planning and agreement in which Hoffa was an active participant."

Having dispensed with the allegations of courtroom impropriety, the court considered and rejected the affidavits alleging juror misconduct during the trial. The decision cited the jurors' alertness and decorum throughout the trial, as well as Judge Wilson's statement that "Not a single affiant purports to have any personal knowledge of the activities or behavior of a single juror in respect to the use of beverages at any time, nor does any affiant identify a single juror or single officer as having done anything wrong in this respect."

After scrutinizing each of the errors claimed by the defense, the Sixth Circuit affirmed the conviction. Disappointed but not surprised, Hoffa and his counsel prepared for their next steps in the fight to capsize the verdict.[25]

––––––

Things were beginning to look desperate. Various efforts to raise public doubt about the verdict had stalled. While their appeals had not been exhausted, each defense motion had been denied, and there was no guarantee that the Supreme Court would even take up the case. As *Time* magazine colorfully described the chief defendant, "Jimmy Hoffa has recently been as nervous as a truck driver at a tea party."[26]

On September 1, 1965, Hoffa swung a flailing sledgehammer in the form of a third motion for a new trial. It was one of the more startling, bare-knuckled tactics in a case already teetering on the edge of credibility. "Some really scurrilous pleadings were filed," law clerk Charlie Gearhiser recalled. "They were absolutely despicable and unbelievable on their face." Accompanying the motion were four affidavits signed by prostitutes claiming US marshals had hired them to entertain jurors during the trial. "The things that they charged were that the deputy marshals at the Read House took the male jurors down to another floor to prostitutes," Mansfield said, "and also that they'd taken one or two of them out to the VFW Post on Riverside Drive to drink beer and stuff like that." Dug up by a pimp and a hotel bellhop, the four women had been trained to identify the jurors with whom they had consorted, as well as the marshals who had made the arrangements.[27]

Under the alias Patsy Jo Harris, twenty-eight-year-old prostitute Catherine Johnson filed an affidavit claiming that bellhop Seymour Ball— whom the Read House had fired in the wake of his prior affidavit—had escorted her to the tenth floor of the hotel and told her to identify herself as a "lady marshal" if asked. Once on the jurors' floor, she had had sex with five jurors. The bellhop gave her $100, which he said had come from "the marshal." Johnson identified two of the men as jurors John Curbow and William Link. "At one orgy involving marshals, three jurors and two or three other girls," she added, a marshal crowed, "We've got the cocky little bastard [Hoffa] now, right where we want him."

Bobbie Ann Sells alleged that she had been at a party at the hotel where a US marshal had danced around the room, wearing only a bra and panties. She also identified juror William Link as having remarked, "We have two Jews, two colored fellows and Hoffa in a pot and we're going to set fire to them." Seymour Ball swore that the third floor of the Read House was a "showroom" where jurors could go to pick out women to be sent up to their rooms. Seven jurors had shelled out twenty dollars a piece for the services of the ladies, he said. As they left, the girls had tipped Virgil Culpepper—the author of one of the earlier affidavits alleging jury shenanigans.[28]

Chuckie O'Brien, among others, had trolled around the underbelly of Chattanooga, finding money-hungry characters willing to make sworn statements in exchange for cash payments. Those individuals had been taken to Harold Brown, who prepared the affidavits. "He was criticized for a long period of time for participating in this," former assistant US attorney Tom Williams explained, "but I don't think Harold is the one that secured those prostitutes initially . . . Harold was merely the lawyer who took their affidavits." Still, other members of the defense team moved quickly to distance themselves from the prostitution allegations.[29]

Undoubtedly, the affidavits were damaging. "But they made one mistake," Mansfield pointed out. In addition to accusing jurors of misconduct, the affidavits claimed that *Judge Wilson* had consorted with prostitutes throughout the trial. Twenty-two-year-old Marie Monday signed her own affidavit claiming that she had met Wilson at the Read House "some time in late January, 1964, or the early part of February, 1964, during the course of the trial of the Hoffa case." Telling her that he was in charge of the trial, the judge was said to have remarked that "Hoffa was going to get what was coming to him this time and that he was going to see to it that he did." "Don't you worry, he is going to be convicted," Wilson had said, because he was "in charge of it." Monday identified the judge by circling his image in a newspaper clipping with black crayon.[30]

No one who knew Judge Wilson believed this incendiary allegation. "I said to myself," Mansfield commented, "'self, this ain't gonna wash,' 'cause everybody that knew Judge Wilson knew that didn't happen. Ever." As Tom Williams echoed, "When they brought Judge Wilson into it everybody felt that was far-fetched and ridiculous." Indeed, when Hoffa attorney Daniel Maher informed the *Washington Post* that he had an even more scandalous tape recording of Monday with Wilson, the editors of the newspaper refused to even listen to it. [31]

Categorically denying the accusations, and without recusing himself from hearing the scandalous motion, Judge Wilson issued a "scathing, ten-page opinion" on September 12, 1965, rejecting the motion for a new trial. The claims, he remarked, were a "complete and total fabrication and fraud" and "patent perjury." Moreover, Wilson concluded that the jurors' and US marshals' denials "are not refuted by the signatures upon the affidavits of four women who admit selling their bodies, if not their signature, for immoral purposes for twenty dollars."[32] Hoffa's lawyers appealed to the Sixth Circuit, which agreed with Wilson and denied the motion. "One would certainly have to be most credulous," the Sixth Circuit found, "to believe that a United States Judge, presiding over a criminal trial, would go to a hotel where the jury was sequestered, meet a prostitute under unexplained circumstances, and confide in her his feelings of bias and prejudice against one of the defendants." The allegations of sexual liaisons between Wilson and "Hoffa's Hookers," as *Time* magazine came to refer to the women, were simply unbelievable.

Hoffa would appeal the decision to the US Supreme Court, but the court declined to hear the case.[33]

That was hardly the end of the matter. FBI agents were dispatched to investigate the "massive perjury" associated with the affidavits. Warrants were issued for Johnson, Sells, and Monday, all of whom had disappeared into the fog. Monday would later recant her affidavit. Johnson would be tracked down after Granville Sertel's wife, who worked for a collection attorney, gave him the address where Johnson could be found.[34]

Seeking a full, truthful accounting, US district judge Robert L. Taylor granted Johnson immunity in exchange for her testimony. However, she failed to testify truthfully and was therefore put on trial for perjury. At the proceedings she chose not to testify. Two of the jurors from the tampering trial (Link and Curbow) appeared to deny the allegations, as did James Kemp, the marshal who had allegedly escorted Johnson to the tenth floor of the hotel. The proof noted that bellman Seymour Ball had been seen around town with O'Brien. Another former bellman who claimed to have obtained prostitutes for jurors admitted that, following his discharge, O'Brien had helped him find a new job in Atlanta.

During Johnson's perjury trial, jurors tested US marshals by asking them to bring up bottles of whiskey. The requests were denied. In the end, Johnson, represented by a Teamsters lawyer, was found guilty and sentenced to three years in prison for testifying falsely before the grand jury.[35] "It's just an ugly side of the case," recalled Williams. "No one, of course, believed it to be true about Judge Wilson, because Judge Wilson was such an honorable person, he was a good Christian man, and no one believed it about him." Jim Neal echoed this sentiment: "Judge Wilson didn't have to fear that anybody believed that." "I think if they had just signed it and got affidavits about jurors and marshals, those are easier targets," Williams added.[36]

Prior disappointments aside, the Hoffa defense received welcome news on January 31, 1966, when the Supreme Court agreed to hear the appeal of the Chattanooga conviction. While Hoffa had cited twenty-one errors, though, the Court limited the hearing to a single issue: whether Partin should have been allowed to testify.[37]

Oral argument took place on October 13, 1966. Two of the nine Supreme Court justices recused themselves from the case; Justice Byron R. White had served as deputy attorney general under Bobby Kennedy in 1962, and Justice Abe Fortas had practiced law at a firm that had represented several dissident Teamsters in a case against Hoffa. Observers doubted the conviction would stick. After all, hanging a guilty verdict on Hoffa had proven to be an elusive goal. The Supreme Court, moreover, had recently held in an unrelated case that the government's use of informants had violated defendants' right to confer with legal counsel. "When the appeal is discussed in legal circles," an article in *Atlantic Monthly* noted, "the usual question is not whether Hoffa will win, but how he will win."

According to Walter Sheridan, in an extremely brazen move a Teamsters official approached the brother of Justice William J. Brennan, warning him that his brewery woud be shut down if Brennan did not "vote right" in the case. The threat, however, did not have the desired effect, and Brennan remained on the panel to hear the case.[38]

On December 12, 1966, the Supreme Court affirmed the conviction. Four justices ruled in favor of the verdict, two concurred with the decision on alternate grounds, and one dissented. Hooker commented, "Judge (Frank) Wilson gave him a fair trial and there was no error in the record. . . . I felt confident the conviction would be affirmed."[39] Justice Potter Stewart issued the court's opinion. The majority rejected the claim that Partin had wormed his way into Hoffa's hotel suite. "Partin did not enter the suite by force or by stealth," Stewart wrote. "He was not a surreptitious eavesdropper. Partin was in the suite by invitation, and every conversation which he heard was either directed to him or knowingly carried on in his presence." With that in mind, the opinion stated, "Neither this Court nor any member of it has ever expressed the view that the Fourth Amendment protects a wrongdoer's misplaced belief that a person to whom he voluntarily confides his wrongdoing will not reveal it."

As for the Fifth Amendment protection from self-incrimination, there was no showing that Hoffa had been compelled or coerced to incriminate himself; all of his comments to Partin were "wholly voluntary." The Court also rejected the claim that Partin's presence violated Hoffa's Sixth Amendment right to consult with his legal counsel: "None of [Hoffa's] incriminating statements which Partin heard were made in the presence of counsel, in the hearing of counsel, or in connection in any way with the legitimate defense of the Test Fleet prosecution."

Finally, the majority took up the hazy claim that, even absent a constitutional violation, the government's conduct should "offend those canons of decency and fairness which express the notions of justice of English-speaking peoples even toward those charged with the most heinous offenses." Partin may have had a motive to lie, the Supreme Court conceded. "But it does not follow that his testimony was untrue, nor does it follow that his testimony was constitutionally inadmissible." The "rigorous cross-examination" to which Partin was subjected presented the jury with sufficient information to rule on his credibility. A mere *motive to lie* was not enough to automatically invalidate his testimony.

Justice Tom C. Clark concurred with the decision, albeit on different grounds. Absent an exceptional showing of error, he explained, the Supreme Court should not overturn reasoned decisions of the lower courts. There was no basis from which to question prior findings that Partin was "knowingly and voluntarily" brought into Hoffa's confidence.

Chief Justice Earl Warren penned a scathing dissent. "Here," he wrote, "Edward Partin, a jailbird languishing in a Louisiana jail under indictments for such state and federal crimes as embezzlement, kidnapping, and manslaughter (and soon to be charged with perjury and assault), contacted federal authorities and told them he was willing to become, and would be useful as, an informer against Hoffa." Partin clearly had a motive for this offer—leniency with respect to his criminal problems. "For his services," Warren continued, "he was well paid by the Government, both through devious and secret support payments to his wife and, it may be inferred, by executed promises not to pursue the indictments under which he was charged at the time he became an informer."

An affidavit signed by Bill Sidney (Billy) Simpson evidently helped the chief justice arrive at his conclusion. Simpson claimed to have shared a Baton Rouge jail cell with Partin in September 1962 after the pair had been arrested on kidnapping charges. Apparently, the Hoffa crew had persuaded Simpson to turn on Partin. "I know a way to get out of here," Partin had reportedly confided to his cellmate. "They want Hoffa more than they want me." Over the next few days, Partin was periodically removed from the cell—for the apparent purpose of meeting with Billy Daniels and the FBI. Simpson asked him why he was betraying Hoffa. "What difference does it make?" Partin replied. "I'm thinking about myself. Aren't you thinking about yourself? I don't give a damn about Hoffa." After a few days of negotiations, Partin had been quietly released. This information was telling. If Partin's motive was betraying Hoffa in order to evade his own legal problems, Chief Justice Warren remarked, "he has been uniquely successful in satisfying it."

In his affidavit, Simpson also claimed that Partin had told him to stay hidden during the Chattanooga trial so that he could not be subpoenaed to testify. Partin took "bennies," he offered. In fact, on one occasion when Partin had accidentally shot himself, he had run away to avoid a possible drug test associated with admission to a hospital, asking Simpson to go to his apartment and throw away drugs that he kept there. As for the Chattanooga trial, Simpson said, Partin had told him that the FBI had drafted and reviewed his testimony with him "several times so that he could remember the exact words."

Partin had filed his own responsive affidavit in February 1965, denying Simpson's allegations. The two men had never shared a cell, he said, and they had never discussed Hoffa. Partin also denied that he ever used dope. "At all times [in Chattanooga]," he added, "I testified to the truth." A supplemental affidavit from Baton Rouge assistant district attorney Billy Daniels confirmed that Partin and Simpson never shared a cell and that, in reality, Simpson himself had told Daniels that Partin had never taken drugs.

Chief Justice Warren did not credit the Partin affidavit against Simpson's claims. After his release, Partin had traveled to Nashville, where he "became the equivalent of a bugging device which moved with Hoffa wherever he went." The chief justice simply could not countenance such a devious plot to undermine an individual's right to privacy. "An invasion of basic rights made possible by prevailing upon friendship with the victim is no less proscribed than an invasion accomplished by force," Warren maintained. "And that is exactly the quicksand upon which these convictions rest." Without Partin, the case against Hoffa was flimsy. It was only through the government's overreaching, unjust actions that the evidence against Hoffa had been procured: "Here, the Government reaches into the jailhouse to employ a man who was himself facing indictments far more serious (and later including one for perjury) than the one confronting the man against whom he offered to inform. It employed him not for the purpose of testifying to something that had already happened, but rather for the purpose of infiltration to see if crimes would in the future be committed. The Government, in its zeal, even assisted him in gaining a position from which he could be a witness to the confidential relationship of attorney and client engaged in the preparation of a criminal defense."

It was not even necessary to examine the case on constitutional grounds, Warren concluded, as the practices of the government were "offensive to the fair administration of justice in federal courts." Due to the "affront to the quality and fairness of federal law enforcement which this case presents," he stated, it was therefore necessary for the Supreme Court to step in. The chief justice would have overturned the conviction.[40] However, the majority had evidently found Partin's testimony persuasive. "I'm proud they saw fit to believe my story," Partin remarked in a television interview, "even though I am not convinced that I want to see Hoffa in jail. I just want him to lose his hold on the locals again."[41]

Hoffa's judicial appeals were at an end. Stating that "[the] fellas don't feel that Jimmy got a fair shake," Detroit Teamsters staged a twenty-four-hour walkout. Hoffa rushed home to calm things down. "Return to your jobs!" he cried. "Don't take the law into your own hands or you'll hurt me! Don't do it! Please!"[42]

––––––

Desperate for proof of government malfeasance, Hoffa placed an ad in Tennessee newspapers offering a $25,000 reward to anyone willing to come forward with evidence of surveillance in the Chattanooga case. Through Bufalino, a group labeled the Friends of James R. Hoffa Committee sweetened the pot, adding $100,000; William Loeb and the *Manchester Union Leader* matched the offer, bringing the total prize to $225,000.

Houston house painter and Chattanooga native James D. East responded, explaining that he knew two bellhops at the Hotel Patten who could confirm that Hoffa's telephones had been bugged. Given an initial payment of $2,150, East proved unable to produce any useful information. The assistant manager of the hotel, moreover, professed that East had made an improper approach to two hotel employees who knew nothing of alleged surveillance. When he was asked to return the money, East lost his nerve and called Fred Hixson at the *Chattanooga Times,* which ran the story of the "blowup" between East and the *Manchester Union Leader.*[43]

The $225,000 reward did yield one additional response in the form of Benjamin David "Bud" Nichols. A self-styled electronics expert from Knoxville, Nichols signed an affidavit swearing that Sheridan had paid him $1,684 to place listening bugs under jurors' mattresses and tap six telephone lines in jurors' rooms at the Read House. By now accustomed to the wild accusations conveniently "unearthed" by the Hoffa team, a dismissive Sheridan denied that he had ever met Nichols and reported that there were no telephones in jurors' rooms.

Nevertheless, buoyed by this promising information, on January 27, 1967, the defense filed with the Supreme Court a "Motion for Relief Because of Government Wiretapping, Electronic Eavesdropping and Other Intrusions." In addition to the Nichols statement, the defense filed twenty other affidavits, including statements from Hoffa and his attorneys confirming that they had used the rooms and telephones Nichols described. Also included were sworn statements from the ubiquitous Frazier, Paden, and Cole, who reported that Sheridan had shared secret tapes of Hoffa's conversations. The flip-flopping Hazel Fulton also reappeared, swearing that Sheridan had showed her audio recordings of discussions between Hoffa and his lawyers.

I. Irving Davidson, a Hoffa confederate whom many considered the Washington, DC, contact for New Orleans mob boss Carlos Marcello, presented one notable affidavit. During a visit to Chattanooga during the 1964 trial, Davidson averred, John J. Hooker warned him "not to call him on the telephone at the Read House where he was staying," as the telephones at that hotel and the Hotel Patten had been bugged. Later, over dinner in Nashville, a regretful Hooker said that "he was sorry he ever agreed to take the Hoffa prosecution," and that "he did not approve of the way the evidence was gathered against Mr. Hoffa, stating that he did not believe in wire-tapping, bugging, or violating people's rights."

US solicitor general Thurgood Marshall directed a memorandum to the Supreme Court reporting that a thorough review of the materials had failed to unearth any evidence of improper surveillance. In a wry side note, on February 9 the *Chattanooga Times* pointed out that Bud Nichols had recently been observed driving a new, white Cadillac around Knoxville.

The Supreme Court directed that the motion should be heard by the district court in Chattanooga, with Judge Wilson presiding. Morris Shenker, Hoffa's attorney at the hearing, learned of rumors that the government had evidence of payments made to some of the affiants in exchange for their statements. Wisely cautious, Shenker requested a postponement so that he could look into the new information. Wilson denied the request for delay, observing that the defense had already had months to prepare for the hearing.[44]

Bud Nichols later admitted that his affidavit had been completely false.[45]

———

The campaign to vindicate Hoffa (and, with far less fanfare, his codefendants) was in its death throes. On March 6, 1967, a last-minute appeal to allow Hoffa to remain free on bond pending the resolution of his appeals was denied. Various trucking companies' requests that Hoffa be given a thirty-day reprieve to complete nationwide contract negotiations was likewise denied.[46] Therefore, at 9:00 a.m. on March 7, 1967, the IBT president surrendered to US marshals at the federal courthouse in Washington. Although he tried to keep the event under the radar, a throng of reporters, tipped off as to the time and place, surrounded Hoffa as he shoved his way toward the courthouse. "This is a very unhappy day in my life," he told them. "The government has wire-tapped, room-bugged, surveilled and done everything unconstitutional it could do." Looking over the crowd, he added, "If they can do this to Hoffa they can do this to any citizen. I urge everyone to beware of the constitutional rights they are losing. That is all I have to say, gentlemen."

He entered the courthouse and telephoned Judge Wilson to make a last unsuccessful request for a delay before surrendering. (A piece of the phone's handset came loose during the call, prompting Hoffa to comment that the office must have been bugged.)[47] Shackled, Hoffa draped his raincoat over his arms in order to hide the handcuffs. He was escorted to the vehicle that would carry him to the medium-security Lewisburg (Pennsylvania) Penitentiary, where he would serve his sentence as Inmate No. 33298. Chained to the floor of the vehicle, he was disconsolate. "As if, for Christ's sake, I was John Dillinger or somebody," he muttered. As the vehicle pulled out of the courthouse garage, Hoffa saw Clark Mollenhoff, the reporter who had first raised the issue of Teamster corruption with Kennedy. His frustrations washing over him, Hoffa spat viciously at the closed window of the car.

As the entourage passed by, a voice called out, "Give the guys in Lewisburg my best, Jimmy."[48]

———

For Hoffa, there were a few subsequent hints that the conviction might yet be overturned. In August 1969, a renewed hearing was held in Chattanooga to determine whether FBI bugs and surveillance had compromised the trial. Hoffa arrived at the federal courthouse in handcuffs, his tie loosened. "When he came in that day," Mansfield said, "the arrogance and his demeanor had changed . . . he patted me on the stomach and said, 'You've been gaining a little weight, haven't you, Marshal?'" A request from local Teamsters to bring Hoffa "good outside food" during a lunch break was approved, and an empty office was set aside for him to talk with his attorneys and visitors during recesses.

The seven-day hearing examined a variety of government recordings, most of which had nothing to do with the jury tampering allegations or the Chattanooga trial. "After the [hearing] was over with," Mansfield said, "I took him [Hoffa] up to the county jail," where he would be held until his return to Lewisburg. The denial of this fourth (and final) motion for new trial was affirmed on January 21, 1971.[49] Undaunted, on May 19, 1971, Hoffa filed another motion demanding that his sentence be vacated because, while Partin had testified that he had no recordings of conversations, he had recorded Ewing King. Finding that Partin had not denied making tape recordings of *King*, Judge Wilson denied the motion on February 11, 1972—more than seven years after the trial had begun, and almost two months after Hoffa had walked out of prison.[50]

The ordeal that had been the Chattanooga trial of Jimmy Hoffa was finally over.

EPILOGUE

"This is a case in which the American system
has been tested and has been victorious."

—*Chattanooga News-Free Press*, March 5, 1964

The lawyers, witnesses, jurors, marshals, and public officials who played a role in the Chattanooga trial took divergent paths after March 1964.[1]

DAVE ALEXANDER, the low-key Franklin, Tennessee, attorney who represented Nicholas Tweel, was "fair with other lawyers, fair with his clients and fair with other people" throughout his career. In one other very public trial, he represented the victims of a 1978 gas explosion in Waverly, Tennessee, caused by the derailment of a freight train that killed sixteen people and injured forty-three others. In 1995, Alexander died at the age of seventy-nine.[2]

HARRY BERKE had a prominent legal practice in Chattanooga for several decades. In 1968, he was disbarred for a two-year period after the Chattanooga and Tennessee Bar Associations brought an action against him, claiming that he had charged usurious interest rates in connection with a series of real estate loans and given false testimony while assisting two ex-convicts in laundering stolen money. Following the reinstatement of his license, Berke continued to practice law until his death in 1999.[3]

MARVIN BERKE met his future wife while she was visiting Chattanooga during the long trial. While the two were on a blind date, a shadowy vehicle tailed them, and Berke made up a story to keep his future wife from becoming spooked. He continues to practice law in the firm his father founded in 1934.[4]

CECIL BRANSTETTER, the longest-surviving primary member of the defense team, was known for his dedication to unpopular causes and the oppressed. In 1969 he and Jack Norman defended former Vanderbilt football star "Big Bill" Powell against charges that he had shot and killed the owner of the auto dealership where he worked. Norman's old adversary John J. Hooker was assigned to the case as special prosecutor, leading to expectations of a sensational showdown between the two grand old men of the bar. The defense made the calculated (if risky) decision to forego closing arguments, thus denying a stunned Hooker the opportunity to charm the jury with his well-planned oration. For months after the not guilty verdict, Hooker could not resist reciting his intended speech for friends. Asked to act as a consultant for the 1992 *Hoffa* film, Branstetter declined, indicating that he wanted nothing to do with the project. He died in 2014, at the age of ninety-three.[5]

HAROLD BROWN, the attorney for Ewing King, struck up a personal friendship with Hoffa, even visiting the penitentiary in Lewisburg every few weeks during his prison term. After his release, Hoffa visited Brown and assured him that, once he was back in power, he would put him on a legal retainer. Brown later practiced law with his son, William, who went on to become a circuit court judge in Chattanooga. "I don't think he regretted being in the Hoffa trial," William Brown reported. "But in general, my dad's connections to labor affected him politically." Harold Brown lost two elections in the 1970s, one for Hamilton County district attorney general and another for city judge. In 1981, Brown collapsed and died while walking to the Hamilton County courthouse. He was only sixty-two years old.[6]

Longtime Hoffa attorney **WILLIAM BUFALINO** objected to reports linking him to underworld figures such as his cousin Russell Bufalino and his father-in-law, Detroit boss Angelo Meli. Following the McClellan hearings, he unsuccessfully sued Kennedy and McClellan for referring to him as a "leech preying on working men and women," insisting that he had never been affiliated with the Mafia or engaged in any criminal enterprise. In the wake of the jury tampering trial, Bufalino distanced himself from Hoffa because "he had concluded that the teamster leader had used other people for his own gain." After the IBT president's disappearance, Bufalino publicly opined that "Hoffa had been killed in order to cover up a CIA plot in which he was involved, which planned the assassination of Fidel Castro by members of the Mafia." Later, he represented several mob figures accused of involvement in Hoffa's disappearance, including Frank Sheeran and "Tony Pro" Provenzano. Bufalino retired from the practice of law in 1982. In 1990, at age seventy-two, he died of leukemia in Ft. Lauderdale.[7]

LARRY CAMPBELL, the first black business agent for Teamsters Local 299 in Detroit, was convicted of jury tampering along with Hoffa in 1964. In March 1967, he began serving a three-year sentence at the Federal Detention Center in Sandstone, Minnesota. Campbell died in 1972 at the age of forty-six.[8]

After his retirement from the US Marshals Service, cigar-chomping **ELMER DISSPAYNE** served as a metro councilman in Nashville. He was later elected as a Democratic member of the Tennessee General Assembly and served for two terms (1979–83). Disspayne died of a heart attack in 1988, at age seventy-four.[9]

Undaunted by his close brush with the law in 1964, **ALLEN DORFMAN** continued to administer the Central States Pension Fund, the "mob bank" used to fund loans for Las Vegas casinos in exchange for generous kick-backs. "He's the guy in charge while I am gone," Hoffa told IBT leaders as he departed for prison. The pension loans proved lucrative, earning Dorfman millions and enabling him to travel in a private jet that he pur-chased from Frank Sinatra. In 1972, Dorfman was convicted of embezzling from the pension fund after approving a $1.5 million loan that came with a $55,000 sweetener. The resulting one-year prison sentence did not prevent him from continuing to make $186 million in loans during the four-year period after his confinement. These earnings included advances intended to fund the Caesar's Palace and Circus Circus casinos.

A 1974 pension fraud charge against Dorfman floundered after the key witness was murdered. In 1979, the FBI instigated "Operation Pendorf" (Pen-etration of Allen Dorfman), tapping phone lines, planting bugs in his office, and monitoring a total of 112,000 calls over six months. With agents listen-ing, the man referred to as the "CFO of the mob" made a critical mistake: in exchange for help killing a bill that would deregulate the trucking industry, Dorfman offered Senator Howard Cannon (D-NV) assistance in preventing a construction project near the senator's Las Vegas home. In December 1982, Dorfman was convicted of bribery. Facing fifty-five years in prison, he became a mob liability, and three days before his sentencing hearing, on January 23, 1983, he was shot and killed in a gangland murder in Lincolnwood, Illinois.[10]

TOMMY EASON, the cameraman whose absence from the trial follow-ing the birth of his daughter was noted by Hoffa, retired from Chattanooga's NBC station in 2010. He had worked in the local television business for fifty years. Reflecting on the Hoffa trial, Eason insisted, "I didn't think it was a big deal. I just had to go down there every day and walk backwards and forth to talk to him [Hoffa]."[11]

In his autobiography, Hoffa listed his rancor with Kennedy as the first of two grave mistakes he had made in his life. The second, the union boss said, "was naming **FRANK FITZSIMMONS** as my successor." Staring down the barrel of an extended prison term, Hoffa named Fitzsimmons general vice president of the Teamsters in 1966. "He's just a peanut-butter sandwich," one disdainful union official commented. The day before Hoffa reported to prison, Fitzsimmons had scrawled out a promise to do whatever he could to get him released. Fitzsimmons was elected to the top post within the

Teamsters Union in 1971 and reelected in 1976. Enticed by the power and prestige of the position, he stressed that Hoffa had agreed to forego the presidency of the IBT as a condition of his release from jail. In so doing, Fitzsimmons ensured the lasting enmity of his outraged former boss. After a lingering illness, Fitzsimmons died of lung cancer in San Diego in 1981. He had never been particularly popular—only four mourners attended his funeral mass in California.[12]

"I certainly was a new law clerk [in 1964]," **CHARLIE GEARHISER** later reminisced. "I guess we started out like novices. Judge Wilson started out like a novice in the sense that he didn't realize the storm that was coming to Chattanooga." Following the 1964 trial, Wilson persuaded Gearhiser to turn down a position at Union Carbide because he was "not suited for the job." Instead, Gearhiser obtained a job in the US Attorney's Office, where he tried a bevy of "white whiskey cases and stolen car cases and the like." During a conspiracy case involving hospital kickbacks, one of the defense attorneys remarked that Gearhiser just wanted "a feather in his cap"; after the successful verdict, jurors appeared at his office to present him with an Indian warbonnet. Gearhiser later served as a part-time US magistrate, and in 1974 he founded his own law firm in Chattanooga. He continued to practice law until his death in 2013.[13]

The colorful **HENRY GRADY**, who teamed up with Dave Alexander to represent Nicholas Tweel in the Chattanooga trial, passed away from cancer only a few years after the trial.

JAMES HAGGERTY died on November 10, 1966. To his dying day, he remained convinced that the federal government had continued its surveillance of the attorneys representing Hoffa in Chattanooga. He advised associates in his law firm to exercise caution in what they said in the office, and whenever he traveled by airplane, he complained that someone had rifled through his bags.

Always frail and in delicate health, **JOSEPHINE HOFFA** was "devastated" by her husband's disappearance in 1975. In 1980, she collapsed and died of a heart attack in Detroit. She was sixty-two years old.[14]

JOHN J. HOOKER SR. reluctantly prosecuted Tommy Osborn for his role in attempting to fix the Test Fleet jury. For the remainder of his life, he felt responsible for Osborn's downfall. After Osborn committed suicide, Hooker received a telephone call at his home. "Well, I hope to hell you're satisfied now, you sonofabitch," the voice on the other end snapped. "Tommy Osborn killed himself this afternoon," Hooker informed his son, "and I believe I may be the cause of it. I'm afraid I'm to blame for it." In 1970, the sixty-seven-year-old Hooker died of a heart attack at his home in Franklin, Tennessee.[15]

NELLIE KENYON, whom one editor referred to as "the best bird dog in the pack so far as news gathering," covered three Hoffa trials in 1962 and 1964. At the conclusion of the Chattanooga trial, she attended the party in Washington celebrating the conviction. She later recalled, "In thanking those who had helped prosecute and convict Hoffa[,] Bobby [Kennedy] had tears in his eyes as he said, 'And the President wants to thank you.'" Kenyon received the Headliner's Award for her coverage of the Chattanooga trial. "Miss Nellie" retired from the *Nashville Tennessean* in 1970 and died in 1982.[16]

Following his conviction, EWING KING served three years in prison in Texarkana, Texas. Letters pleading for his early release on the basis of his wife's cervical cancer diagnosis and his daughter's depression and suicidal tendencies fell flat, and he served the full sentence. When King died in 1990, members of Teamsters Local 480 (Nashville) served as honorary pallbearers at his funeral.[17]

BILL KNOWLES shaved and cut the hair of jurors throughout the Hoffa trial. Several Teamsters subsequently visited his barbershop, inquiring as to what the jurors might have said while there. "I guess they were looking for ways to say something had been compromised," Knowles said later. "But that wasn't the case." In 1974, Knowles became the Hamilton County clerk in Chattanooga, a position he continues to hold to this day.[18]

WILLIAM LOEB, the fiery, archconservative owner of the *Manchester Union Leader* who spilled gallons of ink urging an inquiry into the efforts to get Hoffa, died of cancer in 1981, at age seventy-five. The "petulant, scurrilous and unfailingly infuriating" publisher left the influential New Hampshire newspaper to his wife, Nackey.[19]

MORT LLOYD, regarded as Chattanooga's first television news anchor, returned in 1970 to the local CBS affiliate, WDEF-TV, where he had begun his news career. Four years later, he ran for Congress. While traveling to a victory celebration after winning the Democratic primary on August 20, 1974, Lloyd was killed in a plane crash. He was only forty-three years old. His widow, Marilyn, ran in his place, and she won the election, serving in the US House of Representatives until her retirement in 1995.[20]

"I can't forget that trial," US marshal HARRY MANSFIELD recalled almost five decades later. In the wake of the trial, Kennedy issued Mansfield a letter of commendation for his management of the arduous experience. Later that year, he was asked to set up security for the Hoffa trial in Chicago. "So I guess we did a good job," he remarked. Mansfield continued to serve as a US marshal in Chattanooga until 1969. Later, he returned to the job as an appointee of President Jimmy Carter, continuing in the position until his retirement in 1988. Mansfield died in 2012, at age eighty-six.[21]

After serving his own sentence for jury tampering, **LAWRENCE "RED" MEDLIN** died in 1976 in a Murfreesboro, Tennessee, infirmary.[22]

"Yeah, I love winning," prosecutor **JIM NEAL** was quoted as saying. "But I hate losing even more. Just the thought of losing makes my body shrink from 5'8" to 5'6." Neal was probably the most publicly successful lawyer involved in the Hoffa trial. In 1967, he returned to Chattanooga to defend former Hamilton County sheriff Bookie Turner on charges of involvement in the illegal whiskey trade; Turner was found innocent and subsequently reelected. In 1971, Neal founded a private firm, and on three occasions, he defended Edward Grady Partin during his own legal troubles. "You have to understand that Kennedy people are loyal people," Neal explained, "and Partin stood up for us."

Neal later served as the chief prosecutor in the Watergate case, securing the 1974 convictions of former attorney general John Mitchell and Nixon aides H. R. Haldeman and John Ehrlichman; he also obtained the guilty plea of former White House counsel John Dean. "It was by far the most important case in which I have ever been involved," he remarked, adding, "It is the only time that I have been sad after winning a case." In addition, Neal represented prominent criminal defendants, including director John Landis, charged with manslaughter after a helicopter crash during filming of *The Twilight Zone;* the Ford Motor Company, charged with murder as the result of deaths caused when the Pinto automobile was struck from behind; and Dr. George Nichopoulous, charged with overprescribing medications to Elvis Presley. "I've been lucky to have good cases," Neal understated.

In the 1980s, Neal returned to federal service as a special investigator of the Abscam and Iran-Contra scandals. He defended the Exxon Corporation in 1990 after the *Exxon Valdez* oil tanker spilled thousands of gallons of oil in Alaska; the case was one of his few losses. One of Neal's clients, Johnny Cash, cast him in the 1983 made-for-television movie *Murder in Coweta County.* Neal also played himself in *Watergate,* a 1994 television miniseries. A lifelong cigar aficionado, Neal died of esophageal cancer in 2010, at age eighty-one.[23]

Hoffa's personal aide and "foster son," **CHARLES "CHUCKIE" O'BRIEN**, was convicted of theft from a US Customs Office warehouse in 1965. Haggerty and Bufalino represented him at trial. O'Brien was initially placed on a "protected list" when Hoffa went to prison, but after Hoffa's release, Fitzsimmons banished him to a far-flung union outpost in Alaska. There, he had a drastically reduced salary and expense account. As Hoffa's efforts to regain control of the Teamsters Union became increasingly vocal and divisive, Fitzsimmons lured O'Brien into the "I'm for Fitz" camp, offering him the opportunity to supervise twenty-plus locals around sunny Hallandale, Florida, along with a raise and reactivated credit cards. After Hoffa vanished in 1975, James P. Hoffa confronted O'Brien, claiming that he knew something about the situation. O'Brien has steadfastly denied any involvement in the matter ever since.

In the late 1970s, O'Brien served a year in federal prison for making false statements on a mortgage loan application. In 1991, he was barred from contact with the Teamsters due to his alleged links to organized crime. He bitterly complained that the ban was unfair, preventing him from attending the funerals of his friends and associates. In 2001, O'Brien declined to take a polygraph test for the purpose of clearing his name in the Hoffa disappearance. William Bufalino II, the son of Hoffa's longtime advisor, represented him in the matter.[24]

After exhausting his appeals, **THOMAS EWING PARKS** was incarcerated, along with Ewing King, for three years in the federal correctional facility at Texarkana, Texas. Parks died in Nashville in 1980, with his "very devoted friend" Mattie Mix at his side.[25]

Following the 1964 trial, **EDWARD GRADY PARTIN** maintained his hold on the presidency of Teamsters Local 5. "After the trial was over with," Mansfield explained, "the marshals' service had to guard him for two years." While no attempt was made on Partin's life, however, his legal problems did not go away. For a time, it appeared as though he had benefited from his testimony. New Orleans federal justice E. Gordon West referred to the dismissal of the twenty-six-count indictment against Partin as "a payoff for testimony in the Hoffa case." As the Kennedy administration faded into memory, however, Partin found himself in the cross hairs of a no-longer-grateful DOJ. "Not a week goes by," offered Sheridan at one point, "that I don't hear from Partin once or twice. That man has problems." Still, Partin proved elusive; an old 1961 accusation that he had embezzled union funds crumbled when the six-hundred-pound safe in which the union's records were stored was found at the bottom of a river. Two men who had testified again him were beaten, and one was later run over and killed by a truck. The government persisted, however, conducting an eleven-year investigation into antitrust and extortion charges, and in 1979 Partin was convicted of conspiracy to obstruct justice after it was found that he had hidden witnesses and secured perjured testimony. He nonchalantly commented that he had given the judge $25,000 in exchange for probation instead of incarceration. "This time," brother Doug Partin remarked, "Ed was dead wrong." Ed Partin was shocked when sentenced to three four-year terms in federal prison. Contacted for assistance, Sheridan was pitiless. "You tell Ed Partin that I said he is going to be incarcerated in San Diego, in a federal correctional facility, and he is going to be a prisoner," he replied curtly. "And you tell him that he'd better start acting like a prisoner." The union had initially voted to continue paying his salary while in prison. However, after Partin pled no contest to additional charges of conspiracy, racketeering, and embezzling union funds, he was removed as the business agent of Teamsters Local 5. He was released to a Mississippi halfway house in 1986. In 1990, at age sixty-six, Partin died in a nursing home in Baton Rouge due to complications from diabetes and cardiovascular disease. Heisman Trophy winner Billy Cannon served as a pallbearer at his funeral.[26]

JAMES PASCHAL, the highway patrolman offered a promotion in exchange for assistance in talking with his wife, continued to work for the Tennessee Highway Patrol for the remainder of his career. He died in 1999. Betty Paschal continues to live in the same home in Woodbury, Tennessee, where she and her husband lived during the Test Fleet trial in 1962.[27]

FRANK RAGANO, the defense lawyer whom Judge Wilson castigated for trying to listen in on the jury, continued his association with Hoffa until the disappearance of the former IBT president in 1975. In 1971, Ragano was indicted for tax evasion in connection with a country club investment connected to the mob. "Hung out to dry" by old associate Santo Trafficante, he was convicted, given three years' probation, and suspended from the practice of law. The conviction was overturned in 1981, and at age fifty-eight he was reinstated as a lawyer. In later years, Ragano reportedly came to regret his ties to organized crime. Nevertheless, when Trafficante was charged with racketeering in 1986, Ragano reprised his role defending the Tampa boss. Trafficante was the only one of the thirteen defendants acquitted of the charges.

In 1994, Ragano released a book entitled *Mob Lawyer* detailing his experiences representing organized crime figures. He discussed loans made from Teamster pension funds to enable gangsters in Florida and Louisiana to invest in hotels, trucking companies, and other businesses, with kickbacks paid to Hoffa. Ragano also revealed that in 1963 he had carried a request from Hoffa to Trafficante and Carlos Marcello for John F. Kennedy's assassination. According to Ragano, a dying Trafficante confided to him in 1987, "We shouldn't have killed Giovanni [John] . . . we should have killed Bobby." Today, most critics doubt the legitimacy of Ragano's claims about the Kennedy assassination. In 1990, Ragano was convicted of income tax evasion, and he served ten months in a federal health center due to a heart condition. He died in his sleep in 1998, at age seventy-five.[28]

JACK REDDY, the US attorney for the Eastern District of Tennessee, continued his role in the US Attorney's Office in Chattanooga until his retirement in 1969. He died in 1997, at the age of ninety-one.[29]

Vociferous lawyer **JACQUES SCHIFFER** served his thirty-day sentence for contempt of court at the Maxwell Air Force Base in Alabama. Writing to fellow counsel Harold Brown, he joked, "I've found out these southern boys aren't so bad after all. . . . Everybody I'm in prison with is down here for making whiskey. . . . I've even learned to eat turnip greens, and I like them." The experience, however, did not temper his outrageous courtroom behavior. In July 1965, representing Hoffa stalwart Frank Chavez in Puerto Rico, Schiffer was advised by the presiding judge that "If I ever see you on this island again, I'll have you arrested for practicing law without a license." Schiffer died of cancer in 1970, two days after Hooker. He was only sixty-two years old. Much of his obituary in the *New York Times* was devoted to details of his outbursts during the Chattanooga case in 1964.[30]

"This trial was probably . . . the highlight of his career, no doubt about it," John Sertel recalled of his father, US marshal **GRANVILLE SERTEL**. During the long Chattanooga proceedings, Sertel became an honorary member of the Wilson family, staying at their home on Signal Mountain and taking the young Wilson children fishing. In 1978, when he was forced to retire from the US Marshals Service due to an established age ceiling, Judge Wilson protested, noting that the key requirements for the job were knowing people and having connections—not chasing down crooks. When those complaints proved ineffective, Wilson hired Sertel to serve as a deputy clerk, in which position he stayed until 1987. Sertel passed away in 1994.[31]

Referred to by *Life* magazine as "the foremost lawyer for the mob in the US," **MORRIS SHENKER** assisted in indexing the Chattanooga trial for appeal purposes. Despite his underworld connections, he served at one time as the head of the St. Louis Commission on Crime and Law Enforcement. Shenker was a part owner and chairman of the Dunes Hotel and Casino in Las Vegas, purportedly built with Teamster pension funds. The movies *The Hoodlum Priest* (1961) and *Casino* (1995) contained characters based on Shenker. He died of pneumonia in 1989, at age eighty-two. At the time, he was under a federal indictment for conspiring to conceal hundreds of thousands of dollars from the Internal Revenue Service and his creditors during bankruptcy proceedings.[32]

In 1972, Get Hoffa Squad member **WALTER SHERIDAN** published a book entitled *The Fall and Rise of Jimmy Hoffa*, detailing the efforts to convict the Teamsters boss. From 1965 to 1970, Sheridan was a special correspondent for NBC, where he produced documentaries on drugs, crime, and other issues. He later worked as an aide to the Senate Judiciary and Labor and Human Resources Committees, investigating mine conditions, the exploitation of farmworkers, and drug companies that tampered with data submitted to the FDA. Sheridan died of lung cancer in 1995 in Maryland.[33]

In the wake of the Chattanooga trial, **FRED SHOBE** resurfaced in FBI investigative files exploring claims that he had represented himself as a government agent to shake down numbers operators in the Detroit area. On March 6, 1964, FBI agents were instructed to hold off on the investigation until the conclusion of the Chattanooga trial. Then, on March 19, the agency was authorized to proceed with an inquiry into whether Shobe was guilty of criminal impersonation. Remarks were made during the investigation that "Shobe was not a reliable individual and could never be depended upon," and that "Shobe would do anything for money." Characterized by one witness as "emotionally unstable," Shobe denied the accusations; on July 28, the matter was quietly closed.

In January 1965, the FBI examined possible charges against Shobe for obstruction of justice during Chuckie O'Brien's trial for theft of property from a US Customs Service warehouse. Shobe had allegedly attempted to force an eyewitness to change his testimony. The witness, however, later denied that he had been threatened, and the file was closed due to lack of evidence. In later years, Shobe sold insurance and worked in computer processing for IBM. According to his daughter, he "shed a tear" when he heard of Hoffa's disappearance in 1975. Suffering from emphysema and a heart condition, Shobe moved to California in 1983 to live with his son. He died in 1990.[34]

JOHN SEIGENTHALER took a leave of absence from editing the *Nashville Tennessean* to work on Robert F. Kennedy's 1968 presidential campaign. Later that year, he served as a pallbearer at Kennedy's funeral. Seigenthaler retired from the *Nashville Tennessean* as chairman emeritus in 1991. So closely was the newspaper identified with the civil rights struggle that attorney Jack Norman once derided Seigenthaler as "Nashville's most prominent black leader." Seigenthaler later served as the founding editorial director of *USA Today* (1982). He was "courageous and canny, fearless and tireless," one writer acclaimed. In 1991, Seigenthaler founded the First Amendment Center at Vanderbilt University to "help promote appreciation and understanding for those values so vital in a democratic society." He died in 2014, at age eighty-six. Seigenthaler's obituary noted, "He once danced with Tina Turner, had a bit part in Shakespeare's 'Othello,' and counted the late Johnny Cash as a confidante."[35]

HARVEY SILETS remained in private practice for the remainder of his life, during which he "represented mobsters, corrupt judges and politicians, corporations and hundreds of small businessmen caught up in tax woes." At one time, the *National Law Journal* named him one of the nation's top ten litigators. "He didn't scare the [IRS] agents because he was going to yell at them or he was going to trick them," said one of his longtime legal partners. "They were going to be outsmarted." Silets died in 2007 at age seventy-five.[36]

In a 1966 article entitled "The Big Snoop," *Life* magazine profiled wiretapper **BERNARD SPINDEL**, calling him an "expert pilot, consummate lock-picker, foreign adventurer, electronics wizard and the No. 1 big-league freelance eavesdropper and wiretapper in the US." Reportedly arrested 204 times—mostly for snooping-related offenses—he proudly noted that he had been convicted only once, for eavesdropping, earning a $500 fine. In 1968, Spindel penned an autobiography entitled *The Ominous Ear*. At only forty-seven years of age, Spindel died in 1971 in New York following a heart attack. At the time, he was on parole following a conviction for illegal eavesdropping.[37]

NICHOLAS TWEEL was one of two defendants acquitted of jury tampering in Chattanooga. It would not be the end of Tweel's legal entanglements, although in one such case he would unexpectedly benefit from his connection to Hoffa. In January 1976, a mistrial was declared in an income tax evasion case against Tweel because nine of the twelve jurors had read a newspaper article linking him to Hoffa. Tweel later became a "financial analyst for Holiday Inns in Huntington and Ft. Lauderdale." He died on February 14— Jimmy Hoffa's birthday—in Huntington, West Virginia, in 2009. He was ninety-two years old.[38]

While awaiting the trial of Tommy Osborn, **ROBERT VICK**, the shady Nashville policeman whose secret audiotape would lead to Osborn's disbarment and imprisonment, was made a special patrolman third class and assigned full-time to the US marshal's office. However, the job evaporated after Vick testified in Osborn's trial. It was later discovered that Sheridan had obtained a $3,000 loan for Vick, ostensibly because "he thought it was bad for law enforcement if people who testified for the government were permitted to suffer for it." Two days later, recognizing that the loan could be misinterpreted as a payment for his testimony, Sheridan asked that the money be returned. Vick "was furious and left town mad as hell."

Vick was later given a job working for Teamsters Local 327, where Hoffa enemy Don Vestal had assumed the presidency. This development led to a hearing to address whether Vick had perjured himself. In a puzzling ruling, however, the judge denied Osborn a new trial, finding that "Vick was a notorious liar who often made up stories to convince people he was an important man—except, of course, when he was under oath." Attempts to convince Vick to recant his testimony proved fruitless, despite offers of financial assistance and threats that "some cold night they might drag Vick's body out of the river."[39]

In 1967, **SID ZAGRI** joined the efforts to convince Vick to recant and
"help the boss." A month later, on February 7, 1967, Zagri burned to death in
a restaurant fire in Montgomery, Alabama. In a letter to Alabama governor
Lurleen Wallace, William Loeb reported that Zagri had been in that state to
run down a lead that might have vindicated Hoffa. "Since the agents of that
sinister conspiracy against Mr. Hoffa, in my estimation, will stop at nothing, including murder," he wrote, "and since it seems incredible to me that
a fire should have soared so quickly without artificial stimulation, I would
suggest very careful consideration of this aspect of the tragedy." It was never
determined whether the fire had been deliberately set.[40]

———

The Chattanooga trial had its origins in a personal vendetta, popularly labeled
as a "blood feud," between two powerful men. In time, however, the chief
combatants moved on, leaving the Get Hoffa campaign and its aftermath a
dim memory. **ROBERT F. KENNEDY** was crushed by his brother's assassination. As a result, "he lost all interest in Hoffa" and took no great pleasure
in the jury tampering conviction. He had simply lost his taste for the fight.
During the party celebrating the verdict, the grief-stricken Kennedy advised
one guest that there was "nothing to celebrate."

Kennedy briefly considered turning his back on politics altogether. But in
August 1964 he announced his run for the US Senate seat from New York.
Then, in 1968, in the Caucus Room of the old Senate Office Building—the same
room where he had squared off against Hoffa a decade earlier—he announced
his candidacy for the presidency of the United States. Kennedy won the primaries in Indiana and Nebraska; on June 5, 1968, he won the crucial California
primary before being shot and killed in the kitchen of the Ambassador Hotel.
As might have been expected, Hoffa responded with indifference. "I can't hon-
estly say that I felt bad about it," he wrote later. "Our vendetta had been too
long and too strong. Over the years I'd come to hate him and yet when he got
it I felt nothing." Kennedy was buried at Arlington National Cemetery, near
his brother. In a 1978 biography, it was noted that Kennedy had often inquired
as to how Hoffa was doing in prison. "If he had ever become President," one
aide posited, "the first person he would have let out was Hoffa."[41]

———

In March 1967, **JIMMY HOFFA**, Inmate No. 33298, stepped into a spartan
eight-by-ten foot cell at the federal prison in Lewisburg, Pennsylvania. The

space was furnished with little more than a table, chair, washbasin, toilet, and small radio. Hoffa was assigned to work seven hours a day in the mattress shop or ticketing guards' uniforms for cleaning. It was quite a fall from grace for a man who had risen to unprecedented heights within the IBT.[42]

Despite questions as to what he had done with members' retirement monies, Hoffa somehow retained the support of rank-and-file Teamsters. As one Chicago truck driver commented in 1971, "For what he did for the driver, I'd take a chance on him again. If he robbed a little, what the hell." "Free Hoffa," read bumper stickers affixed to union trucks around the country. Those pleas, however, found barren ground within the legal system. In 1969, Hoffa was disappointed, if not surprised, when his initial parole request was denied. Then, after he resigned from the Teamsters presidency, he was granted a second hearing in August 1971. Although he reportedly possessed a thirty-one-page confession extracted from Partin, his lawyers convinced him not to use it. Hoffa was denied parole again.[43]

Union Leader publisher William Loeb called publicly for a "National Committee to Free James Riddle Hoffa." A supporter of President Nixon who had attended several dinners in the White House, Loeb urged the president to free Hoffa, whom he labeled a political prisoner, "with a stroke of [his] pen."[44] It was a politically expedient idea that would bolster support for Nixon among Teamsters. Hastened along, the request was approved by Attorney General John Mitchell, and Hoffa was released from prison on December 23, 1971, just in time for Christmas. He had served four years, nine months, and sixteen days.[45]

However, Fitzsimmons had inserted a condition into the deal. Desperate to maintain his own grip on the union, he secured the addition of a clause requiring that "the said James R. Hoffa not engage in direct or indirect management of any labor organization prior to March 6 1980." The provision added, "If the aforesaid condition is not fulfilled this commutation will be null and void in its entirety." Hoffa was apoplectic. By 1980, he would be sixty-seven years old. Had he known the conditions placed on his parole, he never would have agreed to it. He would fight, as he had always done, to regain his position atop the union. "I'm not a guy who believes in limited warfare," he threatened, "so the rats better start jumping the ship."[46]

A legal challenge to Nixon's commutation order was heard in Washington in June 1974. Attorney Leonard B. Boudin argued that the restrictions placed upon Hoffa—limiting him for almost nine years from performing the only work that he had ever known—violated his First Amendment right of free association and his Fifth Amendment right of "liberty" to earn a living. Judge John H. Pratt disagreed, however, finding the limitations "reasonable and lawful" in light of Hoffa's prior abuses. The deal served as a fair exchange for the commutation of his prison sentence.

"I *will* be back as president of the Teamsters," Hoffa asserted boldly in 1975. Of course, it was not to be. On July 30, Hoffa pulled up to the Machus Red Fox restaurant outside of Detroit in a dark green Grand Ville Pontiac, expecting to sit down with mobsters Tony Giacalone and "Tony Pro" Provenzano. Finding no one there, Hoffa telephoned his wife to report that no one had shown up for the meeting.

He was never seen or heard from again.[47]

A straight line can be drawn from Hoffa's 1975 disappearance to the events that occurred in a small courtroom in Chattanooga a decade earlier. The 1964 trial set into motion a chain of events that led inexorably to Hoffa's fateful end. The decision of twelve unassuming, average men and women on March 4, 1964 changed history for the Teamsters Union, organized labor, and the United States.

————

The popular legend of the Hoffa trial is that it was the product of a personal vendetta. However, the Chattanooga proceedings evolved into something less salacious yet far more consequential. In the final reckoning, the 1964 trial is the story of the fragility of justice and the quiet perseverance of an isolated, embattled judge. Fairly early on in the proceedings, the defense team determined to secure a mistrial by forcing the presiding judge to lose his temper, make an impertinent remark, or display antagonism toward the defense.

Day after day, US District Court Judge **FRANK WILSON** was hammered relentlessly by lawyers bent on disruption. Over time, the steady barrage of objections and demands for mistrial gave way to snide insinuations that the court itself was a tool of the prosecution. Surely, the young, relatively new judge was tempted to lash out. Judge Wilson had no one in whom to confide, no one to whom he could express his frustrations, no one to shore up his daily resolve. With quiet determination, though, he proved to be equal to the task.

Admiration for Judge Wilson runs deep within the Chattanooga legal community. As attorney Tom Williams pronounced, "[Wilson was] the finest judge I ever had on any case." FBI agent Jim Cole agreed, calling Wilson "one of the most honest gentlemen I ever ran across in my life," inside and outside the courtroom. John Seigenthaler was succinct in his praise: "Oh, man, he was a great human being."[48]

When asked decades later for his opinion of Judge Wilson, Jim Neal did not miss a beat, responding, "the highest." He was, Neal said, "a man of such utter integrity that . . . if I was on the elevator [in the courthouse] and it opened the door, and Judge Wilson was there to get on the elevator, he'd say, 'No, you go on down, I'll catch the next one.'" He would not even risk the appearance of impropriety or partiality.[49] To Harry Mansfield, Wilson was "one of the finest men I have ever known in my life." Law clerk Charlie Gearhiser echoed that sentiment, remembering him as "one of those truly good men that you count yourself privileged to meet once in a lifetime."[50]

"He is both confident and humble," the *Chattanooga Times* editorialized at the close of the trial, asking, "How can you be both at the same time?" The newspaper recounted an incident during the trial in which the judge bumped into a visitor who inquired about his legal philosophy. By that time, Wilson had endured several weeks of bitterness, outbursts, and attempts to derail the proceedings. "In every case," he remarked, "it's not only the defendant who is on trial, but the judicial system as well."

"I've thought quite often about Frank Wilson sitting there on the bench," Seigenthaler mused, "subjected to abuse in ways no other judicial officer in my lifetime suffered." Even members of the defense team were quick to agree. "I don't think I've ever seen a judge provoked as much by lawyers as I did in that trial," Marvin Berke explained, "and it was unbelievable to me that he was able to keep his composure as well as he did."

"I cannot imagine a judge going through more than what Judge Wilson did, and performing in such an outstanding manner," remarked US District Judge Curtis Collier, who for a decade presided over the courtroom that housed the 1964 trial. "The spotlight was on Judge Wilson from the time the case was filed. He was under scrutiny from the media, by the defendants, and by the public at large." Wilson's steadfast calm in the face of relentless pressure validated his motto: "Any day you can leave here and know that you didn't abuse your power is a good day."[51]

The Hoffa verdict did not permit Judge Wilson to sit back, relax, and contemplate the events of the prior months. He had to address the backlog of other cases that had accumulated. The jury tampering case, moreover, would linger before his courtroom for the better part of a decade, sputtering to an end only after Hoffa's release from prison in 1971.

The Hoffa case notwithstanding, probably the most trying suit Wilson handled was *Mapp v. Board of Education of City of Chattanooga*, filed in 1960 to challenge racial segregation in the city's schools. Wilson received "a lot more threats" during that incendiary case, including phone calls where he was denigrated as a "nigger-loving judge." Calm as ever, Wilson would set the handset down, return to his meal, and listen in on the call a few minutes later to find the speaker still ranting on the other end of the line. Various pieces of that case festered until the mid-1980s.[52]

On a somewhat lighter note, Judge Wilson also presided over the trial to determine the fate of the *General*, the locomotive at the heart of the 1862 "Great Locomotive Chase." Displayed in Chattanooga's Union Station for over sixty years, the engine embarked on a national tour to commemorate the centennial of the Civil War. Afterward, the railroad agreed to relocate the locomotive to Georgia. As the train passed through Chattanooga, though, local sheriff's deputies seized it. "In this lawsuit," Wilson mused in his 1969 opinion, "the pursuit of the *General* continues." With detailed deliberation, he denied the city's claims for the locomotive. Expecting admonishment from local citizens, Wilson noted, "The issue before this court is not the appropriateness or inappropriateness of the display of the *General* in Chattanooga, Tennessee or in Kennesaw, Georgia," but rather whether Chattanooga could maintain its legal position with respect to the engine. In 1972, the *General* was released and sent to its present location near Atlanta.[53]

In *Southeastern Promotions v. Conrad,* Judge Wilson heard a First Amendment case involving a showing of the controversial musical *Hair* in Chattanooga. He also presided over the first civil rights case against the Ku Klux Klan, which resulted in a $500,000 verdict in favor of five black women injured by gunfire during a 1980 race riot.[54]

When US Supreme Court justice William O. Douglas retired in 1975, Judge Wilson was one of five finalists to replace him. Wilson knew that he was probably not the favored choice of the Ford administration, and John Paul Stevens was instead chosen. According to the judge's son Randy Wilson, "it was a fun and exciting experience" nonetheless.

Judge Wilson dropped dead of a heart attack in 1981, at age sixty-five, while writing a jury charge for one of his son's law partners. Family members believed the Hoffa trial had foreshortened his life. "He would have loved to have not been the judge [in the 1964 trial]," Randy Wilson said. "[We] realized too that the Wilson family would have been very happy if the Hoffa trial had never come Frank Wilson's way."[55]

———

Whenever the topic of the 1964 jury tampering trial of Jimmy Hoffa arises, inevitable questions are posed: Did Hoffa get a fair trial? Was justice served in Chattanooga? "The trial may have begun as the trial of Jimmy Hoffa," Fred Cook wrote in the *Nation* in the aftermath of the verdict. Yet, he added, "it ended as the trial of the system of justice in the United States."[56]

One question about the case concerns the manner in which the government pursued Hoffa. There is no doubt that the campaign to "Get Hoffa" was unorthodox. Typically, a criminal prosecution begins with a known crime, and the ensuing investigation aims at determining *who* committed that crime. In pursuing Hoffa, the government flipped that approach, beginning with the known individual (Hoffa) and proceeding to try to uncover some violation of the law committed by him.

Of course, the Get Hoffa Squad's crusade was effective. Despite repeated frustrations in the form of unexpected acquittals, Kennedy's team persisted until back-to-back convictions in Chattanooga and Chicago removed Hoffa, whom many perceived as a corrupt, dangerous force within the labor movement, from power. As Arthur Schlesinger summarized, "The methods that sent . . . Hoffa to prison achieved useful social results that might not have been achieved otherwise."

Questions persist, however, as to whether the Get Hoffa Squad's achievements justified the government's *means.* As author Victor Navasky opines in his book *Kennedy Justice,* a prosecutor has the obligation "to refrain from abusing his power by prosecutions that are directed at individuals rather than at crimes." Twenty-five years before the Chattanooga trial, US attorney general Robert H. Jackson explained that the "most dangerous power of the prosecutor" is the possibility that "he will pick people that he thinks he should get, rather than pick cases that need to be prosecuted. . . . It is in this realm . . . that the greatest danger of abuse of prosecuting power lies." It was Kennedy's furious compulsion to pin anything on Hoffa that unsettled some critics of the Get Hoffa Squad.

Neal expressed some reluctance with the strategy, commenting in a 1974 interview, "My own concern was that any time the government goes flat-out to convict a man, it's going to get him—sooner or later." "If you don't think the government can get you if they want you," Judge William Brown agreed, "all you've got to do is remember that Jimmy Hoffa trial, because that was a man that had all the resources, both legal, financial, and otherwise, and he was brought to justice."[57]

"There comes a point," one writer cautioned, "at which the disproportionate allocation of men, monies and time moves from a matter of quantity to a matter of quality, from prosecution to persecution." "There comes a time when prosecution can change to persecution," echoed an article in the *International*

Teamster magazine. "We dislike . . . the unmitigated use of federal judicial power to put [Hoffa] behind bars . . . Yet we now see the US attorney general, Robert Kennedy, making a political career out of the prosecution of Mr. Hoffa."[58]

Hoffa, of course, was an unusual defendant. He possessed the power, influence, and funds to keep the government at bay, beating back for nearly a decade every attempt to put him away. In the IBT president, one writer observed, the government "encountered for the first time a defendant with resources almost as formidable as its own." During the course of the Chattanooga trial, the "Teamsters Bar Association," which Hoffa maintained at great expense, was able to raise serious questions about government tactics, including the manipulation of witnesses through threats, confidential payments, and the forgiveness of criminal indictments in exchange for assistance. Those efforts required a great amount of time, work, and expense.

"The average individual defendant does not have the resources to hire experts to prove wire tapping and surveillance, to engage the high-priced legal counsel which only at long last and by maximum effort extracted the information about the Partin payments and the confidential fund," Cook lamented. "The significance of the Hoffa trial is that, at Chattanooga, two behemoths clashed—the federal government with its overwhelming investigative resources, and Hoffa, heading his own Teamster power complex and able to match power with power. In the collision, basic practices of the Justice Department were exposed; fundamental questions about the processes of justice were raised."

Central to criticism of the federal government is the claim that Hoffa and his attorneys were surveilled throughout the trial. One could point out that a comprehensive hearing was conducted on the topic during the trial; that hearing, as well as numerous appeals of the verdict, produced no conclusive evidence of wiretapping or other unlawful acts.[59]

The defense would never believe it. "I learned more in those two months about the workings of the government, the workings of the FBI, those type of things, than I ever believed," Marvin Berke remarked. "It was unimaginable to me before the trial started that, as a lawyer, somebody would listen to my phone calls to try to prepare themselves for the next day. It was unbelievable to me that I would ever be followed as a lawyer. I thought that lawyers were supposed to be respected by the government. They were not. I think that's the one thing that affected me more than anything else."[60]

Concerns about government overreaching during the Hoffa trial did result in two changes to DOJ procedures. In 1968, restrictions were put in place to limit the circumstances under which law enforcement could obtain a wiretapping order. The second change related to the methods used by the government to pursue Hoffa. "As a result of this case and some other cases,"

Judge Curtis Collier explained, "the Justice Department developed some rules that determine when a case against a politician or a high-profile person can even be initiated . . . This is called predication. There has to be a certain amount of basic information that suggests some crime before you can even initiate an investigation." Each of these developments can be traced to issues that arose during the Chattanooga trial.

———

On the flip side of the coin, many commentators insist that the defense team's disruptive, unprofessional tactics, obviously intended to manufacture a mistrial, were the greatest threat to justice in the Chattanooga trial. "I look on it as the most outrageous assault on the integrity of the US justice system that we've ever had in this country," Seigenthaler concluded. "Judge Wilson," the *Chattanooga News-Free Press* reported, "was himself put on trial by a most vicious and contemptible campaign by some defense attorneys who sought by histrionics and abuse to create a situation that would prevent the proper functioning of the court of justice."

"It is hard to give a man a fair trial when the man is determined to destroy our system of justice," Gearhiser remarked, "and that's what Mr. Hoffa and his associates were determined to do. They were not here to receive a fair trial; they were here to tear down, attack, and discredit the system of justice." He paused. "And Judge Wilson is one of the few people that I know of that could've handled that kind of onslaught."

In the end, it is possible that both the government and the defense played on the edge of propriety—if not over it—during the Chattanooga trial. Nevertheless, the court handled the difficult case by the book and without committing any reversible error. Courtroom personnel who were present during the trial insist that Hoffa and his codefendants received a fair trial in Chattanooga. "There was no question in my mind, and I guess I've told a thousand people since then," Mansfield explained, "that he got a fair trial in Chattanooga, Tennessee, and I don't think he would have got a fairer trial anyplace else in the United States. It was absolutely a fair trial. We did things by the book—and I say by the book, but it was my book, because there was no book [for such an ordeal]."

To those who observed the trial, the credit for ensuring that justice would not be compromised must be laid at the feet of Judge Frank Wilson. "It reminds us again," Seigenthaler said, "just what can happen if the system is not built on integrity, and if there are not judges like Frank Wilson . . . to maintain the highest standards of legal and judicial integrity." "I think justice had been done," Neal commented to reporters in the wake of the verdict. "I think he [Hoffa] got a completely fair trial. In fact, I think Judge Wilson leaned backwards to see that he did get a fair trial."[61]

For US District Judge Sandy Mattice, who succeeded Judge Collier in presiding over the third-floor courtroom in Chattanooga, the significance of the trial of Jimmy Hoffa lies in the resilience of the American justice system, even in the face of dramatic challenges: "What happened in the Hoffa trial is what happens every day in the country. Any time a jury returns a verdict you have taken a very messy, intense dispute between two litigants . . . and you have brought it to a resolution in a forum that hopefully lends some dignity to the dispute resolution process and in the end will produce a resolution—a verdict—that can be accepted, if not agreed to, by the community and the nation. . . . It's just a high-profile example of what we seem to have a genius for here in America, which is lending dignity and bringing a peaceful resolution to human disputes."

"I think this is a very good study in this experiment that we call American democracy," echoed Judge Collier. "The idea that you can take someone with the political and economic power of Jimmy Hoffa, bring him into an American courtroom and have a jury of his peers try him is an extremely intriguing idea. I'm not sure that you could do that in many other countries. In some other countries the nation has been brought down when there has been an effort to try a very powerful person."

Justice should not be a commodity which is available only to those with sufficient funds to obtain it. "It is bad for society for people to believe that there are people who are above and beyond the law," comments Judge Collier. "We have to believe that when people step out of line, there's going to be some accountability for them. . . . So [the Hoffa case] was a demonstration that regardless how powerful you are in this nation, that you still are not above and beyond the law."[62]

"When the heat was on," Seigenthaler concluded, "a jury in Chattanooga did the right thing." Judge Wilson ensured that the twelve men and women of the jury were provided with the opportunity to do so. "Justice," the *Chattanooga Times* proclaimed upon the verdict in the trial of Jimmy Hoffa, "stands tall and proudly in Chattanooga today."[63]

NOTES

Chapter 1

1. Noble F. "Smokey" Stover (1928–2005) was a disc jockey and lyricist whose songs were recorded by George Jones, Loretta Lynn, Ernest Tubb, and Linda Ronstadt. He wrote the mild rockabilly tune "Ballad of Jimmy Hoffa" while working for station KMOP in Tucson, Arizona, in 1960.

2. *Chattanooga Daily Times*, January 19–20, 1964.

3. *Chattanooga Daily Times*, July 15, 1964, December 22, 1962, January 29, 1964, April 2, 1964; *Lovell Field—Municipal Airport—Chattanooga, Local History and Genealogy Department*, Chattanooga Public Library.

4. *Chattanooga Daily Times*, January 31, 1963, January 29, 1964.

5. *Ibid.*, January 19–20, 1964.

6. Arthur A. Sloane, *Hoffa* (Cambridge, MA: MIT Press, 1991), 289.

7. *Chattanooga Daily Times*, January 18, 1964.

8. *Ibid.*, January 20, 1964.

Chapter 2

1. John L. McClellan, *Crime Without Punishment* (New York: Duell, Sloan and Pearce, 1962), 73. John L. McClellan, chair of the McClellan Committee, reported this quotation from one of a multitude of letters from rank-and-file Teamsters imploring the federal government to address the IBT's unlawful and, in their opinion, embarrassing activities.

2. In 2009, in a move that would have left Jimmy Hoffa apoplectic, the US Senate voted to name the Caucus Room in honor of John F. Kennedy, Robert F. Kennedy, and Edward M. Kennedy. The renaming was done "not just as a monument to the things these three brothers did as Senators . . . but in the spirit of compassion and compromise, the fierce advocacy and friendship that Teddy and his brothers brought to this body."

3. Walter Sheridan, *The Fall and Rise of Jimmy Hoffa* (New York: Saturday Review Press, 1972), 36–37.

4. Dan E. Moldea, *The Hoffa Wars: Teamsters, Rebels, Politicians and the Mob* (New York: Charter Books, 1978), 51–53; Sloane, *Hoffa*, 42; Clark R. Mollenhoff, *Tentacles of Power: The Story of Jimmy Hoffa* (Cleveland, Ohio: World, 1965), 13. Throughout his life, Bufalino remained adamant that he had not been involved in any criminal enterprise. He went so far as to sue Robert Kennedy, claiming that the government's publicized attacks had unfairly damaged his reputation.

5. Sloane, *Hoffa*, 42, 44.

6. Moldea, *Hoffa Wars*, 55–56; Sloane, *Hoffa*, 84–85; E. William Henry, *Fatal Alliance: The Prosecution, Imprisonment, and Gangland Murder of Jimmy Hoffa* (Barrington, MA: Andover, 2012), 13. In 1955, the company changed its name to the Hobren Corporation, a combination of the last names of Hoffa and Brennan.

7. Robert F. Kennedy, *The Enemy Within: The McClellan Committee's Crusade Against Jimmy Hoffa and Corrupt Labor Unions* (New York: Harper and Row, 1960), 45; Sheridan, *Fall and Rise of Jimmy Hoffa*, 21; Sloane, *Hoffa*, 45–46; Moldea, *Hoffa Wars*, 56.

8. Sloane, *Hoffa*, 46–47; Sheridan, *Fall and Rise of Jimmy Hoffa*, 23–24. In 1958, Hoffa hired Bender to chair an internal commission investigating racketeering within the IBT. Bender proclaimed the Teamsters "free of corruption" after having been paid almost $60,000 for his services, and he subsequently found that his apparent collusion with the union had irreparably damaged his political reputation. By 1961 he had quietly retired outside of Cleveland, Ohio, where he soon died.

9. Sloane, *Hoffa*, 78, 95–96, 134–35, 137–38, 180; McClellan, *Crime Without Punishment*, 40; James R. Hoffa, *Hoffa: The Real Story* (New York: Stein and Day, 1975), 145; Thaddeus Russell, *Out of the Jungle: Jimmy Hoffa and the Remaking of the American Working Class* (New York: Alfred A. Knopf, 2001), 196; Moldea, *Hoffa Wars*, 82.

10. Sloane, *Hoffa*, 136–37; US Bureau of Labor Statistics, *Union Sourcebook 1947–1983*.

11. Hoffa, *Hoffa: The Real Story*, 32; Moldea, *Hoffa Wars*, 50, 92.

12. Hoffa, *Hoffa: The Real Story*, 21.

13. Moldea, *Hoffa Wars*, 40.

14. Today, organized labor is generally identified with the Democratic Party. In the 1950s and 1960s, however, the Teamsters Union was a firm, unyielding ally of the Republican Party.

15. Sloane, *Hoffa*, 48-49.

16. Charles Brandt, *"I Heard You Paint Houses": Frank "The Irishman" Sheeran and Closing the Case on Jimmy Hoffa* (Hanover, NH: Steerforth, 2005), 89; Russell, *Out of the Jungle*, 179. "Johnny Dio" Dioguardi was tried for conspiracy in connection with the attack on Victor Riesel. At trial, however, the terrified key witness, Gondolfo Miranti, refused to testify (even to the point that he was sentenced to five years in prison for contempt). The charges against Dioguardi were dismissed. James Neff, *Vendetta: Bobby Kennedy Versus Jimmy Hoffa* (New York: Little, Brown, 2015), 73.

17. Sloane, *Hoffa*, 49–50; Mollenhoff, *Tentacles of Power*, 109.

18. Moldea, *Hoffa Wars*, 69–70. Senators Frank Church (ID), Carl T. Curtis (NE), and Homer E. Capehart (IN) later replaced committee members McNamara, McCarthy, and Ives. Moldea, *Hoffa Wars*, 85.

19. United States Senate Select Committee on Improper Activities in Labor and Management (McClellan Committee), First Interim Report, S. Rep. No. 1417, 85th Cong., 2d Sess. (1958), v–vi. Hereafter cited as First Interim McClellan Committee Report.

20. Arthur M. Schlesinger Jr., *Robert Kennedy and His Times* (Boston: Houghton Mifflin, 1978), 144.

21. Ibid., 141–42; *Los Angeles Times*, March 2, 1990; *South Florida Sun-Sentinel*, March 2, 1990.

22. Kennedy, *Enemy Within*, 169.

23. Ibid., 177.

24. Hoffa, *Hoffa: The Real Story*, 13. According to Hoffa, the second of his disastrous mistakes was entrusting his old lieutenant Frank Fitzsimmons with the presidency of the IBT after his own removal from power. Entranced by the power of the position, Fitzsimmons betrayed Hoffa to avoid having to hand back the reins of authority to his former boss.

25. Ibid., 85–92.

26. Kennedy, *Enemy Within*, 41; Sloane, *Hoffa*, 76–78.

27. Hoffa, *Hoffa: The Real Story*, 97–98.

28. Sloane, *Hoffa*, 78.

29. Hoffa, *Hoffa: The Real Story*, 98.

30. Brandt, *"I Heard You Paint Houses,"* 108–9; Sloane, *Hoffa*, 72–73; Neff, *Vendetta*, 45.

31. Moldea, *Hoffa Wars*, 72; Schlesinger, *Robert Kennedy*, 154; Kennedy, *Enemy Within*, 44.

32. Sloane, *Hoffa*, 73–74; Kennedy, *Enemy Within*, 57; Neff, *Vendetta*, 76.

33. Henry, introduction to *Fatal Alliance*, xiii; Mollenhoff, *Tentacles of Power*, 187.

34. Hoffa, *Hoffa: The Real Story*, 107–8.

35. Sloane, *Hoffa*, 75; Henry, *Fatal Alliance*, 37; Mollenhoff, *Tentacles of Power*, 198; Neff, *Vendetta*, 81–82. In response to questions about Jefferson's role in the trial, Hoffa initially said she had come to Washington to talk to him about "peculiar California labor laws." His attorney, however, explained that Jefferson had been retained as a member of the trial team. First Interim McClellan Committee Report, 275–76.

36. Sloane, *Hoffa*, 74–76; Kennedy, *Enemy Within*, 57; Brandt, *"I Heard You Paint Houses,"* 108–9; Henry, *Fatal Alliance*, 40; Neff, *Vendetta*, 87. Although Hoffa denied knowledge of the payment, it was alleged that Louis had been paid $2,500 for his appearance in the courtroom. First Interim McClellan Committee Report, 276.

37. Sloane, *Hoffa*, 169.

38. Ibid., 104–5; Mollenhoff, *Tentacles of Power*, 211; Neff, *Vendetta*, 63.

39. Sloane, *Hoffa*, 114; Schlesinger, *Robert Kennedy*, 158; Henry, *Fatal Alliance*, 69. One result of this case was new federal legislation legalizing telephone wiretapping authorized by a judge's order.

40. Sloane, *Hoffa*, 146–48.

41. Schlesinger, *Robert Kennedy*, 158.

42. Victor S. Navasky, *Kennedy Justice* (New York: Atheneum, 1971), 454.

43. Schlesinger, *Robert Kennedy*, 161; Sloane, *Hoffa*, 157–59.

44. Sloane, *Hoffa*, 159; Moldea, *Hoffa Wars*, 81; Schlesinger, *Robert Kennedy*, 163.

45. Sloane, *Hoffa*, 149; Schlesinger, *Robert Kennedy*, 161; Sheridan, *Fall and Rise of Jimmy Hoffa*, 288; Hoffa, *Hoffa: The Real Story*, 117.

46. First Interim McClellan Committee Report, 267, 270.

47. Kennedy, *Enemy Within,* 166.

48. First Interim McClellan Committee Report, 280.

49. Ibid., x, 280; Kennedy, *Enemy Within,* 73.

50. First Interim McClellan Committee Report, xi, 283–87.

51. McClellan, *Crime Without Punishment,* 36; Sloane, *Hoffa,* 122–23; Sheridan, *Fall and Rise of Jimmy Hoffa,* 128–29.

52. Sloane, *Hoffa,* 80.

53. Kennedy, *Enemy Within,* 74–75. Photographs from the hearings also depict Hoffa's surreptitious tactic of giving Kennedy the middle finger during questioning. Hoffa also employed this trick casually during the criminal trials of the 1960s.

54. Sloane, *Hoffa,* 123.

55. Hoffa, *Hoffa: The Real Story,* 153.

56. Schlesinger, *Robert Kennedy,* 282–83; Sloane, *Hoffa,* 96.

57. Schlesinger, *Robert Kennedy,* 284–85; Sheridan, *Fall and Rise of Jimmy Hoffa,* 4.

58. Sloane, *Hoffa,* 96.

59. Hoffa, *Hoffa: The Real Story,* 103.

60. Moldea, *Hoffa Wars,* 92; Sheridan, *Fall and Rise of Jimmy Hoffa,* 131.

61. Sheridan, *Fall and Rise of Jimmy Hoffa,* 95; Moldea, *Hoffa Wars,* 169.

62. Sheridan, *Fall and Rise of Jimmy Hoffa,* 135; Sloane, *Hoffa,* 164–65.

63. Sheridan, *Fall and Rise of Jimmy Hoffa,* 160; Schlesinger, *Robert Kennedy,* 233.

64. Schlesinger, *Robert Kennedy,* 279–80; Sloane, *Hoffa,* 176.

65. Sheridan, *Fall and Rise of Jimmy Hoffa,* 272; Moldea, *Hoffa Wars,* 125; "Freedom of Speech," *Time* (January 4, 1963); interview with Jim Neal, 2007.

Chapter 3

1. Sheridan, *Fall and Rise of Jimmy Hoffa,* 224–25.

2. Ibid., 181.

3. Ibid., 139; Kennedy, *Enemy Within,* 110.

4. Moldea, *Hoffa Wars,* 58.

5. Ibid., 58–59; Sloane, *Hoffa,* 168; *Orlando Star-Banner,* December 8, 1960.

6. Kennedy, *Enemy Within,* 108–9; Sloane, *Hoffa,* 174; *Orlando Star-Banner,* December 8, 1960.

7. Sheridan, *Fall and Rise of Jimmy Hoffa,* 159–60; Sloane, *Hoffa,* 175; "Government, James Hoffa at Legal Odds Again," *Ocala (FL) Star-Banner,* December 8, 1960; *Wilmington (NC) Morning Star,* September 23, 1958.

8. *Time,* December 19, 1960; Sheridan, *Fall and Rise of Jimmy Hoffa,* 200.

9. Sloane, *Hoffa,* 257–59; Sheridan, *Fall and Rise of Jimmy Hoffa,* 206; Neff, *Vendetta,* 245–46.

10. *Milone v. English,* 306 F.2d 814 (D.C. Cir., July 19, 1962).

11. Sheridan, *Fall and Rise of Jimmy Hoffa,* 206–7, 211. Reportedly, attorney Edward Bennett Williams coined the term "improvers" in a conversation with Walter Sheridan. Neff, *Vendetta,* 252.

12. Sheridan, *Fall and Rise of Jimmy Hoffa*, 210, 212–13.

13. Ibid., 219–20.

14. Ibid., 222–23.

15. Sloane, *Hoffa*, 260, 268; Sheridan, *Fall and Rise of Jimmy Hoffa*, 168–69; *Los Angeles Times*, October 23, 2010; Jim Ridley, "The People vs. Jimmy Hoffa (Part 1)," *Nashville Scene*, March 28, 2002.

16. Sheridan, *Fall and Rise of Jimmy Hoffa*, 167, 201, 223.

17. *New York Times*, May 15, 1990; Sloane, *Hoffa*, 42; Moldea, *Hoffa Wars*, 43.

18. Sheridan, *Fall and Rise of Jimmy Hoffa*, 93, 144, 192–93; Sloane, *Hoffa*, 172.

19. Sloane, *Hoffa*, 260; Sheridan, *Fall and Rise of Jimmy Hoffa*, 222; *Baker v. Carr*, 396 U.S. 186 (1962); Ridley, "People vs. Jimmy Hoffa (Part 1)"; James D. Squires, *The Secrets of the Hopewell Box: Stolen Elections, Southern Politics, and a City's Coming of Age* (Nashville: Vanderbilt University Press, 2012), 208. With respect to *Baker v. Carr*, Chief Justice Earl Warren later called the "one person, one vote" issue it decided the single most important one he considered on the Supreme Court.

20. Sloane, *Hoffa*, 261.

21. Sheridan, *Fall and Rise of Jimmy Hoffa*, 223.

22. Ibid., 228–29.

23. Owen Bert Brennan, whom *Time* referred to as the "mentor and close friend of Jimmy Hoffa," died of cancer in 1961. *Time*, June 9, 1961.

24. Brandt, *"I Heard You Paint Houses,"* 146; Kennedy, *Enemy Within*, 105–6; Sheridan, *Fall and Rise of Jimmy Hoffa*, 244, 249.

25. Sheridan, *Fall and Rise of Jimmy Hoffa*, 227.

26. Ibid., 226; Hoffa, *Hoffa: The Real Story*, 154. Reportedly, Kennedy attempted to dissuade the editor of the *Nashville Banner*, James G. Stahlman, from reporting the incident. The attorney general believed that public reporting of the "Allen from the *Banner*" calls might result in a mistrial in the Test Fleet case. Undaunted, Stahlman publicized the incident, considering it necessary to do so to protect the newspaper's reputation. "A Question of Duty," *Time*, January 11, 1963.

27. Hoffa, *Hoffa: The Real Story*, 154–55.

28. Sheridan, *Fall and Rise of Jimmy Hoffa*, 195.

29. Ibid., 226.

30. Ibid., 210, 216.

31. Ibid., 216–17. According to his younger brother Doug, who worked with him at Teamsters Local 5 throughout his career, Edward Grady Partin "was so good at [lying] that he could fool any lie detector test he was given." He had used that skill to his benefit in 1962 when disclosing his claims about Jimmy Hoffa. While his brother had no real information about Hoffa, Doug Partin related, "he just used that story to get himself out of jail." Doug Partin, *From My Brother's Shadow* (Greenwell Springs, LA: Oak of Acadia, 2013), 90, 111.

32. Sheridan, *Fall and Rise of Jimmy Hoffa*, 217–19; Hoffa, *Hoffa: The Real Story*, 157.

33. Sheridan, *Fall and Rise of Jimmy Hoffa*, 219.

34. Moldea, *Hoffa Wars*, 142.

35. Sheridan, *Fall and Rise of Jimmy Hoffa*, 224–25.

36. Ibid., 227.

37. Hoffa, *Hoffa: The Real Story*, 157.

38. Sheridan, *Fall and Rise of Jimmy Hoffa*, 227–28.

39. Moldea, *Hoffa Wars*, 142.

40. Sloane, *Hoffa*, 262–63; Moldea, *Hoffa Wars*, 142–43; Sheridan, *Fall and Rise of Jimmy Hoffa*, 230, 247–48.

41. Hoffa, *Hoffa: The Real Story*, 156; Sloane, *Hoffa*, 264–65; Sheridan, *Fall and Rise of Jimmy Hoffa*, 246–48; Jim Ridley, "The People vs. Jimmy Hoffa (Part 2)," *Nashville Scene*, April 4, 2002; interview with Neal; Henry, *Fatal Alliance*, 82–83; Mollenhoff, *Tentacles of Power*, 362. Two years later, Jim Neal was appointed US attorney for the Middle District of Tennessee. Learning that Swanson had never been tried (but remained imprisoned), he obtained a court hearing in which it was determined that Swanson was mentally incompetent to stand trial. The would-be assassin was committed to a mental health facility and released some time later. He made no further attempt to contact Hoffa.

42. Sloane, *Hoffa*, 263; Moldea, *Hoffa Wars*, 144; Henry, *Fatal Alliance*, 99.

43. Sheridan, *Fall and Rise of Jimmy Hoffa*, 252; Mollenhoff, *Tentacles of Power*, 366.

44. Sloane, *Hoffa*, 263; Moldea, *Hoffa Wars*, 144; Sheridan, *Fall and Rise of Jimmy Hoffa*, 250.

45. Sloane, *Hoffa*, 266; Sheridan, *Fall and Rise of Jimmy Hoffa*, 252–53; Ridley, "People vs. Jimmy Hoffa (Part 2)."

46. Sloane, *Hoffa*, 267; Henry, *Fatal Alliance*, 87.

47. Sheridan, *Fall and Rise of Jimmy Hoffa*, 253–54.

48. Henry, *Fatal Alliance*, 87.

Chapter 4

1. *Z. T. Osborn, Jr. v. United States*, 385 U.S. 323 (1966).

2. Sheridan, *Fall and Rise of Jimmy Hoffa*, 293–94.

3. Ibid., 259–62.

4. Ibid., 268–69.

5. Ibid., 270.

6. Moldea, *Hoffa Wars*, 111; Kennedy, *Enemy Within*, 174.

7. Transcript of Proceedings, Grand Jury Testimony of Walter J. Sheridan, Case No. 3:09-cv-00375, Document 42-1, 4 (M.D. Tenn., July 9, 2009). Hereafter cited as Transcript, Grand Jury Testimony of Walter J. Sheridan.

8. Ibid., 6. Sheridan also revealed that a second anonymous source, albeit one reportedly unwilling to testify at trial, had supplied him with information.

9. Sheridan, *Fall and Rise of Jimmy Hoffa*, 272, 274.

10. Ibid., 274–75.

11. Ibid., 275.

12. Interview with John Seigenthaler, December 11, 2007. Interview by Tonya Cammon. Nashville. The other was Jack Norman, the alternate Nashville attorney Kennedy considered for the 1964 jury tampering trial.

13. Interview with Seigenthaler; *New York Times,* December 25, 1970; Henry, *Fatal Alliance,* 109–11; Squires, *Secrets of the Hopewell Box,* 221–22.

14. Sheridan, *Fall and Rise of Jimmy Hoffa,* 275–76.

15. Ibid., 276; Roberta W. Greene, recorded interview with Walter Sheridan, June 12, 1970, John F. Kennedy Library Oral History Program, 108–9.

16. Interview with Sheridan, June 12, 1970, 108–10.

17. Sheridan, *Fall and Rise of Jimmy Hoffa,* 277–78.

18. Ibid., 278; interview with Jim Neal, 2007. Interview by Tonya Cammon. Nashville.

19. Moldea, *Hoffa Wars,* 146; Sheridan, *Fall and Rise of Jimmy Hoffa,* 279–80.

20. Sheridan, *Fall and Rise of Jimmy Hoffa,* 280–81.

21. Ibid., 281–82.

22. Ibid., 282–83.

23. Ibid., 280.

24. Ibid., 284–85.

25. Ibid., 283–84.

26. Ibid., 285–86.

27. Ibid., 293; interview with Neal.

28. Sheridan, *Fall and Rise of Jimmy Hoffa,* 293–94.

29. *Osborn,* 385 U.S. 323; *Nashville Banner,* November 21, 1963.

30. Sheridan, *Fall and Rise of Jimmy Hoffa,* 297.

31. Ibid., 297–98.

32. Ibid., 298.

33. Ibid., 298–99; Sloane, *Hoffa,* 277.

34. Interview with Seigenthaler; interview with Neal.

35. Sheridan, *Fall and Rise of Jimmy Hoffa,* 299; Ridley, "People vs. Jimmy Hoffa (Part 2)."

36. Sloane, *Hoffa,* 279–80; Roberta W. Greene, recorded interview with Walter Sheridan, May 1, 1970, John F. Kennedy Library Oral History Program, 2.

37. Sloane, *Hoffa,* 279–81; Schlesinger, *Robert Kennedy,* 616; Sheridan, *Fall and Rise of Jimmy Hoffa,* 299–300.

38. Hoffa, *Hoffa: The Real Story,* 150; Sheridan, *Fall and Rise of Jimmy Hoffa,* 300; Jon Margolis, *The Last Innocent Year: America in 1964, the Beginning of the "Sixties"* (New York: William Morrow, 1999), 29. Kennedy remained attorney general following the abrupt change in administration, but under President Johnson it was clear that his time in that office was limited.

39. Sheridan, *Fall and Rise of Jimmy Hoffa,* 301–2.

40. Ibid., 302–3.

41. Ibid., 303.

42. Brandt, *"I Heard You Paint Houses,"* 165.

43. Patricia E. Brake, *Justice in the Valley: A Bicentennial Perspective of the United States District Court for the Eastern District of Tennessee* (Nashville: Hillsboro, 1998), 192–93; interview with Helen Wilson, November 14, 2007. Interview by Randy Wilson. Signal Mtn., Tennessee.

44. Charles J. Gearhiser, "My Life as a Lawyer: What Makes a Lawyer Succeed?," *Tennessee Bar Journal* 37-Dec TNBJ (December 2001), 3; interview with Charles J. Gearhiser, July 18, 2007; interview with Harry Mansfield, July 18, 2007; *New York Times,* March 13, 1964.

45. Brake, *Justice in the Valley,* 192–93; *Chattanooga Times-Free Press,* June 23, 2015; interview with Randy Wilson, February 14, 2013; *Mapp v. Board of Educ. of City of Chattanooga,* 203 F. Supp. 843 (E.D. Tenn. 1962).

46. Sheridan, *Fall and Rise of Jimmy Hoffa,* 302–3.

47. Ultimately, the decision was made not to call Osborn as a witness. Ibid., 311–12.

48. Ridley, "People vs. Jimmy Hoffa (Part 2)."

49. Ibid.

50. Sheridan, *Fall and Rise of Jimmy Hoffa,* 366.

51. Ridley, "People vs. Jimmy Hoffa (Part 2)."

52. *Capital Times (Madison, WI),* May 30, 1964.

53. *Osborn v. United States,* 350 F.2d 497 (6th Cir. 1965); Squires, *Secrets of the Hopewell Box,* 235.

54. Ridley, "People vs. Jimmy Hoffa (Part 2)."

55. Squires, *Secrets of the Hopewell Box,* 279–80.

Chapter 5

1. Brandt, *"I Heard You Paint Houses,"* 161. Shortly before his death, Frank Sheeran (1920–2003), Hoffa's close associate and sometime bodyguard, claimed responsibility for Hoffa's assassination in 1975.

2. Sheridan, *Fall and Rise of Jimmy Hoffa,* 303; interview with Seigenthaler.

3. *Chattanooga Times-Free Press,* May 4, 2008.

4. *Nashville Tennessean,* January 1, 1964; *Chattanooga Times,* January 1, 1964.

5. *Chattanooga News-Free Press,* January 8, 1964; Moldea, *Hoffa Wars,* 171; Sloane, *Hoffa,* 292.

6. Hoffa, *Hoffa: The Real Story,* 163; interview with Harry Mansfield. Interviewed by Sandy Mattice. Chattanooga.

7. Sheridan, *Fall and Rise of Jimmy Hoffa,* 304; *Detroit News,* January 1, 1964; *New York Times,* January 1, 1964.

8. *Chattanooga News-Free Press,* January 4, 1964; *Nashville Tennessean,* January 5, 1964, January 15, 1964.

9. Interview with Helen Wilson; interview with Gearhiser; Recollections of Granville M. Sertel, 20 (US District Court, E. D. Tenn., 1992). Hereafter cited as Sertel

Recollections. A native of Oak Ridge, Tennessee, Charles "Charlie" Gearhiser attended Austin Peay State College and the University of Tennessee School of Law. While in law school, he worked as a deputy sheriff in Knoxville, where he operated the jail elevator and served as a turnkey and patrol officer. After a brief stint in private practice, in 1961 Gearhiser became Judge Frank Wilson's law clerk. Gearhiser, "My Life as a Lawyer."

10. *Chattanooga Times,* January 7, 1964; *Nashville Tennessean,* January 7, 1964; Moldea, *Hoffa Wars,* 171.

11. *Chattanooga News-Free Press,* January 7, 1964.

12. *Nashville Tennessean,* January 4, 1964, January 7, 1964; Henry, *Fatal Alliance,* 127.

13. *Chattanooga Times,* January 1, 1964; *Nashville Tennessean,* January 7, 1964.

14. Sheridan, *Fall and Rise of Jimmy Hoffa,* 305.

15. *Chattanooga News-Free Press,* January 8, 1964; ibid., 305.

16. *Chattanooga Times-Free Press,* May 4, 2008; interview with Neal; interview with William Brown, 2007. Interviewed by Tonya Cammon. Chattanooga.

17. Henry, *Fatal Alliance,* 47.

18. Sloane, *Hoffa,* 119; interview with Gearhiser.

19. *New York Times,* May 17, 1958, October 8, 1982; "Schoolfields Were Quakers, Fiery Attorneys," Chattanoogan.com, February 13, 2008, www.chattanoogan.com (accessed July 12, 2014); Kennedy, *Enemy Within,* 68; Henry, *Fatal Alliance,* 50; Jerry H. Summers, *Rush to Justice: Tennessee's Forgotten Trial of the Century—Schoolfield 1958* (Walden, TN: Waldenhouse, 2015), 389. Somehow, Schoolfield never lost the support of the local electorate, and he was later elected to a general sessions judgeship, which did not require a law degree. He refused to wear a robe on the bench, from which he smoked continuously. (At one time, the local fire department had to be called to put out a fire in the courtroom that one of his cigarettes may or may not have started.) Schoolfield died on October 6, 1982, of a heart attack; only hours earlier, he had been "the life of the party" at a Love of Chattanooga awards dinner. He had only recently been reelected to another eight-year term as general sessions judge.

20. Kennedy, *Enemy Within,* 68; McClellan, *Crime Without Punishment,* 50–51, 243.

21. *Chattanooga Times,* January 8, 1964.

22. Ibid., January 6, 1964; *Detroit News,* January 9, 1964.

23. *Nashville Tennessean,* January 9, 1964; *Chattanooga News-Free Press,* January 12, 1964.

24. *Chattanooga News-Free Press,* January 9, 1964; *Nashville Tennessean,* January 10, 1964; interview with Cecil Pearce, January 24, 2008; *Tennessee Bar Assoc. v. Berke,* 344 S.W.2d 567 (Tenn. Ct. App. 1960).

25. *Chattanooga Times,* January 10, 1964.

26. Sheridan, *Fall and Rise of Jimmy Hoffa,* 307; Henry, *Fatal Alliance,* 125.

27. Sheridan, *Fall and Rise of Jimmy Hoffa,* 306; *Nashville Tennessean,* January 10, 1964; *Chattanooga News-Free Press,* January 10, 1964.

28. *Nashville Tennessean,* January 13, 1964.

29. Hoffa, *Hoffa: The Real Story,* 164–65.

30. *Chattanooga News-Free Press,* January 14, 1964; *Nashville Tennessean,* January 14, 1964.

31. *Nashville Tennessean,* January 9, 1964.

32. *Chattanooga Times,* January 16, 1964; *Chattanooga News-Free Press,* January 15, 1964.

33. *Chattanooga Times,* January 17, 1964; *Chattanooga News-Free Press,* January 16, 1964.

34. Sloane, *Hoffa,* 289; Moldea, *Hoffa Wars,* 172; Brandt, *"I Heard You Paint Houses,"* 169; *Detroit News,* January 17, 1964; *Chattanooga Times,* January 17, 1964.

35. *New York Times,* January 17, 1964.

36. Interview with Neal; *Detroit News,* January 18, 1964; *Chattanooga Times,* January 18, 1964.

37. *Chattanooga News-Free Press,* January 18, 1964.

38. Sheridan, *Fall and Rise of Jimmy Hoffa,* 308; interview with Tommy Eason, January 28, 2013.

39. Interview with Jim Cole, November 15, 2007. Interview by John Medearis. Chattanooga.

40. Sheridan, *Fall and Rise of Jimmy Hoffa,* 310; Neff, *Vendetta,* 313; ibid.; Henry, *Fatal Alliance,* 124–25.

41. Kyle J. Wilson, "An Enduring Symbol of Hope, History, and Justice: The Joel W. Solomon Federal Building," *Federal Lawyer* 60, no. 5 (June 2013), 32–35; Gavin Townsend, *R. H. Hunt: Master Architect of Chattanooga* (Chattanooga: Cornerstones, 2010), 102–4. The New Deal–era federal courthouse (1933), composed of white Georgia marble and aluminum detailing, cost $493,000 to construct. Consulting on the project was the New York architectural firm of Shreve, Lamb and Harmon. In the same time frame, the company cut the ribbon on its Empire State Building, which shares several interior features with the Chattanooga courthouse (the hallways, in particular, bear a remarkable similarity to those of the iconic New York building).

42. Sheridan, *Fall and Rise of Jimmy Hoffa,* 309.

43. Fred J. Cook, "The First Full Account of a Fateful Trial That Raises the Disturbing Question: Can Jungle Warfare Subvert American Justice?," *Nation,* April 27, 1964, 422.

44. *Official Transcript of Proceedings, United States v. James R. Hoffa, et al.,* Case No. 11,989, 18 (E.D. Tenn. 1964). Hereafter cited as *Official Transcript, United States v. James Hoffa, et al.*

45. Ibid., 19, 24–25.

46. Ibid., 20.

47. Ibid., 25.

48. Ibid., 26–27.

49. Ibid., 29–30.

50. Derived from a Latin phrase meaning "to say what is true," *voir dire* refers to the process of selecting the jury to hear a legal proceeding.

51. *Official Transcript, United States v. James Hoffa, et al.*, 50, 65.

52. Ibid., 81–91.

53. Wilson, "Enduring Symbol of Hope," 33.

54. Ibid., 33–34; Brake, *Justice in the Valley*, 92; Carroll Van West, *Tennessee's New Deal Landscape: A Guidebook* (Knoxville: University of Tennessee Press, 2001), 60.

55. *Official Transcript, United States v. James Hoffa, et al.*, 99.

56. *Time*, January 31, 1964; *New York Times*, January 19, 1964; *Chattanooga Times*, January 19, 1964.

Chapter 6

1. Interview with Marvin Berke, 2007. Interviewed by Tonya Cammon. Chattanooga.

2. June N. Adamson, "*Selected Women in Tennessee Newspaper Journalism*" (master's thesis, University of Tennessee [Knoxville], August 1971), 123, 125–27, 129, 133, 135, 139, 141, 143; *Chattanooga Times*, February 15, 1982; "The Girl Reporter Gets Her Man," *The Illustrated Detective Magazine*, November 1931.

3. Interview with Gearhiser; *Chattanooga Times*, February 17, 1982.

4. Interview with Mike Pare, December 8, 2015. Interview by author. Chattanooga; Carl Sessions Stepp, "A Dying Breed," *American Journalism Review*, December 1994.

5. *Chattanooga Times*, January 20, 1964; interview with Mansfield; interview with Etta Williams, November 14, 2007. Interview by Shelley Rucker. Chattanooga.

6. Sertel Recollections, 16–17.

7. *Detroit News*, January 20, 1964; *Chattanooga News-Free Press*, January 18, 1964; ibid., 33.

8. Interview with Mansfield; interview with Cecil Pearce, January 24, 2008. Interview by Tonya Cammon. Chattanooga; *Chattanooga Times-Free Press*, August 25, 2012; interview with John Sertel, December 21, 2007.

9. Interview with Mansfield.

10. Ibid.

11. Sertel Recollections, 19; interview with Mansfield.

12. Interview with John Sertel, December 21, 2007. Interview by author. Chattanooga; interview with Mansfield.

13. Interview with Pearce.

14. Sheridan, *Fall and Rise of Jimmy Hoffa*, 310–11; interview with Mansfield; *Detroit News*, January 20, 1964.

15. Interview with Etta Williams; *Chattanooga Times*, January 21, 1964.

16. *Official Transcript, United States v. James Hoffa, et al.*, 123–24, 127–28.

17. United States District Court, Eastern District of Tennessee, *Court Historical Society Newsletter* (March 2010).

18. Interview with Berke, 2007; Henry, *Fatal Alliance*, 126; Sheridan, *Fall and Rise of Jimmy Hoffa*, 309.

19. *Chattanooga Times,* January 21, 1964; *Chicago Tribune,* January 24, 2007.

20. *Official Transcript, United States v. James Hoffa, et al.,* 141–42, 153.

21. Ibid., 141–42; *Chattanooga News-Free Press,* January 20, 1964.

22. *Official Transcript, United States v. James Hoffa, et al.,* 138–39, 172–73, 175, 179–82, 188, 199.

23. Ibid., 143, 203–5, 209.

24. Ibid., 210.

25. *New York Times,* December 27, 1970; Henry, *Fatal Alliance,* 126–27.

26. *Official Transcript, United States v. James Hoffa, et al.,* 210–12.

27. Ibid., 111–20, 222–23.

28. Ibid., 225.

29. Ibid., 234–35.

30. Ibid., 237, 240.

31. Ibid., 246–48, 255; *Chattanooga News-Free Press,* January 21, 1964; *Chattanooga Times,* January 21, 1964.

32. *Official Transcript, United States v. James Hoffa, et al.,* 265.

33. Ibid., 278.

34. Ibid., 280, 282, 286.

35. Ibid., 293, 295; *Chattanooga News-Free Press,* January 21, 1964.

36. *Official Transcript, United States v. James Hoffa, et al.,* 310, 313–14, 316–17; Summers, *Rush to Justice,* 322; interview with Jerry Summers, November 24, 2015. Interview by author. Chattanooga.

37. *Official Transcript, United States v. James Hoffa, et al.,* 323, 325.

38. Ibid., 326–37.

39. Ibid., 340–44.

40. *Chattanooga Times,* January 21, 1964; *Detroit News,* January 21, 1964.

41. Interview with Patrick Haverty, 2008. Interview by author. Chattanooga.

42. Interview with Mansfield; interview with Haverty; interview with Neal; Sertel Recollections, 21.

43. *Official Transcript, United States v. James Hoffa, et al.,* 440.

44. Interview with Mansfield; interview with Haverty; Bill Knowles, *Journal (1964),* 13–14.

45. *Chattanooga Times,* January 22, 1964; interview with Mansfield; interview with Haverty; *Official Transcript, United States v. James Hoffa, et al.,* 430; Knowles, *Journal,* 13–14.

46. Interview with Mansfield; interview with Gearhiser; *USA Today,* February 12, 1988.

47. *Official Transcript, United States v. James Hoffa, et al.,* 347.

48. Ibid., 349–50, 353.

49. Interview with Haverty; ibid., 355.

50. *Official Transcript, United States v. James Hoffa, et al.,* 359–60, 362, 365.

51. Interview with Haverty; ibid., 368.

52. *Official Transcript, United States v. James Hoffa, et al.*, 369.

53. Ibid., 386.

54. *Chattanooga Times*, January 22, 1964.

55. *Official Transcript, United States v. James Hoffa, et al.*, 387, 522, 532, 534, 536, 539, 541–42, 545, 551–52, 571, 582.

56. Ibid., 388, 393, 417–18. At one point, Neal made a similar objection to questions Harry Nerke posed as to "government persecution and persecution by the Attorney General." Neal pointed out that the case was initiated not by the Department of Justice, but by the federal court in Nashville. Judge Wilson overruled the objection. Ibid., 504.

57. Ibid., 442, 468, 519–21; *Chattanooga News-Free Press*, January 21, 1964.

58. *Official Transcript, United States v. James Hoffa, et al.*, 603, 605.

59. *Chattanooga News-Free Press*, January 21, 1964; *Detroit News*, January 26, 1964.

60. *Detroit News*, January 22, 1964; *Chattanooga News-Free Press*, January 22, 1964; *Chattanooga Times*, January 22, 1964; *Time*, January 31, 1964.

61. Sheridan, *Fall and Rise of Jimmy Hoffa*, 311; interview with Berke, 2007.

62. *Official Transcript, United States v. James Hoffa, et al.*, 607; *Chattanooga Times*, January 22, 1964.

63. *Official Transcript, United States v. James Hoffa, et al.*, 612–13.

64. Ibid., 613–15.

65. Ibid., 617–18, 620–21.

66. Ibid., 692–93.

67. Ibid., 750.

68. Ibid., 754–55, 759–60.

69. *New York Times*, January 23, 1964; *Detroit News*, January 23, 1964.

70. *Chattanooga City Directory* (1964); Sheridan, *Fall and Rise of Jimmy Hoffa*, 308.

71. *Chattanooga News-Free Press*, January 24, 1964.

72. Hoffa, *Hoffa: The Real Story*, 164.

73. Sheridan, *Fall and Rise of Jimmy Hoffa*, 312.

74. *Official Transcript, United States v. James Hoffa, et al.*, 831, 841, 960.

75. Ibid., 965–66, 969.

76. Ibid., 970–88.

77. *Chattanooga Times*, January 24, 1964.

78. *Chattanooga News-Free Press*, January 23, 1964.

79. Ibid., January 24, 1964; *New York Times*, January 24, 1964; *Detroit News*, January 24, 1964.

80. Sheridan, *Fall and Rise of Jimmy Hoffa*, 312; *New York Times*, January 24, 1964.

81. *Chattanooga News-Free Press*, January 23, 1964.

82. *Official Transcript, United States v. James Hoffa, et al.*, 1030–31.

83. Ibid., 1031.

84. Ibid., 1169–73. Silets' concerns were echoed in later years by Marvin Berke. "The real problem was that after a period of time," he opined, "the jury was together all that time, they were surrounded by federal marshals, the newspapers were trying to report

the most sensational things that they could . . . all of those things I thought played a part in the psyche of the jurors that were hearing the case." Interview with Berke, 2007.

85. Ibid., 1075, 1082, 1091, 1098, 1105, 1217–20. Hoffa's attorneys made nine of the defense's peremptory challenges, showing the degree to which the IBT president and his counsel would direct the case. One challenge was made on behalf of Larry Campbell, one on behalf of Nicholas Tweel, and one on behalf of Ewing King. Counsel for Thomas Ewing Parks and Allen Dorfman did not exercise any peremptory challenges during the jury selection process.

86. *Chattanooga News-Free Press,* January 25, 1964.

87. *Official Transcript, United States v. James Hoffa, et al.,* 1225–27; Hoffa, *Hoffa: The Real Story,* 164.

88. Interview with Berke, 2007; interview with Neal.

89. Interview with Brown, 2007.

90. *Detroit News,* January 25, 1964; *Official Transcript, United States v. James Hoffa, et al.,* 1313, 1318.

91. *Official Transcript, United States v. James Hoffa, et al.,* 1332, 1351–52.

92. Ibid., 1377.

93. Ibid., 1361, 1372–75, 1382.

94. Ibid., 1380.

95. Ibid., 1381, 1383, 1385, 1389–90, 1394–95.

96. Ibid., 1135, 1153, 1293, 1324.

97. *Chattanooga News-Free Press,* January 28, 1964.

98. *Detroit News,* January 26, 1964; *Official Transcript, United States v. James Hoffa, et al.,* 1401, 1412.

99. *Official Transcript, United States v. James Hoffa, et al.,* 1420.

Chapter 7

1. Ridley, "People vs. Jimmy Hoffa (Part 2)," 13.

2. *Detroit News,* February 2, 1964; interview with Mansfield; *New York Times,* January 25, 1964.

3. *Official Transcript, United States v. James Hoffa, et al.,* 1450, 1457–58.

4. Transcript, Grand Jury Testimony of Walter J. Sheridan, 4.

5. *Detroit News,* January 28, 1964.

6. *Official Transcript, United States v. James Hoffa, et al.,* 1465–66, 1470–71, 1475.

7. *Chattanooga News-Free Press,* January 28, 1964; *Chattanooga Times,* January 28, 1964; *Official Transcript, United States v. James Hoffa, et al.,* 1484–88, 1501.

8. *Official Transcript, United States v. James Hoffa, et al.,* 1511.

9. Ibid., 1517.

10. Ibid., 1519.

11. Cook, "First Full Account of a Fateful Trial," 426–27.

12. *Official Transcript, United States v. James Hoffa, et al.,* 1522.

13. Ibid., 1524–27, 1529, 1542–43, 1545, 1547, 1593.

14. Ibid., 1546.

15. Ibid., 1547, 1550.

16. Ibid., 1550–51.

17. Ibid., 1551.

18. Ibid., 1553, 1556–57.

19. Ibid., 1557, 1559.

20. Sheridan, *Fall and Rise of Jimmy Hoffa*, 315; *Chattanooga Times*, January 29–30, 1964; *Detroit News*, January 28, 1964.

21. *Official Transcript, United States v. James Hoffa, et al.*, 1571; *Detroit News*, January 28, 1964; *Chattanooga News-Free Press*, January 29, 1964.

22. *Official Transcript, United States v. James Hoffa, et al.*, 1605–6, 1608, 1610–11, 1701; *Chattanooga News-Free Press*, January 28, 1964.

23. *Official Transcript, United States v. James Hoffa, et al.*, 1690.

24. Ibid., 1717.

25. Ibid., 1722, 1724–29, 1731.

26. Ibid., 1732–34, 1737.

27. Ibid., 1740–41.

28. Ibid., 1743, 1762.

29. Ibid., 1763–64; *New York Times*, January 29, 1964.

30. *Official Transcript, United States v. James Hoffa, et al.*, 1769.

31. Ibid., 1623, 1664–65, 1668, 1708. The Jencks Act, 18 U.S.C. § 3500, mandates that the government must produce any statement made by government witnesses that relates to the subject matter of that witness's testimony (after the account has been provided). *United States v. Greco,* 298 F.2d 247 (2d Cir. 1962), *cert. denied,* 369 U.S. 820.

32. *Official Transcript, United States v. James Hoffa, et al.*, 1836, 1839, 1842, 1849–50, 1855–56; Sheridan, *Fall and Rise of Jimmy Hoffa,* 314.

33. *Official Transcript, United States v. James Hoffa, et al.*, 1856.

34. Ibid., 1774, 1807–8, 1813.

35. *Tennessee Bar Journal* 50, no. 6 (June 2014); *Nashville Tennessean,* May 9, 2014; Summers, *Rush to Justice,* 248.

36. Leading questions, which tend to suggest to the witness the answer the questioning attorney is seeking, are not allowed during direct examination.

37. *Official Transcript, United States v. James Hoffa, et al.*, 1780–81, 1800.

38. Ibid., 1817, 1822.

39. *New York Times,* January 30, 1964.

40. *Chattanooga Times,* January 30, 1964; Sheridan, *Fall and Rise of Jimmy Hoffa,* 315; *Official Transcript, United States v. James Hoffa, et al.*, 1883.

41. *Official Transcript, United States v. James Hoffa, et al.*, 1884.

42. Ibid., 1894–95; Sheridan, *Fall and Rise of Jimmy Hoffa,* 315; *Chattanooga Times,* January 30, 1964.

43. Sheridan, *Fall and Rise of Jimmy Hoffa,* 315; *Official Transcript, United States v. James Hoffa, et al.*, 1897; *Chattanooga Times,* January 30, 1964.

44. *Official Transcript, United States v. James Hoffa, et al.*, 1900, 1907–8.

45. *New York Times,* January 30, 1964; *Chattanooga Times,* January 30, 1964; ibid., 1913.

46. *Chattanooga Times,* January 30, 1964; *Official Transcript, United States v. James Hoffa, et al.,* 1904, 1914–15; Henry, *Fatal Alliance,* 129.

47. Sheridan, *Fall and Rise of Jimmy Hoffa,* 315; *Chattanooga Times,* January 30, 1964; *Official Transcript, United States v. James Hoffa, et al.,* 1901, 1931, 1933–35, 1939, 1941.

48. *Chattanooga Times,* January 30, 1964; Transcript, Grand Jury Testimony of Walter J. Sheridan, 1950, 1981.

49. Sheridan, *Fall and Rise of Jimmy Hoffa,* 316; *Chattanooga Times,* January 30, 1964; *Official Transcript, United States v. James Hoffa, et al.,* 1972, 1974, 1979–80, 1982.

50. Sheridan, *Fall and Rise of Jimmy Hoffa,* 316; *Official Transcript, United States v. James Hoffa, et al.,* 1985, 1987–88, 1994, 1996, 2003, 2007. Larry Campbell was employed by Teamsters Local 299; the reference to his "boss" may be interpreted as a reference to Hoffa.

51. *Official Transcript, United States v. James Hoffa, et al.,* 2009–10.

52. Sheridan, *Fall and Rise of Jimmy Hoffa,* 316; ibid., 2011.

53. Sheridan, *Fall and Rise of Jimmy Hoffa,* 316; *Chattanooga Times,* January 30, 1964; *Official Transcript, United States v. James Hoffa, et al.,* 2065, 2069, 2071, 2075–76.

54. *Chattanooga Times,* January 30, 1964; *Official Transcript, United States v. James Hoffa, et al.,* 2076, 2087.

55. Sheridan, *Fall and Rise of Jimmy Hoffa,* 316–17; *Detroit News,* January 30, 1964; *Official Transcript, United States v. James Hoffa, et al.,* 2069, 2115–16, 2122–25, 2135–37, 2155–56, 2172.

56. *Official Transcript, United States v. James Hoffa, et al.,* 2177, 2198, 2200.

57. Interview with Neal.

Chapter 8

1. Interview with Haverty; interview with Mansfield; *Chattanooga Times,* March 5, 1964.

2. *Chattanooga Times,* January 31, 1964; Sheridan, *Fall and Rise of Jimmy Hoffa,* 317; *Official Transcript, United States v. James Hoffa, et al.,* 2209–10, 2213–15, 2219–20, 2225.

3. *Official Transcript, United States v. James Hoffa, et al.,* 2236, 2239, 2241–42; *Detroit News,* January 31, 1964; *Chattanooga Times,* February 3, 1964.

4. *New York Times,* January 31, 1964; *Official Transcript, United States v. James Hoffa, et al.,* 2246–47, 2270, 2277; Sheridan, *Fall and Rise of Jimmy Hoffa,* 318.

5. *Official Transcript, United States v. James Hoffa, et al.,* 2288–93, 2330; *Chattanooga News-Free Press,* January 31, 1964.

6. Interview with William Brown, January 21, 2015; interview with Sandy Mattice, December 2007. Interview by author. Chattanooga; interview with Summers; interview with Mansfield.

7. *Official Transcript, United States v. James Hoffa, et al.,* 2342.

8. *Chattanooga News-Free Press,* January 29, 1964.

9. *Chattanooga Times,* January 30, 1964, February 1, 1964.

10. *Chattanooga News-Free Press,* January 29, 1964.

11. Sheridan, *Fall and Rise of Jimmy Hoffa,* 318; ibid., January 31, 1964; *Official Transcript, United States v. James Hoffa, et al.,* 2355, 2359–61.

12. *Official Transcript, United States v. James Hoffa, et al.,* 2372, 2398, 2480.

13. *New York Times,* February 1, 1964; ibid., 2404–5; *Chattanooga News-Free Press,* January 31, 1964.

14. Sheridan, *Fall and Rise of Jimmy Hoffa,* 319; *Detroit News,* February 1, 1964; *Official Transcript, United States v. James Hoffa, et al.,* 2439, 2455, 2462, 2475, 2479; *Chattanooga News-Free Press,* January 31, 1964.

15. *Detroit News,* January 31, 1964.

16. *Official Transcript, United States v. James Hoffa, et al.,* 2484–85, 2488, 2490, 2492-2494, 2503.

17. Ibid., 2506–7; *Detroit News,* February 1, 1964.

18. *Official Transcript, United States v. James Hoffa, et al.,* 2518, 2522, 2536.

19. Knowles, *Journal,* 1–5; *Chattanooga Times Free-Press,* May 9, 2008.

Chapter 9

1. Interview with Eason; "Tommy Eason Retiring After 52 Years in Local TV," *chattanoogan.com,* March 17, 2009; interview with Haverty; interview with Mansfield; Summers, *Rush to Justice,* 366.

2. Transcript, Grand Jury Testimony of Walter J. Sheridan, 13; *Official Transcript, United States v. James Hoffa, et al.,* 2570, 2576–77.

3. *Official Transcript, United States v. James Hoffa, et al.,* 2658.

4. Ibid., 2753.

5. Ibid., 2659–60, 2666.

6. Ibid., 2679; Cook, "First Full Account of a Fateful Trial," 424; *Chattanooga News-Free Press,* February 3, 1964; *Detroit News,* February 4, 1964; *Chattanooga Times,* February 4, 1964; State of Michigan, Record of Fred Shobe (November 8, 1961), in Case File, *United States v. James R. Hoffa, et al.,* File No. 11-989 (E.D. Tenn. 1964). Even Shobe's family history is shrouded in mystery. According to his daughter, Shobe's father was a US soldier of Sicilian heritage who met his Japanese wife during World War II. Animosity toward his father is said to have led Shobe to change his last name from Sarocino. After Shobe's death, however, his son found some information indicating that his parents were both black and from Missouri. Interview with Joanne Shobe, June 8, 2016.

7. *Official Transcript, United States v. James Hoffa, et al.,* 2680.

8. Ibid., 2686, 2688; *Chattanooga News-Free Press,* February 3, 1964.

9. *Official Transcript, United States v. James Hoffa, et al.,* 2692.

10. Ibid., 2693; *Chattanooga News-Free Press,* February 3, 1964.

11. *Official Transcript, United States v. James Hoffa, et al.,* 2834–35.

12. Ibid., 2841.

13. Sheridan, *Fall and Rise of Jimmy Hoffa*, 322, 323; ibid., 2671.

14. *Official Transcript, United States v. James Hoffa, et al.*, 2702–3, 2705–6.

15. Ibid., 2707–8.

16. Sheridan, *Fall and Rise of Jimmy Hoffa*, 322-323; ibid., 2709, 2712.

17. Cook, "First Full Account of a Fateful Trial," 420; *Official Transcript, United States v. James Hoffa, et al.*, 2757, 2766.

18. *Official Transcript, United States v. James Hoffa, et al.*, 2778.

19. Ibid., 2728, 2731–32, 2734, 2740, 2742, 2748, 2750–52, 2787, 2793; Cook, "First Full Account of a Fateful Trial," 421.

20. *New York Times*, February 4, 1964.

21. *Official Transcript, United States v. James Hoffa, et al.*, 2804, 2807–8, 2810–11.

22. Ibid., 2816–17.

23. Ibid., 2820–21.

24. Ibid., 2822, 2824.

25. *Chattanooga News-Free Press*, February 4, 1964.

26. *Official Transcript, United States v. James Hoffa, et al.*, 2849–50, 2852.

27. Ibid., 2854–55, 2869.

28. Ibid., 2867, 2876–77, 2908, 2917, 2921–25; Sheridan, *Fall and Rise of Jimmy Hoffa*, 324.

29. *Official Transcript, United States v. James Hoffa, et al.*, 2876.

30. Ibid., 2870–71, 2875.

31. Ibid., 2925–27. As he had replied when asked about Oscar Pitts, Governor Frank Clement responded to reports of Paschal's testimony by asserting, "I don't know the trooper, have never met him and wouldn't know him if he walked through the door." *Chattanooga News-Free Press*, February 4, 1964.

32. Interview with Betty Paschal, October 9, 2014. Interview by author by telephone.

Chapter 10

1. Cook, "First Full Account of a Fateful Trial," 417.

2. *Official Transcript, United States v. James Hoffa, et al.*, 2929–50.

3. Interview with Neal; *Detroit News*, January 31, 1964; *New York Times*, January 31, 1964; Sloane, *Hoffa*, 293–94.

4. *Chattanooga Times*, February 5, 1964; interview with Neal.

5. Brandt, *"I Heard You Paint Houses,"* 170; Sloane, *Hoffa*, 294; interview with Neal; interview with Mansfield.

6. Interview with Berke; Sheridan, *Fall and Rise of Jimmy Hoffa*, 324–25.

7. *Detroit News*, February 5, 1964; Sheridan, *Fall and Rise of Jimmy Hoffa*, 325; interview with Mansfield.

8. Interview with Haverty; Sloane, *Hoffa*, 294.

9. *Official Transcript, United States v. James Hoffa, et al.*, 2954–55, 2957, 2960; interview with Mansfield.

10. *Official Transcript, United States v. James Hoffa, et al.*, 2965; *Chattanooga Times,* February 5, 1964.

11. *Chattanooga Times,* February 5, 1964; *Official Transcript, United States v. James Hoffa, et al.*, 2967–68, 2973, 2975, 2978; interview with Berke, 2007.

12. *Chattanooga News-Free Press,* February 5–6, 1964; interview with Berke, 2007.

13. *Chattanooga Times,* February 6, 1964; *Wellman, et al. v. United States,* 227 F.2d 757, 770 (6th Cir. 1955); *United States v. Thomas,* 303 F.2d 561, 563 (6th Cir. 1962); Navasky, *Kennedy Justice,* 473, 475, 477.

14. *Official Transcript, United States v. James Hoffa, et al.*, 2982.

15. Ibid., 3029.

16. Ibid., 3054–55, 3058, 3066–67.

17. Moldea, *Hoffa Wars,* 43; ibid., 3072, 3075, 3077, 3083–84, 3088, 3091–93, 3205; Hoffa, *Hoffa: The Real Story,* 157–58.

18. *Official Transcript, United States v. James Hoffa, et al.*, 3100–3101.

19. Ibid., 3192, 3197, 3203; Mollenhoff, *Tentacles of Power,* 192; *Chattanooga Times,* February 6, 1964.

20. *New York Times,* January 15, 1995, December 31, 1995; Pam Sohn, "Hoffa Trial Spying Still a Mystery," *Chattanooga Times-Free Press,* May 10, 2008.

21. *Official Transcript, United States v. James Hoffa, et al.*, 3134, 3145, 3152, 3160, 3167.

22. *Chattanooga News-Free Press,* February 5, 1964.

23. *Detroit News,* February 5, 1964.

24. Interview with Helen Wilson; *Detroit News,* February 5, 1964; *Official Transcript, United States v. James Hoffa, et al.*, 6311.

25. *Chattanooga News-Free Press,* February 5, 1964; *New York Times,* February 6, 1964; *Official Transcript, United States v. James Hoffa, et al.*, 3212.

26. *New York Times,* February 6, 1964; *Chattanooga News-Free Press,* February 5, 1964.

27. Hoffa, *Hoffa: The Real Story,* 157; *Official Transcript, United States v. James Hoffa, et al.*, 3395–96; Sloane, *Hoffa,* 294.

28. *Official Transcript, United States v. James Hoffa, et al.*, 3581; Transcript, Grand Jury Testimony of Walter J. Sheridan, 3, 6–7.

29. *Official Transcript, United States v. James Hoffa, et al.*, 3219, 3330–33, 3338, 3375; *Detroit News,* February 6, 1964.

30. Hoffa, *Hoffa: The Real Story,* 170–71.

31. Cook, "First Full Account of a Fateful Trial," 419, 427–28.

32. *Official Transcript, United States v. James Hoffa, et al.*, 3222, 3232, 3236, 3238.

33. Ibid., 3240, 3244, 3246, 3247.

34. Ibid., 3268–69.

35. Ibid., 3250, 3254, 3256–57, 3279, 3286.

36. Ibid., 3298, 3305–7, 3309.

37. Ibid., 3284–85.

38. Interview with Haverty.

39. *Official Transcript, United States v. James Hoffa, et al.*, 3311–12, 3314.

40. *Chattanooga News-Free Press,* February 5, 1964; Moldea, *Hoffa Wars,* 172; Brandt, *"I Heard You Paint Houses,"* 171.

41. *Chattanooga Times,* February 5–6, 1964; *Chattanooga News-Free Press,* February 5, 1964; *New York Times,* February 6, 1964; Henry, *Fatal Alliance,* 133; Sloane, *Hoffa,* 296; Hoffa, *Hoffa: The Real Story,* 170–71; *Official Transcript, United States v. James Hoffa, et al.,* 3683.

42. *Chattanooga News-Free Press,* February 6, 1964; *Chattanooga Times,* February 6, 1964; interview with Mansfield.

43. *Official Transcript, United States v. James Hoffa, et al.,* 3261, 3263, 3267; Partin, *From My Brother's Shadow,* 75.

44. *Official Transcript, United States v. James Hoffa, et al.,* 3398–99.

45. Sheridan, *Fall and Rise of Jimmy Hoffa,* 330.

46. *Detroit News,* February 6, 1964.

Chapter 11

1. Ibid., February 9, 1964.

2. Partin, *From My Brother's Shadow,* 29, 37–38, 45, 47–49, 51, 54, 89–90, 101, 103, 105–8, 113.

3. Interview with Berke, 2007.

4. *Official Transcript, United States v. James Hoffa, et al.,* 3462, 3473; *Chattanooga News-Free Press,* February 5, 1964.

5. *Official Transcript, United States v. James Hoffa, et al.,* 3474–75; *Chattanooga News-Free Press,* February 6, 1964; Sloane, *Hoffa,* 299.

6. *Chattanooga Times,* February 7, 1964; *Chattanooga News-Free Press,* February 7, 1964; Cook, "First Full Account of a Fateful Trial," 428–29.

7. *Official Transcript, United States v. James Hoffa, et al.,* 3467, 3488.

8. Ibid., 3481.

9. Ibid., 3491, 3493, 3497.

10. Interview with Haverty.

11. *Official Transcript, United States v. James Hoffa, et al.,* 3503–4, 3510, 3512–13, 3518, 3524, 3532; Brandt, *"I Heard You Paint Houses,"* 144; *New York Times,* February 7, 1964; *Detroit News,* February 7, 1964, February 9, 1964; Hoffa, *Hoffa: The Real Story,* 170–71.

12. *Official Transcript, United States v. James Hoffa, et al.,* 3552, 3554–55, 3559–62. According to Doug Partin, his brother had been involved in smuggling activities as the defense alleged. "Once, when he [Ed Partin] was trying to make some quick cash," he explained, "he actually made an arms deal with Fidel Castro in Cuba. He went to Cuba twice and met with Castro both times." Partin, *From My Brother's Shadow,* 242.

13. *Official Transcript, United States v. James Hoffa, et al.,* 3587, 3589; Sloane, *Hoffa,* 300.

14. *Official Transcript, United States v. James Hoffa, et al.,* 3646–47, 3812; *Chattanooga News-Free Press,* February 7, 1964. The following day, Schiffer raised the issue again, complaining, "Before this witness answers questions on cross examination he looks either at Mr. Hooker or Mr. Neal or Mr. Reddy and after he finishes his answer he

looks to them for approbation of what he has testified to." For their part, the prosecutors adamantly denied trying to coach Partin while he was on the stand.

15. Sheridan, *Fall and Rise of Jimmy Hoffa*, 331.

16. *Official Transcript, United States v. James Hoffa, et al.*, 3766.

17. Ibid., 3760.

18. Sheridan, *Fall and Rise of Jimmy Hoffa*, 334; interview with Neal; interview with Sertel; interview with Berke, 2007; interview with Gearhiser.

19. *Official Transcript, United States v. James Hoffa, et al.*, 3791.

20. Ibid., 3837, 3851–52.

21. Ibid., 3859.

22. *Chattanooga News-Free Press*, February 7, 1964.

23. Wilson, "Enduring Symbol of Hope"; interview with Randy Wilson; *Chattanooga News-Free Press*, January 30, 1964; interview with Helen Wilson.

24. *Detroit News*, February 16, 1964.

25. Interview with Gearhiser; interview with Berke, 2007; interview with Mansfield; interview with Seigenthaler.

26. *Official Transcript, United States v. James Hoffa, et al.*, 3264–65.

27. Ibid., 3345–46.

28. Ibid., 3838–46; *Chattanooga News-Free Press*, February 7, 1964.

29. Interview with Seigenthaler; interview with Berke, 2007.

30. *Official Transcript, United States v. James Hoffa, et al.*, 3789–90.

31. Ibid., 3798.

32. Ibid., 3817–18, 4075, 4120; Sheridan, *Fall and Rise of Jimmy Hoffa*, 306.

33. *Official Transcript, United States v. James Hoffa, et al.*, 3397–98, 4144, 4148–49, 4152–53, 4240; Navasky, *Kennedy Justice*, 477–78; *Chattanooga News-Free Press*, February 11, 1964; *New York Times*, February 11, 1964.

34. Sohn, "Hoffa Trial Spying"; Navasky, *Kennedy Justice*, 464, 467; Hoffa, *Hoffa: The Real Story*, 164; Schlesinger, *Robert Kennedy*, 270–72.

35. Interview with Seigenthaler; interview with Neal.

36. Interview with Cole; Cook, "First Full Account of a Fateful Trial," 416; interview with Neal; interview with Berke, 2007; interview with Pearce.

37. Hoffa, *Hoffa: The Real Story*, 167–68; interview with Neal; Sertel Recollections, 19–20.

38. *Official Transcript, United States v. James Hoffa, et al.*, 3443–44, 3447.

39. Ibid., 3860–62, 3873–76, 3878.

40. Ibid., 3879–80.

41. Ibid., 3862; Cook, "First Full Account of a Fateful Trial," 432.

42. Interview with Pearce.

43. Sheridan, *Fall and Rise of Jimmy Hoffa*, 332; *Chattanooga News-Free Press*, February 11, 1964; *Chattanooga Times*, February 11, 1964; interview with Pearce; Affidavit of Daniel B. Maher, *United States v. James R. Hoffa, et al.*, Case No. 11,989 (E.D. Tenn. 1964).

44. Interview with Mansfield.

45. *Official Transcript, United States v. James Hoffa, et al.*, 3881–84; *Chattanooga Times*, February 11, 1964; *Chattanooga News-Free Press*, February 11, 1964.

46. *Official Transcript, United States v. James Hoffa, et al.*, 3886; *Chattanooga News-Free Press*, February 9, 1964.

47. *Official Transcript, United States v. James Hoffa, et al.*, 3905.

48. Sheridan, *Fall and Rise of Jimmy Hoffa*, 334; interview with Neal.

Chapter 12

1. Knowles, *Journal*, 6–7, 10–11; "Chattanooga: Knowles' Journal Gives Glimpse into Hoffa Trial," *Chattanooga Times-Free Press*, May 9, 2008.

2. *Detroit News*, February 9, 1964; *Chattanooga Times*, February 9, 1964; Knowles, *Journal*, 18; interview with Brown, 2007.

3. *Chattanooga News-Free Press*, February 8, 1964.

4. "Chattanooga's premier movie and variety theater," the ornate, Beaux Arts–style Tivoli Theater opened in 1921. It became the first air-conditioned public building in the South in 1926, enabling the theater to operate throughout the year, including the hot, humid summer months. Declining in importance due to the advent of television, the theater was closed in 1961, but a local grant enabled it to be reopened in 1963, shortly before the rally hosting Jimmy Hoffa. It remains in operation today as one of the cultural gems of Chattanooga. Maury Nicely, *Chattanooga Walking Tour & Historic Guide* (Chattanooga: Stillhouse Hollow, 2005), 170–71.

5. *Chattanooga Times*, February 9–10, 1964; *Detroit News*, February 10, 1964; *Chattanooga News-Free Press*, February 9, 1964; *Official Transcript, United States v. James Hoffa, et al.*, 3865.

6. Reportedly, Partin told attorney Charlie Shaffer that he had arranged for the shotgun blasts himself. "That was pure Partin," Shaffer said. "It was a shocking revelation about Partin and his ingenuity." Neff, *Vendetta*, 319.

7. *Chattanooga Times*, February 8, 1964.

8. Cook, "First Full Account of a Fateful Trial," 415–16, 439; Benjamin P. Harper, "A Highway, a Hill, the Automobile, and the Use of Space in the Urban Context: The Golden Gateway Urban Renewal Project, Chattanooga, Tennessee, 1955–1977" (thesis, Covenant College, 2002).

9. Interview with Berke, 2007.

10. *Official Transcript, United States v. James Hoffa, et al.*, 4038, 4155–57, 4162.

11. *Chattanooga News-Free Press*, February 11, 1964; ibid., 4243, 4284–86.

12. *Official Transcript, United States v. James Hoffa, et al.*, 4304–5.

13. Ibid., 4018; Moldea, *Hoffa Wars*, 54; Sloane, *Hoffa*, 89, 104–5; Kennedy, *Enemy Within*, 61; *Chattanooga Times*, February 12, 1964; interview with Berke, 2007.

14. *Chattanooga Times*, February 12, 1964; Sohn, "Hoffa Trial Spying"; interview with Gearhiser.

15. *Official Transcript, United States v. James Hoffa, et al.*, 4464, 4468, 4478, 4617, 4619; 47 U.S.C. § 605, Federal Communications Act of 1934.

16. Interview with Cole.

17. *Chattanooga Times*, February 11, 1964.

18. *Official Transcript, United States v. James Hoffa, et al.*, 4503, 4518–19, 4534, 4546.

19. *Chattanooga News-Free Press*, February 11, 1964; *Chattanooga Times*, February 11, 1964.

20. *Official Transcript, United States v. James Hoffa, et al.*, 4605–10; *Chattanooga News-Free Press*, February 12, 1964; *Detroit News*, February 12, 1964.

21. *New York Times*, February 11, 1964; *Detroit News*, February 11, 1964; Sloane, *Hoffa*, 306; interview with Berke.

22. *Chattanooga News-Free Press*, February 12, 1964; *New York Times*, February 12, 1964; *Detroit News*, February 12, 1964; CBS News Feed, February 11, 1964.

23. Interview with Seigenthaler; *Official Transcript, United States v. James Hoffa, et al.*, 4588, 4598, 4660–62, 4664-4665, 4667, 4675, 4711, 4717–18, 4731. In a light moment, when Partin commented offhand that his wife had been satisfied with the expenses paid to her, Branstetter asked, "You don't think that women just complain, is it because they don't have enough money, is that the only time she complained now?" "No, sir," Partin responded. "I would be living with her now if that was the case."

Chapter 13

1. *Chattanooga Times*, February 12, 1964; *Chattanooga News-Free Press*, February 13, 1964.

2. *Official Transcript, United States v. James Hoffa, et al.*, 4965, 4967, 4986, 4990, 4996–98.

3. Ibid., 5000, 5008, 5010, 5014–15, 5018, 5020, 5060; *Chattanooga News-Free Press*, February 13, 1964; *Detroit News*, February 14, 1964.

4. *Official Transcript, United States v. James Hoffa, et al.*, 5062, 5065–66, 5068, 5075–79; *Detroit News*, February 14, 1964.

5. *Official Transcript, United States v. James Hoffa, et al.*, 5103; *Detroit News*, February 14, 1964; *Chattanooga Times*, February 14, 1964; Cook, "First Full Account of a Fateful Trial," 419.

6. Interview with Seigenthaler.

7. Interview with Mansfield; *Chattanooga Times*, February 14, 1964; Charles Bartlett, "Hoffa Nears Crucial Fork in Career," *Chattanooga Times*, March 1, 1964; Sheridan, *Fall and Rise of Jimmy Hoffa*, 339.

8. *Chattanooga Times*, February 13–14, 1964; *Chattanooga News-Free Press*, February 14, 1964.

9. *Official Transcript, United States v. James Hoffa, et al.*, 5135–36, 5141, 5143, 5152–55.

10. Ibid., 5144–46, 5149.

11. Ibid., 5245–63.

12. Ibid., 5263–81.

13. Ibid., 5282–5304.

14. State of Tennessee General Assembly, "A Resolution to Honor the Memory of Dave A. Alexander, Sr.," Senate No. SJR0149 (March 29, 1995).

15. *Official Transcript, United States v. James Hoffa, et al.*, 5305–30.

16. Ibid., 5331.

17. Ibid., 5333–34.

18. Ibid., 5335–45.

19. Ibid., 5381; Sheridan, *Fall and Rise of Jimmy Hoffa*, 339–40.

20. *Chattanooga Times*, February 15–16, 1964.

Chapter 14

1. *Official Transcript, United States v. James Hoffa, et al.*, 5437.

2. Interview with Gearhiser; interview with Mansfield; interview with Randy Wilson; interview with Helen Wilson; interview with Sertel; "Chattanooga: Jimmy Hoffa Jury Tampering Trial Tested Legal System," *Chattanooga Times-Free Press*, May 4, 2008; Sertel Recollections, 1, 6, 12, 29–30; United States District Court, Eastern District of Tennessee, *Court Historical Society Newsletter* (July 2006).

3. *Official Transcript, United States v. James Hoffa, et al.*, 5352–76; *Chattanooga News-Free Press*, February 15, 1964.

4. *Official Transcript, United States v. James Hoffa, et al.*, 5388–92.

5. *Chattanooga News-Free Press*, February 26, 1964.

6. *Chattanooga News-Free Press*, February 25, 1964.

7. *Official Transcript, United States v. James Hoffa, et al.*, 5384, 5387, 5542–45, 5548–49; *Chattanooga Times*, February 18, 1964; *Chattanooga Times*, February 19, 1964.

8. *Chattanooga News-Free Press*, February 15, 1964.

9. *Official Transcript, United States v. James Hoffa, et al.*, 5394; *Detroit News*, February 2, 1964.

10. *Official Transcript, United States v. James Hoffa, et al.*, 5398–5400.

11. Ibid., 5401–5.

12. Ibid., 5406–8, 5410, 5448.

13. Ibid., 5410, 5414–16.

14. Ibid., 5418–19.

15. Ibid., 5420, 5422, 5429, 5434.

16. Ibid., 5435, 5437, 5438; *Chattanooga News-Free Press*, February 17, 1964.

17. *Official Transcript, United States v. James Hoffa, et al.*, 5444–46.

18. Ibid., 5451, 5459, 5463-5464.

19. Ibid., 5464, 5466–67, 5487–88, 5496, 5501, 5517–18.

20. Ibid., 5556.

21. Ibid., 5586.

22. Ibid., 5588.

23. Ibid., 5608–12, 5618–19, 5627-5629, 5631, 5634, 5640, 5644–45, 5658–61.

24. Kennedy, *Enemy Within*, 86; Brandt, *"I Heard You Paint Houses,"* 105; Lester Velie, "Stakes in the Struggle Against Hoffa," *Reader's Digest*, March 1964, 96; Moldea, *Hoffa Wars*, 97–98.

25. *Official Transcript, United States v. James Hoffa, et al.*, 5676–77; *Detroit News*, February 2, 1964.

26. *Official Transcript, United States v. James Hoffa, et al.*, 5678, 5681, 5686.

27. Ibid., 5693–95, 5697, 5699–5700.

28. Ibid., 5700, 5702–3, 5707, 5709, 5713, 5715–16. The court reporter at the trial mistakenly transcribed this information. Neal was referring to Felix Aldirisio (1912–71), an underboss to Chicago ganglord Sam Giancana. Due to his connections to criminal activity in Wisconsin, Aldirisio was nicknamed "Milwaukee Phil."

29. Ibid., 5746–48, 5764, 5802.

30. Ibid., 5803, 5805.

31. Ibid., 5807, 5810, 5813, 5815, 5817; *Chattanooga Times-Free Press*, February 18, 1964.

32. Sheridan, *Fall and Rise of Jimmy Hoffa*, 341.

Chapter 15

1. *Official Transcript, United States v. James Hoffa, et al.*, 5829, 5834, 5836–37.

2. *New York Times*, January 26, 1983.

3. *Official Transcript, United States v. James Hoffa, et al.*, 5848–49, 5854, 5858, 5862, 5868, 5874, 5879, 5881, 5884, 5891, 5895, 5899.

4. Ibid., 5871, 5906, 5912, 5914, 5916.

5. Ibid., 5925–27, 5929–34; *Detroit News*, February 2, 1964.

6. *Official Transcript, United States v. James Hoffa, et al.*, 5935, 5937, 5939, 5943–44, 5946–55.

7. Ibid., 6050–54.

8. Ibid., 6277, 6280–82, 6284, 6287, 6290–91.

9. Ibid., 6055–57, 6471.

10. Ibid., 6062–66, 6071, 6099–101.

11. Ibid., 6075–79, 6082, 6084. The colorful characters Shobe referenced were not imaginary. Henry "Good Jelly" Jones was a tavern operator and booking agent (known for running out on his acts when it came time to pay them) in Nashville's black community. A series of photographs documenting Jones's arrest for possession of untaxed (bootleg) whiskey was published in the *Nashville Tennessean* on February 12, 1965.

12. Ibid., 6104–7.

13. Ibid., 6121–26.

14. "Black Members Protest Bias Charge, July 1959," accessed July 10, 2014, www .teamster.org; *Detroit News*, February 2, 1964.

15. *Official Transcript, United States v. James Hoffa, et al.*, 6128–29, 6133–34, 6139, 6144, 6147, 6156–57, 6160, 6162; *Detroit News*, February 2, 1964.

16. *Official Transcript, United States v. James Hoffa, et al.*, 6165, 6168, 6173–75, 6184–85.

17. Hoffa, *Hoffa: The Real Story*, 14; *New York Times*, May 7, 1981; Moldea, *Hoffa Wars*, 185; Sloane, *Hoffa*, 316–18.

18. *Official Transcript, United States v. James Hoffa, et al.*, 6212, 6214.

19. Ibid., 6950–69, 6984–7004.

20. Ibid., 6293, 6730–31, 6734–36, 6738, 6747; *Chattanooga News-Free Press*, February 21, 1964; Offer of Proof, Norma Jean Partin, *United States v. James R. Hoffa, et al.*, Case No. 11,989 (E.D. Tenn. 1964).

21. *Official Transcript, United States v. James Hoffa, et al.*, 6313–15.

Chapter 16

1. It should be noted that the autobiography of Doug Partin contains several factual errors and inconsistencies. By way of example, in discussing the Chattanooga trial Partin notes, "In another hotel, Bobby Kennedy and his FBI team were staying. Kennedy and the FBI agents played football outside the hotel nearly every day." Kennedy was never in Chattanooga during the trial. One is advised to use some measure of circumspection (and caution) when relying on Partin's recounting of events related to the Chattanooga trial. As for his allegations of a brawl at the Farmer's Curb Grill Room, no such establishment is listed anywhere in the 1964 *Chattanooga City Directory*. Whether this error is simply the product of faulty recollections after a half century's time, or an indication of the desire to artificially inflate accounts of the incident, one may question whether this incident is apocryphal.

2. *Chattanooga News-Free Press*, February 22, 1964; Partin, *From My Brother's Shadow*, 120–25. Described as a "convict with a long record," Billy Simpson later became a government informant in an alleged plot to assassinate Louisiana governor John McKeithen in retaliation for his investigation into organized labor. Sent to Angola Prison on a burglary charge, Simpson was released an hour later after McKeithen, learning of an alleged plot to murder Simpson, prevailed upon the parole board to set him free. *New Orleans States-Item*, June 24, 1968.

3. *Official Transcript, United States v. James Hoffa, et al.*, 6321–25; *Detroit News*, February 2, 1964; *New York Times*, February 21, 1964; Squires, *Secrets of the Hopewell Box*, 218.

4. *Official Transcript, United States v. James Hoffa, et al.*, 6332–36, 6339–40, 6342, 6347.

5. Ibid., 6332, 6344, 6346.

6. Ibid., 6351; *Chattanooga Times*, February 21, 1964.

7. *Official Transcript, United States v. James Hoffa, et al.*, 6367.

8. Ibid., 6398.

9. Ibid., 6402, 6419–20.

10. Ibid., 6433.

11. Ibid., 6435–36, 6438–41, 6444.

12. Ibid., 6495–6500, 6505–11, 6534; *Chattanooga New-Free Press*, February 21, 1964.

13. *Official Transcript, United States v. James Hoffa, et al.*, 6539–41, 6547, 6557–71, 6578–83, 6600.

14. *Detroit News*, February 21, 1964; *Chattanooga News-Free Press*, February 21, 1964.

15. *Official Transcript, United States v. James Hoffa, et al.*, 6628–58; *Chattanooga News-Free Press*, February 19–21, 1964; *Chattanooga Times*, February 20, 1964; Cook, "First Full Account of a Fateful Trial," 425; *Detroit News*, February 20, 1964.

16. *Official Transcript, United States v. James Hoffa, et al.*, 6887.

17. Ibid., 6665–74, 6680–82, 6698–702.

18. Ibid., 6706–16.

19. Ibid., 6741, 6745, 6748.

20. Ibid., 6758–67. Later, Bloomenstiel filed an affidavit contending that Doug Partin instructed him that Ed Partin wanted him to take the Fifth Amendment in Chattanooga. On his way to the courtroom, Bloomenstiel added, he was threatened with retaliation if his testimony was adverse to Partin. Affidavit of Lester Bloomenstiel (October 20, 1964), in Case File, *United States v. James R. Hoffa, et al.*, File No. 11-989 (E.D. Tenn. 1964).

21. *Official Transcript, United States v. James Hoffa, et al.*, 6792–803. Doug Partin wrote in his autobiography that Ed Partin did, in fact, take "lots of prescription pills." He did not, however, corroborate his brother's use of narcotics. Partin, *From My Brother's Shadow*, 76.

22. *Official Transcript, United States v. James Hoffa, et al.*, 6821–24, 6856–60.

23. Ibid., 6827–38.

24. Ibid., 6771–89.

25. Ibid., 6840–51.

26. Ibid., 6867–70.

27. Ibid., 6925.

28. Ibid., 6806–9, 6873–89.

29. Ibid., 7071–99, 7118–32.

30. Ibid., 7133–47, 7210–50.

Chapter 17

1. Interview with Neal; interview with Seigenthaler.

2. *Chattanooga Times*, February 23, 1964; *Chattanooga News-Free Press*, February 24, 1964; "Witness for the Prosecution," *Time Magazine*, February 28, 1964.

3. *Chattanooga News-Free Press*, February 25–26, 1964; *Chattanooga Times*, February 26, 1964.

4. *Chattanooga Times*, February 26, 1964; *Official Transcript, United States v. James Hoffa, et al.*, 7254, 7262.

5. *Official Transcript, United States v. James Hoffa, et al.*, 7267, 7269–71, 7313–16.

6. Ibid., 7271–73, 7275, 7278, 7308–9.

7. *Chattanooga Times*, February 26, 1964; ibid., 7279-82, 7286–90.

8. *Official Transcript, United States v. James Hoffa, et al.*, 7292–7301, 7305.

9. CBS News Feed, February 11, 1964.

10. Henry, *Fatal Alliance*, 136–37; Brandt, *"I Heard You Paint Houses,"* 172; *Official Transcript, United States v. James Hoffa, et al.*, 7376–77, 7388–89, 7399–7400.

11. *Chattanooga Times,* February 26, 1964; *Chattanooga News-Free Press,* February 26, 1964.

12. *Chattanooga News-Free Press,* February 26, 1964; *Official Transcript, United States v. James Hoffa, et al.,* 7332.

13. *Official Transcript, United States v. James Hoffa, et al.,* 7330–31, 7365, 7370–71.

14. Ibid., 7339.

15. Ibid., 7394–95.

16. Ibid., 7405–6.

17. Ibid., 7360–61, 7406.

18. *Chattanooga News-Free Press,* February 26, 1964.

19. CBS News Feed, February 25, 1964.

20. *Chattanooga Times,* February 28, 1964.

21. *Official Transcript, United States v. James Hoffa, et al.,* 7409–10, 7425, 7427.

22. Ibid., 7428, 7440–42.

23. Ibid., 7434–38.

24. Ibid., 7431–34.

25. Ibid., 7532, 7535.

26. Ibid., 7456.

27. Ibid., 7467–73.

28. Ibid., 7557, 7561, 7565–69, 7573.

29. Ibid., 7595–99; *Chattanooga News-Free Press,* February 26, 1964.

30. *Official Transcript, United States v. James Hoffa, et al.,* 7599, 7606–7.

31. Ibid., 7688–92, 7694, 7703–4.

32. Ibid., 7782, 7785–95, 7813, 7865, 7868, 7890–92; *New York Times,* February 28, 1964; *Chattanooga News-Free Press,* February 27, 1964. Amazingly, in his own cross-examination of Bussie, Silets also tried to address the Mississippi rape allegation. An objection to the question was quickly sustained.

33. *Official Transcript, United States v. James Hoffa, et al.,* 7817–20; *Chattanooga News-Free Press,* February 27, 1964; *Chattanooga Times,* February 28, 1964.

34. *Official Transcript, United States v. James Hoffa, et al.,* 7824–27.

35. Ibid., 7828.

36. Ibid., 7831–35.

37. Ibid., 7837.

38. Interview with Haverty; Knowles, *Journal,* 18–19.

39. *Official Transcript, United States v. James Hoffa, et al.,* 7847–48; Velie, "Stakes in the Struggle Against Hoffa," 92, 96.

40. *Chattanooga News-Free Press,* February 29, 1964. The 1962 film *Trial by Jury,* starring Laurence Olivier, depicts a milquetoast alcoholic schoolteacher accused of molestation by a student whose romantic advances he had rejected.

41. *Official Transcript, United States v. James Hoffa, et al.,* 7837–41.

42. *American Justice: Defending the Mob* (television broadcast), season 4, episode 3, March 15, 1995, A&E Television.

43. *Official Transcript, United States v. James Hoffa, et al.*, 7852–54, 7858.

44. Ibid., 7918–19, 7925, 7929, 7941, 7948.

45. Ibid., 7954–66, 7970, 8026–28, 8036, 8042–43, 8073, 8082.

46. Ibid., 8150; *Chattanooga News-Free Press,* February 28, 1964.

47. *Official Transcript, United States v. James Hoffa, et al.*, 8093–95.

48. Ibid., 8159, 8167, 8180.

49. Ibid., 8193–96.

50. Ibid., 8207–8.

51. *Chattanooga News-Free Press,* February 25, 1964; *Chattanooga Times,* February 28, 1964; *New York Times,* February 28, 1964.

Chapter 18

1. *Chattanooga Times,* February 29, 1964, March 4, 1964, March 7, 1964.

2. Knowles, *Journal,* 20.

3. Bartlett, "Hoffa Nears Crucial Fork in Career."

4. *Official Transcript, United States v. James Hoffa, et al.*, 7708–12, 7722–26.

5. Ibid., 8251–52.

6. Ibid., 8256.

7. Ibid., 8262; interview with Etta Williams.

8. *Official Transcript, United States v. James Hoffa, et al.*, 8266–68.

9. Ibid., 8311.

10. Ibid., 8268, 8274.

11. Ibid., 8270–71.

12. Ibid., 8264; *Chattanooga Times,* March 2, 1964; interview with Etta Williams.

13. *Official Transcript, United States v. James Hoffa, et al.*, 8271–73.

14. Ibid., 8274.

15. Ibid., 8274–75.

16. Ibid., 8278–79.

17. Ibid., 8308.

18. Ibid., 8282–83.

19. Ibid., 8293–96.

20. Ibid., 8306.

21. Ibid., 8297.

22. Ibid., 8302.

23. Ibid., 8313; *Chattanooga Times,* March 3, 1964.

24. *Official Transcript, United States v. James Hoffa, et al.*, 8317–18; *Chattanooga Times,* March 3, 1964.

25. *Official Transcript, United States v. James Hoffa, et al.*, 8320, 8324.

26. Ibid., 8325; *Chattanooga Times,* March 3, 1964.

27. *Official Transcript, United States v. James Hoffa, et al.*, 8329.

28. Ibid., 8330, 8335.

29. Ibid., 8335–36.

30. Ibid., 8336–38.

31. Ibid., 8340.

32. Ibid., 8340–41.

33. Ibid., 8341–42.

34. Ibid., 8351–52.

35. Ibid., 8353–54.

36. Ibid., 8358.

37. Ibid., 8360, 8362–65.

38. Ibid., 8367–68.

39. Ibid., 8361.

40. Ibid., 8365–66.

41. Ibid., 8371.

42. Ibid., 8372.

43. Ibid., 8375.

44. Ibid., 8381–82.

45. Ibid., 8382–83.

46. Ibid., 8383–84.

47. Ibid., 8387–88.

48. Ibid., 8388–90.

49. Ibid., 8393.

50. Ibid., 8395; *Chattanooga Times,* March 3, 1964.

51. *Official Transcript, United States v. James Hoffa, et al.,* 8395–96.

52. Ibid., 8396–97.

53. Ibid., 8401–2.

54. Ibid., 8405.

55. Ibid., 8406–8.

56. Ibid., 8416.

57. Interview with Haverty; ibid., 8419–20; *Chattanooga News-Free Press,* March 3, 1964.

58. *Official Transcript, United States v. James Hoffa, et al.,* 8426.

59. Ibid., 8423.

60. Ibid., 8427–28.

61. Ibid., 8427–28, 8430–32.

62. Ibid., 8438–39; *Chattanooga News-Free Press,* March 3, 1964.

63. *Official Transcript, United States v. James Hoffa, et al.,* 8439.

64. Ibid., 8442–45.

65. Ibid., 8447, 8453.

66. Ibid., 8454.

67. Ibid., 8458.

68. *Chattanooga Times,* March 4, 1964.

69. *Official Transcript, United States v. James Hoffa, et al.,* 8462–63.

70. Ibid., 8465.

71. Ibid., 8465–69.

72. Ibid., 8471–72; *Chattanooga News-Free Press,* March 3, 1964.

73. *Chattanooga News-Free Press,* March 3, 1964.

74. *Official Transcript, United States v. James Hoffa, et al.,* 8477–80.

75. Ibid., 8482–83, 8490.

76. Ibid., 8486.

77. Ibid., 8490–93, 8504.

78. Ibid., 8503–4.

79. Ibid., 8512–14.

80. Ibid., 8525–40.

81. Interview with Gearhiser.

82. *Official Transcript, United States v. James Hoffa, et al.,* 8555–56.

83. Ibid., 8556, 8562.

84. Ibid., 8572.

85. Ibid., 8575.

86. Ibid., 8580–81.

87. Ibid., 8581.

88. Ibid., 8583.

89. Ibid., 8585.

90. Ibid., 8585–86.

91. Ibid., 8587.

92. Ibid.

93. Ibid., 8593–94.

94. Ibid., 8600.

95. Ibid., 8240–42, 8245, 8248; *Chattanooga News-Free Press,* February 29, 1964; *Chattanooga News-Free Press,* March 4, 1964. Initially, Judge Wilson had proposed a rare Saturday session to go over the jury charge with the attorneys for both sides. This brought an objection from Harvey Silets, who declared, "On behalf of myself and my client Allen Dorfman, for religious reasons we will not be present." Silets instead suggested a Sunday session. "No, sir," Judge Wilson responded, "We will not hold Court upon Sunday." In the end, the parties agreed to allow Judge Wilson to determine the instructions to be provided to the jury, after which the attorneys could present any objections on behalf of their clients.

96. *Official Transcript, United States v. James Hoffa, et al.,* 8722–24; *Chattanooga Times,* March 4, 1964.

97. Henry, *Fatal Alliance,* 141; Sheridan, *Fall and Rise of Jimmy Hoffa,* 352.

98. *Official Transcript, United States v. James Hoffa, et al.,* 8730–31.

Chapter 19

1. Interview with Haverty.

2. Interview with Mansfield; interview with Randy Wilson.

3. *Official Transcript, United States v. James Hoffa, et al.,* 8749, 8761–71; *Chattanooga News-Free Press,* March 3, 1964.

4. *Official Transcript, United States v. James Hoffa, et al.,* 8743.

5. Ibid., 8775–77.

6. Ibid., 8778–79.

7. Ibid., 8783–86.

8. Ibid., 8791.

9. Ibid., 8804–40, 8847, 8855, 8861–64.

10. *Chattanooga Times,* March 5, 1964.

11. *Official Transcript, United States v. James Hoffa, et al.,* 8866–69.

12. Ibid., 8867–69; interview with Mansfield; *Chattanooga News-Free Press,* March 5, 1964; *New York Times,* March 5, 1964.

13. *Official Transcript, United States v. James Hoffa, et al.,* 8877–79.

14. Ibid., 8882–83.

15. Interview with Mansfield. According to the *Chattanooga News-Free Press,* Josephine Hoffa's attending physician informed her of the verdict, and "she took the news calmly." Convinced of her husband's innocence, she expressed confidence that the verdict would be overturned on appeal. "She is most anxious to get back to be with him," the article added. *Chattanooga News-Free Press,* March 5, 1964.

16. Sloane, *Hoffa,* 301; *Chattanooga Times,* March 5, 1964; *Chattanooga News-Free Press,* March 5, 1964; *New York Times,* March 5, 1964.

17. *Chattanooga Times,* March 5, 1964; *New York Times,* March 5, 1964.

18. *Chattanooga Times,* March 5, 1964; *Chattanooga News-Free Press,* March 5, 1964; CBS News Feed, March 4, 1964.

19. *Chattanooga News-Free Press,* March 5, 1964.

20. *Time Magazine,* March 13, 1964; *Chattanooga Times,* March 5, 1964; *Chattanooga News-Free Press,* March 5, 1964.

21. *Official Transcript, United States v. James Hoffa, et al.,* 8894–95, 8900.

22. Ibid., 8905–6.

23. Ibid., 8907–8, 8915–16.

24. Ibid., 8909–14.

25. Ibid., 8937.

26. Ibid., 8938.

27. Ibid., 8980–83, 8996, 9000, 9008, 9016, 9028.

28. Ibid., 9050–57, 9064; *Life Magazine,* May 20, 1966.

29. *Official Transcript, United States v. James Hoffa, et al.,* 9059–66, 9134–35; *Chattanooga Times,* February 12, 1964; interview with Berke, 2007.

30. *Official Transcript, United States v. James Hoffa, et al.,* 9068–73.

31. Ibid., 9078–80, 9086–87.

32. Ibid., 9089–91.

33. Ibid., 9093–97.

34. Ibid., 9112–13.

35. Ibid., 9115–16.

36. Ibid., 9127; Exhibit 249, *United States v. James R. Hoffa, et al.,* Case No. 11,989 (E.D. Tenn. 1964).

37. *Official Transcript, United States v. James Hoffa, et al.*, 9139, 9143, 9146–48, 9195–96.

38. Ibid., 9206–12.

39. Ibid., 9220–34.

40. Ibid., 9243–48.

41. Ibid., 9251–59.

42. Ibid., 9260–61.

43. Ibid., 9281–83.

44. Interview with Cole; interview with Neal.

45. *Chattanooga Times*, March 7, 12, 1964; Hoffa, *Hoffa: The Real Story*, 172; *Chattanooga Times*, March 5, 1964.

Chapter 20

1. Interview with Eason.

2. *Chattanooga Times*, March 5, 1964; interview with Mansfield; interview with Haverty.

3. Sertel, 29; *Chattanooga Times*, March 7, 1964.

4. Interview with Berke, 2007.

5. *Official Transcript, United States v. James Hoffa, et al.*, 9288–89; *New York Times*, March 13, 1964; Mollenhoff, *Tentacles of Power*, 8.

6. *Official Transcript, United States v. James Hoffa, et al.*, 9290–93; *Chattanooga Times*, March 13, 1964; *New York Times*, March 14, 1964.

7. *Official Transcript, United States v. James Hoffa, et al.*, 9294–96.

8. Ibid., 9296–98.

9. Ibid., 9299–9300.

10. *Chattanooga Times*, March 13, 1964; *United States v. Schiffer*, 351 F.2d 91 (6th Cir. 1965), *cert. denied*, 384 U.S. 1003 (1966), *reh'g denied*, 385 U.S. 890 (1966); interview with Gearhiser.

11. *Official Transcript, United States v. James Hoffa, et al.*, 9302–21.

12. Interview with Sheridan, May 1, 1970, 5–6; Sertel Recollections, 36–37; interview with Mansfield; Hoffa, *Hoffa: The Real Story*, 173.

13. *Chattanooga Times*, March 13, 1964.

Chapter 21

1. Squires, *Secrets of the Hopewell Box*, 147; *Nashville Tennessean*, April 2, 1964; *United States v. Medlin*, 353 F.2d 789 (6th Cir. 1965); *Medlin v. United States*, 384 U.S. 973 (1966); *New York Times*, April 4, 1964; *Chattanooga Times*, November 23, 1966; *Chattanooga News-Free Press*, November 23, 1966, November 29, 1966.

2. *United States v. Bell*, 351 F.2d 868 (6th Cir. 1965); Squires, *Secrets of the Hopewell Box*, 147; *Nashville Banner*, April 9, 1964; Sheridan, *Fall and Rise of Jimmy Hoffa*, 360.

3. *Chattanooga News-Free Press,* March 2, 1964; Sheridan, *Fall and Rise of Jimmy Hoffa,* 220, 259–61, 270–71, 280, 287, 385.

4. *Nashville Tennessean,* April 15, 19, 1964; *Nashville Banner,* April 15, 1964; *United States v. Schiffer,* 351 F.2d 91 (6th Cir. 1965), *cert. denied,* 384 U.S. 1003 (1966), *reh'g denied,* 385 U.S. 890 (1966).

5. Moldea, *Hoffa Wars,* 173–75; Sloane, *Hoffa,* 305–12, 320–21; interview with Sheridan, May 1, 1970, 8; Sheridan, *Fall and Rise of Jimmy Hoffa,* 360–77, 395, 398, 416, 429–30, 488, 510; Henry, *Fatal Alliance,* 174–75; Navasky, *Kennedy Justice,* 479–81; *United States v. Hoffa,* 273 F. Supp. 141 (N.D. Ill. 1967); *United States v. Hoffa,* 367 F.2d 698 (7th Cir. 1966); *Chattanooga News-Free Press,* March 5, 1964; *Nashville Tennessean, April 2, 1964; New York Times,* August 23, 1967.

6. *Chattanooga Times,* March 7, 12–13, 1964.

7. *Chattanooga News-Free Press,* March 5, 1964.

8. *Chattanooga Times,* March 8, 1964; ibid., March 5, 1964; Henry, *Fatal Alliance,* 179–80.

9. *New York Times,* March 8, 1964.

10. Ibid., March 11, 1964; *Chattanooga Times,* March 11, 1964; Affidavits of Ezeil Evrons (March 9, 1964), Johnnie Brown (March 8, 1964), Virgil Culpepper (March 8, 1964), William Narrimore (March 10, 1964), Hal Bullen (March 11, 1964), Emolene Akers (March 14, 1964), Edsel Morrison (March 11, 1964), Mrs. Sam Oliver (March 11, 1964), John Curbow (March 11, 1964), Harry Mansfield (March 16, 1964), Anthony Charles Bradford (March 16, 1964), Dorothy Vaughn (March 11, 1964), Jack Irwin (March 14, 1964), in Case File, *United States v. James R. Hoffa, et al.,* File No. 11-989 (E.D. Tenn. 1964); *United States v. Hoffa, et al.,* 235 F. Supp. 611 (E.D. Tenn. 1964); Sheridan, *Fall and Rise of Jimmy Hoffa,* 354; Cook, "First Full Account of a Fateful Trial," 439; *Nashville Tennessean,* April 2–3, 1964; *Nashville Banner,* April 3, 1964.

11. Sheridan, *Fall and Rise of Jimmy Hoffa,* 356.

12. Ibid., 354.

13. Cook, "First Full Account of a Fateful Trial," 439; *Nashville Tennessean,* April 2–3, 1964; *Nashville Banner,* April 3, 1964. At the time, O'Brien was already under two other indictments, one for breaking and entering into a US Customs warehouse to steal salvaged materials, and the other for embezzling $900 from the union to buy a car for Frank Meli, William Bufalino's father-in-law.

14. Sheridan, *Fall and Rise of Jimmy Hoffa,* 346–47, 357–58; *Chattanooga Times,* March 3, 1964; *Chattanooga News-Free Press,* March 4, 1964; Henry, *Fatal Alliance,* 164, 168–69, 171–72, 175–76.

15. Moldea, *Hoffa Wars,* 175; Sheridan, *Fall and Rise of Jimmy Hoffa,* 255, 386, 396, 405, 416; *Time,* June 2, 1967; *Independent Press-Telegram* (Long Beach, CA), May 26, 1967; Dana L. Spitzer, "The Hoffa Taint," *New Republic,* June 10, 1967.

16. Henry, *Fatal Alliance,* 178–79; Moldea, *Hoffa Wars,* 283–84; Sheridan, *Fall and Rise of Jimmy Hoffa,* 386–88, 518.

17. *Chattanooga News-Free Press,* August 20, 1966.

18. Sheridan, *Fall and Rise of Jimmy Hoffa,* 389.

19. Partin, *From My Brother's Shadow*, 161–62.

20. Sheridan, *Fall and Rise of Jimmy Hoffa*, 408–12; Moldea, *Hoffa Wars*, 179; Henry, *Fatal Alliance*, 215; ibid., 168.

21. A mistrial occurred in the first trial on July 8, 1971. Jim Neal then agreed to represent Partin in the case, which was relocated to Atlanta. Although Partin was convicted, a motion for mistrial was granted, and a new trial was ordered. Sheridan, *Fall and Rise of Jimmy Hoffa*, 415, 420–24, 433–35, 441–43, 445, 458, 466, 475–77; Moldea, *Hoffa Wars*, 180, 279.

22. Partin, *From My Brother's Shadow*, 168–69.

23. Moldea, *Hoffa Wars*, 279–80, 285; Sloane, *Hoffa*, 215; ibid., 173–74, 229–31; Sheridan, *Fall and Rise of Jimmy Hoffa*, 491, 499, 511–14, 516, 519–20, 524–25, 535; Henry, *Fatal Alliance*, 215.

24. Sloane, *Hoffa*, 303; *Chattanooga News-Free Press*, March 5, 1964.

25. Sheridan, *Fall and Rise of Jimmy Hoffa*, 389–90; *United States v. Hoffa, et al.*, 349 F.2d 20 (6th Cir. 1965); *Nashville Banner*, April 11, 1964; *Nashville Tennessean*, April 12–13, 1964.

26. "Hoffa's Hookers," *Time*, October 1, 1965.

27. Interview with Gearhiser; Sheridan, *Fall and Rise of Jimmy Hoffa*, 390–91; interview with Mansfield. Also attached to the motion were six affidavits from purported coworkers and associates of various jurors who attributed prejudicial comments to those members of the jury. The court was not persuaded, Judge Wilson said, "by the affidavits of fellow employees of two jurors who view themselves as union sympathizers and believe such jurors to be hostile to unions." *United States v. Hoffa, et al.*, 247 F. Supp. 692 (E.D. Tenn. 1965).

28. *Time Magazine*, October 1, 1965; Motion for New Trial (September 1, 1965), in Case File, *United States v. James R. Hoffa, et al.*, File No. 11-989 (E.D. Tenn. 1964); *United States v. Johnson*, 414 F.2d 22 (6th Cir. 1969), *cert denied*, 397 U.S. 991 (1970); interview with Tom Williams, November 15, 2007.

29. Interview with Tom Williams; interview with Berke, 2007.

30. Interview with Mansfield; "Hoffa's Hookers"; *United States v. Hoffa, et al.*, 382 F.2d 856 (6th Cir. 1967), *cert. denied*, 390 U.S. 854 (1968).

31. Interview with Tom Williams; interview with Mansfield; Sheridan, *Fall and Rise of Jimmy Hoffa*, 391; interview with Gearhiser.

32. "Hoffa's Hookers"; Sheridan, *Fall and Rise of Jimmy Hoffa*, 390–91; *United States v. Hoffa, et al.*, 247 F. Supp. 692 (E.D. Tenn. 1965).

33. *United States v. Hoffa, et al.*, 382 F.2d 856 (6th Cir. 1967); interview with Tom Williams. The court of appeals found that Judge Wilson had erred by refusing to recuse himself from the case. The court also determined that prejudicial post-trial remarks attributed to one juror, Mrs. Emolene Akers, could not have been made as alleged, as she had been in Florida, not Tennessee, at the time the comments were said to have been made.

34. "Hoffa's Hookers"; interview with Sertel; Sheridan, *Fall and Rise of Jimmy Hoffa*, 391.

35. Interview with Tom Williams; *United States v. Johnson*, 414 F.2d 22 (6th Cir. 1969); *Chattanooga News-Free Press*, January 25, 1966; interview with Mansfield.

36. Interview with Tom Williams; interview with Neal.

37. Sheridan, *Fall and Rise of Jimmy Hoffa*, 393.

38. Ibid., 393, 399; Sloane, *Hoffa*, 315, 321–23, Henry, *Fatal Alliance*, 179, 181–85; interview with Sheridan, June 12, 1970, 105.

39. *Chattanooga Times*, December 13, 1966.

40. Judge Wilson had previously rejected Sidney Simpson's testimony in denying the second motion for new trial on April 15, 1965. As a procedural matter, the judge concluded, the defense had secured Simpson's affidavit in 1964. Because the information had been available previously but had not been submitted to the court, it was untimely and unusable by the defense. *United States v. Hoffa, et al.*, 385 U.S. 293 (1966); Affidavits of Bill Sidney Simpson (December 1, 1964), Edward Grady Partin (February 18, 1965), and William H. Daniels (February 17, 1965), in Case File, *United States v. James R. Hoffa, et al.*, File No. 11-989 (E.D. Tenn. 1964).

41. *Chattanooga Times*, December 13, 1966.

42. "A Pragmatic View of Privacy," *Time*, December 23, 1966; *Chattanooga Times*, December 15, 1966.

43. Sheridan, *Fall and Rise of Jimmy Hoffa*, 397, 400; *Chattanooga News-Free Press*, July 30, 1966; *Chattanooga News-Free Press*, December 31, 1966.

44. Affidavits of Bud Nichols (January 1967) and I. Irving Davidson (December 1966), in Case File, *United States v. James R. Hoffa, et al.*, File No. 11-989 (E.D. Tenn. 1964); Sheridan, *Fall and Rise of Jimmy Hoffa*, 414–16.

45. Sheridan, *Fall and Rise of Jimmy Hoffa*, 416.

46. Ibid., 413; Sloane, *Hoffa*, 327.

47. Moldea, *Hoffa Wars*, 185–86; Henry, *Fatal Alliance*, 192–94.

48. Moldea, *Hoffa Wars*, 185–86; Henry, *Fatal Alliance*, 192–94; CBS News Feed, March 7, 1967.

49. Sheridan, *Fall and Rise of Jimmy Hoffa*, 459–65, 489–90; interview with Mansfield.

50. Sheridan, *Fall and Rise of Jimmy Hoffa*, 489–90, 513, 524.

Epilogue

1. Note: Some of the figures who played roles in the Hoffa trial effectively disappeared in the years afterward. Efforts to research the whereabouts of the trial participants have in some cases failed to turn up any reliable information.

2. State of Tennessee General Assembly, "A Resolution to Honor the Memory of Dave A. Alexander, Sr.," Senate No. SJR0149 (March 29, 1995).

3. *Berke v. Chattanooga Bar Association*, 436 S.W.2d 296 (Tenn. Ct. App. 1968); Sheridan, *Fall and Rise of Jimmy Hoffa*, 392, 397.

4. Interview with Berke, 2007.

5. *Tennessee Bar Journal*, 50, no. 6 (June 2014), 9; *Nashville Tennessean*, May 9, 2014; interview with Hayden Mauk, August 27, 2013; Bob Holladay, "'Big Bill' Powell Takes the Stand," *Nashville Scene*, August 31, 1995.

6. Interviews with Brown, 2007, January 21, 2015; interview with Summers; Monica Mercer and Pam Sohn, "Chattanooga: Jimmy Hoffa Jury Tampering Trial Tested Legal System," *Chattanooga Times-Free Press*, May 4, 2008.

7. *New York Times*, May 15, 1990; Sloane, *Hoffa*, 172; Moldea, *Hoffa Wars*, 43; Henry, *Fatal Alliance*, 261–62.

8. *New York Times*, February 1, 1972. Campbell filed various legal appeals from jail. One was a habeus corpus motion alleging that the rejection of his defense in Chattanooga demanded a finding that any remedy the court fashioned would be inadequate or ineffective. Another was a Sixth Amendment motion claiming that allowing statements about Campbell by his coconspirators (Hoffa and Parks) had violated Campbell's rights to confrontation and cross-examination. The courts rejected both arguments, finding with regard to the second that the remarks constituted admissible statements of coconspirators made in the course of the conspiracy. *Campbell v. Clark*, 274 F. Supp. 556 (D. Minn. 1967); *Campbell v. United States*, 415 F.2d 356 (6th Cir. 1969).

9. *USA Today*, February 12, 1988.

10. Brandt, *"I Heard You Paint Houses,"* 105; *United States v. Dorfman*, 335 F. Supp. 675 (S.D.N.Y. 1971); *United States v. Dorfman*, 532 F. Supp. 1118 (N.D. Ill. 1981); *United States v. Dorfman*, 542 F. Supp. 355 (N.D. Ill. 1982), aff'd, 690 F.2d 1217 (7th Cir. 1982); *Mafia's Greatest Hits: Allen Dorfman, The Mob's Banker* (documentary series), season 1, episode 9 (July 13, 2012).

11. Interview with Eason; "Tommy Eason Retiring After 52 Years in Local TV," *Chattanoogan.com*, March 17, 2009.

12. Hoffa, *Hoffa: The Real Story*, 13; Sloane, *Hoffa*, 316–18; "Jimmy's Nemesis," *Time Magazine*, March 17, 1967; Moldea, *Hoffa Wars*, 185; Brandt, *"I Heard You Paint Houses,"* 185; "Fitzsimmons Rites Held With Few in Attendance," *United Press International*, May 8, 1981.

13. Gearhiser, Charles J., "A Career Full of Memorable Cases," 38-MAY Tenn. B.J. 3 (2002); interview with Gearhiser.

14. *Chicago Tribune*, June 9, 1991.

15. *New York Times*, December 25, 1970; Squires, *Secrets of the Hopewell Box*, 221–22, 280.

16. Adamson, "Selected Women in Tennessee Newspaper Journalism," 123, 126, 128, 137–38; *Chattanooga Times*, February 15, 1982.

17. *Nashville Tennessean*, November 29, 1990; Letters re. Kathy King (May 24, 1967) and Margaret King (May 18, 1967) in Case File, *United States v. James R. Hoffa, et al.*, File No. 11-989 (E.D. Tenn. 1964).

18. *Chattanooga Times-Free Press*, May 9, 2008.

19. *New York Times*, September 14, 1981; *Time*, September 28, 1981.

20. "Marilyn Lloyd," in *Women in Congress, 1917-2006* (Washington: Government Printing Office, 2006).

21. Interview with Mansfield; *Chattanooga Times-Free Press*, August 25, 2012.

22. *Nashville Tennessean*, July 11, 1976.

23. Mark Curriden, "Jim Neal," *American Bar Journal* (March 9, 2009), www.american bar.org; *Los Angeles Times,* October 23, 2010; *Nashville Scene,* October 22, 2010; *New York Times,* October 22, 2010; *Chattanooga Times-Free Press,* May 9, 2008.

24. Sloane, *Hoffa,* 239–41; Henry, *Fatal Alliance,* 221–23; *Baltimore Sun,* September 11, 2001; *St. Augustine Record,* May 30, 2006; *Orlando Sentinel,* May 21, 1991; *Los Angeles Times,* July 27, 1985.

25. *Nashville Tennessean,* October 28, 1980.

26. Interview with Mansfield; Navasky, *Kennedy Justice,* 491; Partin, *From My Brother's Shadow,* 170, 182–83, 198, 211, 254–55, 262; Neff, *Vendetta,* 319; *New York Times,* March 13, 1990; *Baton Rouge Morning Advocate,* March 12, 1990; interview with Keith Partin, January 16, 2013.

27. Interview with Betty Paschal, October 9, 2014.

28. *New York Times,* May 18, 1998; *American Justice: Defending the Mob,* season 4, episode 3.

29. United States District Court, Eastern District of Tennessee, *Court Historical Society Newsletter* (March 2010).

30. *New York Times,* December 27, 1970; interview with Brown, 2007; Sheridan, *Fall and Rise of Jimmy Hoffa,* 389.

31. Interview with Sertel; interview with Randy Wilson; United States District Court, Eastern District of Tennessee, *Court Historical Society Newsletter* (July 2006).

32. Interview with Berke; *New York Times,* August 11, 1989.

33. *New York Times,* January 15, 1995.

34. Federal Bureau of Investigation, "Frederick M. Shobe," Bureau File No. 47-51422 / Field Office File No. 47-4944 (1964); Federal Bureau of Investigation, "Frederick M. Shobe," Bureau File No. 72-1653 / Field Office File No. 72-92 (1965); interview with Joanne Shobe. Interview by author by telephone, June 8, 2016.

35. *New Yorker,* July 15, 2014; *Nashville Tennessean,* July 11, 2014; Squires, *Secrets of the Hopewell Box,* 239.

36. *Chicago Tribune,* January 24, 2007.

37. *Life,* May 20, 1966; *Putnam County Courier (Carmel, NY),* February 10, 1971.

38. *New York Times,* January 16, 1976; *Herald Dispatch (Huntington, WV),* February 17, 2009.

39. Navasky, *Kennedy Justice,* 488–91; Squires, *Secrets of the Hopewell Box,* 241, 278; Sheridan, *Fall and Rise of Jimmy Hoffa,* 386–88, 392.

40. Sheridan, *Fall and Rise of Jimmy Hoffa,* 395, 405.

41. Schlesinger, *Robert Kennedy,* 637, 666, 904, 914; Hoffa, *Hoffa: The Real Story,* 208; Mollenhoff, *Tentacles of Power,* 404. The comments about Kennedy letting Hoffa out of jail stand in stark contrast to Kennedy's actual comments to an aide (and his brother Edward) during the Democratic primaries: "If I'm ever elected president of the United States, he has a darn slim chance of ever getting out of jail." Neff, *Vendetta,* 338.

42. "Jimmy's Nemesis," *Time,* March 17, 1967; Moldea, *Hoffa Wars,* 185–86, 264.

43. *Time,* March 17, 1967; Russell, *Out of the Jungle,* 224; Brandt, *"I Heard You Paint Houses,"* 200–201, 206, 208.

44. Henry, *Fatal Alliance*, 116–17, 207; Sheridan, *Fall and Rise of Jimmy Hoffa*, 280, 388–89, 454–56, 487, 519.

45. Brandt, *"I Heard You Paint Houses,"* 209.

46. Sloane, *Hoffa*, 400; Brandt, *"I Heard You Paint Houses,"* 236; Hoffa, *Hoffa: The Real Story*, 24, 215–16; "Who Killed Jimmy Hoffa?" (television series episode), *History Detectives: Special Investigations*, July 22, 2014, PBS.

47. Hoffa, *Hoffa: The Real Story*, 15, 238, 240–41; Brandt, *"I Heard You Paint Houses,"* 3.

48. Interview with Tom Williams; interview with Cole; interview with Seigenthaler; interview with Berke, 2015; interview with Curtis Collier, December 21, 2007. Interviewed by author, Chattanooga; interview with Mattice.

49. Interview with Neal.

50. Interview with Mansfield; interview with Gearhiser.

51. *Chattanooga Times*, March 13, 1964; interview with Berke, 2007; interview with Seigenthaler; interview with Haverty; interview with Collier.

52. Interview with Collier; Brake, *Justice in the Valley*, 121–23; *New York Times*, December 14, 1986; *Mapp v. Board of Educ. of City of Chattanooga*, 525 F.2d 169 (6th Cir. 1975); interview with Randy Wilson.

53. *City of Chattanooga, Tennessee v. Louisville & Nashville Railroad Co.*, 298 F. Supp. 1 (E.D. Tenn. 1969), *aff'd*, 427 F.2d 1154 (6th Cir.), *cert. denied*, 400 U.S. 903 (1970); *State of Georgia v. City of Chattanooga, Tennessee*, 406 F.2d 800 (6th Cir. 1969); Russell S. Bonds, *Stealing the General: The Great Locomotive Chase and the First Medal of Honor*, (Yardley, PA: Westholme, 2008), 367–68.

54. Brake, *Justice in the Valley*, 192–93.

55. Mercer and Sohn, "Chattanooga: Jimmy Hoffa Jury Tampering Trial"; interview with Randy Wilson; interview with Tom Williams.

56. Cook, "First Full Account of a Fateful Trial," 438.

57. Schlesinger, *Robert Kennedy*, 239, 283, 285; Navasky, *Kennedy Justice*, 446–47; Moldea, *Hoffa Wars*, 175; interview with Brown, 2007.

58. Navasky, *Kennedy Justice*, 492; *International Teamster*, March 1964 (reprint of *Escanaba (MI) Daily Press*, February 1, 1964); Hoffa, *Hoffa: The Real Story*, 173.

59. Navasky, *Kennedy Justice*, 447.

60. Cook, "First Full Account of a Fateful Trial," 438; interview with Berke, 2007; Moldea, *Hoffa Wars*, 175.

61. Interview with Gearhiser; interview with Collier; interview with Mansfield; interview with Seigenthaler; *Chattanooga Times*, March 5, 1964; *Chattanooga News-Free Press*, March 5, 1964.

62. Cook, "First Full Account of a Fateful Trial," 417, 439; interview with Collier.

63. Interview with Mattice; interview with Collier; interview with Seigenthaler; *Chattanooga Times*, March 5, 1964; *Chattanooga News-Free Press*, March 5, 1964.

BIBLIOGRAPHY

Primary Sources

American Bar Association Journal

American Bar Journal

American Journalism Review

Baker v. Carr. 396 U.S. 186 (1962).

Baltimore Sun

Baton Rouge Morning Advocate

Berke v. Chattanooga Bar Association. 436 S.W.2d 296 (Tenn. Ct. App. 1968).

Campbell v. Clark. 274 F. Supp. 556 (D. Minn. 1967).

Campbell v. United States. 415 F.2d 356 (6th Cir. 1969).

Capital Times (Madison, WI)

Case File, *United States v. James R. Hoffa, et al.,* File No. 11-989 (E.D. Tenn. 1964).

CBS News Feed. February 11, 1964.

CBS News Feed. February 25, 1964.

CBS News Feed. March 7, 1967.

Chattanooga City Directory (1964).

Chattanooga Daily Times

Chattanooga News-Free Press

Chattanooga Times

Chattanooga Times-Free Press

chattanoogan.com

Chicago Tribune

City of Chattanooga, Tennessee v. Louisville & Nashville Railroad Co. 298 F. Supp. 1
    (E.D. Tenn. 1969). *Aff'd,* 427 F.2d 1154 (6th Cir.). *Cert. denied,* 400 U.S. 903 (1970).

Clipping Files: Lovell Field (Airport). Local History and Genealogy Department. Chat-
    tanooga Public Library.

Continental Baking Co. v. United States. 281 F.2d 137 (6th Cir. 1960).

Detroit Free Press

Detroit News

11 FCC 1033. 1947 WL 58823 (March 24, 1947). Use of recording devices in connection
    with telephone services.

Federal Bureau of Investigation. "Frederick M. Shobe." Bureau File No. 47-51422 / Field
    Office File No. 47-4944 (1964).

———. "Frederick M. Shobe." Bureau File No. 72-1653 / Field Office File No. 72-92 (1965).

47 C.F.R. § 64.501. Recording of telephone conversations with telephone companies.

Gray v. Board of Trustees of Univ. of Tenn., et al. 342 U.S. 517 (1952).

Herald Dispatch (Huntington, WV)

Illustrated Detective Magazine

Independent Press-Telegram (Long Beach, CA)

Inquirer (Philadelphia)

International Teamster

Jencks Act. 18 U.S.C. § 3500.

Knowles, Bill. *Journal* (1964). Copy in author's possession.

Life Magazine

Los Angeles Times

Mapp v. Board of Educ. of City of Chattanooga. 203 F. Supp. 843 (E.D. Tenn. 1962).

Mapp v. Board of Educ. of City of Chattanooga. 525 F.2d 169 (6th Cir. 1975).

Medlin v. United States. 384 U.S. 973 (1966).

The Michigan Labor Legacy Project. "Labor's Legacy: A Landmark for Detroit" (2003).
    mlhs.wayne.edu.

Milone v. English. 306 F.2d 814 (D.C. Cir. July 19, 1962).

Morning Call (Allentown, PA)

Nashville Banner

Nashville Scene

Nashville Tennessean

New Orleans States-Item

New Republic

New York Times

New Yorker

Ocala (FL) Star-Banner

Official Transcript of Proceedings, United States v. James R. Hoffa, et al. Case No. 11,989
    (12 vols.) (E.D. Tenn. 1964).

Orlando Sentinel

Orlando Star-Banner

Osborn v. United States. 350 F.2d 497 (6th Cir. 1965).

Osborn v. United States. 385 U.S. 323 (1966).

Putnam County Courier (Carmel, NY)

Reader's Digest

Saturday Evening Post

Section 605, Federal Communications Act of 1934. 47 U.S.C. § 605.

South Florida Sun-Sentinel

St. Augustine Journal

St. Augustine Record

State of Georgia v. City of Chattanooga, Tennessee. 406 F.2d 800 (6th Cir. 1969).

State of Tennessee General Assembly. "A Resolution to Honor the Memory of Dave A.
    Alexander, Sr." Senate No. SJR0149 (March 29, 1995).

Tech (Cambridge, MA)

Tennessee Bar Assoc. v. Berke. 344 S.W.2d 567 (Tenn. Ct. App. 1960).

Tennessee Bar Journal

Time

Toledo Blade

Transcript of Proceedings, Grand Jury Testimony of Walter J. Sheridan. Case No. 3:09-cv-00375, Document 42-1 (M.D. Tenn., July 9, 2009).

United Press International

United States District Court, Eastern District of Tennessee. *Court Historical Society Newsletter.* March 2010.

United States Senate, Committee on Improper Activities in Labor and Management (McClellan Committee). First Interim Report. S. Rep. No. 1,417. 85th Cong., 2d Sess. (1958).

United States Senate Select Committee on Improper Activities in Labor and Management (McClellan Committee). Second Interim Report. S. Rep. No. 621. 86th Cong., 1st Sess. (1959).

United States Senate Select Committee on Improper Activities in Labor and Management (McClellan Committee). Final Report. S. Rep. No. 1,139. 86th Cong., 2d Sess. (1960).

United States v. Bell. 351 F.2d 868 (6th Cir. 1965).

United States v. Campbell. 386 U.S. 970 (1967).

United States v. Dorfman. 335 F. Supp. 675 (S.D.N.Y. 1971).

United States v. Dorfman. 532 F. Supp. 1118 (N.D. Ill. 1981).

United States v. Dorfman. 542 F. Supp. 355 (N.D. Ill. 1982). *Aff'd,* 190 F.2d 1217 (7th Cir. 1982).

United States v. Essex. 275 F. Supp. 393 (E.D. Tenn. 1967). *Rev'd,* 407 F.2d 215 (6th Cir. 1969).

United States v. Greco. 298 F.2d 247 (2d Cir. 1962). *Cert. denied,* 369 U.S. 820.

United States v. Hoffa. 205 F. Supp. 710 (S.D. Fla. 1962).

United States v. Hoffa. 273 F. Supp. 141 (N.D. Ill. 1967).

United States v. Hoffa. 367 F.2d 698 (7th Cir. 1968).

United States v. Hoffa. 386 U.S. 970 (1967).

United States v. Hoffa, et al. 196 F. Supp. 25 (S.D. Fla. 1961).

United States v. Hoffa, et al. 235 F. Supp. 611 (E.D. Tenn. 1964).

United States v. Hoffa, et al. 247 F. Supp. 692 (E.D. Tenn. 1965).

United States v. Hoffa, et al. 349 F.2d 20 (6th Cir. 1965).

United States v. Hoffa, et al. 382 F.2d 856 (6th Cir. 1967). *Cert. denied,* 390 U.S. 854 (1968).

United States v. Hoffa, et al. 385 U.S. 293 (1966).

United States v. Johnson. 414 F.2d 22 (6th Cir. 1969). *Cert. denied,* 397 U.S. 991 (1970).

United States v. King. 386 U.S. 971 (1967).

United States v. Medlin. 353 F.2d 789 (6th Cir. 1965).

United States v. Parks. 386 U.S. 970 (1967).

United States v. Schiffer. 351 F.2d 91 (6th Cir. 1965). *Cert. denied,* 384 U.S. 1003 (1966). *Reh'g denied,* 385 U.S. 890 (1966).

United States v. Thomas. 303 F.2d 561 (6th Cir. 1962).

US Bureau of Labor Statistics. *Union Sourcebook 1947–1983.*

USA Today

Washington Evening Star
Washington Post
Wellman, et al. v. United States. 227 F.2d 757 (6th Cir. 1955).
Western Political Quarterly
Wilmington (NC) Morning Star
Z. T. Osborn, Jr. v. United States. 385 U.S. 323 (1966).

Secondary Sources

Adamson, June N. "Selected Women in Tennessee Newspaper Journalism." Master's thesis, University of Tennessee (Knoxville), August 1971.

Bonds, Russell S. *Stealing the General: The Great Locomotive Chase and the First Medal of Honor*. Yardley, PA: Westholme, 2009.

Brake, Patricia E. *Justice in the Valley: A Bicentennial Perspective of the United States District Court for the Eastern District of Tennessee*. Nashville: Hillsboro, 1998.

Brandt, Charles. *"I Heard You Paint Houses": Frank "The Irishman" Sheeran and Closing the Case on Jimmy Hoffa*. Hanover, NH: Steerforth, 2005.

Brill, Steven. *The Teamsters*. New York: Simon and Schuster, 1978.

Cook, Fred J. "The First Full Account of a Fateful Trial That Raises the Disturbing Question: Can Jungle Warfare Subvert American Justice?" *Nation*. April 27, 1964.

Englade, Ken. *Hoffa*. New York: Harper Paperbacks, 1992.

Gearhiser, Charles J. "My Life as a Lawyer: What Makes a Lawyer Succeed?" *Tennessee Bar Journal* 37 no. 3 (December 2001).

Goldfarb, Ronald. *Perfect Villains, Imperfect Heroes: Robert F. Kennedy's War on Organized Crime*. New York: Random House, 1995.

Greenwalt, Kent. "The Consent Problem in Wire Tapping and Eavesdropping: Surreptitious Monitoring with the Consent of a Participant in a Conversation." 68 Columb. L. Rev. 819 (February 1968).

Guthman, Edwin O., and Jeffrey Shulman, eds. *Robert Kennedy in His Own Words: The Unpublished Recollections of the Kennedy Years*. New York: Bantam Books, 1988.

Harper, Benjamin P. "A Highway, a Hill, the Automobile, and the Use of Space in the Urban Context: The Golden Gateway Urban Renewal Project, Chattanooga, Tennessee, 1955–1977." Undergraduate Thesis, Covenant College, 2002.

Henry, E. William. *Fatal Alliance: The Prosecution, Imprisonment and Gangland Murder of Jimmy Hoffa*. Barrington, MA: Andover, 2012.

Hoffa, *James R. Hoffa: The Real Story*. New York: Stein and Day, 1975.

Humphreys, Adrian. *The Weasel: A Double Life in the Mob*. Missisauga, Ontario: John Wiley and Sons Canada, 2012.

Hunt, Keel. *Coup: The Day the Democrats Ousted Their Governor, Put Republican Lamar Alexander in Office Early, and Stopped a Pardon Scandal*. Nashville: Vanderbilt University Press, 2013.

Kennedy, Robert F. *The Enemy Within: The McClellan Committee's Crusade Against Jimmy Hoffa and Corrupt Labor Unions*. New York: Harper and Row, 1960.

Langsdon, Phillip. *Tennessee: A Political History*. Franklin, TN: Hillsboro, 2000.

Livingood, James W. *A History of Hamilton County, Tennessee*. Memphis: Memphis State University Press, 1981.

Mamet, David. *Hoffa*. Shooting script. 1992.

Margolis, Jon. *The Last Innocent Year: America in 1964, the Beginning of the "Sixties."* New York: William Morrow, 1999.

Martin, John Bartlow. *Jimmy Hoffa's Hot*. New York: Fawcett World Crest, 1959.

McClellan, John L. *Crime Without Punishment*. New York: Duell, Sloan and Pearce, 1962.

Moldea, Dan E. *The Hoffa Wars: Teamsters, Rebels, Politicians and the Mob*. New York: Charter Books, 1978.

Mollenhoff, Clark R. *Tentacles of Power: The Story of Jimmy Hoffa*. Cleveland: World, 1965.

Navasky, Victor S. *Kennedy Justice*. New York: Atheneum, 1971.

Neff, James. *Vendetta: Bobby Kennedy Versus Jimmy Hoffa*. New York: Little, Brown, 2015.

Nicely, Maury. *Chattanooga Walking Tour & Historic Guide*. Chattanooga: Stillhouse Hollow, 2005.

Norman, Jack, Sr. *The Nashville I Knew*. Nashville: Rutledge Hill, 1984.

Partin, Douglas Wesley. *From My Brother's Shadow*. Greenwell Springs, LA: Oak of Acadia, 2013.

Ragano, Frank, and Selwyn Raab. *Mob Lawyer*. New York: Charles Scribner and Sons, 1994.

Raymond, Barbara Bisantz. *The Baby Thief: The Untold Story of Georgia Tann, the Baby Seller Who Corrupted Adoption*. New York: Carroll and Graf, 2007.

Reception Celebrating the Unveiling of a Study for the Historic Mural *Allegory of Chattanooga*. Chattanooga: Historical Society of the US District Court for the Eastern District of Tennessee, Chattanooga Chapter of the Federal Bar Association, April 27, 2010.

Ridley, Jim. "The People vs. Jimmy Hoffa (Part 1)." *Nashville Scene*. March 28, 2002.

———. "The People vs. Jimmy Hoffa (Part 2)." *Nashville Scene*. April 4, 2002.

Russell, Thaddeus. *Out of the Jungle: Jimmy Hoffa and the Remaking of the American Working Class*. New York: Alfred A. Knopf, 2001.

Schlesinger, Arthur M., Jr. *Robert Kennedy and His Times*. Boston: Houghton Mifflin, 1978.

Sertel, Granville M. *Recollections of Granville M. Sertel*. US District Court, Eastern District of Tennessee, 1992.

Sheridan, Walter. *The Fall and Rise of Jimmy Hoffa*. New York: Saturday Review Press, 1972.

Sloane, Arthur A. *Hoffa*. Cambridge, MA: MIT Press, 1991.

Sohn, Pam. "Hoffa Trial Spying Still a Mystery." *Chattanooga Times-Free Press*. May 10, 2008.

Spindel, Bernard B. *The Ominous Ear*. New York: Award House, 1968.

Spitzer, Dana L. "The Hoffa Taint." *New Republic*. June 10, 1967.

Spritzer, Ralph S. "Hoffa v. United States: A Retrospective Viewing." 39 Ariz. St. L.J. 377 (Summer 2007).

Squires, James D. *The Secrets of the Hopewell Box: Stolen Elections, Southern Politics, and a City's Coming of Age*. Nashville: Vanderbilt University Press, 2012.

Stover, Noble F. "Smoky." *The Ballad of Jimmy Hoffa*. 1960.

Summers, Jerry H. *Rush to Justice: Tennessee's Forgotten Trial of the Century—Schoolfield 1958*. Walden, TN: Waldenhouse, 2015.

Thomas, Evan. *The Man to See: Edward Bennett Williams—Ultimate Insider, Legendary Trial Lawyer*. New York: Simon and Schuster, 1991.

"Tommy Eason Retiring After 52 Years in Local Television." *chattanoogan.com*. March 17, 2009.

Townsend, Gavin. *R. H. Hunt: Master Architect of Chattanooga*. Chattanooga: Cornerstones, 2010.

United States District Court, Eastern District of Tennessee. *Court Historical Society Newsletter*. July 2006.

United States District Court, Eastern District of Tennessee. *Court Historical Society Newsletter*. March 2010.

Velie, Lester. "Stakes in the Struggle Against Hoffa." *Reader's Digest*. March 1964.

West, Carroll Van. *Tennessee's New Deal Landscape: A Guidebook*. Knoxville: University of Tennessee Press, 2001.

Wilson, John. *Chattanooga's Story*. Chattanooga: Chattanooga News-Free Press, 1980.

Wilson, Kyle J. "An Enduring Symbol of Hope, History, and Justice: The Joel W. Solomon Federal Building." *Federal Lawyer* (June 2013).

Witwer, David. *Corruption and Reform in the Teamsters Union*. Urbana: University of Illinois Press, 2003.

Women in Congress, 1917–2006. Washington, DC: Government Printing Office, 2006.

Oral Interviews

Marvin Berke (2007). Interview by John Medearis. Chattanooga.

William Brown (2007; January 21, 2015). Interviews by Tonya Cammon, author. Chattanooga.

Jim Cole (November 15, 2007). Interview by John Medearis. Chattanooga.

Curtis Collier (December 21, 2007). Interview by author. Chattanooga.

Tommy Eason (January 28, 2013). Interview by author. Chattanooga.

Charles J. Gearhiser (July 18, 2007). Interview by Tonya Cammon. Chattanooga.

Patrick Haverty (2008). Interview by author. Chattanooga.

Harry Mansfield (July 18, 2007). Interview by Sandy Mattice. Chattanooga.

Sandy Mattice (December 2007). Interview by author. Chattanooga.

Hayden Mauk (August 27, 2013). Telephone interview by author. Chattanooga.

Jim Neal (2007). Interview by Tonya Cammon. Nashville.

Mike Pare (December 8, 2015). Telephone interview by author. Chattanooga.

Keith Partin (January 16, 2013) Telephone interview by author. Chattanooga.

Betty Paschal (October 9, 2014). Telephone interview by author. Chattanooga.

Cecil Pearce (January 24, 2008). Interview by Tonya Cammon. Chattanooga.

John Seigenthaler (December 11, 2007). Interview by Tonya Cammon. Nashville.

John Sertel (December 21, 2007). Interview by author. Chattanooga.
Walter Sheridan. Recorded interview by Roberta W. Greene. March 23, 1970. John F. Kennedy Library Oral History Program.
———. Recorded interview with Roberta W. Greene. April 1, 1970. John F. Kennedy Library Oral History Program.
———. Recorded interview with Roberta W. Greene. May 1, 1970. John F. Kennedy Library Oral History Program.
———. Recorded interview with Roberta W. Greene. June 12, 1970. John F. Kennedy Library Oral History Program.
Joanne Shobe (June 8, 2016). Interview by author. Chattanooga.
Jerry Summers (November 24, 2015). Interview by author. Chattanooga.
Etta Williams (November 14, 2007). Interview by Shelley Rucker. Signal Mountain, TN.
Tom Williams (November 15, 2007). Interview by John Medearis. Chattanooga.
Helen Wilson (November 14, 2007). Interview by Randy Wilson. Signal Mountain, TN.
Randy Wilson (February 14, 2013). Interview by author. Chattanooga.

Television

American Justice: Defending the Mob (television broadcast). Season 4, episode 3. March 15, 1995, A&E Television.
Balancing the Scales: The Chattanooga Trial of U.S. v. James R. Hoffa (documentary). 2008, Federal Bar Association, Chattanooga Chapter.
Biography: Jimmy Hoffa—The Man Behind the Mystery. July 26, 2005, A&E Home Video.
Blood Feud (television movie). April 25, 1983, Twentieth Century Fox Television.
Mafia's Greatest Hits: Allen Dorfman, The Mafia's Banker (documentary series). Season 1, episode 9. July 13, 2012, World Media Rights Productions.
"Who Killed Jimmy Hoffa?" (television series episode). *History Detectives: Special Investigations*. July 22, 2014, PBS.

INDEX

Page numbers in **boldface** refer to illustrations.

www.ingramcontent.com/pod-product-compliance
Lightning Source LLC
Chambersburg PA
CBHW031934090426
42811CB00002B/183